CRITICAL INSIGHTS

T. S. Eliot

CRITICAL INSIGHTS
T. S. Eliot

Editor
John Paul Riquelme
Boston University

Salem Press
Pasadena, California   Hackensack, New Jersey

High School Media Center
Northfield, MN 55057
507-645-3414

Cover photo: AP/Wide World Photos

Published by Salem Press

© 2010 by EBSCO Publishing
Editor's text © 2010 by John Paul Riquelme
"The *Paris Review* Perspective" © 2010 by Gemma Sieff for *The Paris Review*

All rights in this book are reserved. No part of this work may be used or reproduced in any manner whatsoever or transmitted in any form or by any means, electronic or mechanical, including photocopy, recording, or any information storage and retrieval system, without written permission from the copyright owner except in the case of brief quotations embodied in critical articles and reviews or in the copying of images deemed to be freely licensed or in the public domain. For information about the print edition address the publisher, Salem Press, http://salempress.com. For copyright information, contact EBSCO Publishing, 10 Estes Street, Ipswich, MA 01938.

∞ The paper used in these volumes conforms to the American National Standard for Permanence of Paper for Printed Library Materials, Z39.48-1992 (R1997).

Library of Congress Cataloging-in-Publication Data
T.S. Eliot / editor, John Paul Riquelme.
    p. cm. -- (Critical insights)
    Includes bibliographical references and index.
    ISBN 978-1-58765-606-4 (alk. paper)
    1. Eliot, T. S. (Thomas Stearns), 1888-1965--Criticism and interpretation.
I. Riquelme, John Paul.
    PS3509.L43Z872436 2010
    821'.912--dc22
                                                            2009026434

PRINTED IN CANADA

Contents

About This Volume, John Paul Riquelme   vii

Career, Life, and Influence

On T. S. Eliot, John Paul Riquelme	3
Biography of T. S. Eliot, R. Baird Shuman	8
The *Paris Review* Perspective, Gemma Sieff for *The Paris Review*	15

Context, Reception, Comparison, Critical Lens

Cultural Contexts, Neil Heims	23
Critical Reception and Influence, John Paul Riquelme	40
T. S. Eliot and Robert Browning's Dramatic Monologues, Matthew J. Bolton	55
Voices and Language in T. S. Eliot's *The Waste Land*, Allan Johnson	74

Critical Readings

Eliot as Critic

"Poetry as Poetry," Louis Menand   93

Eliot as Poet

Playing at Relationship, John T. Mayer	123
"Prufrock," "Gerontion," and Fragmented Monologues, John Paul Riquelme	166
"Unknown terror and mystery": *The Waste Land*, Ronald Bush	184
'The Word Within the World': *Ash-Wednesday* and the 'Ariel Poems,' Nancy K. Gish	224
The Soul's Mysterious Errand, Lee Oser	267

Eliot as Dramatist

Fear in the Way: The Design of Eliot's Drama, Michael Goldman   294

v

Resources

Chronology of T. S. Eliot's Life	319
Works by T. S. Eliot	321
Bibliography	323
About the Editor	331
About *The Paris Review*	331
Contributors	333
Acknowledgments	336
Index	337

About This Volume

John Paul Riquelme

This collection of essays on the work of T. S. Eliot contains a variety of materials for approaching the writings of one of the twentieth century's most influential writers: overviews of his career and his importance in the opening section; followed by a group of original essays focusing on relevant contexts and critical reception and illustrating interpretive choices; and the longest section, devoted to previously published essays by established scholars on Eliot's critical writing, his drama, and the whole range of his poetry from early to late in his career. A section of "Resources" rounds out the collection, including a chronology of Eliot's life, a list of his works, and a bibliography.

I have written an introductory note for each of the essays in the two main sections, sketching the direction of the argument, some of its salient moments, and tits relevance for understanding the importance and the implications of Eliot's writings. As a way of providing a different kind of navigational aid for readers, I want to take the opportunity here to explain briefly the organization of the Critical Readings section and to comment on some connections and contrasts among the collection's essays. As I explain in more detail below, the seven essays are arranged by the genre that they address and chronologically with regard to the period of Eliot's career that they investigate.

In the first essay of Critical Readings, Louis Menand discusses key concepts from Eliot's criticism, mostly formulated in Eliot's early essays, that come up regularly in critical writings about Eliot's poetry and drama, including several that appear in this collection. His concern to interpret Eliot's relation to nineteenth-century precursors is one that Matthew Bolton shares in his essay comparing Eliot and Robert Browning, and also one that I share in my contribution on Eliot's poetry through *The Waste Land*, which deals in part with William Wordsworth and with Eliot's transformation of the dramatic monologue. In the closing essay, Michael Goldman focuses on a different stage of Eliot's career and on quite a different genre, verse drama, which Eliot wrote in the middle of his career and later. Goldman's concern with a recurring gothic element, the ghost, is related to Ronald Bush's commentary on the nightmare situation in *The Waste Land*.

Between these opening and closing pieces, the five middle essays of Critical Readings span the chronological range of Eliot's poetic career, starting with John T. Mayer's consideration of early unpublished and published poems and ending with Lee Oser's commentary on *Four Quartets*, Eliot's last and most ambitious poem, written mostly during World War II. The intervening essays work between those poles. Mine deals with early poetry and briefly with *The Waste Land*, while Ronald Bush concentrates on that poem (as does Allan Johnson in his lens commentary in the preceding section). Nancy Gish's essay deals with poems written between *The Waste Land* and *Four Quartets*. You will find commonalities and divergences among these essays. Mayer and Bush both argue for interpretations that emphasize character and psychology, while my poststructural reading finds Eliot thoroughly challenging the notions of self and person. Oser and Gish are both concerned with Eliot's spirituality, but Oser argues for Eliot's American cultural roots, while Gish compares Eliot's writing to religious and mystical sources that are British and European.

Whatever period or genre of Eliot's career interests the reader is covered by one or more of our essays. I join with my colleagues whose essays on Eliot are published here in expressing the hope that our essays send you back to Eliot's writings with new perspectives.

CAREER, LIFE, AND INFLUENCE

On T. S. Eliot
John Paul Riquelme

Poet, critic, dramatist, editor, Nobel laureate—Thomas Stearns Eliot (1888-1965) was an uncompromising, prolific author whose writings in several genres held the attention of other writers and of a wide audience during his lifetime. Eliot had more influence on his "contemporaries and younger fellow writers than perhaps anyone else of our time," as Gustaf Hellström of the Swedish Academy remarked in introducing Eliot when he accepted the Nobel Prize for Literature in 1948.[1] Hellström also compared Eliot's effect on literature to the revolutionary impact of Sigmund Freud's contribution to our understanding of the mind. The public recognition that he achieved during his lifetime is hard for us to imagine now. When Eliot lectured or read from his poetry while visiting the United States in the 1950s, the crowds were so large that some of the events were held in sports stadiums filled with thousands of people. The remarkable impression that Eliot produced was still strong when he died in 1965. It had arisen primarily because his poetry was permanently revolutionary in character and his essays insistently challenged and displaced dominant nineteenth-century views on literature and literary history. The literary canon changed, for example, after Eliot made a case for the modern relevance of John Donne and other Metaphysical poets of the seventeenth century.

The Waste Land and "Tradition and the Individual Talent" may well be the most widely reprinted and discussed longer poem and literary essay of the twentieth century. When *The Waste Land* appeared in 1922, its revolutionary quality and its accomplished, memorable intensity turned Eliot overnight from a poet appreciated by the avant-garde into a writer widely recognized for his enigmatic, daunting, but also unforgettable, poetry. The poem becomes even more strangely memorable when we hear the unusual intonations that Eliot adopts on recordings. *The Waste Land* won a substantial cash prize from *The Dial*, the journal that published it in the United States. Eliot's fame persisted when, over the next decades, he continued to write distinctive poetry that was widely read and soon widely taught, and to publish influential essays and verse dramas that drew audiences in London theatres. In addition, Eliot edited his own journal, *The Criterion*, for nearly twenty years, until ceasing publication when he knew that World War II was imminent. As an editor at Faber and Faber he had decisive influence on the selection of contemporary writers to be brought out by this major British publishing house. He helped, for instance, to keep Ezra Pound in print at Faber.

Eliot's poetry is experimental, intellectual, and not overtly personal. The intellectuality of the verse comes in part from his knowledge of philosophy. During his graduate studies at Harvard, Eliot wrote while living in England an accomplished doctoral dissertation on the British philosopher, F. H. Bradley, but he never returned to Harvard to defend the thesis and receive the degree. The decision not to return reflected the expense and danger of crossing the Atlantic during World War I, but the choice was also a determined break with his family and with a career in academic philosophy that awaited him in the United States. Instead, he remained in England to pursue his vocation as a poet and essayist. He admired Dante and Metaphysical poets as precursors whose poems were not personal, that is, not primarily and explicitly about the poet's emotions and feelings. Eliot objected to the tradition of British Romantic poetry, as it had developed by the early twentieth century into a debased popular preference for the subjective and the expressive.

Eliot advocated poetry that included and invited thinking about ideas, poetry that could overcome the dissociation of sensibility, the division of thought from feeling that he attributed to John Milton and Milton's Romantic descendants. His writing, however, is not poetry of ideas, narrowly speaking—not logical, philosophical argument in the form of discursive verse. Instead it is highly fragmented, elliptical, enigmatic, and allusive, often including jarring juxtapositions of different kinds of language and experiences. It yokes opposites, sometimes aggressively, in a modern version of Metaphysical poetry. Rather than being discursive and rational, Eliot's writing can be gothic and surreal, with many moments that seem a matter of chance, not of intelligible intention, in a way that bears comparison with Edgar Allan Poe and with Dada and its aftermath. Marcel Duchamp and René Magritte were his contemporaries, and Salvador Dalí and Samuel Beckett were only half a generation younger. They were his fellow travelers in producing strange, challenging work that makes a lasting impression but does not yield to easy explanations that emphasize the personal or the rational.

What is permanently revolutionary about Eliot's work? The diversity and multiplicity of the writing, both in form and in language, provide a large part of the answer. Eliot gives us no stable place to stand in responding to his career or to its individual parts. He was chameleonic and kaleidoscopic, a shape changer who could publish articles in academic philosophical journals, turn the dramatic monologue into a hardly recognizable fragmented modernist form, write self-less incantatory verse, create drawing-room comedies for the British stage, write children's poems about cats, and produce a long poetic sequence late in his career that is both musical and spiritual in its elaborate poetic translation of pre-Socratic philosophical fragments. It is not possible to reconcile the multiplicity into a single human being who was the writer.

Eliot's arguments about literature and the details of his poetic language also resist reduction to single perspectives. His perspectives are multiple and oscillating. Eliot's meditation on creativity in "Tradition and the Individual Talent" circles around the conundrum of the individual and the inheritance from the past, a conundrum that cannot be coherently simplified to either the person only or the historical only. It ambiguously and complexly involves both. The famous comparison, in "Prufrock"'s opening, of the evening to a patient anesthetized (we know not how fully) on a table is a prime example of his poetic language's complex, ambiguous, multiply suggestive qualities. The odd comparison can take us in many directions, including ones that raise questions about the relation of nature to the human, about consciousness, and about the way the speaker, concerning whom we know little, thinks. Eliot's poetic language regularly challenges the stability of identity in his speakers and in us. His persistent dissolving of the *I* that many of us assume to be stable makes the poetry perpetually enigmatic and disconcerting. In *S/Z* Roland Barthes claims that literature always prevents the question *Who speaks?* from ever being answered. Eliot provides compelling evidence for this claim. If we do not know who or what speaks, we also do not know who or what is being addressed. It is ourselves who overwhelmingly come into unanswerable question in the mirror of Eliot's poetry.

After Eliot's death, there was a backlash in the academy against his work, and against literary modernism in general, as it was understood then. Modernist writers, with the exception of a few, such as Virginia Woolf and James Joyce, were demoted from the place of prominence that they had held, but no one else as drastically as Eliot. Lightning always strikes the tallest tree on the mountain most frequently. The strength of the belated negative reaction is a testament to Eliot's importance during his lifetime and an indication of his continuing, long-term significance. A new generation's adjustment in views about writing that have held sway for decades is normal. Eliot himself had participated aggressively in his own generation's rebuke of nineteenth-century precursors. The vehemence of the reversal in views about Eliot on the part of some scholars was, however, surprisingly strong. In the 1970s and 1980s, he was frequently assailed as reactionary (even fascist), anti-feminist, and anti-Semitic. For a time, at major literary conferences speakers sometimes included negative asides about Eliot even when they were dealing with subjects that did not involve his work. From the perspective of some who were affected by the social and sexual liberation that developed in the late 1960s, Eliot was a dead white European male to be exorcised, a conservative rather than a liberatory force.

Since the late 1990s, modernist studies have burgeoned, and revised descriptions of literary modernism have emerged along with changed historical and intellectual insights that help provide provisional answers to new questions. Within the revivified attention to a literary modernism now more broadly defined than fifty years ago, Eliot is still a central figure, still a large presence, but on a larger canvas. More than half a century after Eliot's death, we are in a better position than either Eliot's contemporaries or those who immediately followed them in making meaningful, defensible sense of his remarkable writings.

Note
1. Hellström, Gustaf. Nobel Prize in Literature. Presentation Speech. http://nobelprize.org/nobel_prizes/literature/laureates/1948/eliot-speech.html

Biography of T. S. Eliot

R. Baird Shuman

Early Life

Although Thomas Stearns Eliot was born in and lived his early life in St. Louis, his family was so New England in its outlook that it can hardly be identified as Midwestern. Eliot's grandfather, William Greenleaf Eliot, was a Unitarian clergyman whose religious zeal brought him to St. Louis in 1834, shortly after graduation from Harvard's Divinity School. He founded a Unitarian church in St. Louis and then went on to establish three schools, a poor fund, and a sanitary commission in the city. His crowning triumph, however, was in founding Washington University in 1872.

Eliot was the youngest of seven children, one of whom died in infancy. His sister Abigail was nineteen when Eliot was born, his only brother, Henry, nine. Eliot's parents, Henry Ware and Charlotte Champe Stearns Eliot, were in their forties when their last child was born. They had been married for twenty years. The father was president of the Hydraulic-Press Brick Company. Both of Eliot's parents lived in the shadow of the renowned grandfather. Eliot's father suffered the guilt of not having become a clergyman. Charlotte Eliot, an accomplished person by most standards, believed that she was a failure because she had not attended college and because her verse, written mostly for friends but occasionally published in local newspapers, had brought her no recognition. Charlotte was not comfortable around infants, so during Eliot's early years, a nurse looked after him.

The family spent summers in Gloucester, Massachusetts, at Eastern Point, the summer home Eliot's father built in 1896. Eliot knew early that regardless of where he lived, he was a New Englander. Although he was a Unitarian as well, his nurse had exposed him to services in the Roman Catholic Church, to which she belonged. In 1927, the year Eliot became a British subject, he was also confirmed in the Anglican Church.

Eliot received a solid classical education at Smith Academy in St.

Louis. In preparation for his entrance to Harvard in 1906, Eliot attended Milton Academy in Massachusetts. At Harvard, he finished his bachelor's degree in three years. Eliot stayed on from 1909 to 1914 as a graduate student in English and philosophy. Following the lead of Arthur Symons' *The Symbolist Movement in Literature* (1899), Eliot read the French Symbolists, especially Jules Laforgue, in whose literary tracks he followed.

Awarded a Sheldon Travelling Fellowship in 1914, Eliot planned to travel on the Continent, then to take up residence at Merton College, Oxford, to write his thesis on F. H. Bradley. In July, 1914, he went to Marburg, Germany, for a summer program in philosophy but left after two weeks because war was imminent. He married Vivien Haigh-Wood in 1915. Eliot, five feet, eleven inches tall, was handsome and slender, although stooped, sallow, and sad-eyed. Always meticulously dressed and polished, he fit easily into British life. He visited the United States only occasionally after 1915.

Shortly after Eliot arrived in England from Marburg, his Harvard classmate, Conrad Aiken, introduced him to Ezra Pound, who became the most influential literary influence in Eliot's life. Pound identified "The Love Song of J. Alfred Prufrock," written on Eliot's first trip to Europe in 1910-1911, as the poem most likely to establish Eliot's literary reputation. Pound persuaded Harriet Monroe to publish the poem in *Poetry*, which she did, in June, 1915. Subsequently, Eliot's poems appeared often in *Poetry*. In 1917, his first book, *Prufrock and Other Observations*, was published in London.

Life's Work

At thirty, Eliot had two books in print: *Prufrock and Other Observations* and *Ezra Pound: His Metric and Poetry* (1917). By his fortieth birthday, he had twenty-three more books in print, including collections of his poetry, several books of criticism that dislocated many entrenched ideas about literature, and three dramatic works, *Sweeney*

Agonistes (1932; verse play), *The Rock* (1934), and *Murder in the Cathedral* (1935).

The most influential of his books was *The Waste Land* (1922), a long poem dedicated to Ezra Pound, who suggested the extensive revisions Eliot made in the manuscript. The poem, which deals largely with the question of human alienation and estrangement in the post-World War I era, is a series of closely related sections whose unifying allegorical thread is the search for the Holy Grail. It depicts pessimistically humankind's greed and lust, its need and desire for redemption. No poem could have been more right for its time.

The Waste Land was unique in that Eliot supplied extensive notes and references for it, leading readers to view it as a more formidable document than it actually is. Eliot later confessed that he added the documentation, much of which is misleading, to fill space. The poem is more important for its fresh and vigorous use of language and for its control of metrics than early critics, misled by the documentation, had credited it. *The Waste Land* broke totally from the post-Romantic literary tradition, and it had obvious roots in such French Symbolists as Paul Verlaine and Arthur Rimbaud, in the philosophical quest for salvation found in the works of Dante and Vergil, and in the English metaphysical poetry of John Donne and John Dryden.

The Waste Land is the first truly modern poem in English in the twentieth century.

It is remarkable that during Eliot's most productive period he was variously a teacher, a bank employee, and, for more than thirty years, a member of the publishing house of Faber and Gwyer, after 1929 known as Faber and Faber. Eliot could write for no more than three hours a day, usually composing directly to his typewriter as he stood at a lectern. He continued his work in publishing because he was never convinced that his writing was of sufficient quality that he should give over his life to it. As an editor, he was generous with his time and advice to young writers.

Religiously orthodox, Eliot declared himself to be also a neoclassicist and a royalist, stands that were uncommon among many intellectuals of his day. Viewed against the backdrop of the late twentieth century, Eliot, despite the heterodoxy of his poetic style and of his critical judgments, seems conservative, often to the point of being reactionary.

Religious identity was a continuing theme in Eliot's poetry and drama, reflecting the personal religious conflicts he experienced. Eliot's Ariel poems and *Ash-Wednesday* (1930) express some of the concerns he had about the acceptance of religious belief and about the discipline such belief requires. His early dramas, most notably *Murder in the Cathedral*, a play in the Greek tradition that uses a chorus, reflect his own religious search.

Eliot's philosophical stance and literary methodology were antithetical to Romanticism, which emphasizes emotion over intellect. Eliot's artistic aim was to be as objective as possible but to produce writing that would serve a social function. This aim led him to experiment with drama in the 1930s, a decade in which *Murder in the Cathedral* was his greatest triumph. His Orestian *The Family Reunion* (1939), although it contains some superb writing, confused audiences and enjoyed little popular success.

With the onset of World War II, Eliot wrote more poetry than drama, resurrecting "Burnt Norton" (1936) as the first poem of *Four Quartets* (1943), which also contained "East Coker" (1940), "The Dry Salvages" (1941), and "Little Gidding" (1942), poems that deeply reflect his own past and, by extension, the collective past of the human race. Each of the four poems is autonomous, but taken collectively, they make a statement about humankind that has an encompassing philosophical and anthropological impact.

Eliot received the Nobel Prize for Literature in 1948, the same year in which he received the Order of Merit from King George VI. By that time, Eliot was generally considered the most important poet writing in English. He heard of his selection for the Nobel Prize while he was in Princeton as a fellow at the Institute for Advanced Studies. There, he worked on *The Cocktail Party* (1949), which he had begun before he left England.

The play, which enjoyed enormous popular acceptance, was followed by *The Confidential Clerk* (1953) and *The Elder Statesman* (1958). The later plays were concerned with the philosophical and moral issues with which Eliot had long been grappling, but they avoided the pitfalls of *The Family Reunion* and delivered their didactic messages indirectly.

The Cocktail Party, witty and delightfully farcical, was Eliot's greatest commercial success, although the musical extravaganza, Andrew Lloyd Webber's *Cats* (1981), based on Eliot's *Old Possum's Book of Practical Cats* (1939), has become one of the most commercially successful shows of the twentieth century, hav-ing far surpassed *The Cocktail Party* in popular appeal.

Eliot, ever the gentleman in appearance and actions, was clearly an elitist. This austere posture, however, did not prevent his helping young writers of promise throughout his life, which was neither easy nor happy. His first wife, Vivien, from whom he was separated in 1932, was mentally unstable and was institutionalized for much of their married life. She died in 1947.

On January 10, 1957, Eliot married Valerie Fletcher, who had worked for him at Faber and Faber for eight years. In their nearly eight years together before Eliot's death, Valerie, who keenly understood and appreciated Eliot's work, brought more light and joy into his life than he had experienced since he reached adulthood.

From *Dictionary of World Biography: The 20th Century* (Pasadena, CA: Salem Press, 1999): 1058-1061. Copyright © 1999 by Salem Press, Inc.

Bibliography

Ackroyd, Peter. *T. S. Eliot: A Life*. New York: Simon & Schuster, 1984. The first comprehensive biography based on Eliot's published and unpublished writing as well as on extensive interviews with his friends and associates. Ackroyd has been praised in several reviews for his handling of both Eliot's life and work, especially the poet's disastrous first marriage and *The Waste Land*.

Bloom, Harold, ed. *Murder in the Cathedral*. New York: Chelsea House, 1988. A collection of the most significant articles, by a variety of critics, on one of Eliot's most famous plays. Some of the articles tend toward obscurity, but most are helpful in placing the play in the larger context of poetic drama. Includes a helpful introduction by Bloom and a bibliography.

Browne, Elliott Martin. *The Making of T. S. Eliot's Plays*. London: Cambridge University Press, 1969. The most exhaustive textual study of Eliot's plays available, this book analyzes the early typescript and manuscript versions of Eliot's dramas, identifying and commenting on all major changes. Browne attempts to reconstruct Eliot's writing process, and so any reader interested in that aspect of Eliot's art might begin here.

Childs, Donald J. *From Philosophy to Poetry: T. S. Eliot's Study of Knowledge and Experience*. London: Athlone Press, 2001. Childs analyzes Eliot's literary works with emphasis on how he expressed his philosophy through his poetry. Bibliography and index.

Davidson, Harriet, ed. *T. S. Eliot*. New York: Longman, 1999. A collection of literary criticism regarding Eliot and his works. Bibliography and index.

Donoghue, Denis. *Words Alone: The Poet, T. S. Eliot*. New Haven, Conn.: Yale University Press, 2000. A wide-ranging critical examination in the form of an intellectual memoir, and an illuminating account of Donoghue's engagement with the works of Eliot. Includes bibliographical references and index.

Eliot, Valerie, ed. *The Letters of T. S. Eliot, 1898-1922*. Vol. 1. New York: Harcourt Brace Jovanovich, 1988. Includes all the poet's significant extant correspondence up to the age of thirty-four. An important addition to the biographical and critical literature on Eliot, none of which had access to this complete collection of letters. His correspondence contains drafts of poems and reveals both his extremely correct and whimsical sides.

Gordon, Lyndall. *Eliot's Early Years*. New York: Oxford University Press, 1977. Reviewed by Richard Ellmann and other critics as the most thorough treatment of Eliot's early career, Gordon's study is a superb meld of biography and criticism, drawing upon unpublished diaries, letters, and poems by the poet's mother. Should be read in conjunction with Peter Ackroyd's equally important biography.

_____. *Eliot's New Life*. New York: Farrar, Straus & Giroux, 1988. A continuation of Gordon's biography of the early years, concentrating on the religious phase of the poet's life, his separation from his first wife, his friendships with two other women, and his marriage to Valerie Fletcher in 1957. Gordon is equally sound on Eliot's later poetry, especially on the development of *Four Quartets*.

_____. *T. S. Eliot: An Imperfect Life.* New York: Norton, 1999. (See *Magill's Literary Annual* review.) In this exhaustive biography Gordon builds on the efforts from her first two books covering Eliot's early years. She assiduously tracked down Eliot's correspondence and manuscripts to address the issue of Eliot's anti-Semitism and misogyny. Gordon reinforces her thesis that Eliot's poetic output should be interpreted as a coherent spiritual biography.

Habib, Rafey. *The Early T. S. Eliot and Western Philosophy.* New York: Cambridge University Press, 1999. A look at the philosophical beliefs held by Eliot and how they found their way into his literary works. Bibliography and index.

Litz, A. Walton, ed. *Eliot in His Time: Essays on the Occasion of the Fiftieth Anniversary of* The Waste Land. Princeton, N.J.: Princeton University Press, 1973. Eight essays by eminent poets and scholars on the development, the achievement, and the impact of Eliot's great poem. Each essay assesses Eliot's place in literary history and examines not only his published poetry but also the facsimile publication of Eliot's manuscripts of *The Waste Land.*

Malamud, Randy. *T. S. Eliot's Drama: A Research and Production Sourcebook.* New York: Greenwood Press, 1992. A close look at the production of Eliot's dramatic works. Bibliography and indexes.

_____. *Where the Words Are Valid: T. S. Eliot's Communities of Drama.* Westport, Conn.: Greenwood Press, 1994. A critical analysis and interpretation of Eliot's plays. Bibliography and index.

Moody, A. David, ed. *The Cambridge Companion to T. S. Eliot.* New York: Cambridge University Press, 1994. A comprehensive reference work dedicated to Eliot's life, work, and times. Bibliography and index.

Schuchard, Ronald. *Eliot's Dark Angel: Intersections of Life and Art.* New York: Oxford University Press, 1999. A critical study demonstrating how Eliot's personal voice works through the sordid, the bawdy, the blasphemous, and the horrific to create a unique moral world. Schuchard works against conventional attitudes toward Eliot's intellectual and spiritual development by showing how early and consistently his classical and religious sensibility manifests itself in his poetry and criticism.

The *Paris Review* Perspective

Gemma Sieff for *The Paris Review*

Thomas Stearns Eliot (1888-1965) was a man not easily categorized: his life and his writing present a range of ultimately unresolvable juxtapositions. Eliot was a St. Louis native with a New England sensibility. He worked simultaneously as both a poet and a banker. He was a naturalized British citizen, but his work remained, he claimed late in his life, American "in its sources, in its emotional springs." His life, in short, mirrored his work—unapologetically complex and preoccupied with the incongruous scraps and bigger mysteries of the human predicament.

Eliot would probably balk at the notion of any overt connection between his life and his poetry. He thought that the best literature should be objectively resonant and considered his oeuvre to be somehow distant from himself, free from the entrapments of ego. The trick is not "reducing Eliot to his noncreative, dental-chair self," as Irvin Ehrenpreis accused those who mined his biography to read his poetry of doing, but rather to mark the way that his varied life helped create a body of work that was wide-ranging, catholic even, in its genre and scope. His major works of poetry—"The Love Song of J. Alfred Prufrock" (1915); "Gerontion" (1920); *The Waste Land* (1922); "The Hollow Men" (1925); *Ash-Wednesday* (1930); and *Four Quartets* (1936-42)—suggest, in their startling stylistic range, the unrelenting drive of his artistic ambition. Where "Prufrock" took on the mired, wistful, aging consciousness of one man, "The Hollow Men" conveyed the broken and brutalized consciousness of an entire land following the Great War. His poems contain a multitude of voices—from the priggish Prufrock to the blunt pubgoer of *The Waste Land* to the gnomic, symmetrical utterances in *Four Quartets*—and take a variety of forms: the same man who sought to bring together Western and Indic philology would also compose the whimsical *Old Possum's Book of Practical Cats*, stating gamely, "One wants to keep one's hand in, you know, in every type of poem, serious and frivolous and proper and improper." Eliot's penetrating critical mind strongly influenced the school of New Criticism—a year after his death, Philip Rahv called him "the finest literary critic of this century in the English language"—yet his work strays far beyond the bounds of his decrees as a critic.

Despite his poetry's presumed difficulty, there is great pleasure to be found in reading it, in experiencing the rawness and charge of Eliot's language, its ebbs and torrents, hairpin turns, and incantatory rhythms. One wants to get the beauty of it hot. Like his friend Ezra Pound, who helped refine some of Eliot's best early work, he showed no compunction about making something new out of strands of allusion and outright, thrilling theft. "When the poem has been made," Eliot wrote, "something new has happened, something that cannot be wholly explained by *anything that went before*. That, I believe, is what we mean by 'creation.'" To trace Eliot's dizzying array of references is a formidable challenge, but the reader can also simply revel in what Louis Menand describes as the poet's "extraordinary mysteriousness," a "vast sensorium of word music . . . oscillating between clarity and utter obscurity." The critic Michael Wood has noted that for Eliot "discontinuities are the life of the poems. . . . Things are together in the poem, however violently they have been yoked to each other," a comment that echoes Eliot's own estimation of Dante's genius: Dante knew "the real right thing, the power of establishing relations between beauty of the most diverse sorts: it is the utmost power of the poet."

The daring and ambition of Eliot's poems can seem at odds with their mild-mannered creator, whose controlled self-presentation (Siegfried Sassoon remarked that Eliot had "cold-storaged [his] humanity") concealed the fact, manifest in his writing, that he was intimately acquainted with misery. In Eliot's poetry, shreds of specificity give way to a universal howl that Wood characterizes as "inhabit[ing] a zone beyond personal anguish." He channeled the despair of post-World War I Europe, the syncopations of the Jazz Age, and the roar of the London Blitz. He would ultimately write some of the most mournful verses of modernism:

>Is it like this
>In death's other kingdom
>Waking alone
>At the hour when we are
>Trembling with tenderness
>Lips that would kiss
>Form prayers to broken stone.

And, more famously:

>*This is the way the world ends*
>*This is the way the world ends*
>*This is the way the world ends*
>*Not with a bang but a whimper.*

Eliot was raised Unitarian but he joined the Anglican Church in 1927, and it is challenging to reconcile the fluid near-nihilism of these lines from "The Hollow Men" with the redemptive message of Christianity—much less the ritualized trappings of High Anglicanism. He once declared himself a "classicist in literature, royalist in politics, and Anglo-Catholic in religion," and while this statement was almost certainly a little bit arch, it also gets at his deeply felt traditionalism in opposition to what he saw as the vulgarity of contemporary life.

So many of Eliot's motifs concern emptiness, deprivation, isolation. Even after renewing his dedication to Christianity, he was preoccupied with the futility of life on earth, reminding his readers of their impotence, the necessity of their surrender. And so we believe him when he implores in "Ash-Wednesday":

> Teach us to care and not to care
> Teach us to sit still.

The lines are tied up in Eliot's faith, but they are also a testament to the enduring power of poetry—of the written word—in the world, even as the world fights against it:

> Against the Word the unstilled world still whirled
> About the centre of the silent Word.

In 1948 he accepted the Nobel Prize in Literature by saying, "I stand before you, not on my own merits, but as a symbol, for a time, of the significance of poetry." Certainly his work stands alone, independent of the reputation that precedes it: full of feather-light, generative, never-leaden erudition; responsive to the complicated world he observed; a product of the nuanced and expansive reach of his perception. That his perception felt, and continues to feel, *true* for so many suggests the influence and incredible authority of his work.

Works Cited

Ackroyd, Peter. *T. S. Eliot*. New York: Simon & Schuster, 1984.
Craft, Robert. "Eliot's English Usage." *The New York Review of Books*, June 10, 1976.
_____. "The Perils of Mrs. Eliot." *The New York Review of Books*, May 23, 2002.
Ehrenpreis, Irvin. "Art, Life, and T. S. Eliot." *The New York Review of Books*, June 28, 1984.
Eliot, T. S. "The Art of Poetry No. 1." Interview with Donald Hall. *The Paris Review* 21 (Spring/Summer 1959).
_____. *Collected Poems: 1909-1962*. New York: Harcourt Brace, 1963.
Kermode, Frank. "Bearing Eliot's Reality." *The Guardian*, September 27, 1984.
Menand, Louis. "How Eliot Became Eliot." *The New York Review of Books*, May 15, 1997.
_____. "The Women Come and Go." *The New Yorker*, September 30, 2002.
Rahv, Philip. "Eliot's Achievement." *The New York Review of Books*, March 3, 1966.

Spender, Stephen. "In Eliot's Cave." *The New York Review of Books*, September 19, 1974.
"T. S. Eliot," from *Nobel Lectures, Literature 1901-1967*, ed. Horst Frenz. Amsterdam: Elsevier Publishing Company, 1969. http://nobelprize.org/nobel_prizes/literature/ laureates/1948/eliot-bio.html
Wood, Michael. "Bleistein and Mr. Eliot." *The New York Review of Books*, February 15, 1990.
———. "The Struggles of T. S. Eliot." *The New York Review of Books*, May 13, 1976.

CONTEXT, RECEPTION, COMPARISON, CRITICAL LENS

Cultural Contexts

Neil Heims

Neil Heims sketches significant intellectual, spiritual, literary, and professional contexts, influences, and events in Eliot's life through the 1948 award of the Nobel Prize. As he explains, Eliot's family were easterners who had displaced themselves to the Midwest, to St. Louis, where his paternal grandfather, William Greenleaf Eliot, was an influential, socially engaged minister. He traces Eliot's sense of self-discipline back to his grandfather's attitudes as reinforced by those of his parents. Because of the family's roots, Eliot studied at Harvard, where, as Heims tells us, he came under the influence of strong-minded professors, including Irving Babbitt, an important humanist with whom Eliot studied the history of thought. He also read Dante and the Metaphysical poets, especially John Donne. Heims introduces one of Eliot's key notions, the objective correlative, as an outcome of his thinking about the tendencies of Metaphysical poetry, by contrast with later Romantic poetry and its emphasis on personal, or subjective, expression. Eliot's quarrel with the Romantics, especially William Wordsworth, is deep. About Eliot's discovery of Jules Laforgue, the French Symbolist poet, on his own at Harvard, Heims makes the suggestive point that Eliot adopted an ironic stance, like Laforgue's, as a way to be honest about poetic attempts to project sincerity, a central Victorian virtue. According to Heims, Eliot adopts a stance of modernist sincerity, in which self-irony contributes to a double attitude that keeps the pose from being sentimental and uncritical. Eliot's intellectual and aesthetic ambitions took him to Paris, Germany, and, for the long term, England, where he acquired new contexts for his thinking and writing. As a graduate student in philosophy, before his departure for Germany and England, Eliot studied, among other subjects, Eastern thought and the anthropological work of Sir James Frazer, whose multivolume *The Golden Bough* influenced a generation of intellectuals. The traces of that influence are clear in *The Waste Land*. In England, while he pursued his career as a poet and critic, Eliot worked as a teacher, then a bank clerk (who could put to use his knowledge of European languages), and finally an editor at Faber and Faber, a major publisher. He also edited his own journal, *The Criterion*, for almost twenty years between the two world wars, halting publication when he realized that World War II was imminent. As Heims rightly asserts, he encountered a variety of strong, influencing contexts, but Eliot's attitudes and his work were so innovative that they transformed the contexts he encountered as much as the contexts shaped him. —J.P.R.

The poetry of the dead is in his bones and at the tips of his fingers: he has the rare gift of being able to weave . . . an echo or even a line of the past into the pattern of his own poem. (Leonard Woolf)

. . . making this new poetry flower on the stem of the oldest. (Virginia Woolf, "Is This Poetry?" *Athenaeum*, June 20, 1919)

Family

In 1669, Andrew Eliot left the English village of East Coker in Somerset—where T. S. Eliot, one of his many descendants, was buried nearly three hundred years later, in 1965—to sail for Massachusetts. There he became one of the first citizens of the colony and, as one of the judges presiding over the Salem witch trials, he condemned nineteen of his neighbors to be hanged for witchcraft. Andrew Eliot's family took root, prospering in Massachusetts and exerting religious and cultural power as preachers and educators. Charles William Eliot (1834-1926), for example, a third cousin once removed from T. S. Eliot's grandfather, was the president of Harvard from 1869 to 1909. T. S. Eliot's grandfather, William Greenleaf Eliot (1811-1887), was a Unitarian minister. His wife, Abigail Adams Cranch, was a great-niece of the wife of the second president of the United States, John Adams.

Although W. G. Eliot died in 1887, the year before T. S. Eliot's birth, he exerted a formidable influence on his grandson's life. In 1904 Eliot's mother, Charlotte, published *William Greenleaf Eliot: Minister, Educator, Philanthropist*, which she wrote, as she indicated in the dedication, "for my Children / Lest They Forget."

After graduating from Harvard Divinity School in 1834 and being ordained a Unitarian minister, W. G. Eliot, following an inner calling, left Boston for St. Louis, Missouri. There he founded the first Unitarian church west of the Mississippi, the Church of the Messiah, now called the First Unitarian Church of Saint Louis, and the Eliot Seminary, which became Washington University. He also helped establish the St. Louis public schools, the St. Louis Art Museum, the Mission Free School, the South Side Day Nursery, the Colored Orphans' Home, the Soldiers' Orphans' Home, the Memorial Home, the Blind Girls' Home, the Women's Christian Home, and the Western Sanitary Commission, which furnished medical care and supplies during the Civil War. He was active, too, prior to the war, in keeping Missouri in the Union. He was vehement in his condemnation of tobacco use, alcohol consumption, and prostitution. W. G. Eliot was a man of great public spirit, a stern moralist dedicated to public service in the interest of the social good. As a Unitarian, a Christian who accepts the unity rather than the trinity of God and for whom Jesus is thus exemplary rather than divine, it was a matter of principle for him that people can be helped to be better people and that social institutions, spiritual, educational, and eleemosynary, are the means to that end. He believed that religion and reason were not antithetical but could and did function cooperatively together.

T. S. Eliot thus came from a tradition of engaged citizens focusing their individual intelligence and resources on social issues in order to shape the world around them to match an idea within them. Unlike his grandfather, who believed in the perfectibility of mankind, Eliot despaired of natural goodness and promoted the virtues of subduing the flesh to the rule of the chastened spirit. Like his grandson, W. G. Eliot was the author of a number of books.

Among his books, the *Life of Archer Alexander: From Slavery to Freedom* (1885), an account of a runaway slave whom W. G. Eliot harbored and protected, reads most like a novel, but W. G. Eliot was wary of novels. The genre that was his specialty was the sermon or lecture, and he published several volumes, including *Lectures to Young Women* and *Lectures to Young Men*, published in Boston in 1854 by the International Historical Library of Y.M.C.A. [the Young Men's Christian Association] Publications. These books were placed in every room rented in the Ys. Regarding novels, W. G. Eliot wrote in a lecture called "Leisure Time," "One might as well expect to gain strength to his body from sweetmeats and confectionary, as for his mind from works of fiction. The very best of them should be used as an occasional refreshment; considered as a daily food, they are absolutely pernicious" (Miller, 15).

At least as pernicious as novels were intoxication, breaking the Sabbath, and the "lewd and lavish act of sin," in other words, sexual activity outside the boundaries of marriage. T. S. Eliot's grandfather wrote, "Of all the influences in society, calculated to purify and elevate man's character, that of virtuous and well-educated women is perhaps the strongest. . . . An essential part of the education of a young man is in a woman's society. He needs it as much as he needs the education of books, and its neglect is equally pernicious. . . . He who betrays her from her innocence is not less hateful in the eyes of God, than the serpent who brought sin into Paradise. He who is upon terms of friendship with her after she is betrayed, unless for the purpose of restoring her to virtue, is helping her to sink lower in her degradation, and himself goes down with her to the gates of hell" (Miller, 15-16). Strictures, boundaries, rules, proprieties, territories beyond which it was dangerous to stray: these concepts and guides to decorum were fundamental to the character of virtue according to W. G. Eliot, and they are the props for the doctrines and declarations at the heart of T. S. Eliot's beliefs and writing, whether poetry or criticism.

T. S. Eliot's father, William Greenleaf's son, Henry Ware Eliot, disappointed *his* father only in refusing to become a Unitarian minister and became, instead, a prosperous manufacturer of bricks. Otherwise he was true to his father's values, perhaps exceeding his father's condemnation of sexual expression. To his brother, Thomas Ware Eliot, who did become a Unitarian Minister, Henry Ware wrote, "I cannot get up sympathy with Sex Hygien[e]. . . . I do not approve of public instruction in sexual relations. When I teach my children to avoid the Devil I do not begin by giving them a letter of introduction to him and his crowd. I hope that the cure for syphilis will never be discovered. It is God's punishment for nastiness. Take it away and there will be more nastiness, and it will be necessary to emasculate our children to keep them clean" (Miller, 16). Nor was T. S. Eliot's mother, Charlotte, of very different opinion regarding the root of sin in appetite. In *Savonarola*, her long dramatic poem, which Eliot arranged to be published in 1926, Charlotte Eliot wrote, "Can penitence alone forgiveness earn? / Or must I not in purgatorial fire/ Atone the baser promptings of desire?" (Miller, 21).

That these family lessons of youth were formative, Eliot attests in a confidence he imparted in his last years to William Turner Levy. In the 1950s, Eliot's doctors ordered him to stop smoking, and he tried to substitute eating candy but "his puritanical upbringing had left him permanently scarred with an inability to indulge this pleasure. Indeed, when he was a boy, . . . although he had money he could never bring himself to enter a candy store and actually purchase a box of candy for himself" (Miller, 18). This is a noteworthy testament not only to the force of the Eliot family's Puritanism but also to the power of tobacco, which despite its interdiction was not as easily boycotted as candy.

His family setting and his family's values and traditions constitute Eliot's first culture and first context, the "accumulated sensations" of youth essential to a writer, as Eliot called them in a 1917 essay in *The Egoist* on the Russian author Ivan Turgenev (Howarth, 36). His family provided a culture and a context that drew upon, organized, and united a number of cultural contexts, especially Christian, Classical, Aristocratic, and Calvinistic, each element tempering and defining the others, but all sharing the discipline and severity that give backbone to Eliot's work. The culture of Eliot's lineage was also a culture defined by the values of social engagement and stern personal discipline. Eliot fits well as a member into his line. In fact, it is his family that gave him first the sense of line, of being an individual in a tradition, a sense to which he returns with regard to writing in his influential 1921 essay "Tradition and the Individual Talent."

The young T. S. Eliot was protected not only from the weakness of the spirit as it might be vanquished by desire but also from a bodily frailty that forbade athletics and vigorous movement and encouraged bookishness. Because of a congenital double hernia, Eliot from early youth was made to wear a truss, a kind of corset designed to protect the herniated area.

In contrast to the austerity and reserve of his family's culture, there was St. Louis itself. After the Civil War, St. Louis became a thriving city. Its commerce, industry, and culture were developed by its leading citizens in an attempt to secure for the city a special place in the United States, because of its geographical situation, as a link between the eastern and newly opening western sections of the country. For a while St. Louis achieved the prominence its leading citizens sought, but by the beginning of the twentieth century it had been overtaken as the major midwestern city by Chicago. In addition, it fell victim to a political corruption that became famous as the story of election fraud became the matter of the first chapter of Lincoln Steffens' muckraking exposé, *The Shame of the Cities* (1904). With the exposé came a renewed effort to clean up the city, and the Eliots were in the advance guard of the effort.

Harvard

Eliot left his family home in St. Louis in 1906 for Cambridge, Massachusetts, and Harvard College. While Boston, during the first years of the twentieth century, offered a bohemian haven for the gender-slippery dandyism and the aestheticism of models like the Pre-Raphaelites and Oscar Wilde, it was Harvard's academic culture that made Eliot the man of letters he became. Learning, by its very nature, is transmission of culture, and when it occurs, learning is always formative, shaping the individual by an encounter with traditions that reconfabulate the narrative of identity that is derived from any dialogue with the surrounding world. At Harvard, the world around him was composed of the great works of literature and philosophy and a handful of professors, the men of high eminence who thought about them.

Among the courses that Eliot took were medieval history, Greek literature, constitutional government, German grammar and prose, English literature and drama, French prose and poetry, art history, philosophy, continental literature, Latin poetry, the Roman novel, French literary criticism, and the "Ideals of Society, Religion, Art, and Science, in Their Historical Development." Even cursory familiarity with Eliot's poetry and his prose criticism reveals how much his course work at Harvard filled his thought and suffused his work. Harvard laid in Eliot the intellectual foundation for his poetry and his criticism.

Every student knows that the content of a course, whatever value it may have, becomes transformative when it is given momentum by a teacher for whom it has existential significance, when someone who cares about literature and thought can make the concern immediate to the student. At Harvard, Eliot had several such teachers whose influence upon his thinking, his character, and his subsequent work was decisive and recognizable. First among them was the philosopher Irving Babbitt.

Babbitt's lectures, Eliot wrote in *The Criterion* in October 1933, following Babbitt's death, ostensibly were about "French Literary Criticism; but they had a great deal to do with Aristotle, Longinus and Dionysius of Halicarnassus; they touched frequently upon Buddhism, Confucius, [Jean Jacques] Rousseau, and contemporary political and religious movements. Somehow or other one read a number of books . . .

just because Babbitt assumed that any educated man had already read them" (Miller, 82). It sounds like a preparation for reading *The Waste Land*. The goal of such study, according to Babbitt, was "not to encourage the democratic spirit, but on the contrary to check the drift to pure democracy," for, Babbitt asserted, "what is needed is not democracy alone, nor . . . an unmixed aristocracy but a blending of the two—an aristocratic and selective democracy" (Miller, 81). Consequently, Babbitt decried the scientific progressivism of Sir Francis Bacon and the Romantic optimism of Rousseau. They were "humanitarians," whose thought could only mislead, not "humanists," whose virtue is to see that "what is important in man . . . is not his power to act on the world, but his power to act upon himself." It is the "true principle of restraint," and, accordingly, "that man is most human who can check his faculty . . . in its mid-career and temper it by its opposite" (Miller, 83). Such reservations about democracy and progress and such beliefs in aristocracy and restraint permeate Eliot's work, and he gives them voice even more bluntly than his teacher in his 1933 essay, when he writes, "We insist on 'educating' too many people; and Heaven knows for what" (Miller, 84).

The second significant influence on Eliot at Harvard was Barrett Wendell, author of *A Literary History of America*. Wendell did not hold American literature in high regard and was not only in his literary judgments but in everything a fervent Anglophile, as Eliot himself became. Eliot also ultimately adopted his monarchical, anti-democratic stance. "The American Revolution, then," Wendell wrote, "disuniting the English-speaking race, has had on history an effect which those who cherish the moral and political heritage of our language may well grow to feel in some sense tragic" (Miller, 86). Of slavery in America, Wendell wrote, "the institution of slavery was honestly regarded by many people as one more phase of the more comprehensive institution which really lies at the basis of modern civilization; namely, property. Property in any form involves deprivation. Property in land, for example, deprives many human beings of access to many portions of the earth"

(Miller, 86). Wendell concluded his defense of slavery by lamenting the historical valorization of the abolitionists. "In so far as this legend [of the righteousness of the abolitionists] has led the growing generation of American youth to assume that because you happen to think a given form of property wrong, you have a natural right to confiscate it forthwith, the antislavery movement has perhaps tended to weaken the security of American institutions. At least in Massachusetts, too, the prevalence of this movement seems permanently to have lowered the personal dignity of public life, by substituting for the traditional rule of the conservative gentry the obvious dominance of the less educated classes" (Miller, 87).

Wendell's influence was also significant for the evolution of Eliot's thought about and practice of religion. Eliot strayed from his family's optimistic Unitarianism into a gloomy intellectual atheism. From Wendell, Eliot heard an attack on Unitarianism that deplored its reducing Jesus to a perfect model of virtue, which denied His being as a Divine Incarnation. Wendell attacked the Unitarian belief in the perfectibility of mankind. He argued that it led people to abandon their belief in the need for a savior. A savior is necessary only when mankind is seen as inherently wicked. Parallel to his later shift to favoring monarchy in government, Eliot came to Wendell's religious position, in 1930, when he joined the Church of England.

Eliot also absorbed from his Harvard teachers attitudes about poetry and poetics, along with the poetry itself that was being taught. The poets upon whom Eliot's attention was concentrated at Harvard were Dante, John Donne and the English Metaphysical poets, William Wordsworth and the Romantic poets, and the French Symbolists, particularly Jules Laforgue. All but the Symbolists were matter for courses at Harvard. Of Dante, at the time of Eliot's matriculation, there was something of a cult at Harvard. Dante's poetic vision moved away from the flesh to the spirit and suggested a progressive refinement of beauty, a concept that fit nicely with the aestheticism of the Pre-Raphaelite poets that was part of the dominant spirit of the time.

John Donne's poetry was of a defining significance for Eliot's own. "A thought to Donne," Eliot wrote in 1921, in an essay called "The Metaphysical Poets," "was an experience; it modified his sensibility. When a poet's mind is perfectly equipped for its work, it is constantly amalgamating disparate experience . . . always forming new wholes" from the several experiences that impinge upon him separately and simultaneously. Donne and the Metaphysical poets, Eliot argued, were "trying to find the verbal equivalent for states of mind and feeling" (quoted in Miller, 109). This attempt essentially removes poetry from the realm of the poet's personal expression. By being transformed into a linguistic representation of reality as the poet experienced it, poetry becomes what Eliot came to call an "objective correlative" of the state of mind and the emotional condition produced in the poet by that experience.

Depersonalization in poetry was emphasized by William Allan Neilson, with whom Eliot studied the Romantic poets. Referring to Wordsworth's famous definition of poetry as "the spontaneous overflow of powerful feelings," Neilson argued that "The term 'emotion' . . . is not an entirely happy one. It points in the right direction, but hardly hits the mark. . . . The quality aimed at may . . . more fitly be termed intensity" (Miller, 92). Eliot extended this way of thinking in "Tradition and the Individual Talent" when he wrote that Wordsworth's description of poetry as "'emotion recollected in tranquility' is an inexact formula. . . . [I]t is neither emotion, nor recollection, nor . . . tranquility. It is a concentration, and a new thing resulting from the concentration, of a very great number of experiences which to the practical and active person would not seem to be experience at all; it . . . does not happen consciously or of deliberation" (quoted in Miller, 93). Poetry, accordingly, is the recurring new growth of a tradition that is tended by the midwifery of the poet.

Rather than being the emotionally expressed center of his poem, the poet is a catalyst through which various complex experiences are transformed into language that enables a transmutation by the reader into something new. The poet, then, can be represented as a persona or a masked figure who uses himself for the purpose of effecting the transmutation of experience into poetry. For Eliot, the supreme poet of masks is the French Symbolist, Jules Laforgue. His ironic stance involves apparent sincerity that is, nevertheless, the result of the poet's awareness of experiencing the emotions he is distilling into poetry by displaying them through a language that represents the poses conveying those emotions. Laforgue's irony is of particular importance to Eliot because Laforgue's poetry conveys sincerity despite the reader's sophisticated understanding that sincerity is a literary illusion. The double attitude responds to the great intimate and personal poems of the nineteenth century, such as Percy Bysshe Shelley's *Adonais*, Alfred Tennyson's *In Memoriam*, or Robert Browning's dramatic monologues, whose effects depended on the sincerity or, in Browning's case, the masking of the poet's feelings. The poetry of sentiment often risks becoming sentimental poetry. Thus an ironic attitude, in Laforgue and in Eliot, paradoxically, becomes the signal for sincerity, whereas sincerity itself, without irony, can seem to be calculating and straining for emotional effect, or even false.

Eliot did not discover Laforgue through his course work at Harvard. He read about him in the Harvard library in Arthur Symons' (1865-1945) book *The Symbolist Movement in Literature*, 1899, and sent to Paris for a collection of Laforgue's poetry. The lure of Paris existed not only in its poetry. Europe and its major capitals exerted a strong pull on many American artists and intellectuals. Writers like Henry Adams and Henry James, and the philosopher George Santayana, one of Eliot's teachers at Harvard, all abandoned what appeared to be the cultural wasteland of the United States for the cultural refinement and complexity of a tradition-rich Europe. In 1910, encouraged by Irving Babbitt, T. S. Eliot began the migration back to Europe for himself when he went to spend a year in Paris and to study at the Sorbonne. Some fifty-five years later, in his autobiography, the Pulitzer Prize-winning literary critic and historian Van Wyck Brooks explained how

Harvard had shaped Eliot's disposition. "When one added these tastes together, the royalism and the classicism, the Anglo-Catholicism, the cults of Donne and Dante, the Sanskrit, the Elizabethan dramatists and the French Symbolist poets, one arrived at T. S. Eliot, the quintessence of Harvard" (quoted in Miller, 113-4).

One of the lasting friendships Eliot formed at Harvard was with the poet Conrad Aiken, to whom, in his letters, Eliot often included the kind of verse that might hardly have been expected of him. He sprinkled witty and obscene, even pornographic, verse throughout his letters to Aiken. Despite being "the quintessence of Harvard," Eliot had command of a demotic idiom and a fascination with sexuality that he knew how to use in his poetry.

Paris

Paris in 1910 offered the kind of complex cultural climate just suited for the Eliot who had been formed at Harvard. Paris sheltered a historic cultural, intellectual, and political tradition that Eliot held still to be vital and a new movement in poetry that Eliot considered to be essential for its robust continuation. Writing in 1944, Eliot described his year in Paris, saying, "Sometimes Paris was all the past; sometimes all the future; and the two aspects combined in a present perfect" (Miller, 147). Eliot attended lectures at the Collège de France by Henri Bergson, the philosopher noted for his theories of time's relativity and of consciousness. Through his French tutor, the novelist Alain-Fournier, he met Jacques Rivière, the secretary of *La Nouvelle Revue Française*, the literary journal founded in 1909 by André Gide to spread the new post-Symbolist poets. Eliot was in the center of advanced guard culture. But he also admired Charles Maurras, imprisoned in 1948 for collaboration with the Nazis during the German occupation, and his organization Action Française, a right-wing, monarchist, anti-Semitic, Catholic group—repudiated by the Catholic Church itself—which worked to retard the movement of democracy and restore the monarchy. His admiration put Eliot in the center of rear guard, reactionary culture. In Paris, Eliot's work came to first full blossom as he composed among other poems, "The Love Song of J. Alfred Prufrock" and "Portrait of a Lady." Paris clearly had a determining influence on Eliot.

In Paris, too, Eliot met Jean Verdenal, a medical student who was lodging at the *Pension Casaubon*, the same house in which Eliot was renting a room. Despite his course of study, Verdenal's interests were nearly identical to Eliot's, including the poetry of Laforgue and the politics of Maurras. He and Eliot developed a loving friendship which remained strong in Eliot's remembrance long after Verdenal was killed in the war in 1915. "Prufrock" is dedicated to him, and this epigraph, in the original Italian, taken from the twenty-first canto of Dante's *Purgatory*, is attached to that dedication, as if illuminating it: "Now can you understand the quality of love that warms me towards you, so that I forget our vanity, and treat the shadows like the solid thing." Some critics also regard *The Waste Land* as an elegy for Verdenal.

The climate of discrimination against homosexuality provides one relevant cultural context for Eliot's work. Such a context illuminates that work's attempts to present a depersonalized escape from emotion and to show emotional and sexual relations as buried, as in "Prufrock," "Portrait of a Lady," and *The Waste Land* or as surmounted, as in "Ash-Wednesday." In "Ash-Wednesday," the first line "Because I do not hope to turn again," suggests the Shakespearean double entendre which invests "turn" with a sexual connotation; the poet has removed himself from the hope of human, erotic love and celebrates his assumption of the spiritual love offered by the precepts and discipline of the Anglican Communion.

Eliot returned to Harvard after his year in Paris and resumed his study of philosophy, concentrating on Asian and Indian philosophy and on mythological anthropology of the kind developed by Sir James Frazer in *The Golden Bough*. One of the major assertions in that encyclopedic work is that the progress of culture is driven by the clash of the new with the old, wherein the new both destroys and incorporates the old. Frazer presents the idea by using images drawn from the vegetation cycle and stories of a young god slaying an ancient god.

It was becoming clear to Eliot at Harvard that literature rather than philosophy was his calling, and it was also becoming clear to him that if he were going to enter the literary tradition with any seriousness, it would not be in the United States but in Europe. On June 14, 1914, Eliot left Harvard on a Sheldon Traveling Fellowship and returned to Europe. After traveling on the continent and studying in Germany, with the outbreak of World War I, Eliot returned to England at the end of August 1914 and settled in London.

London

Conrad Aiken, Eliot's friend from Harvard and destined to become an important poet in his own right, preceded Eliot to London, bringing with him not only pieces of his own poetry, but several works by Eliot, including "Prufrock," which he showed with no success to several poetry magazine editors. When Eliot arrived in London, Aiken recommended he go to see an American poet who had been living in Europe, particularly in Italy, since 1908. Ezra Pound had published several volumes of poetry and had served as secretary to the Irish poet William Butler Yeats. He had been one of the leading figures in several new poetry movements, including Imagism and Vorticism, which repudiated the lengthy, discursive, and sentimental elements of nineteenth-century poetry. Pound had literary connections and influential friends. Living in London in 1914, he was the liaison to the American magazine *Poetry*, published, since 1912, by Harriet Monroe, in Chicago.

Eliot and Pound met on September 22, 1914, in one of the most important literary encounters of the twentieth century. Even without seeing any of his poetry, Pound was impressed by Eliot, and when Eliot did show him "Prufrock" and several other poems, Pound began a campaign on his behalf that brought Eliot to the attention of those who made careers and shaped the public perception of poetry. It was Pound who sent "Prufrock" to Harriet Monroe at *Poetry*, writing that "Prufrock" was "the best poem I have yet had or seen from an American" and that Eliot was "the only American poet I know who has made . . . adequate preparation for writing" (quoted from Humphrey Carpenter, *A Serious Character: The Life of Ezra Pound*, Boston, Houghton Mifflin, 1988, in Miller, 199). And it was Pound who overcame Monroe's early reservations and made sure she published the poem, which appeared in June 1915. With Pound backing him, Eliot was drawn into the culture of the new poetry that was being introduced through the little magazines published by a circle of literary figures all connected to Pound. In July, Wyndham Lewis, along with Pound a founder of Vorticism and a painter as well as an editor, published two poems by Eliot, "Preludes (I-IV)" and "Rhapsody on a Windy Night," in his magazine, *Blast*. In September "Portrait of a Lady" appeared in *Others*; in October, three more poems, "The Boston Evening Transcript," "Aunt Helen," and "Hysteria," appeared in *Poetry*; and in November, Pound republished five of these poems, including "Prufrock," in his *Catholic Anthology*. (Pound used the word "catholic" not in its religious sense but in its pure lexical sense, meaning "universal.") Eliot was on the map. He was being published, and he had become part of an important circle of artists and intellectuals. Eliot also became close with the noted twentieth-century philosopher and mathematician Bertrand Russell, the model for Eliot's poem "Mr. Apollinax," printed in *Poetry* in September 1916. Russell put Eliot and his new wife, Vivien, up in his own apartment (and in all likelihood had an affair with Vivien). Eliot's marriage to Vivien was not happy. Although it lasted for sixteen years until her death, much of that time the Eliots lived apart. During her last years Vivien was confined to a mental hospital. Marrying Vivien Haigh-Wood, however, did serve as one of the determining factors that kept Eliot in London once he had decided that he did not want to return to the United States or to follow an academic career teaching philosophy but to be a poet.

Marrying Vivien and abandoning his intended career also ensured that Eliot would live for a time in poverty. Since his father objected both to the marriage and to the scuttling of his career, he not only stopped Eliot's allowance but also kept his inheritance from him, putting it in a trust that would revert to the estate after his son's death. Consequently, Eliot became an extension lecturer for Oxford University. That "forced him," according to Ronald Schuchard, "into a three year period of intensive reading and selective organizing. His courses required him to articulate his developing critical concepts, to exercise his taste, and to reorder the poems of the English tradition into his own aesthetic and moral hierarchy.... His preparations expanded the obvious erudition that he brought to his first critical efforts, and they provided a tremendous personal storehouse of allusions for his poetry" (quoted in Miller, 262). In other words, Eliot was consolidating his cultural context and making the literature of the past his own.

Even while Eliot was engaged in lecturing, in 1917 he began to work also as a clerk in Lloyd's Bank, a position he held until 1925, when he became an editor at the newly founded English publishing house Faber and Gwyer, which soon became Faber and Faber, still an important publisher. In 1917, too, through Pound's efforts, Eliot became the assistant editor of a literary magazine, *The Egoist*, a position he retained until 1919, when *The Egoist* stopped publication. Eliot then became the London correspondent for the New England journal *The Dial*, for which he wrote a series of eight letters and in which in November of 1922, *The Waste Land* was first published in the United States. The first appearance of the poem was, however, a month earlier in *The Criterion*, a magazine Eliot himself edited from 1922 until 1939 and one that helped define the cultural, literary, and political issues of the twenties and thirties.

Through his poetry and criticism, his association with Pound, Russell, Virginia Woolf, and many other influential contemporaries, and his work as an editor, Eliot became, and remained until his death, a literary figure who transformed his cultural context for later writers and readers, whether they admired or deplored his example. The award of the Nobel Prize for Literature in 1948 indicates clearly the high public regard in which Eliot was held internationally during his own lifetime. His surprising work and his alterations in views, as when he announced his conversion to Anglo-Catholicism, reflected in his poem "Ash-Wednesday," shaped the culture around him, equally for those who would enter it as practitioners or understand it as readers.

Works Cited

Howarth, Herbert. *Notes on Some Figures Behind T. S. Eliot*. Boston: Houghton Mifflin Company/The Riverside Press, 1964.

Miller, James E., Jr. *T. S. Eliot: The Making of an American Poet, 1888-1922*. Philadelphia: Pennsylvania State University Press, 2005.

Critical Reception and Influence
John Paul Riquelme

The Waste Land (1922) marks the moment of Eliot's recognition by a wider audience than the avant-garde in England (and to a lesser extent in America) who had been appreciating his earlier poetry and essays. Eliot had already published three volumes of shorter poems and a collection of essays, but these had attracted only moderate attention. Despite, or perhaps because of its difficulty, *The Waste Land* captured the imagination of a public that was experiencing the wasted aftermath of a terribly destructive war. Its disjointed, apparently alienated and pessimistic character resonated with strong feelings about the difficulties, social and individual, of the time in England and in Europe. The poem's perceived pessimism stood in sharp contrast to conventional Victorian, Edwardian, and American optimism. The challenge resonated with other important writings of the moment, including Oswald Spengler's *Untergang des Abendlandes* (1919-22), translated into English as *The Decline of the West* (1926-28). In the United States, the poem won a large cash award from *The Dial*, the American journal in which it was published.

Eliot was able to take advantage of his newfound recognition by establishing his own journal, *The Criterion*, which he edited for nearly two decades until 1939, when the unmistakable approach of a second world war made him decide, as he explained movingly in a final editorial, to cease publication, the goals of the journal being impossible to attain in the midst of the social upheaval. After the appearance of *The Waste Land*, he left his work at Lloyd's Bank and became an adviser for the new publishing firm Faber and Gwyer, which soon became Faber and Faber. Eliot was an influential editor at this important publisher until he retired. The fact that Eliot's writings were met with interest by journalists, patrons, intellectuals, and many writers beginning with *The Waste Land* constitutes an important aspect of the reception and the influence of his work, though it is not narrowly *critical*, in the sense of a scholarly response.

Starting with the publication of *The Waste Land*, the reception of Eliot's work has run on multiple tracks, with, eventually, voluminous critical writing about it, significant responses from other writers and artists, and abundant attention from a wider audience of readers. It is important to remember that the wider audience has been more continuously positive than some critics and writers have at times been. In the 1940s, for example, Eliot's long poem *Four Quartets*, a much longer and in many regards more pacific poem than *The Waste Land*, sold many thousands of copies, a highly unusual occurrence in the publishing of poetry in the twentieth century, especially when the poetry is difficult. *Four Quartets* opens with epigraphs in Greek and proceeds in a nonlinear, musical way. The situation is in some regards parallel to the public reception of the earlier, darker poem. But in the later instance, the audience was encountering writing that can reasonably be called healing, though not easy, by contrast with the jagged fragmentation of 1922. The award of the Nobel Prize in 1948 is also part of the reception, one that indicates the overwhelmingly positive reaction to Eliot's writings in various genres and its substantial influence.

As is the case with any strong-minded artist whose work is distinctive, opinion was not unanimously positive among intellectuals. Culturally conservative readers of the poetry and essays that Eliot wrote through the mid-1920s resisted his attack on conventional values. His rejection of nineteenth-century optimism and poetic attitudes was resented by some. Eliot's declaration of his Anglican religious faith and his taking of British citizenship gave rise to responses that were split in the opposite way. Former admirers who saw him as critical of cultural orthodoxies considered that he had betrayed the cause of iconoclasm, while culturally conservative denigrators of his iconoclasm could celebrate his commitment to established values. Like Bob Dylan leaving folk music behind, Eliot turned his back on a large audience on principle. The decision to do so could not have been easy. In the 1930s, Eliot came under strong criticism for prejudicial racial attitudes and for being politically to the right. His *After Strange Gods* (1934) contained remarks that were considered anti-Semitic, as were references in some of his poems, including "Gerontion" and "Burbank with a Baedeker: Bleistein with a Cigar." Eliot never allowed the book to be republished. The controversy about his alleged anti-Semitism continues in some interpretive responses to his work. Although we do not have all the evidence yet (letters and other papers remain to be published, as I indicate in more detail below), it appears that Eliot was not an anti-Semite in the sense that he wanted to see harm done to Jews. But he did hold prejudicial views that he voiced from time to time in statements that were, at the least, insensitive. He was also known to admire the French intellectual Charles Maurras, authoritarian head of the reactionary *Action Française*, a monarchist, counter-revolutionary political movement. In *Culture and Society*, Raymond Williams presents a particularly cogent response from the left to Eliot's cultural views.

The controversy about Eliot's anti-Semitism continued sporadically after World War II, and another controversy developed when Eliot took legal action against a critic, John Peter, who published an essay in which he suggested there were homoerotic elements in *The Waste Land*. Eliot's response stopped for a time the critical discussion of the homosocial and homoerotic aspects of his work, but the topic has been developed since his death, particularly in the recent past, with the flourishing of gender studies from both feminist and queer perspectives. Important poets also eventually rejected in their own work the kind of impersonal writing that Eliot advocated. The confessional movement in poetry in the 1950s, for example, which included Robert Lowell, John Berryman, Sylvia Plath, and others, was emphatically a return to personal poetry. As I mention in "On T. S. Eliot," earlier in this volume, there was a strong critical reaction against Eliot in particular and literary modernism in general in the 1970s and 1980s. Eliot was demoted from his place of eminence and often vilified. The recent resurgence of modernist studies, often called the *new* modernist studies, has raised probing questions and brought innovative, suggestive perspectives to bear. The results are revised views about literary modernism's character and about individual writers, including Eliot. There is every indication that his writings will continue to be studied and reevaluated.

* * *

Readers wanting more information about Eliot or wanting to explore responses to Eliot by critics and other artists are faced with a great deal of material to choose from and various avenues to pursue. Though the list of works I provide here is lengthy, it is also necessarily selective. There is much more of value to be consulted about Eliot, as well as a considerable amount of commentary that is less helpful. In order to provide ways to organize the list for further focused reading about Eliot, I provide comments below concerning groups of individual titles by considering for the most part in turn: annotations for texts, biographical resources, early responses, introductory commentaries, collections of essays, general studies, treatments of the longer poems, studies of the drama, commentaries on more specialized topics, responses by recent critics (who are asking new questions), the appearance of previously unpublished writings, and work by selected writers and artists influenced by Eliot.

Annotations can often be helpful in elucidating passages in which Eliot has alluded to earlier writing, echoed it, or quoted from it in ways he could have expected readers to recognize; and they can explain now obscure nonliterary references that would have been more recognizable when the works were first published. Glosses can also distract us from engaging with the elliptical, enigmatic qualities of Eliot's writings. It is important to keep in mind that no one will recognize all the sources, including the scholarly annotators; that Eliot would not have been consciously referring to some of the sources that scholars have identified; and that the sources are not explanations. Once we think we have a source, the implications of its use remain to be formulated. The fact of alluding as a process involving both the writer and the reader is often as important as the source for a specific allusion. With these caveats in mind, readers are likely to find B. C. Southam's *Student's Guide*, which has been through multiple editions, a reliable guide. Lawrence Rainey's annotation of some of Eliot's poetry, essays, and drama in his *Annotated Waste Land* and in his *Modernism* anthology is quite thorough, particularly for *The Waste Land*. A practical resource of a different kind, for readers interested in tracing Eliot's language among his writings, is J. L. Dawson's *Concordance*.

Because of Eliot's desire for privacy and his aversion to biographical readings of literature, reliable published biographical discussions are still limited. Caroline Behr provides a detailed chronology of Eliot's life that constitutes a small book. More than a chronological list of major events, it mentions in relation to those events the publication of numerous works by Eliot and provides references for them. The biographies by Peter Ackroyd and Lyndall Gordon are the most reliable, and Gordon's is based on more material than Ackroyd was able to consider. The two volumes edited by Valerie Eliot, the poet's widow, are revealing, essential sources of information. Her facsimile edition of *The Waste Land* includes a lengthy introduction, and the early letters and their annotations are fascinating.

Readers interested in early critical responses to Eliot's writing will be well served by Jewel Spears Brooker's edition of the contemporary reviews and Michael Grant's two-volume *T. S. Eliot: The Critical Heritage*. Grant reprints significant reviews and criticism from the beginning of Eliot's career through the appearance of *Collected Poems* in 1962, the last collected volume before Eliot's death.

Two brief book-length interpretive introductions to Eliot's career that would repay close attention are Northrop Frye's *T. S. Eliot* (1963) and John Xiros Cooper's *The Cambridge Introduction to T. S. Eliot* (2006). Despite its early date and its sometimes obvious lack of sympathy with Eliot, Frye's commentary is a cogent response by a distinguished Canadian critic and theorist. Cooper's lucidly written, well-informed, more recent book is, of course, more useful concerning current critical attitudes toward Eliot. His review of the criticism and his annotated selected bibliography are salutary.

Numerous collections of essays have been published about Eliot, some that reprint existing criticism and others composed of new essays. Among the older collections, those by Hugh Kenner, A. Walton Litz, and Allen Tate are of particular interest, in part because the editors were all distinguished critics. Litz's collection is made up of essays by a particularly stellar group of scholars, including Kenner and Richard Ellmann, the most prominent commentators on literary modernism during the 1950s and 1960s, when it was turning from contemporary literature into literature of the past. They contributed in a significant way to defining how modernism was understood at the time of Eliot's death in 1965. Laura Cowan's collection (1990) includes commentaries from some critics of that earlier generation who were still active, but most of the essays are by well-regarded scholars of the next generation, who would have been the students of Kenner, Ellmann, Litz, and their contemporaries. A. D. Moody's *Cambridge Companion* is part of a respected series of substantial volumes on important writers, all composed of new essays by established scholars. The essays focus on the whole range of Eliot's writings. The review of Eliot studies (through the early 1990s) by Jewel Brooker in the *Companion* is quite detailed. Brooker's *Approaches to Teaching* is made up of short original essays designed for teachers, but the essays would be illuminating for anyone interested in Eliot. Harriet Davidson's collection of reprinted essays emphasizes critical attitudes that she characterizes as postmodern, by which she means attitudes that yield readings of Eliot that resonate with the humanistic theory, mostly originating in Europe, that came to the fore in Anglo-American literary studies soon after Eliot's death. She considers Eliot himself to be a kind of theorist, whose works yield new insights when considered in relation to ideology, poststructuralism, sexuality, and cultural studies. She organizes her bibliography for further reading according to these categories. Although the retrospective reading of Eliot from the perspective of humanistic theory of the past half century can easily become exaggerated and tendentious (and a distraction from textual details), the questions and approaches that inform this volume are illuminating. I should mention that my essay for the current collection and the book from which it is drawn take directions that are informed by poststructuralism.

Many worthwhile book-length interpretive considerations of Eliot's career are available. Besides those by Ronald Bush, Nancy K. Gish, John T. Mayer, Lee Oser, and myself (all represented by excerpts in the current collection), Hugh Kenner's *T. S. Eliot: The Invisible Poet* is the first important book on Eliot. Its arguments remain provocative. Moody's lengthy book focuses on the poetry, with some attention to the drama. Donoghue deals more exclusively with the poetry, though he does include a chapter on Eliot's *The Idea of a Christian Society*. Stephen Spender brings to bear the perspective of an English poet and essayist of the generation after Eliot's.

There are numerous accomplished, illuminating commentaries on Eliot's longer poems. I have already mentioned Rainey's annotations. Rainey's *Revisiting "The Waste Land"* presents a detailed account of the poem's composition. Michael North's edition of *The Waste Land* includes background material and critical commentaries. Lois Cuddy and David Hirsch's collection reprints important essays on the poem published before 1990. Calvin Bedient's book provides a close reading of the poem that argues for a single speaking voice, neither the voice of Tiresias nor that of the poet but that of a stand-in for the poet. Peter Middleton's lively essay offers a refreshingly skeptical perspective on the academic use (and distortion) of the poem, but it is primarily valuable for his conclusion that *The Waste Land* is a Dadaist text, comparable with the work of Tristan Tzara, Eliot's contemporary who was a founder of the Dada movement. As I suggest in "On T. S. Eliot," Eliot deserves to be interpreted in the context of twentieth-century avant-garde art. David Chinitz's brief essay is particularly clear about the poem's pessimism and its continuing relevance. The two books by Gardner both include accomplished commentaries on *Four Quartets*, one about themes, structure, and language, the other about its composition. Keith Alldritt considers Eliot's use of sonata form. The longest chapter of my book treats the poem(s) as an extended translation of Heraclitus's fragments that is essentially postmodernist in character.

Eliot's drama has been less admiringly received by critics than his poetry or his criticism. The books by D. E. Jones, Carol Smith, and Denis Donoghue are all early studies of continuing value. Donoghue presents Eliot in the context of other attempts to reestablish verse drama. Michael Goldman's essay from Litz's volume (reprinted in the current collection) makes clear the interest and significance of the plays, largely by bringing out their gothic dimension and their careful structuring. The two chapters (of six) that David Chinitz devotes to Eliot's dramatic works are the most engaging and revealing new writing about the plays. He presents the unfinished *Sweeney Agonistes* as Eliot's attempt to create a crossover genre by turning to vernacular sources. He then traces the competing impulses in Eliot's later drama, a vanguardist tendency toward ritual and the contrary populist, theatrical tendency that tries not to be literary.

Those interested in Eliot's relation to nineteenth-century British poetry will find ample discussion in the books by Frank Kermode, Robert Langbaum, Loy Martin, and myself, all of which take positions about how discontinuous, if at all, literary modernism is from its immediate precursors. Kermode's *Romantic Image* is an early seminal contribution to the study of modernist poetry and attitudes by comparison with Romantic and Victorian antecedents. The studies by Louis Menand (who is represented in this collection), Michael Levenson, Michael North (especially *Reading 1922*), and Sanford Schwartz frame Eliot's work within the larger contexts of society, history, and the development of modernism. Roy Harvey Pearce, Lee Oser, and Eric Sigg present Eliot in relation to American traditions, as does Anita Patterson, though America for her is actually the Americas, including the Caribbean. Of the many books on Eliot's intellectual development and attitudes, those by Manju Jain, M. A. R. Habib, Jeffrey Perl, and John D.

Margolis are particularly cogent on the range, character, and implications of Eliot's studies and his thinking. Habib concludes his commentary on Eliot and Western philosophy with a reading of *The Waste Land*. Cleo Kearns by contrast investigates Eliot's considerable knowledge of non-Western traditions. Dante was such an important figure for Eliot that he published three essays about him in his major collections. Dominic Manganiello's book provides a detailed assessment of Dante's place in Eliot's thought and his writing. Grover Smith's early book, updated in a second edition, continues to be valuable for its discussion of significant sources for Eliot's writing.

In his review of Joyce's *Ulysses* in *The Dial* in 1923, Eliot formulated a new principle by which modern writing could proceed, the *mythical method*, which he felt Joyce had brought to maturity in his modern epic. Eliot cited William Butler Yeats, an earlier writer who had produced works in which contemporary situations and classical myths were coordinated, mixed, and merged. Eliot had already practiced the method himself in poems such as "Sweeney among the Nightingales" (1918), with its Greek epigraph from Aeschylus, and *The Waste Land* (1922), whose epigraph comes from Petronius and whose integral notes include a long citation in Latin from Ovid. Later, he wrote verse plays for the popular stage that had choral elements and Greek sources, and *Four Quartets* meditates on its epigraphs and other fragments from the pre-Socratic philosopher Heraclitus's. William Arrowsmith, a distinguished classicist, wrote vividly about Eliot and the classics, and both David Chinitz and I consider Eliot's relationship to Greek precursors, as do all the critics who write about the plays. Once understood by critics in a one-sided way as primarily ironic about a debased modern world, Eliot's evocations of classical myth are as ironic about idealized versions of the past as they are about current realities.

Christopher Ricks considers the extent to which Eliot's successful poems were bound up with prejudicial attitudes that he either held himself or used to engage his readers. Anthony Julius is more accusatory and prosecutorial about Eliot and prejudice. Craig Raine's book includes an appendix in which he reviews the evidence in order to defend Eliot. When more biographical information is available, including correspondence after 1922, we may be in a better position to make unambiguous judgments about Eliot's racial attitudes.

The issue of Eliot's sexuality and his attitudes toward sex, gender, and women were not widely pursued during his lifetime, but they have been since his death, starting most prominently with James Miller's book, which picks up where John Peter had to leave off. In Colleen Lamos's more recent study, Eliot is the central figure in defining what she means by *deviant modernism*. She undertakes lengthy, suggestive commentaries on gender anxieties and perverse desire in Eliot's criticism, his poetry, and his drama. The essays in the collection edited by Nancy K. Gish and Cassandra Laity focus on matters pertaining to homoeroticism, desire, and early twentieth-century feminism in Eliot's writing.

Recent commentators have considered Eliot's relation to race and to popular culture, including jazz. David Chinitz's book is a groundbreaking study of Eliot and popular culture. North's *The Dialect of Modernism* contains an important chapter on Eliot and racial masquerade. In making the important point that modernism is not simply Anglo-American, Charles Pollard's book focuses on Eliot's influence on Caribbean poets and their transformations of elements of his writing. In her recent book about transatlantic modernism, Anita Patterson considers Eliot in relation to poets of the Americas, including African-American and Caribbean writers for whom migration was a central issue. As she cogently points out, the Nobel laureate Saint-John Perse, whose *Anabasis* Eliot translated, was French, but he was born and raised in Guadaloupe. In turning to Perse's work, Eliot is aligning himself with a writer who is transnational, a writer with mingled roots in Europe and in the Americas.

Our understanding of Eliot has changed in the past decade and a half in part because of the publication of some of Eliot's writings that had previously been unavailable to the public. More new material will appear in the near future. Ronald Schuchard's thoroughly annotated edition of Eliot's lectures on Metaphysical poetry has given us a new sense of Eliot's thinking about the strengths and the limits of Metaphysical writing at an important moment in his career. Christopher Ricks's edition of Eliot's unpublished early poems from manuscripts in the collection of the New York Public Library provides access to Eliot's poetic workshop and to unguarded moments that Eliot chose not to print during his lifetime. Further volumes of Eliot's letters are being co-edited by Valerie Eliot and Hugh Haughton. Ronald Schuchard's multivolume edition of Eliot's complete prose will appear through Faber and Faber in the United Kingdom and from Johns Hopkins University Press in the United States. These will be major publishing events for modernist studies and for Eliot's readers in particular.

I want to close by emphasizing that the reception of Eliot's work and its influence deserve to be measured not only by the scholarly response to his writing but also by the testimony of artists who have been moved to create because of their encounter with Eliot or else have written about his importance. I have already mentioned Stephen Spender's book. Ted Hughes, who was British Poet Laureate from 1984 until his death in 1998, calls Eliot *"the* poet of our times" in *A Dancer to God.* I have included as well an essay by Seamus Heaney, another Nobel Laureate, about Eliot. In 2006, Heaney was awarded the T. S. Eliot Prize, given annually since 1993 to the best collection of new verse published in the United Kingdom or Ireland. His collection of essays *The Government of the Tongue* includes the T. S. Eliot Memorial Lectures delivered at Eliot College of the University of Kent in 1986. Another Nobel Prize winner, the Russian poet Joseph Brodsky, marked Eliot's passing with "Verses on the Death of T. S. Eliot."

Eliot's influence continues to be visible in genres outside poetry, including popular culture. Martin Rowson produced a wonderfully engaging graphic novel version of *The Waste Land,* which translates the poem into a film-noir narrative. Andrew Lloyd Webber, the highly successful composer of musical theater, decided to stage a version of

Eliot's poems for children, *Old Possum's Book of Practical Cats*, a book that he remembered from childhood. The result was the award-winning dance musical *Cats*, whose songs are based on the cat poems, "Rhapsody on a Windy Night," and a passage from *Four Quartets*. The show has been translated into more than twenty languages and performed worldwide. It had 8,949 performances in London, where its concluding performance, on the twenty-first anniversary of its opening, was projected onto a big screen in Covent Garden. It also ran for eighteen years on Broadway.

The Irish actress Fiona Shaw, considered one of the finest classical actresses of her generation (who appears as well in the Harry Potter films), staged *The Waste Land* under the direction of Deborah Warner in 1995 in London's East End to rave reviews. The one-person show, in which she passionately rendered all the poem's voices, then went on a world tour, which included New York and Sydney, and a film version was shown at the Cannes Film Festival in 1996.

There is every reason to expect that Eliot's work will continue to generate such memorable performances and writing of all kinds, not just academic commentaries, that will confirm Eliot's significance while also redefining and redirecting it.

Further Reading

Ackroyd, Peter. *T. S. Eliot*. New York: Simon & Schuster, 1984.

Alldritt, Keith. *Eliot's Four Quartets: Poetry as Chamber Music*. London and Totowa, NJ: Woburn Press, 1978.

Arrowsmith, William. "Daedal Harmonies: A Dialogue on Eliot and the Classics." *Southern Review* 13, no. 1 (Winter 1977): 1-47.

Bedient, Calvin. *He Do the Police in Different Voices: "The Waste Land" and Its Protagonists*. Chicago: University of Chicago Press, 1986.

Behr, Caroline. *T. S. Eliot: A Chronology of His Life and Works*. London: Macmillan, 1983.

Brooker, Jewel Spears, ed. *Approaches to Teaching Eliot's Poetry and Plays*. New York: Modern Language Association, 1988.

_____. *T. S. Eliot: The Contemporary Reviews*. Cambridge: Cambridge University Press, 2004.

Bush, Ronald. *T. S. Eliot: A Study of Character and Style*. New York: Oxford University Press, 1983.
Chinitz, David E. *T. S. Eliot and the Cultural Divide*. Chicago: University of Chicago Press, 2003.
_____. "T. S. Eliot: *The Waste Land*." In *A Companion to Modernist Literature and Culture*, ed. David Bradshaw and Kevin J. H. Dettmar. Oxford: Blackwell, 2006.
Cooper, John Xiros. *The Cambridge Introduction to T. S. Eliot*. Cambridge: Cambridge University Press, 2006.
Cowan, Laura. *T. S. Eliot: Man and Poet, Volume I*. Orono, ME: National Poetry Foundation, 1990.
Cuddy, Lois, and David H. Hirsch, eds. *Critical Essays on T. S. Eliot's "The Waste Land."* Boston: G. K. Hall, 1991.
Davidson, Harriet, ed. *T. S. Eliot*. London and New York: Longman, 1999.
Dawson, J. L., P. D. Holland, and D. J. McKitterick, eds. *A Concordance to the Complete Poems and Plays of T. S. Eliot*. Ithaca: Cornell University Press, 1995.
Donoghue, Denis. *The Third Voice: Modern British and American Verse Drama*. Princeton, NJ: Princeton University Press, 1959.
_____. *Words Alone: The Poet T. S. Eliot*. New Haven, CT: Yale University Press, 2000.
Eliot, T. S. *Inventions of the March Hare, Poems 1909-1917*. Ed. Christopher Ricks. New York: Harcourt Brace & Co., 1996.
_____. *The Varieties of Metaphysical Poetry*. Ed. Ronald Schuchard. New York: Harcourt Brace & Co., 1993.
Eliot, Valerie, ed. *The Letters of T. S. Eliot, Volume I, 1898-1922*. New York: Harcourt, Brace, Jovanovich, 1988.
_____. *The Waste Land: A Facsimile and Transcript of the Original Drafts, Including the Annotations of Ezra Pound*. New York: Harcourt, Brace, Jovanovich, 1971.
Frye, Northrop. *T. S. Eliot: An Introduction*. New York: Grove Press, 1963.
Gardner, Helen. *The Art of T. S. Eliot*. New York: Dutton, 1950.
_____. *The Composition of "Four Quartets."* London: Faber and Faber, 1978.
Gish, Nancy K. *Time in the Poetry of T. S. Eliot: A Study in Structure and Theme*. London: Macmillan, 1981.
Gordon, Lyndall. *T. S. Eliot: An Imperfect Life*. New York: W. W. Norton, 1999.
Grant, Michael. *T. S. Eliot: The Critical Heritage*. Vols. 1-2. London and Boston: Routledge & Kegan Paul, 1982.
Habib, M. A. R. *The Early T. S. Eliot and Western Philosophy*. Cambridge: Cambridge University Press, 1999.
Heaney, Seamus. "Learning from Eliot." T. S. Eliot Centenary Lecture, Harvard University, 1988. Pp. 28-41 in *Finders Keepers, Selected Prose 1971-2001*. New York: Farrar, Straus and Giroux, 2002.
_____. *The Government of the Tongue: The 1986 T. S. Eliot Memorial*

Lectures and Other Critical Writings. London: Faber and Faber, 1989. Published in the United States as *The Government of the Tongue: Selected Prose, 1978-1987*. New York: Farrar, Straus and Giroux, 1989.

Hughes, Ted. *A Dancer to God: Tributes to T. S. Eliot*. New York: Farrar, Straus and Giroux, 1993.

Jain, Manju. *T. S. Eliot and American Philosophy: The Harvard Years*. Cambridge: Cambridge University Press, 1992.

Jones, D. E. *The Plays of T. S. Eliot*. Toronto: University of Toronto Press, 1960.

Julius, Anthony. *T. S. Eliot, Anti-Semitism, and Literary Form*. Cambridge: Cambridge University Press, 1995.

Kearns, Cleo McNelly. *T. S. Eliot and Indic Traditions: A Study in Poetry and Belief*. Cambridge: Cambridge University Press, 1987.

Kenner, Hugh. *The Invisible Poet: T. S. Eliot*. New York: Harcourt, Brace, 1959.

_____, ed. *T. S. Eliot, A Collection of Critical Essays*. Englewood Cliffs: Prentice-Hall, 1962.

Kermode, Frank. *Romantic Image*. New York: Vintage, 1957.

Laity, Cassandra, and Nancy K. Gish, eds. *Gender, Desire and Sexuality in T. S. Eliot*. Cambridge: Cambridge University Press, 2004.

Lamos, Colleen. *Deviant Modernism: Sexual and Textual Errancy in T. S. Eliot, James Joyce, and Marcel Proust*. Cambridge: Cambridge University Press, 1998.

Langbaum, Robert. *The Poetry of Experience: The Dramatic Monologue in Modern Literary Tradition*. New York: Random House, 1957.

Levenson, Michael. *A Genealogy of Modernism: A Study of English Literary Doctrine, 1908-1922*. Cambridge: Cambridge University Press, 1984.

Litz, A. Walton, ed. *Eliot in His Time: Essays on the Occasion of the Fiftieth Anniversary of "The Waste Land."* Princeton, NJ: Princeton University Press, 1973.

Manganiello, Dominic. *T. S. Eliot and Dante*. New York: St. Martin's Press, 1989.

Margolis, John D. *T. S. Eliot's Intellectual Development, 1922-1939*. Chicago: University of Chicago Press, 1972.

Martin, Loy D. *Browning's Dramatic Monologues and the Post-Romantic Subject*. Baltimore: Johns Hopkins University Press, 1985.

Mayer, John T. *T. S. Eliot's Silent Voices*. New York: Oxford University Press, 1989.

Menand, Louis. *Discovering Modernism: T. S. Eliot and His Context*. New York: Oxford University Press, 1987.

Middleton, Peter. "The Academic Development of *The Waste Land*." In *Demarcating the Disciplines: Philosophy, Literature, Art*, ed. Samuel Weber. Minneapolis: University of Minnesota Press, 1986.

Miller, James E., Jr. *T. S. Eliot's Personal Waste Land: Exorcism of the Demons*. University Park: Pennsylvania State University Press, 1977.

Moody, A. D. *The Cambridge Companion to T. S. Eliot*. Cambridge: Cambridge University Press, 1994.

_____. *Thomas Stearns Eliot, Poet*. Cambridge: Cambridge University Press, 1979.

North, Michael. *The Dialect of Modernism: Race, Language, and Twentieth-Century Literature*. Oxford: Oxford University Press, 1994.

_____. *Reading 1922: A Return to the Scene of the Modern*. New York: Oxford University Press, 1999.

_____, ed. *"The Waste Land": Authoritative Text, Contexts, Criticism*. New York: W. W. Norton, 2001.

Oser, Lee. *T. S. Eliot and American Poetry*. Columbia: University of Missouri Press, 1998.

Patterson, Anita. *Race, American Literature and Transnational Modernism*. Cambridge: Cambridge University Press, 2008.

Pearce, Roy Harvey. *The Continuity of American Poetry*. Princeton, NJ: Princeton University Press, 1961.

Perl, Jeffrey M. *Skepticism and Modern Enmity: Before and After Eliot*. Baltimore: Johns Hopkins University Press, 1989.

Pollard, Charles W. *New World Modernisms: T. S. Eliot, Derek Walcott, and Kamau Brathwaite*. Charlottesville: University of Virginia Press, 2004.

Raine, Craig. *T. S. Eliot*. New York: Oxford University Press, 2006.

Rainey, Lawrence, ed. *The Annotated Waste Land with Eliot's Contemporary Prose, Second Edition*. New Haven, CT: Yale University Press, 2006.

_____, ed. *Modernism: An Anthology*. Oxford: Blackwell, 2005.

_____. *Revisiting "The Waste Land."* New Haven, CT: Yale University Press, 2005.

Ricks, Christopher. *T. S. Eliot and Prejudice*. Berkeley and Los Angeles: University of California Press, 1988.

Riquelme, John Paul. *Harmony of Dissonances: T. S. Eliot, Romanticism, and Imagination*. Baltimore: Johns Hopkins University Press, 1991.

Rowson, Martin. *The Waste Land*. New York: Harper and Row, 1990.

Schwartz, Sanford. *The Matrix of Modernism: Pound, Eliot, and Early Twentieth-Century Thought*. Princeton, NJ: Princeton University Press, 1985.

Sigg, Eric. *The American T. S. Eliot: A Study of the Early Writings*. New York: Cambridge University Press, 1989.

Smith, Carol H. *T. S. Eliot's Dramatic Theory and Practice*. Princeton, NJ: Princeton University Press, 1963.

Smith, Grover. *T. S. Eliot's Poetry and Plays: A Study in Sources and Meaning*. 2d ed. Chicago: University of Chicago Press, 1974.

Southam, B. C. *A Student's Guide to the Selected Poems of T. S. Eliot*. 6th ed. London and Boston: Faber and Faber, 1994.

Spender, Stephen. *T. S. Eliot*. Ed. Frank Kermode. New York: Viking, 1976.

Tate, Allen, ed. *T. S. Eliot: The Man and His Work, a Critical Evaluation by Twenty-Six Distinguished Writers*. New York: Delacorte Press, 1966.

Williams, Raymond. *Culture and Society, 1780-1950*. New York: Columbia University Press, 1958. 227-43.

T. S. Eliot and Robert Browning's Dramatic Monologues

Matthew J. Bolton

Matthew Bolton explores the nineteenth-century literary background of Eliot's early poems by reading them by comparison with the dramatic monologue tradition, specifically in relation to the work of Robert Browning, the Victorian poet usually identified as the defining poet for that tradition. In so doing, Bolton identifies Eliot's centrality for literary modernism, which responded, often trenchantly, to Romantic and Victorian traditions in poetry and to the realistic tradition in fiction. Bolton also affirms Eliot's influence as both poet and critic during the whole of the twentieth century, mentioning, for example, Eliot's key notion of "dissociation of sensibility," a split between thought and feeling that Eliot argued affected nineteenth-century English poetry in adverse ways, by contrast with the notion of "wit" (not to be confused with Romantic imagination), which is visible as a strength in English poetry before John Milton. He argues that Eliot borrows and transforms Browning's use of a poetic mask, that is, a speaker not to be identified with the poet, disturbed characters, and silent listeners, to whom the speaker reveals motives and attitudes. The transformation involves what Bolton calls a deconstruction of the dramatic monologue, one that involves specifically Eliot's interiorizing and textualizing the language. Instead of (or in addition to) overhearing a speaker who addresses a silent listener in a believable scene that proceeds in a conversational way, we may be overhearing an interior dialogue. Rather than only or primarily a speaking voice, we encounter language that is highly allusive, language that calls attention to itself as written rather than spoken. We might add to Bolton's cogent comments that Eliot's transformation includes fragmenting the language with gaps and unexplained juxtapositions that break the illusion of a continuous speaking voice. In "Prufrock," Bolton discerns the morbid sensibility of some of Browning's speakers, though presented in ways that run counter to the speaking conventions of Browning's monologues. In "Portrait of a Lady," Bolton brings out the way that aspects of Prufrock's situation and character are divided between the female speaker and her silent male listener, as part of an experiment with the dramatic monologue that frames spoken language within an interior monologue. As he rightly suggests, the destructive context of World War I and its social aftermath affected Eliot's thinking and writing, as they did the attitudes of the whole European populace beginning in 1914. Within that violent context of dislocations, traditional forms of poetry and of thinking were displaced by other attitudes and strategies of writing, including challenging language, such as Eliot's, that undoes conventions of the past not just to destroy them but to build something new from the fragments. —J.P.R.

Upon reading several unpublished chapters of James Joyce's *Ulysses* (1922), T. S. Eliot told Virginia Woolf that the novel "would be a landmark, because it destroyed the whole of the nineteenth century" (Woolf, 57). This was not lamentation but praise, for in his criticism and his poetry Eliot was undertaking much the same process of destruction. Throughout the 1910s and 1920s, he was razing literary monuments to clear ground for his own work and for that of his contemporaries, notably Joyce, Woolf, and Pound. The literary movement that would come to be termed Modernism was in no small part predicated on a rhetorical destruction of Victorian modes of thought and expression, content and form, sentiment and syntax. To "make it new," as Pound exhorted, one must do away with the old. No single writer more deliberately, systematically, or convincingly undertook this process of redefining the literary tradition than did Eliot. In speaking of Joyce as a destroyer, Eliot therefore tacitly identifies himself as one, too. For 1922 saw the publication not only of *Ulysses*, but also of Eliot's poem *The Waste Land*. What Joyce's work did to the English novelistic tradition, Eliot's did to the poetic one. Indeed, twentieth-century poetry and criticism has largely been defined in relation to Eliot's poetry and to his writings on poetry. Eliot is responsible for what Isobel Armstrong terms "a great redirection of energy" away from the Victorian poets and toward both Modernism itself and those poets whom Eliot singled out for praise, notably the seventeenth-century Metaphysical poets, the Jacobean playwrights, and the French Symbolists. Through argumentation in his essays and literary allusions in his poetry, Eliot succeeded in locating himself in a poetic tradition of his own making—a tradition that displaced Tennyson, Robert Browning, Arnold, and the other English poets of his parents' and grandparents' generations.

Yet Eliot's repeated efforts to downplay the Victorian poets may belie the importance of that generation of artists to Eliot's own art. Eliot's professed disregard for his poetic forerunners can be read as a form of subterfuge by which he minimizes what Harold Bloom terms "the anxiety of influence." Bloom argues that poetic influence "always proceeds by a misreading of the prior poet, an act of creative correction that is actually and necessarily a misinterpretation" (Bloom, 32). Eliot has a vested interest in minimizing or deflecting the importance of some of his poetic predecessors, and his literary criticism is one of the modes by which he "misreads" the writers who influenced him. One of Eliot's most important misreadings is his notion of the "dissociation of sensibility," which he first lays out in his essay "The Metaphysical Poets" (1921). By comparing a passage from the seventeenth-century poet George Chapman with one from the Victorian poet Robert Browning, Eliot claims to identify

> ... something which happened to the mind of England between the time of Donne ... and the time of Tennyson and Browning; it is the difference between the intellectual poet and the reflective poet. Tennyson and Browning are poets, and they think, but they do not feel their thought as immediately as the odour of a rose. (*Selected Essays*, 287)

The Victorian poets, Eliot argues, are too cerebral: they can think and feel, but they cannot "feel their thought." Their intellectual and emotional facilities are wholly severed in a way they were not for poets two and a half centuries before, and Victorian poetry therefore lacks "direct sensuous apprehension of thought, or a recreation of thought into feeling." Eliot's essay "Andrew Marvell" similarly treats a quality possessed by the seventeenth-century Cavalier poets, but lost to their inheritors: "wit, a tough reasonableness beneath the slight lyric grace" (*Selected Prose*, 102). Eliot claims, "You cannot find it in Shelley or Keats or Wordsworth . . . still less in Tennyson or Browning" (102). What came naturally for men of the seventeenth century—a natural and spontaneous integration of the intellectual and emotional lives—men of the nineteenth century could only approach through great, doomed effort. Eliot argues that Romantics such as Keats and Shelley "in one or two passages . . . struggle toward unification of sensibility," but "Keats and Shelley died, and Tennyson and Browning ruminated" (288). This is a damning indictment of nineteenth century verse, particularly when one remembers the primary definition of "ruminate": the cow's action of chewing his half-digested cud. Yet ultimately, the theory of the dissociation of sensibility says as much about Eliot's own work as it does about that of either the Victorians or the Metaphysicals. Carol T. Christ writes, "Eliot's criticism throws up a smokescreen . . . which at one and the same time produces a climate of appreciation for his own work and obscures the genuine continuities between him and his immediate predecessors" (Christ, 157). Nor was Eliot himself blind to this process. Four decades after writing "The Metaphysical Poets," he admitted, in his book *To Criticize the Critic*, "In my earlier criticism, both in my general affirmations about poetry and in writing about authors who had influenced me, I was implicitly defending the sort of poetry that I and my friends wrote" (16).

Rather than taking Eliot's excoriation of the Victorian poets at face value, therefore, one would do better to read Eliot's poetry in light of theirs. Comparing Eliot's early monologues to those of Alfred Tennyson or Robert Browning, for example, one finds startling parallels that reveal Eliot's familiarity with the poets whom he so roundly criticized.

This process of comparison therefore challenges Eliot's own representation, in his criticism, of his relationship to the great Victorian poets. For Modernism did not so much destroy the nineteenth century as transform it. As Jessica Feldman argues:

> It is important to tell critical stories of both destruction *and* preservation, and one way to do so is to bring the mid-century high Victorian into relation with high modernism. As we do so, a Victorian modernist aesthetic of both rupture and continuity, of stark differences and relations across gaps, develops. (Feldman, 453)

One way to bring "the high Victorian into relation with high modernism" is to read Eliot's early monologues alongside those of Browning, who has often been credited with inventing the dramatic monologue and who was by far the Victorians' most prolific practitioner of the form. Eliot's first published collection of poems, *Prufrock and Other Observations*, can in this spirit be read not only as breaking from Victorian conventions but also as transforming them into something new and strange.

Although he would eventually become the most popular poet of his generation, Browning was for the first several decades of his career dogged by charges of obscurity. His earliest poetic efforts, the long blank-verse poems *Pauline* and *Sordello*, were critically excoriated for being deliberately inaccessible and arcane. Perhaps many modern readers would continue to find these first poems so, but the shorter monologues that would follow them—poems such as "My Last Duchess," "Meeting at Night," "Soliloquy of the Spanish Cloister," "Fra Lippo Lippi," and "Childe Roland to the Dark Tower Came"—now seem as clear as day. Yet these, too, were charged with being too obscure, and even *Men and Women* (1855), arguably Browning's greatest collection of monologues, met with bafflement and anger upon its first publication. Browning is difficult, a reviewer argues in *Fraser's* magazine of January 1856, out of "willfulness, caprice, and carelessness," and his obscurity is bent on "making a fool of the public."

What was Browning doing in these dramatic monologues, as his characteristic form came to be called, that the English reading public found so baffling and obscure? Perhaps the first problem that confronted the common reader was that the poet had adopted a voice that was not his own. Indeed, Browning's speakers are radically different: his poems are peopled and voiced by murderers, monsters, and self-flagellating martyrs. Nor do these unsavory characters directly address the reader; in most cases, they speak to silent, and presumably sympathetic, auditors within the world of the poem. The reader becomes the proverbial fly on the wall, hearing the speech of a single character who is speaking in a detailed context. In "My Last Duchess," an urbane duke takes a messenger on a tour of his art collection, only gradually revealing that he has had the duchess whose picture they are admiring put to death. The reader must work to complete the poem's meaning. The duke says of his duchess:

> Oh sir, she smiled, no doubt,
> Whene'er I passed her; but who passed without
> Much the same smile? This grew; I gave commands;
> Then all smiles stopped together. There she stands
> As if alive.

There is a tremendous gap in the duke's story: he does not specify of what his commands consisted. The reader must supply the unsaid word "murder." This gradual process of self-incrimination, whereby a character who seems to view himself as sympathetic gradually confesses to the most heinous of crimes, is a thread that runs through many of Browning's poems.

Perhaps, then, it was as much the poems' content as their form that so disturbed Victorian audiences. In his seminal 1864 essay "Wordsworth, Tennyson, and Browning; or Pure, Ornate, and Grotesque Art in English Poetry," Walter Bagehot identifies Browning as "the prolific master" of the grotesque manner, one who "shows you what ought to be by what ought not to be . . . reminds you of the perfect image, by showing you the distorted and imperfect image" (Litzinger and Smalley, 274). When Wordsworth's narrator speaks to us in "The Prelude," we feel we are in the presence of someone very similar in temperament and outlook to the poet and to our better selves. We identify strongly with the confessional aspects of Romantic poetry, hearing, as Wordsworth put it, "a man speaking to men." Browning, on the other hand, takes the Romantic confessional mode in a very different direction. No longer is the poet speaking to us in something resembling his own voice. Rather, he has lent his voice to a speaker who is radically different from both himself and us. We should not mistake the mad monk of "Soliloquy of the Spanish Cloister" or Porphyria's homicidal lover—who strangles the beautiful girl with her own golden hair—for Browning. This melding of challenging forms with disturbing themes helps explain why Browning was so unappealing to his contemporaries for so many decades. It was better to write him off as obscure than to delve into that obscurity, for in so doing one might have to confront the darker parts of the soul from which Browning's voices emanate.

Here, then, may be the source of Eliot's anxiety concerning Browning's achievement: the older poet had already charted a formal and thematic territory that Eliot saw as lying too close to his own. Browning was a poet of the voice who tended to speak from behind the masks of various dramatis personae, masks that allowed him to display great formal rigor while exploring his preoccupation with the grotesque, the diseased, and the dreadful. An intensely private, intensely self-conscious young man, Eliot must have seen the freedom that speaking from behind a mask, as in Browning's monologues, would allow him. After all, his first published poem, "The Love Song of J. Alfred Prufrock," announces in its very title that its words should be ascribed to a character rather than to the poet himself. Browning and Eliot therefore adopted the same strategy, distancing themselves from the sentiments of their own poems by speaking in the voice and name of a fictive speaker. This distancing provides a way to negotiate Romantic subjectivity, the "inward turn" that threatens to lead to solipsism (Bornstein, 1976). The poet escapes himself by creating a double, a second name with a second voice. Yet the dramatis persona is more than a pseudonym: it is a mask that becomes a face. For both Browning and Eliot, the dramatis personae through which they speak become fully formed characters, with their own cadences and peculiarities.

In Eliot's earliest poems, recorded longhand in the notebook he labeled *Inventions of the March Hare*, a number of efforts are in the mode of Browning. The 1996 publication of the notebook reveals an indebtedness to Browning that Eliot carefully effaced in his published work of the 1910s. The volume's editor, Christopher Ricks, cites eleven instances of Eliot alluding to lines from Browning's poetry. An obvious and extensive allusion occurs in "A Song for St. Sebastian." This psychological monologue about an obsessive lover who thinks of strangling his beloved in order to possess her is clearly a variation on Browning's "Porphyria's Lover." Richard Kaye notes of the two poems:

> In addition to echoing the rhymes of Browning's poem ("I would flog myself until I bled" would seem to mimic Browning's "The smiling rosy little head / So glad it has its utmost will, / That all it scorned at once is fled."), several sentences of Eliot's poem recast both the subjectively rendered morbidity of "Porphyria's Lover" and the theme of unspecified betrayal by a woman who has caused her lover to turn murderous. (Kaye, 111)

Had "The Love Song of St. Sebastian" been published before "Prufrock," its Victorian origins would have been readily understood—in a way "Prufrock" was not—by an audience long accustomed to Browning's dramatic monologues and to decadent imitations of them.

While Browning the poet uses dramatis personae to escape from his own personality—to write in a confessional mode without necessarily revealing himself—many of his speakers fail to effect such an escape. The prototypical Browning speaker is as caged in his own ego as any prisoner in his cell. Browning made this point emphatically in his 1842 volume *Dramatic Lyrics*, in which he linked two previously published poems, "Johannes Agricola in Meditation" and "Porphyria's Lover," under the heading "Madhouse Cells." One could imagine the voice of the mad martyr and that of the mad murderer echoing down the same prison hall. But the real "madhouse cells" are made not of iron and stone, but of sinew and synapse. Even those speakers who are powerful and free, like the duke of "My Last Duchess," are contained within the bounds of their own consciousnesses. The text of "My Last Duchess"—which begins with "My" and ends with "me!"—makes such containment literal: the duke is surrounded by his own ego. In telling and retelling a story of himself ("not the first / are you to turn and ask thus"), he only further immures himself in selfhood. The poem therefore becomes a descent into solipsism, and when one peels back the duke's refined exterior, one begins to realize that he is no less mad than Porphyria's lover.

The prison of the self is likewise a central concern of Eliot. It appears as a central image in *The Waste Land*: "We think of the key, each in his prison, / thinking of the key, each confirms a prison." In a note to this line, Eliot quotes Bradley's *Appearance and Reality*: "My external sensations are no less private to myself than are my thoughts or my feelings. In either case my experience falls within my own circle, a circle closed on the outside . . . the whole world for each is peculiar and private to that soul." Louis Menand points out that Bradley posited this as only one of several possible relationships between consciousness and the external world, and that the lines that Eliot quotes are "not really representative of Bradley's position" (Menand, 47). Carol Christ sees the threat of solipsism as a link between Browning and Eliot:

> Like Tennyson and Browning, Eliot uses the dramatic monologue to explore man's imprisonment within his own consciousness. Phenomena in the early poems exist only as the reflex of the perceiving self. (Christ, 46)

The notion that one is imprisoned in one's own consciousness is terrifying, for it puts the socialized man, the alienated man, and the madman on the same spectrum. No one can definitively confirm that his own perceptions of reality are consonant with reality itself. To return to Bradley, every man lives in a world that is "peculiar and private." The disturbing quality of many of Browning's monologues comes from the reader's realization that a speaker's representation of reality is very different from *objective* reality. This is true not only of Browning's madmen and murderers but of his would-be heroes as well. Consider the knight in "Childe Roland to the Dark Tower Came." Roland crosses a terrain that is by his account grotesque and wasted. Indeed, this Victorian wasteland seems to look forward to the infernal landscape that would undergird London in Eliot's famous poem some seventy-five years later. Yet the flora and fauna that evoke Roland's disgust seem pedestrian enough: a horse, an unseen water rat, a stand of willows, grass. Roland's revulsion reveals as much about himself as it does of the land through which he walks. As Herbert Tucker observes about another Browning poem, "the external enters the poem only as subject to the speaker's lyric sovereignty over interpretation" (190-1). The reader has no access to the terrain through which Roland walks other than through Roland's representation of it.

Roland's morbidity of vision expresses itself in his grotesque metaphors. For metaphor-making is a form of translation; indeed, the words "metaphor" and "translation," Greek and Latin respectively, are literally equivalent in meaning: to carry across. Roland's metaphors thus serve as a Rosetta Stone, enabling one to read Roland's psychological "translation" of any given external phenomenon. The setting sun, for Roland, "shot one grim / Red leer to see the plain catch its estray" (47-8). The reader can take it on faith that the sun did indeed set as Roland walked across the plain. That the sun was maliciously pleased to see the plain "catch" the straying Roland is less readily believable. To what extent is Roland's positing of malign agency on the sunset a "bad translation"? All metaphors say something about their creators: the issue is not merely whether Roland's descriptions of his surroundings are reliable, but what they reveal about his own inner life. His metaphors exhibit a morbidity and fatalism that translate his surroundings into images of the grotesque. Roland regularly conjures grotesque images of death and decay. He says, "As for the grass, it grew as scant as hair / In leprosy; thin dry blades pricked the mud / Which underneath looked kneaded up with blood" (73-75). The scant grass serves as a kind of Rorschach test for Roland, stimulating him to impose meaning upon itself. Roland's monologue is rife with examples of this associative process that couples the landscape that he observes with images of the grotesque, such as "A sudden little river crossed my path / As unexpected as a serpent comes" (109-10) or "Drenched willows flung them headlong in a fit / Of mute despair, a suicidal throng" (119-20). Roland's fatalistic thoughts render even rivers and trees menacing and ill-intentioned.

Eliot's J. Alfred Prufrock shares Roland's morbidity of vision. The sunset is as ominous for him as it is for Roland: "the evening is spread out against the sky / Like a patient etherised upon a table" (4). C. S. Lewis would parody these famous lines in a short lyric, "A Confession":

> For twenty years I've stared my level best
> To see if evening, any evening, would suggest
> A patient etherized upon a table;
> In vain. I simply wasn't able.
>
> (1-4)

Lewis might mean to undercut the poem, but he succeeds only in confirming its essential truth: he cannot see the sky as an etherized patient precisely because he is not Prufrock. Prufrock's perceptions of the world are "peculiar and private" to himself, and the poem is less a representation of any external landscape or cityscape than it is a representation of a man's inner reality. Everything Prufrock sees and hears is filtered through his own crippling self-consciousness. John T. Mayer's description of Prufrock's wanderings could be applied with equal validity to that of Roland: "The spirit that shadows his quest is Narcissus, who threatens to narrow his self-consciousness into a prison from which escape is impossible and to transform the preoccupation with self into psychic hell" (Mayer, 17). Roland's gray plain and Prufrock's dusky streets could be located on the same map.

Yet despite these parallels, Eliot does not in "Prufrock" merely imitate Browning's dramatic monologues. Rather, he utterly deconstructs the form. Eliot takes Browning's essentially dramatic, spoken form and sinks it into the depths of the psyche, where conscious reflection, self-conscious reflex, and subconscious impulse mingle. In turning the dramatic monologue inward, Eliot renders it, to use Matthew Arnold's term, the dialogue of the mind with itself (Arnold, 282). Prufrock begins his poem, "Let us go then, you and I." This could be the opening gambit of a Browning poem, in which a speaker addresses an unseen auditor; yet the "you" and the "I," one soon realizes, seem to be the speaking and listening aspects of Prufrock's own psyche. One might think of them as the public and the private selves, or as the conscious and the subconscious mind. Prufrock's monologue represents not an act of communication with some outside auditor, but the man's communion with himself. The two aspects of Prufrock's psyche will fleetingly become one in the poem's last image of a return to a womblike state: "We have lingered in the chambers of the sea. . . ."

This inward turn has profound implications for the nature of the monologue. Plot diminishes in importance in Eliot's monologues precisely because processes of thought, even when the thinker deliberately tries to cast his thoughts dramatically, are less containable and plottable than speech. This is not to say that Browning's characters are able to control the implications of their speech; indeed, many of the monologues are ironically self-revelatory. Rather, in representing processes of thought, Eliot's emphasis shifts from linear plot to diffuse characterization. The field of thought contains other texts and voices, the recalled snatches of poetry, song, and conversation that pass through the thinking mind—or perhaps through the scribbling pen—but do not pass into speech. For Prufrock, as for the governing consciousness of *The Waste Land*, processes of thought are inherently intertextual.

"Prufrock" is not the only poem in Eliot's 1917 *Prufrock and Other Observations* to restructure the themes and conventions of the dramatic monologue. "Portrait of a Lady" is of particular interest both for the degree to which it is interwoven with a Prufrock-like field of consciousness and for its deft manipulation of Browning's poetic monologue form. A Boston grand dame invites a young man to tea, during which she makes a halting confession to having once hoped that their relationship might become something more intimate. The young man listens silently while in his own mind he ridicules the fustian lady. It is as if Prufrock himself sits across from her, veiling the hostile gaze and stifling the laughter he fears will be directed at him in his own poetic love song. The Prufrockian field of consciousness expands to incorporate and ridicule the speeches of a hostess who is, as Prufrock knows himself to be, "At times, indeed, almost ridiculous— / Almost, at times, the Fool." Of the poem's 124 lines, fifty are spoken by the lady and nearly seventy-five by the young man. Thus "Portrait of a Lady" could be described as an interior monologue which frames a spoken monologue. Without the framing, the quoted language resembles a dramatic monologue. In comparing Eliot's poem with "My Last Duchess," Cory Davies writes, "The real theater in 'Portrait' is the theatre of the young man's mind. The lady's words exist only for and through his thoughts" (Davies, 32).

In her repetitions, ellipses, interjections, and fractured syntax, the lady's speaking role decidedly evokes Browning:

> "You do not know how much they mean to me my friends,
> And how, how rare and strange it is, to find
> In a life composed so much, so much of odds and ends,
> [For indeed I do not love it . . . you knew? You are not blind!
> How keen you are!]
> To find a friend who has these qualities.
>
> (19-24)

It is worth considering the fifty lines of "Portrait" presented in quotation marks as if they were independent of the young man's interior monologue which frames them. Even without the silent commentary of the young man, the lady's discourse is double-voiced. There is a discrepancy between the way she sees herself—full of high seriousness and sentiment—and the way her guest sees her.

It is worth comparing the lady of Eliot's poem with her original, Adelaine Moffatt, the Bostonian hostess who was in the habit of inviting Eliot and other Harvard undergraduates to tea. Eliot wrote to Ezra Pound in February 1915 that he had received a "Christmas card from the lady, bearing the ringing greeting of friend to friend at this season of high festival" (*Letters*, 86). The language of Moffatt's greeting card is as clinging and maudlin as any sentiments Eliot's lady voices; Miss Moffatt makes herself an easy target for mimicry. Therefore one has to ask a rather absurd question to underscore the artifice behind Eliot's portrait: does Adelaine Moffatt habitually speak in rhyme? If not, then rhyme is an intervention on the part of the Prufrockian narrator, the fundamental way in which he turns her monologue back upon her. As many critics have noted, simplistic, end-stopped rhymes help render the lady's speech trite and rehearsed: "We must leave it now to fate. / You will write, at any rate. / Perhaps it is not too late" (105-107). Elizabeth Howe says of this triplet: "Her shameless persistence is mocked by the insistent rhyme and by the abruptness of the short sentences" (85). However, rhyme does more than make the lady an object of ridicule: it makes her a threat. She would end her young caller's independence, and so here rhyme—sounds which are dependent upon each other for effect—is equated with conformity.

Rhyme is only one of the modes by which the narrator renders the lady both ridiculous and threatening. He scrupulously represents the lady's repeated phrases ("But what have I, but what have I, my friend"), phrases that might seem less affected in spoken English than they do transcribed. Her gratuitous peppering of her speech with French words—such as her use of *cauchemar*, rhyming insipidly with "you are"—further signals her pretension and affectation. Yet it is the allusion to Arnold's poem "The Buried Life" that identifies the real source of fascination for the younger man. The lady says:

> Yet with these April sunsets, that somehow recall
> My buried life, and Paris in the Spring,
> I feel immeasurably at peace, and find the world
> To be wonderful and youthful, after all.
>
> (52-55)

Compare the lady's vision of the sunset with that of Roland or Prufrock. She attributes a facile moral implication to the beauty of nature that Eliot's narrator will not or cannot. She claims to have an epiphany revealing, to quote Browning's Pippa, that "God's in his heaven, all's right with the world." Thus she is not entirely wrong when she says, "I am always sure that you understand / My feelings" (58-9). Eliot's narrator understands her feelings only too well: they are the *reductio ad absurdum* of his own inherited poetic tradition. Like the "mechanical and tired" street piano he hears in the park, the lady "reiterates some worn-out common song" (79-80). This is why the narrator is both fascinated and revolted by the lady, why he returns to visit her despite himself: she is an embodiment of Victorian sensibilities that he must either flee or accept.

"Portrait of a Lady" can therefore be read as Eliot's negotiations with and containment of Victorian themes and forms. The internal monologue of Eliot's narrator satirizes and reacts to the spoken monologue of the fustian Victorian lady. Eliot's internal monologue modifies, responds to, and contains Browning's dramatic monologue by framing and incorporating the spoken monologue. Where the lady claims to find meaning in the light of April sunsets, the narrator's own element is one of obscuring vapors. He moves through "the smoke and fog of a December afternoon," takes the air in "a tobacco trance," writes "pen in hand / With the smoke coming down above the housetops" on an "afternoon grey and smoky." He likens his own psychological processes to a guttering—and hence smoke-producing—candle: "My self-possession flares up for a second. . . . My self-possession gutters; we are really in the dark" (94, 101). While the lady's candles burn steadily, casting "four rings of light on the ceiling overhead," the narrator's imagined candle leaves him in smoke and darkness (5). As in "Prufrock," the narrator walks veiled in fog and smoke, an ether through which he perceives all of the objects and people that make up his private and peculiar world.

The conclusion of "Portrait of a Lady" finds the narrator speculating ". . . what if she should die some afternoon. . . . Would she not have the advantage, after all?" (114, 121). The poem's two references to smiles may look forward to *The Waste Land*'s equation of the smile and the skull: "But at my back in a cold blast I hear / The rattle of the bones, and chuckle spread from ear to ear" (185-6). When the narrator says "I feel like one who smiles and turning shall remark / Suddenly, his expression in a glass," he may, like Eliot's speaker in "Whispers of Immortality," have seen "the skull beneath the skin; / and breastless creature under ground / Leaned backward with a lipless grin" ("Portrait," 99-100; "Whispers of Immortality," 2-4). Encoded then in his consideration of the lady's eventual death is a consideration of his own death. In the poem's final lines, dying and the smile are coupled: "This music is successful with a 'dying fall' / Now that we talk of dying— / And should I have the right to smile?" (122-4). Eliot's narrator can sit politely in a well-furnished parlor, taking tea and making proper conversation, but his mind returns always to waste, death, and destruction.

Let us return, then, to Eliot's observation to Virginia Woolf that *Ulysses* "destroyed the whole of the nineteenth century." "Destroy" is an appropriately violent verb to describe the art of the twentieth century, a century of great progress and foment, and equally great destruction. It is quite fitting, in fact, that *The Waste Land* is the most influential poem of a century that gave birth to the trench, the concentration camp, and the atom bomb. Eliot and Woolf had seen real destruction just a few years earlier during World War I, and it had left its scars on both of them. Eliot dedicated *Prufrock and Other Observations* to Jean Verdenal, his French friend who died in the trenches at Flanders. Some twenty years later, when it was clear that England would enter a second world war, Woolf chose to destroy herself rather than again to be a witness to destruction. During World War I, Eliot, young but unhealthy, was not accepted into the American army. His memories of the war would be not of the muddy trenches, but of a London emptied of its young men: the purgatorial, unreal city that Prufrock wanders and that overlies the infernal landscape of *The Waste Land*. During World War II, however, Eliot would see the devastation of the conflict firsthand, serving as a fire warden during the London blitz. The collapsing houses and flash fires of the German aerial bombardment will make their way into his great final cycle of poems, *Four Quartets*: "dust in the air suspended / marks the place where a story ended / dust inbreathed was a house, / the wall, the wainscot, and the mouse."

Yet Eliot does not ultimately succumb to destruction; he does not see the destructive impulse as inherently more powerful than the creative one. J. Robert Oppenheimer, the physicist who headed the Manhattan Project, recalls watching the atom bomb test he called Trinity and thinking of a line from the *Bhagavad-Gita*, "I am become death, destroyer of worlds." Oppenheimer, like Eliot, studied Sanskrit at Harvard and counted the *Bhagavad-Gita*—as well as Eliot's *The Waste Land*—among his favorite books. Eliot would allude to this same passage in the "The Dry Salvages," one of his *Four Quartets*. But Eliot would get the translation right—Vishnu claims not to have become death, but time—and would choose a line a little later in the passage, one that carries a decidedly more nuanced meaning: "Time the destroyer is time the preserver." This perhaps is a good model for reading the literature of one time in relation to that of a previous one. Eliot's rending of Victorian monologue forms in "Prufrock," "Portrait of a Lady," and *The Waste Land* is at once destructive and creative. The young Eliot defined his own work and that of his peers in opposition to that of the Victorians, but the older man admits that in art, the act of destruction is simultaneously an act of creation.

Works Cited

Armstrong, Isobel. *Victorian Poetry: Poetry, Poetics and Politics*. New York: Routledge, 1993.

Arnold, Matthew. *Irish Essays, and Others*. London: Smith, Elder, 1882. Accessed through the New York Public Library.

Bagehot, Walter. "Wordsworth, Tennyson, and Browning; or Pure, Ornate, and Grotesque Art in English Poetry." 1864. *Literary Studies*. London: Longmans, Green, 1879.

Bloom, Harold. *The Anxiety of Influence*. New York: Oxford University Press, 1973.

Bornstein, George. *Transformations of Romanticism in Yeats, Eliot and Stevens*. Chicago: University of Chicago Press, 1976.

Browning, Robert. *Robert Browning's Poetry: Authoritative Texts, Criticism*. Norton Critical Edition, ed. James F. Loucks. New York: Norton, 1979.

Christ, Carol T. "T. S. Eliot and the Victorians." *Modern Philology* 79 (1981): 157-165.

Davies, Cory Bieman. "'Natural Evolution' in 'Dramatic Essences' from Robert Browning to T. S. Eliot." *Browning Institute Studies: An Annual of Victorian Literary and Cultural History* 11 (1983): 23-37.

Eliot, T. S. *The Complete Poems and Plays, 1909-1950*. New York: Harcourt, Brace & World, 1962.

_____. *Inventions of the March Hare*. Ed. Christopher Ricks. New York: Harcourt Brace, 1996.

_____. *Selected Essays: 1917-1932*. New York: Harcourt, Brace and Company, 1932.

_____. *Selected Prose of T. S. Eliot*. Ed. Frank Kermode. New York: Harcourt Brace Jovanovich, 1975.

_____. *To Criticize the Critic*. London: Faber and Faber, 1965.

_____. *The Waste Land: A Facsimile and Transcript of the Original Drafts including the Annotations of Ezra Pound*. Ed. Valerie Eliot. New York: Harcourt Brace Jovanovich, 1971.

Eliot, Valerie, ed. *The Letters of T. S. Eliot*. New York: Harcourt Brace Jovanovich, 1988.

Feldman, Jessica R. "Modernism's Victorian Bric-a-Brac." *Modernism/Modernity* 8 (2001): 453-470.

Howe, Elisabeth A. *The Dramatic Monologue*. New York: Twayne Publishers, 1996.

Kaye, Richard A. "'A Splendid Readiness for Death': T. S. Eliot, the Homosexual Cult of St. Sebastian, and World War I." *Modernism/Modernity* 6 (1999): 107-134.

Litzinger, Boyd, and Donald Smalley. *Robert Browning: The Critical Heritage*. London: Routledge, 1995.
Mayer, John T. *T. S. Eliot's Silent Voices*. Oxford: Oxford University Press, 1989.
Menand, Louis. *Discovering Modernism: T. S. Eliot and His Context*. New York: Oxford University Press, 1987.
Tucker, Herbert F. *Browning's Beginnings: The Art of Disclosure*. Minneapolis: University of Minnesota Press, 1980.
Woolf, Virginia. *A Writer's Diary*. London: Hogarth Press, 1975.

Voices and Language in T. S. Eliot's
*The Waste Land*_____
Allan Johnson

    Allan Johnson provides an illuminating reading of *The Waste Land* by attending to the difficulty of identifying a continuous speaking voice as an organizing thread in the poem. Through selective close reading, he comments on all five parts, moving from the opening voice and the voice of Marie in part one through the voice of the thunder in part five. As Johnson points out, from early in the writing of the poem Eliot had in mind the multiple voices of reading aloud from Dickens' *Our Mutual Friend*. The vocal multitude is ambiguous in character because the voices are often not clearly demarcated and they do not merge into any single figure that provides unity, despite Eliot's identification of Tiresias as the poem's central figure in one of his notes. For Johnson, Tiresias has no more authority as a prophet than does the Cumaean Sibyl in the poem's epigraph. Eliot presents or projects death, destruction, waste, and detritus throughout the poem, but the voices are made up of language that enables the reader to do many things, while the language also prevents the voices from coalescing into a single unifying thread. Johnson provides examples of details that cannot be taken in simply one way or another. Instead the potentials for meaning blur and merge in ways that are not meaningless. If anything there is too much rather than too little meaning in *The Waste Land*. Allusions from different periods of literature are juxtaposed, as are the voices of members of different social classes. Among the various texts in the foreground and the background of the poem, Johnson attends to the Buddha's Fire Sermon because of its physical and thematic centrality. As he reads part three, however, he brings out the echoes that link its elements to other passages. This kind of cross-referencing as the act of reading the poem makes it clear that we are not following a single thread. Instead moving forward is also a process of moving back, in a way that anticipates effects that Eliot creates again later at greater length in *Four Quartets*. Johnson emphasizes the projection of chaos and disorder in the poem and the recurring issue of the difficulty of making sense of images that the poem itself evokes. The difficulty is in part a matter of dread, as Johnson's references to psychically damaged soldiers from World War I indicate. The dread also involves gothic, vampiric voices, ghostly cultural voices from the past that are no longer living but not completely dead. But he does not interpret the poem as representing absolute alienation in the modern world, as many critics once did in a widespread reading not only of *The Waste Land* but of literary modernism in general. Instead, he finds rich meanings in the enigmatic voices that are full even when they seem to be empty, like the "voices singing out of empty cisterns" in part five. —J.P.R.

T. S. Eliot's *The Waste Land* (1922) has become infamous for its ostensible linguistic impenetrability and thematic elusiveness, but the difficulty of the text can be seen as a calculated stylistic choice made by Eliot in order to develop the poem's central theme of chaos and disorder in the modern world. When Eliot began work on the first draft of *The Waste Land* in the autumn of 1921, he titled his work *He Do the Police in Different Voices*, a line from Charles Dickens' *Our Mutual Friend* (1864-1865), which offers a valuable insight into the consternating construction of this poem. Like Sloppy in *Our Mutual Friend* (who is praised for reading the crime section of the newspaper aloud in different voices), the narrative voice of *The Waste Land* recounts a series of often surprising, unconventional independent character monologues, and the poem's organizing motif of waste is enacted by the text's own mysterious incoherence and accumulation of disparate voices.

Eliot argues in his 1921 essay "The Metaphysical Poets" that "poets in our civilization, as it exists at present, must be *difficult* . . . more comprehensive, more allusive, more indirect," and certainly we can recognize the way in which *The Waste Land* serves as the true acme of this high modernistic attitude (*Selected Prose*, 65). Yet this is not an impenetrable poem; indeed, the "comprehensive" infrastructure of metaphors, motifs, and allusions that characterizes this poem serves as an analytical route through the text. Perhaps the most challenging aspect of reading *The Waste Land* is learning to accept the undecipherable and to view the voices of the many residents of the wasteland not as inconsistent, but disjointed and reaching toward one goal.

In his notes to the text (which are highly allusive and sometimes misleading), Eliot suggests that the voice of the sage Tiresias, who first appears in the third section of the poem, "although a mere spectator and not indeed a 'character,' is yet the most important personage in the poem . . . what Tiresias *sees*, in fact, is the substance of the poem" (*Waste Land*, 23). There are multiple problems that emerge, however, when we seek to read Tiresias as the singular voice of the poem, and many critics have emphasized the specificity and individuality of each of the voices of the poem. Bonamy Dobrée, literary scholar and intimate friend of Eliot, has convincingly argued that there are two speakers—a man and a woman, or perhaps, the male and female aspect of the hermaphroditic Tiresias—who take on roles as a series of doomed lovers (Dobrée, 113), while John Mayer has described the narrative voice of *The Waste Land* as a "psychic monologue," a reading that, on one level, accepts Eliot's suggestion that Tiresias is the single framing voice, while also highlighting the uncanny and mystical way in which the narrative voice bifurcates and reforms itself like a psychic channeling spirits (Mayer, 241). The question of the voice behind *The Waste Land* can be answered in one way by the poem's curious epigraph, taken from Petronius' *Satyricon*, which is obscure in both its language and its direct implications to Eliot's work. Here the Cumaean Sibyl, an ancient oracle and prophetess, begs for death after not having the insight to recognize the foolishness of requesting eternal life without eternal youth. Eliot's poem makes much of this theme, turning thwarted, incomplete, or inaccurate prophecy into an emblem of the futile structures and systems that seek to find coherence within the chaos of the world. As a consequence, the text gives us no specific reason to accept the validity of the sage Tiresias or his visions.

Yet the many voices of *The Waste Land* do converge in several central themes. *The Waste Land* is, in many ways, a response to the destruction caused across Europe during World War I and the dramatic impact this had on Britain specifically. Although the poem is characterized by its images of futility, barrenness, and death, the debris and waste scrutinized by the residents of the wasteland remain part of a deeply rational poem that challenges readers to encounter language in new ways as they move through a modern, postwar world.

The First Four Voices

With a coherent narrative voice and unambiguous poetic images, the first seven lines of "The Burial of the Dead" are among the most immediately accessible moments in the entire poem, but already Eliot is beginning to advance his complex inspection of death and detritus in the modern world. Even the title—simply taken from a service in the Anglican Book of Common Prayer—alerts us to the motifs of burial and death that predominate in this section. The traditional association of spring with birth, growth, and renewal has been inverted, and here, in the opening line, April becomes "the cruellest month" because of the frightful way in which nature creates life out of death (I.1). This is not a traditional cycle of death and rebirth, but an uncanny and deeply esoteric notion of death followed by fearsome transmogrification. The poem takes for its theme the typical modernist preoccupations of innovation and inheritance and the singular moment of deathly stasis that falls between them. It is vital to understand that this initial eloquent speaker is buried beneath the ground—where "Winter kept us warm, covering / Earth in forgetful snow"—and that with these lines we find the first instance of the motif of burial in earth, water, or fire that runs throughout *The Waste Land* (I.5-6). Spring *is* fearful to the corpse because growing flowers feed off of the buried dead, and the body becomes, once again, preyed upon.

With the turn in line 8 signaled by the first instance of the personal "you," the poem moves from a fearful burial scene to a series of tender childhood memories of Marie, the first named character in *The Waste Land*. Is it perhaps Marie who voiced the legendary first lines of this poem before reminiscing about childhood happiness? Or is this the voice of Tiresias, who can see both through the eyes of the dead and through the memories of a woman? Critics have demonstrated that the source of the Marie story is an autobiography written by Countess Marie Larisch, one of many texts that influence and infiltrate Eliot's poem like ghostly voices themselves. Certainly the opening section of "The Burial of the Dead" has a clear memoir-quality, reminding both Marie and the reader of happier times before the fear and death that choked Europe during World War I.[1] In the midst of this narrative clarity, however, we encounter a disorientating moment in line 12, and even in translation ("I'm not Russian at all, I come from Lithuania, a true German") this line in German remains bewildering. Much can be made later of Marie's movement from fear to freedom while "in the mountains" and this curious line about Marie's Lithuanian roots that is perhaps suggestive of the poem's concern with geographical boundaries and national identity. But the images that will bring Marie's story into greater focus will not be found until the later sections of the poem (I.17). In this first encounter with Marie, the reader's attention is focused on the final line—which comes as a devastating conclusion to Marie's charming story—and Marie's return to a present moment that is characterized by monotony and barrenness. The adventurous action of the sledding story is contrasted with the unfussiness of reading at night and leaving the snow-covered mountains of her childhood to go south in the winter.

The narrative voice of Marie quickly fades, and the second section of "The Burial of the Dead" opens with a pseudo-Biblical declaration from a new voice:

> What are the roots that clutch, what branches grow
> Out of this stony rubbish? Son of man,
> You cannot say, or guess, for you know only
> A heap of broken images.
>
> (I.19-22)

This passage presents us with the true analytical challenge of *The Waste Land*: how much, if at all, are we meant to interpret, rationalize, and categorize the "heap of broken images" and disjointed voices that constitute this poem? What, if anything, can grow out of the infertile wasteland of "this stony rubbish" (I.20)? The question posed by the narrative voice remains unanswerable. Although the many inhabitants of the wasteland struggle to find coherence and order within their fractured worlds, the passage issues a general warning that no such order can ever be found.

The connection between this haunting voice that promises to "show you fear in a handful of dust" and the story of the hyacinth girl that follows is unclear (I.30). Scholars, including Jewel Spears Brooker and Joseph Bentley, have suggested that the passages from Wagner's *Tristan und Isolde* (1865) that appear in lines 31-34 and line 42 can be seen as a contextual frame that sets apart the story of the hyacinth girl and her undead lover (Brooker and Bentley, 69). Even without knowledge of Wagner's opera or the complex thematic connections Eliot is suggesting between these two works, we can easily recognize the emphasis placed upon thwarted love. The hyacinths recall the lilacs of line 2 that grew "out of the dead land" (I.2), and the mysterious return of the hyacinth girl's lover perhaps suggests the return of soldiers from World War I, an image explored later in the Unreal City passage. As her lover explains, "when we came back . . . I could not / Speak," and it is uncertain whether "we" is used to signify these two lovers, or the speaker and a group of others, such as the crowds of dead and undead soldiers that will appear later in the Unreal City (I.37). We may see in this section the account of a soldier returning, either dead or suffering from severe post-traumatic stress disorder, who feels *"Oed' und leer das Meer"* ("desolate and empty the sea," I.42). The potential for romantic love is upset by the fact that the man is "neither / Living nor dead," and we find a clear example of the barren, unfulfilled relationship that exists between all of the lovers in *The Waste Land* (I.39-40).

This motif of futility is further developed by the Madame Sosostris section that follows. Unenlightened divination, a topic already introduced by the epigraph to the poem, is a clear theme here. A notable stylistic feature of this section is the sardonic tone the speaker adopts when describing the fortune-teller: even though the "famous clairvoyante / Had a bad cold" she is still "known to be the wisest woman in Europe" (I.43-45). A particularly intriguing aspect of this tone is achieved in the final lines of this section:

> Thank you. If you see dear Mrs. Equitone,
> Tell her I bring the horoscope myself:
> One must be so careful these days.
>
> (I.57-59)

The absurdity here (as with the earlier comment about Madame Sosostris' cold) undermines the fortune-teller's credibility, but these lines are additionally significant because they make clear that Madame Sosostris, like the Cumaean Sybil of the epigraph, is unable to see clearly enough into the future to recognize a threat. Although divination is presumably a way to achieve order, coherence, and command, the random shuffling of the Tarot cards and Madame Sosostris' questionable reliability again emphasize randomness and futility—meaning cannot be found.

Much can be made of the archetypal images on the Tarot cards that Madame Sosostris reveals, and it is helpful to recognize how the images on the cards provide a cast list for the rest of the poem: we can reasonably be reminded of Marie and her mountain adventure by "the Lady of the Rocks"; the "one-eyed merchant" is later embodied by Mr. Eugenides in a scene of homosexual burlesque in "The Fire Sermon";

the "drowned Phoenician Sailor" becomes the central figure in "Death by Water." The generally accurate, if not particularly extraordinary, predictions that Madame Sosostris makes from the arrangement of these specific cards are, in one sense, nothing more than the game of a fraudulent fortune-teller. The fear of drowning is a general human attribute, and there is as yet no specific prediction of an actual death by water; "crowds of people" is a commmon enough sight, especially in London, where most of this poem is set (I.56)—but in the world of the poem, these predictions acquire multiple profound significances. Madame Sosostris' vision of "crowds of people, walking round in a ring" seems to melt into and provide the central dramatic action in the final section of "The Burial of the Dead." We are left to wonder how the narrator of this final section is related to the narrator of the previous three sections—is this Tiresias mocking the foresight of a crude fortune-teller? The "crowds of people" foretold by the fortune-teller are manifested in the swarm of people that "flowed over London bridge" in the startling image created of London as an "Unreal City" (I.60, 62).

As is often the case with interpretations of this poem, critics remain divided on the significance of this flow of dead, undead, or unresponsive crowds across London Bridge. In his highly influential work *The Intellectuals and the Masses*, John Carey has suggested that this passage evokes what Eliot saw as the numbing effects of mass culture: we find a stream of lower-middle-class clerks commuting from their suburban homes into the City for work (Carey, 10). This interpretation is strengthened when, in "The Fire Sermon," Tiresias voyeuristically watches an aggressive clerk in a sexual encounter that highlights the emptiness of modern life. We might also be wise to recognize in this passage allusions to the return of the wounded and maimed from World War I, a reading strengthened by the hyacinth girl episode and by the general historical context of the work. The thematic intensity of *The Waste Land* is a product of, firstly, the multiple interpretations that willingly emerge from the text; moments such as this have multiple thematic resonances that speak to the broader goals of the poem as a whole. For example, we find, again, a discussion of buried bodies that perhaps alludes to the buried and semi-buried dead in the trenches of World War I but also reminds us of the opening narrative voice that spoke from beneath the ground. Is the body that Stetson "planted last year" the speaker of the first seven lines of "The Burial of the Dead" (l.71)? If so, we find the answer to the intriguing question presented by the speaker: yes, the body has begun to sprout and is now feeding the spring flowers. But, of course, Eliot doesn't make interpretations of this poem as simple as that, and we are left to contend with a remarkable anachronism: the Battle of Mylae mentioned in line 70 took place in 206 B.C.E. These cannot simply be soldiers returning from a recent battle, nor can they be simply clerks going to or coming from their office: they are clerks *and* contemporary soldiers *and* ancient soldiers *and* everyone else moving through the endless, unbreakable cycle of death and despair predicted by Madame Sosostris in her vision of the "crowds of people, walking round in a ring" (I. 56).

The Two Queens

The growing importance of the motif of the destruction caused by World War I—an effect achieved through Eliot's use of repeated images and phrases—helps to make sense of the narrative formula in "A Game of Chess." Chess is a sterilized and neutered game of war that retains none of the life-and-death stakes involved in real battle. Like Tarot, it provides a system of rules and regulations that attempt to govern the otherwise ungovernable. "A Game of Chess" is very much concerned with the opposition between the orderly and the disorderly, and we find in this section two women squared off against each other like opposing queens on a chess board: an upper-middle-class woman observed in the private space of a luxurious bathroom, bedroom, or boudoir, and a Rabelaisian working-class woman who is mercilessly gossiped about in the open social setting of a pub. Although the socioeconomic difference between these women is emphatic and each has a different understanding of order and control, these figures are linked through their entrapment in bleak relationships in a postwar world. The two queens in "A Game of Chess," have been protected by the pawns and chess pieces that surround them, but the only outcome is lifeless, loveless, barren romantic relationships.

"A Game of Chess" opens with a paraphrase of a line from Shakespeare's *Antony and Cleopatra* that draws immediate attention to the stateliness and majesty of the first female character and her environment. The style the narrative voice adopts in these initial thirty lines mirrors the opulence of the setting. The diction here is elegant and lush. Even the "strange synthetic perfumes, / Unguent, powdered, or liquid" are described with rich, evocative assonance that emphasizes the sumptuousness of this room (II.87-88). This description will make a stark contrast to the setting of the second half of this section. This woman is described only through her relationship to the space that she inhabits until a much later description of her dry hair, which "spread out in fiery points" (II.109). We may be reminded here of the hyacinth girl and her wet hair, suggesting a parallel between these two figures of thwarted love and perhaps suggesting a movement of time: wet hair has now become dry. This nameless, faceless figure is able to exert complete control over the safe confines of her dressing room, but her sense of safety and order is destroyed when her husband enters her space. Although she begs this man to "Stay with me. / Speak to me," he seems to do neither, and remains silent and mortally distant (II.111-12). Witnessing the panic and fear of this woman's loneliness (again, perhaps, reminding us of Marie), the man is only able to ponder meaningless thoughts that are perhaps suggestive of the despondency and mental disorder caused by post-traumatic stress disorder. He imagines that he and the female speaker are "in rats' alley / Where the dead men lost their bones," which can be seen as, again, a reference to the horrors of the trenches in World War I. As the female speaker continues to wonder and worry, all that is left for this returning soldier to imagine is the banality of life before him: "hot water at ten" for breakfast tea, rides in a motorcar, "a game of chess," and waiting for something to happen (II.135-38). This is a fruitless relationship that neither figure is able to interpret or control.

The change of speaker that occurs between lines 138 and 139 is signaled only by a new diction that is suggestive of British working-class dialect: "When Lil's husband got demobbed, I said— / I didn't mince my words, I said to her myself . . . Now Albert's coming back, make yourself a bit smart" (II.139-42). Unlike the private scene that comprised the first half of this section, the action has moved to the public space of a pub at closing time, with a barman impatiently telling the customers to "HURRY UP PLEASE ITS TIME" (II.141). Like the faceless woman in the first half of "The Game of Chess," Lil is never seen by the reader but is observed only indirectly through the narrative eyes of her nameless friend. Although Lil's husband Albert, who is coming back from the war, gave her money for false teeth to improve her appearance, she has spent it on an abortion, after which her health and her body have "never been the / same" (II.161-62). Although Eliot does not appear to be making any specific comment on abortion here, it connects to the topic of barrenness developed throughout this poem. As in the first section of "The Game of Chess," there is no consummation, and Lil remains in a barren relationship that is beyond her control.

Interpreting the Voices

Of the crowd of literary, historical, and religious texts that inform and provide a thematic grounding within *The Waste Land* (only a sampling of which have been mentioned here), one that is vital to understanding the work is the Buddha's Fire Sermon, from which the third section of *The Waste Land* takes its name. In his sermon to a group of devoted followers, the Buddha evokes the fearsome image of fire to demonstrate the danger of being bound to the material world. Our sensory organs are made of fire, the Buddha explains, along with all of the images around us, and the only way to escape this fire is to reject the material in favor of the spiritual. With this powerful metaphorical image, the Buddha suggests that a rejection of earthly desire is the only way to be released from *samsara*, the cycle of birth and death that is the suffering characteristic of humanity. The implications of this allusion to the Buddha's Fire Sermon seem clear: if, as the voice in "The Burial of the Dead" warned, the world is simply "a heap of broken images," then only a release from a preoccupation with these images will bring enlightenment. Although Tiresias the sage is a shade, he is tied to earthly passions and continues to gaze voyeuristically at other characters. Like the Cumaean Sybil and Madame Sosostris, Tiresias can be viewed as a fraudulent sage who makes errors and misjudgments that expose his assumed enlightenment to questions of legitimacy.

Although the central motif of this section is fire, the settings of all the major vignettes in "The Fire Sermon" involve water, including, prominently, the bank of the Thames. As the section opens, the narrator is sitting near the Thames during early winter, when "the last fingers of leaf / Clutch and sink into the wet bank," and observing the destruction and waste of London (III.173-74). This mysterious figure is eloquent and well read—this opening monologue includes allusions to the Psalms, Edmund Spenser, Andrew Marvell, and William Shakespeare—and conjures many of the images and motifs explored earlier in *The Waste Land*, including, significantly, rats and bones. We can begin to see here how *The Waste Land* is built around a structure of repeated images that accumulate significance with each successive appearance—the "rattle of bones" in line 186 can remind us of the scene with Stetson in "The Burial of the Dead," and the rat in line 187 can remind us of trenches, "rats' alley" in "A Game of Chess." That these two earlier images can be associated with the destruction caused by World War I reinforces the importance of that contextual framework at this later point in the poem.

Interpretation becomes an increasingly difficult task from this point forward, and the narrative through-line of *The Waste Land* begins to move rapidly in and out of focus. Approximately halfway through the poem, we find three short vignettes that reemphasize the significance of unfruitful, mechanical, or barren relationships introduced first in "The Burial of the Dead" and "A Game of Chess." The onomatopoeic passage in lines 203-06 evokes the painting of the "sylvan scene" that hung in the dressing room of the woman in "A Game of Chess" (II.98), and "Mr. Eugenides, the Smyrna merchant" can remind us of the one-eyed merchant in Madame Sosostris' Tarot reading. But a crucial turning point in the poem comes when Tiresias is finally identified and named in line 218. Eliot suggests in his notes that Tiresias is the true narrator of the entire poem, and we see here how invasive and penetrating the voyeuristic eye of Tiresias really is (*Waste Land*, 23). He watches as "The typist home at teatime, clears her breakfast, lights / Her stove, and lays out food in tins" and continues to watch as this woman's lover comes and "Endeavours to engage her in caresses" (III.222-23, 237). Like each of the earlier pairs of lovers shown in the poem, this couple has a mechanical, emotionless relationship that mirrors the waste and debris that characterize this wasteland.

The remaining sections of "The Fire Sermon" recede into complex meditations on the destruction of London and scattered waste. The fragmented, cubistic pieces of images anticipate the style and diction of the dramatic conclusion to "What the Thunder Said," the final section of the poem. Traditional modes of narration melt away, and the stress of the poem is transferred into the staccato rhythms used to describe the Unreal City:

> The river sweats
> Oil and tar
> The barges drift
> With the turning tide
> Red sails
> Wide
> To leeward, swing on the heavy spar.
> (III.267-72)

We can observe in passages such as this, though, a keen interest in the materiality of the world, something that the Buddha's Fire Sermon explicitly teaches against. Is this what Tiresias sees? If so, the voyeuristic way in which he moves in and around the private, often highly sexualized lives of these characters leads to a consumption by fire and an enactment of the central image of the Buddha's Fire Sermon:

> Burning, burning, burning, burning
> O Lord Thou pluckest me out
> O Lord Thou pluckest
>
> burning
> (III.308-11)

This consumption by fire is, in many ways, reminiscent of the burials elsewhere in the poem, and it presents burial as a central problem image in the text. In the aptly named "Death by Water," the burial at sea fulfills Madame Sosostris' vision of the "drowned Phoenician Sailor" and her warning to "Fear death by water" (I.47, 55). As in earlier treatments of burial, the burial in water brings not renewal or rebirth but a frightful rebirth as the undead. The body of the dead sailor Phlebas is personified, making the corpse into a sentient participant in its own decomposition and memorably blurring the line between the living and the dead:

> A current under sea
> Picked his bones in whispers. As he rose and fell
> He passed the stages of his age and youth
> Entering the whirlpool.
> (IV.315-18)

During the process of decomposition, his body moves rapidly from youth to old age, linking Phlebas to the procession of the ageless undead that haunt the world of the poem. Bodies become only another aspect of the waste and detritus, and just as the body of the narrative voice in the first section of "The Burial of the Dead" is feeding the spring flowers, the body of Phlebas is feeding the water, which cruelly "picked his bones" (IV.316).

While the overarching theme of *The Waste Land* deals with the rigors and perhaps impossibility of the interpretation of poems, "What the Thunder Said" is the poem's thematic climax. After riding down a mountain with Marie in "The Burial of the Dead" in order to enter the world of the wasteland, the poem follows the delirious movement of the speaker back up a mountain and away from the danger and death in the valley between. After a series of hallucinatory images that recount a treacherous movement up from the ocean in search of fresh water, the speaker is at the top of the sacred mountain Ganga to receive a message from God, which ultimately comes in the form of the thunder's simple statement: "DA" (V.400). This is a meaningless, onomatopoetic phrase— a poetic estimation of the sound of thunder, such as the treatment of bird calls in "The Fire Sermon" and in lines 356-57. Meaning can be attributed to this word and to its sound only through a process of interpretation. Eliot adapts the subsequent attempts at interpreting the voice of the thunder from the *Brihadaranyaka Upanishad*, a sacred Hindu text in which three divine interpreters are made to explain this mysterious, meaningless syllable. They each suggest that it is the first part of an incomplete word: *datta*, or "give"; *dayadhvam*, or "sympathize"; *damyata*, or "control." Although giving, sympathizing, and controlling are critical aspects in the thematic architecture of *The Waste Land*, this section emphasizes the value and role of interpretation. Like the mysterious syllable from the thunder, the text of *The Waste Land* provides only a structure for interpretation. Eliot's poem holds simultaneous meanings—it is present and past, general and specific, personal and private—that can be appreciated *simultaneously* and in varying combinations. Like the voice of the thunder, Eliot has provided hints, codes, and beginnings that invite and enable the reader, along with the three religious men on the mountain, to recognize meaning within the apparently meaningless.

Note
1. For an analysis of this source, see George L. K. Morris, "Marie, Marie, Hold on Tight," *Partisan Review* 21 (1953): 231-33.

Works Cited
Brooker, Jewel Spears, and Joseph Bentley. *Reading "The Waste Land": Modernism and the Limits of Interpretation*. Amherst: University of Massachusetts Press, 1990.

Carey, John. *The Intellectuals and the Masses: Pride and Prejudice Among the Literary Intelligentsia, 1880-1939*. London: Faber and Faber, 1992.

Dobrée, Bonamy. *The Lamp and the Lute*. New York: Barnes & Noble, 1964.

Eliot, T. S. *Selected Prose of T. S. Eliot*, ed. Frank Kermode. New York: Harcourt, 1975.

_____. *The Waste Land*. Norton Critical Edition, ed. Michael North. New York: Norton, 2000.

Mayer, John. *T. S. Eliot's Silent Voices*. Oxford: Oxford University Press, 1989.

Morris, George L. K. "Marie, Marie, Hold on Tight," *Partisan Review* 21 (1953): 231-33.

CRITICAL READINGS

"Poetry as Poetry"

Louis Menand

Louis Menand's meditation on several of Eliot's most influential critical essays links the poet-critic's thinking to that of contemporaries and nineteenth-century precursors. Menand argues for more of an affinity between them and Eliot than has often been suggested. He sees specific concepts, such as the *objective correlative* and the *dissociation of sensibility*, not as originating with Eliot in a narrow way, though Eliot's specific formulations of them captured the imagination of literary intellectuals of his time. Taken in isolation, these and other aspects of Eliot's thinking do resemble concepts that were already in circulation, but creativity consists often in fitting together existing elements into new configurations, and Eliot's arranging of existing ideas into new relationships and arguments made him the most influential poet-critic of his day. "Tradition and the Individual Talent" is arguably the most widely circulated and discussed literary essay in English of the twentieth century, the sibling of *The Waste Land*, which may well be the most widely reprinted and discussed long poem in English of the century. Menand suggests early in his essay that in taking anti-Romantic positions Eliot may have been adopting an avant-garde pose or that he was perhaps deluded in not recognizing his own kinship to nineteenth-century British precursors. Eliot can also be understood, however, to have taken his stances against Romanticism for polemical reasons, in order to make his points in emphatic rather than qualified ways, as part of a cultural debate in which he was challenging accepted popular thinking. Whatever the case in that regard, his critical formulations contributed substantially to bringing the distinctive character of literary modernism into focus for the public and for other writers. Menand rightly places Eliot among the Imagists of the early part of the century. He also brings out the fuzziness of Eliot's famous essay on *Hamlet* in which Eliot used the term *objective correlative*. Despite the essay's uneven quality, Eliot's insistence on

> the *objective* rather than the *subjective* comes through clearly. As Menand explains, Eliot held the radical position, by contrast with the popular heritage of Romanticism, that there was no inner life to be expressed. Poetry was for Eliot a matter of impersonality, not of personality. His anti-expressive view, most famously stated in "Tradition," did not occur in a vacuum, and Menand sketches its appearance in other writers. He does the same for the dissociation of sensibility, which Eliot presents in objecting to the influence of John Milton, a major precursor of Romantic poetry, and in praising John Donne and Metaphysical poetry. Menand claims that Eliot merely refines what he found in circulation already, but the question of modernism's relation to British Romanticism, as either a continuity or a sharp break, is still open. The extent to which the ideas Eliot worked with were known and accepted is also worth considering. They may have been well received already by some other intellectuals, but they certainly were not by the reading public in general. After Eliot, alternatives to nineteenth-century attitudes were much more widely known and accepted. His essays changed the way we think about literature and literary history.   —J.P.R.

Eliot devoted himself in his early critical essays to debunking a good deal more of the nineteenth century than he could reasonably have expected to get along without, which is one of the reasons it is not surprising that many of the celebrated phrases in those essays have been discovered in various nineteenth-century settings. It gives any commentator satisfaction, of course, to be able to produce antecedent versions of a particular aesthetic prescription from the very tradition that prescription was apparently aimed at discrediting—as when, to take an especially well-turned example, something like Eliot's historical theory of the dissociation of sensibility, invented in part to disparage Tennyson, is shown to have once been proposed by Arthur Hallam.[1] And Eliot's polemical overreaching has made him seem an easy target for revisionists bent on exposing his profession of anti-

Romanticism as either an avant-garde pose (when the interest is sympathetic) or (when it is not) a piece of protective self-deception.

But revisionism works so well with Eliot because Eliot was a reshaper of attitudes and not, by design, a redefiner of things. His own motto for the essays in *The Sacred Wood* (1920)—"when we are considering poetry we must consider it primarily as poetry and not another thing"[2]—seems an instance of misplaced concreteness (for what *is* poetry apart from what we consider it to be?) because like any ironist Eliot worked best with received ideas. His conception of what literature is as a thing in itself generally coincided with the contemporary conception, and his best-known critical judgments were arrived at by giving a traditional aesthetic vocabulary untraditional jobs to do. Praise for a poet's "direct sensuous apprehension of thought," for instance, is Romantic praise of an unexceptional sort, and would hardly have drawn attention applied (as in fact, in the nineteenth century, it was applied[3]) to Keats. It was not even much worth noticing applied, as Eliot of course did apply it, to Donne. Such things had often been said about the metaphysical poets in the later nineteenth century and had been repeated in Eliot's own time by even so moderate a literary progressive as Rupert Brooke.[4] But the trick of praising Donne in this manner *at the expense of* Keats and the Keatsians was an ingenious feat of critical partisanship, not least because of its willingness to take forensic advantage of the unverifiability of its own aesthetic standard. For once we begin to argue over which poet's thought is in fact "felt thought," we risk exposing the purely rhetorical nature of such judgments.

This was strategy of a kind that seems to have occurred frequently to Eliot, and it is what makes his early critical writing a kind of skeptic's guide to the literary values of early modernism —which is to say in many cases to the literary values, in boiled-down or attenuated forms, of the nineteenth century. There was, of course, another side to Eliot's formulations as well: they were for many of his contemporaries positive articulations of the distinctive aesthetic principles of twentieth-century writing. But these aspects of Eliot's importance as a critic are not unrelated; for the thing that gives a statement prescriptive force for one reader is the same as the thing that gives it ironic force for another—its reliance upon what is already taken for granted. And Eliot was never a writer to pass up the chance to draw upon the authority of what already exists. But to say only this does not do justice to the real character of his genius, for Eliot was also a writer who tended to find his greatest opportunities in ideas whose authority was already slightly discredited or whose applications seemed used up.

Notions very like the one named by the term "objective correlative" have been located in a number of nineteenth-century texts: in Pater's chapter on Botticelli in *The Renaissance*; in the *Lectures on Art* (1850) of the American painter Washington Allston, whose work Coleridge admired and made the occasion for a famous series of essays on aesthetics; in a formulation used by Coleridge himself; and (now we are deep inside the enemy camp) in a letter from Schiller to Goethe.[5] But there is no need to look even as far as Pater for the origins of Eliot's term; it derives from a standard item in contemporary definitions of proper poetic procedure: it is the recipe for an image. Eliot got a spectacular use out of it—one imagines him keeping the formula in his pocket until the most unlikely occasion should present itself—because while the notion of a dramatic image was current when the essay on *Hamlet* was written (1919),[6] no one had quite thought to administer an Imagist test to not merely a line or a scene, but an entire Elizabethan play.

Eliot might have run across the general formulation almost anywhere. Ford, for instance, explained the poems in Pound's *Cathay* (1915) to readers of his column in *The Outlook* by invoking what he called "a theory and practice of poetry that is already old—the theory that poetry consists in so rendering concrete objects that the emotions produced by the objects shall arise in the reader";[7] and Pound, always a great clipper of his own notices, gave Ford's review to Eliot, who dutifully quoted from it in his promotional pamphlet, *Ezra Pound: His Metric and Poetry* (1917). But the same argument appeared wherever

Imagist practices needed justification. Richard Aldington, a Pound protégé, in *The Egoist* (1914):

> We convey an emotion by presenting the object and circumstance of that emotion without comment.... [W]e make the scene convey the emotion.[8]

John Gould Fletcher, an ally of Amy Lowell, in *The Little Review* (1916):

> The Imagist . . . presents the sum-total of the emotions in any given subject in such a way that the reader experiences the self-same emotions.[9]

And by 1918, the formula had become enough of a fixture in the critical vocabulary of the avant-garde to be relied on to explain artistic activity generally. We find, for instance, Dora Marsden, one of *The Egoist*'s original editors, defining Rebecca West's literary method as "imagism in its widest sense," and her talent as

> the power to sense a complex situation, and to take such an accurate and assured grip of the situation's essential attitude that the mental image of some sense-form embodying the precise attitude would spring into the mind by a simple act of association.[10]

These explanations are floated on the notion that every object has an inherent emotional value, cashable in a work of art by presenting the object as it truly is—a notion whose authority the man who wrote "Experience and the Objects of Knowledge in the Philosophy of F. H. Bradley" would of course hardly have been disposed to respect, for it is empiricism's epistemological equation—the right mix of sensations produces the correct mental picture of the external object—read backward. We are likely to be skeptical as well, to feel that the effectiveness of "In a Station of the Metro" has as little to do with the actual faces Pound saw in the Paris subway as the effectiveness of *In Memoriam*

VII's "bald street" has to do with the real Wimpole Street where Arthur Hallam lived. But the formula is a match for the practice it was designed to justify; it is a minimalist theory of the imagination, the sentence that remains after what the twentieth-century theorists of the image regarded as the transcendentalist extravagances of Romantic theories of art has been edited out. "Nature" has been reduced to "objects," and the poet's mind figures as a kind of high-frequency receiver of stimuli.[11] Imagism is a theory that tries not to look theoretical (as an Imagist poem is a work of literature that tries not to look literary), and it poses the reductionist's challenge: if this is not acceptable as an explanation of the way art works, what sort of claims can be made for theories that explain art's effect on us by its success at tapping into some more elaborately defined chunk of experience—such as the natural world, whose mode of being art's form imitates; or the moral life, whose values its seriousness preserves; or the vision within, whose lineaments its style evokes? For once we have determined to point to something as the true source of legitimate aesthetic effects, we will end with a reproduction of the Imagist formula: we will have isolated an object and loaded it up with value.

If we want to make good on our skepticism by doing without this theoretical paradigm, however, we will find that we cannot quite say that art works in some entirely different way. We can only say that at a cultural moment when art is understood to get its effects from the objects (however defined) it represents (by whatever means), it will succeed only if it can give the impression of having done so. And Eliot's revision of the conventional prescription does not resist such a gloss:

> The only way of expressing emotion in the form of art is by finding an "objective correlative"; in other words, a set of objects, a situation, a chain of events which shall be the formula of that *particular* emotion; such that when the external facts, which must terminate in sensory experience, are given, the emotion is immediately evoked.[12]

Eliot has rewritten the Imagist scenario by having the original emotion appear unaccompanied by any object and then depicting the artist looking about for an object that will do the trick of expressing it. And the right object, in his version, is the object that works; a more metaphysical criterion is not supplied.

The word "only" is what gives Eliot's formula its prescriptive appearance, and it is a good instance of Eliot's critical manner. It announces a discovery where most writers would be content to state a preference ("The most efficient way of expressing emotion . . ."), and thereby places the entire formulation at the brink of tautology. Efforts to read Eliot's sentence as saying something more specific than "The emotion expressed by a work of art is the product of the elements of that work" do not even need to venture into the waters of experience to spring a leak. Eliot punctures his definition as soon as he provides an example: "Hamlet (the man)," he explains, "is dominated by an emotion which is inexpressible, because it is in *excess* of the facts as they appear."[13] Which leaves, of course, the question, If Hamlet can be said to feel such an emotion, how did Shakespeare manage to convey it?

Few critics, I suppose, have ever wished to defend Eliot's judgment of *Hamlet*, but many seem to have been convinced of the usefulness of Eliot's formula (the success of "Hamlet and His Problems" can be measured by the number of attempts to prove it in error by asserting that Shakespeare did in fact create an objective correlative in *Hamlet*). These critics might want to answer the charge of tautology by suggesting that Eliot (wrong though he may have been in this particular case) knows that Hamlet is possessed by some emotion only because Hamlet says he is, or acts as though he is, and that the theory of the objective correlative requires that the play should not *talk* about an emotion, but should *present* one. But Eliot states quite explicitly that this is not the problem: "We find Shakespeare's *Hamlet*," he says, "not in the action, not in any quotations that we might select, so much as in an unmistakable tone which is unmistakably not in the earlier play."[14] Well, it might be argued, this "unmistakable tone" indicates the point of Eliot's objection: the phrase "*particular* emotion" must mean an emotion we can give a description to, and though Shakespeare did, in Eliot's view, somehow succeed in whipping up an atmosphere of emotionality, the specific emotion Hamlet is meant to be in the grip of remains indefinite. To this one can only reply that Eliot claims to know exactly the emotion he understands Hamlet to be feeling: "The intense feeling, ecstatic or terrible, without an object or exceeding its object," he informs us, "is something which every person of sensibility has known; it is doubtless a subject of study for pathologists."[15] The unexpected conclusion appears to be that *Hamlet* expresses a particular emotion well enough—it is just not an emotion that is proper for art.

Coming from another critic, this judgment might seem merely pedantic: the distinction being asserted between what qualifies as a work of art and what does not has not been shown to make a difference to our understanding of the play. Eliot's reading of Hamlet as a man who cannot match up his emotions with the objects his world provides is after all a perfectly standard one; it is the reading that makes, for instance, the scene with the players, Hamlet's leap into Ophelia's grave, and Fortinbras's conquest of Poland aspects of a unified action. If Shakespeare contrived to make his play intelligible to this extent without the benefit of an objective correlative, we might conclude, so much the worse for the formula. But coming from the author of "Prufrock" and the "Preludes," the line of argument is curious to say the least—it seems a sort of self-castigation—and the theory of the objective correlative, from the perspective of those early poems, looks less like a truth about poetic language, or even a principle of decorum, than a complaint about the limitations of art disguised as a compliment. Art is a machine for reproducing with economy and precision emotions blurred and attenuated in experience, is the good news; emotions that cannot be made proportionate to the objects the world provides cannot be satisfactorily expressed in art, is the hidden grievance.

This is a view of art that many poets, in moments of frustration, have no doubt held, but it is not a view one would think any poet could be content to rest with. It implies that the poet's estimate of an object's emotional value must be the world's—that the significance a poem ascribes to the relations among its images is somehow answerable to the significance the world gives to the relations among the objects those images represent—and it makes the artifice poetry has customarily relied on to make its kind of discourse work seem illegitimate, a sort of cheating on behalf of the self against the way things really are. Nothing is more revealing of Eliot's flickering suspicion of poetry's claim to be a privileged way of knowing than his willingness to endow this attitude with the authority of a critical standard. And the theory of the objective correlative is nicely paradigmatic, too, of the way modernism sometimes seems to have been determined to transform poetry, in the name of a purer style, from a manner of speaking to a mode of symptomizing. Eliot had reservations, as we have seen, about the possibility of a purified, non-"literary" style, but he had deeper doubts about the writer's ability to exert control over his own meanings. And these doubts surface in the notion of impersonality.

Eliot offers, in the *Hamlet* essay and elsewhere, a single corollary to his utilitarian proposition about objects and emotions: solving the equation correctly, he suggests, relieves the artist of a psychic distress. Thus the essay makes an identification of Hamlet's feelings with Shakespeare's which would otherwise be insupportable—"Hamlet's bafflement at the absence of objective equivalent to his feelings is a prolongation of the bafflement of his creator in the face of his artistic problem"—and indulges in speculation about the emotional circumstances of Shakespeare's life which would otherwise be pointless— "we should like to know whether, and when, and after or at the same time as what personal experience, he read Montaigne, II. xii., *Apologie de Raimond Sebond*."[16] This notion of the nature of creativity had a consistent appeal for Eliot—it turns up often in his critical writings, particularly where he is describing his own experience as a poet[17]— and it has the proper Imagist look to it. The writer knows his solution is the right one in the same way that the reader knows the result is a work of art: he tests it on his nerves. But efforts to give Eliot's account of art-making a theoretical shape, and thus an interpretive usefulness, are compelled in the end to make some improvements on the suggestions he provides; for at the same time that he was hypothesizing in *The Athenaeum* about Shakespeare's feelings, Eliot was busy discrediting the traditional justification for such hypotheses in *The Egoist*.

Those hypotheses depend, "Tradition and the Individual Talent" advises, on "the metaphysical theory of the substantial unity of the soul"—the belief that personality is a thing definitive enough to sustain coherent expression. And it is, of course, precisely the point of this most famous of Eliot's arguments that to say that for something to happen aesthetically to the person who reads the poem something must first have happened emotionally to the person who wrote it (which is what Eliot does say) is not the same thing as to say that the successful work of art expresses the inner life of the artist who produced it. For there is, in Eliot's view, nothing that might properly be called an inner life to be expressed. If we could examine the artist's mental contents, we would find simply the usual unorganized assortment of experiential odds and ends, a warehouse of "numberless feelings, phrases, images," uninteresting in themselves and distinguished from the contents of nonartistic minds only by their being less easily effaced (this appears to be the essay's version of the Romantic *agon*) by the ordinary processes of forgetting. To read back, therefore, from the nicely particularized emotion of the finished work of art, firmly grounded in its aesthetic "object," to the untidy mass of sensation in the unstable construct of the artistic self is to undertake a journey with the wrong map; for

> Impressions and experiences which are important for the man may take no place in the poetry, and those which become important in the poetry may play quite a negligible part in the man, the personality.

The essay asks us, in short, to accept the proposition that the reader's experience of a genuine "art emotion" depends on the writer's execution of an authentic escape from some troublesome "'personal'"[18] emotion, and then to regard the connection as, for all practical purposes, a coincidence.

But it is not a coincidence, of course, or else why require the artist to suffer at all? It plainly does not matter to the notion of the objective correlative in its Aristotelian aspect—the audience derives pleasure from the perception of a fitness between situation and emotion—what the private tribulations were of the artist who managed that effect. The principle presents itself, in the manner of the Poetics, as a straightforward deduction from the evidence of art that works. It is the suggestion that for the effect to be what "Tradition and the Individual Talent" calls "significant"[19] there *must* have been a tribulation, itself properly managed, that gives the concept its nineteenth-century spin. The emotions of the audience are now tied up to the feelings of the artist. The problem with Eliot's formulation is the problem of how, on a view of the integrity of the subject that had grown increasingly skeptical from Pater to Vorticism to "Tradition and the Individual Talent," the presumption of such a connection can be shown to be necessary—can be shown, that is, to make an interpretive difference.

The difficulty consists in coming up with a description of the relation that is weak enough. For though we may find in the work of art figures of speech, or symbols, or images, it is too ambitious to say that these refer us to anything belonging to the artist, since personality is not to be considered, in Eliot's conception, as a container of things as stable and intelligible as thoughts, or unconscious archetypes, or even recollections of discrete moments of sensory experience—things private and discriminable which might, by the right representational trick, be expressed. We are confronted with a relation that is at every point contiguous but at no point correspondent: we have the work of art, considered in its totality as effective or not, and we have the artist, considered as an undifferentiated state of psychic affairs, in balance or out of it. To say that one refers to the other is no more true or false than to say that rosy cheeks refer to health. If they do, the relation has nothing to do with intention. The artist may or may not say what he means, but he cannot help meaning what he says.[20] The "doctrine of impersonality" is the nineteenth-century doctrine of sincerity at its most extreme stage of attenuation: being has become a physiological condition, and its sentiment a symptom.

Like the formula of the objective correlative, the notion of a necessary but obscure connection between the resolution of an unspecified inner crisis on the part of the artist and the enjoyment of a significant "art emotion" on the part of the audience can be found elsewhere in the period. Clive Bell, for instance, was a writer for whom Eliot seems to have had little respect—he once referred to him as "the *boutonnière* of post-1900 culture"[21]—but the argument of Bell's *Art* (1913) runs along the same lines as Eliot's essay of six years later. What all genuine works of art have in common, Bell proposed, is the ability to produce something called an "aesthetic emotion," and they have this ability because they possess "significant form": "In each, lines and colours combined in a particular way, certain forms and relations of forms, stir our aesthetic emotions."[22] These emotions belong to art alone. They are not copies of what we are evidently to think of as "life emotions": "to appreciate a work of art," Bell explained, "we need bring with us nothing from life, no knowledge of its ideas and affairs, no familiarity with its emotions."[23] This is a journey a good distance in the formalist direction, but Bell did not, it turns out, cut every cord, and one tie to the world remains; he calls it his "Metaphysical Hypothesis":

> That which orders the work of art is, I suggest, the emotion which empowers artists to create significant form.... To make the spectator feel, it seems that the creator must feel too.

Still, the self is a muddle, and having made this concession to experience (or borrowed this much from experience to buttress his theory), Bell posted the warning Eliot's essay would make famous: "Let no one imagine that the expression of emotion is the outward and visible sign of a work of art." The critic who heads back from the art to the artist is condemned to wander endlessly: "it is because they [works of art] express an emotion that the artist has felt," Bell concluded, "though I hesitate to make any pronouncement about the nature or object of that emotion."[24] Eliot, too, was not disposed to pronounce on that subject, but he was—as long as the matter was understood to remain ultimately a mystery—highly disposed to speculate, as in the case of the relation between Shakespeare's experiences and *Hamlet*'s failure. His theory was, in fact, the ideal license for such speculation: since nothing can ever really be explained by knowledge of the writer's "personal emotion"—since no coherent knowledge of a "personal emotion" is in fact possible—no damage can be done to the impersonal nature of the "art emotion" by indulging in some suggestive discussion.

We can find the same view of the relation between art and emotion, expressed in a manner even closer to that of "Tradition and the Individual Talent" than Bell's and a year before Eliot's essay, in Dora Marsden's article on Rebecca West:

> ... when one says that a writer is under the emotional necessity of expressing an experience, one can only mean that the experience has assumed a determining control enabling it to outbalance and command all that remains of the forces of the mind. The emotional part is driving the conscious whole. When, however, in submission to such driving force, the mind takes up its task with the adequate courage and strength, this overbalance in powers at once corrects itself. ... An overpowering subjective condition has been compelled in fact to shed its subjectivity and become an object: a true entity, capable of being expelled from the exclusiveness of the individual and made current as a universal possession. By making it so intimately personal it has indeed become impersonal. ... Whatever the condition be, by stating it justly the mind makes an escape from its absolute thrall.[25]

Or, in other words, "only those who have personality and emotions know what it means to want to escape from these things."[26]

We can see how far Eliot's thinking goes in the direction of skepticism about the value of literature as a form of knowledge by comparing his view of art as escape from emotion with one more antecedent—the view offered in Nordau's *Degeneration*:

> Artistic activity . . . satisfied the need of [the artist's] organism to transform its emotions into movement. He creates the work of art, not for its own sake, but to free his nervous system from a tension. The expression, which has become a commonplace, is psycho-physiologically accurate, viz., the artist writes, paints, sings, or dances the burden of some idea or feeling off his mind.[27]

It is one of the ironies of literary history that some twenty-five years after Nordau used this analysis of the artistic process as the basis for an attack on the forerunners of modernism, "Tradition and the Individual Talent" made the same notion of creativity part of an argument that seemed to many readers a defense of art's autonomy and value. And Nordau's evolutionary model of cultural change can be detected in the background of Eliot's theory of the dissociation of sensibility as well—a theory that depends on the hypothesis that literary history can be explained not by changes in literary form or in the things writers become interested in, but by changes in the way the brain works.

The argument for impersonality in "Tradition and the Individual Talent" makes an attractive proposition: in return for giving up the desire to express himself, the poet is offered the chance to express something far greater—the shape the tradition takes as it passes through his time. But the structure of this argument is familiar. For if we open up "Tradition and the Individual Talent" and replace "tradition" with "experience," the sequence of texts with the stream of sensations, we will find ourselves with something very like Pater's essay on "Style"; and we will discover at the center of both arguments a similar model of the mind, one that seems both reductive, because such passivity is ascribed to it, and extravagant, because it is required to generate such an exalted kind of truth. The mental eyeball Pater borrowed from the empiricists to explain how the input of random sense data is corrected against the fixed structure of the "inner vision" reappears in "Tradition and the Individual Talent" as the famous "shred of platinum,"[28] the catalyst that adjusts the experience of the contemporary world to the "ideal order" of tradition and guarantees that the result will be "impersonal."

Making the metaphor mechanical instead of organic is a modernist refinement, one we have noticed already in Pound's "vortex":

> The best artist is the man whose machinery can stand the highest voltage. The better the machinery, the more precise, the stronger, the more exact will be the record of the voltage and of the various currents which have passed through it.[29]

For a theorist interested in an "exact record," a machine (like a shred of platinum) makes a better analogy than an eyeball precisely because it is inhuman. It is not of the same stuff as the material it processes, and it can therefore be expected to distinguish reliably between the real and the merely mutable. The metaphor was also, of course, intended to shock; it is the language of the Futurists, whom the Vorticists publicly despised, but whose controversiality they emulated—*Blast* was patterned after a Futurist manifesto, Apollinaire's "L'Antitradition Futuriste" (1913)—and some of whose antihumanist postures they found it useful to adopt. Futurism seems to have had for Pound around the time of his *Blast* manifesto something of the same interest it was having for D. H. Lawrence, who used it to explain to Edward Garnett, in the well-known letter on *The Rainbow*, his new conception of character: "what is interesting in the laugh of the woman is the same as the binding of the molecules of steel or their action in heat: it is the inhuman will, call it physiology, or like Marinetti—physiology of matter, that fascinates me."[30]

The main "character" in a literary work on the Paterian model is the writer. The danger of the model—as Pound became convinced—was that the chief virtue of literature would be taken to be the expression of the writer's "personality," the assortment of moods, tastes, and opinions that go to make up the conscious self. Pater had taken care to distinguish this type of self-expression from the brand of sincerity he endorsed:

> The style, the manner, would be the man, not in his unreasoned and really uncharacteristic caprices, involuntary or affected, but in absolutely sincere apprehension of what is most real to him. . . .
> If the style be the man, in all the colour and intensity of a veritable apprehension, it will be in a real sense "impersonal."[31]

But there is little in Pater to help us identify the point at which the accident of personality ends and radical individuality begins: in the double vision of the "Conclusion" to *The Renaissance*, everything is either entirely outside or entirely inside. And since an avant-gardist will need such a distinction to underwrite his claim that the traits conventional opinion prizes as original with the individual are actually surface markings conforming to society's impress, Futurism's description of the mind as a piece of machinery gave some of the modernists a useful notion of how such a thing as the "impersonal" or "pre-personal" self might be conceived: the metaphor rediscovered a structure where all structure had been threatening to dissolve. Thus Lawrence contrived to dispense with the artifice of "the old stable *ego*—of character" in his novel by announcing a prior structure of real stability, the transindividual structure of generation, to which all character could be made relative; and thus the mind figures in Pound's theory of poetry as sheer pattern-producing energy, an autonomous entity whose highest function is to leave a sort of mental fingerprint on experience.

Readers have sometimes complained that much of what is presented as "impersonal" in modernist writing looks like nothing more than the moods, tastes, and opinions of the writer, deliberately fragmented, rearranged, and invested with a metapersonal significance—that what

Lawrence's novels take to be elemental in human life is a reflection of their author's special convictions about sexual relations, that the *Cantos'* picture of what is lasting in the history of culture is a mosaic of Pound's aesthetic and political enthusiasms, that *The Waste Land* offers as a report on a general spiritual condition a composition of bits of Eliot's favorite reading that surreptitiously refer to private anxieties about his marriage and career. One can respond to these complaints only by asking what else, given the requirements of a generally diffused aesthetic that condemned the expression of personal "views" but tied the value of a literary work to the intensity of the author's private experience, an "impersonal" work could have looked like.

In giving the self so little to express, in making the literary work the symptom of conditions, inner and outer, for which the writer's pen served only as a kind of unconscious conduit, Eliot gave his criticism a powerful vocabulary for revisionism, since what the writer *intended* to say could now be safely ignored in favor of what he could not *help* saying. The vocabulary might be called a rhetoric of hygiene: the metaphor is sometimes neurological, sometimes psychological, sometimes—as in the case of Henry James's mind—sexual; and the pieces collected in *The Sacred Wood* are filled with critical judgments that turn on this vocabulary's key terms. Thus, Coleridge's "feelings are impure," while Aristotle "had [no] impure desires to satisfy";[32] comparing the *Education sentimentale* to *Vanity Fair* shows us "that the labour of the intellect consisted largely in a purification, in keeping out a great deal that Thackeray allowed to remain in"[33] (the judgment derives, of course, from Pater's praise of Flaubert in "Style"; but most of the essays in *The Sacred Wood*—even "The Perfect Critic," which tries to rescue Arnold from Paterianism—are Paterian[34]); Elizabethan rhetoric "pervaded the whole organism; the healthy as well as the morbid tissues were built up on it";[35] Swinburne's "intelligence is not defective, it is impure";[36] and in Massinger we find an unrefined nervous system and the record of "the decay of the senses."[37]

The vocabulary is a nice example of what a sociologist of knowledge might call a negative ideology—an ideology that avoids declaring itself by adopting a rhetoric whose notions of good and bad seem unarguable. Who would be "impure"? Only someone already admitting to being perverse. Part of the appeal of "pure" and "impure" as terms of judgment perhaps had something to do with their professionalist associations: the professional worker is defined by his ability to keep his researches from adulteration by the corrupting forces of the ideological marketplace. But the rhetoric was appealing for a more practical reason as well. It seemed to encode a set of judgments on a whole range of nonliterary matters, and to do so using a framework of values that appeared to be ideologically neutral. For by describing not only the writer's physiological condition but the condition of his time—the condition of the time *through* the physiological condition— Eliot's vocabulary made an extraordinarily effective tool for putting cultural history into whatever order the critic wished or was able to claim for it. The essay on Massinger in *The Sacred Wood* provided some hints in this direction by setting a comparison of Jacobean dramatists according to the development of their nervous systems next to remarks about the devolution of the Puritan moral system. But the project was most strikingly carried out in the essays on seventeenth-century poetry Eliot wrote just after the publication of *The Sacred Wood*.

The three essays eventually published by the Hogarth Press in 1924 as *Homage to John Dryden* were originally written for the *Times Literary Supplement*, where they appeared in 1921. They are the tours de force of Eliot's early criticism, for later readers found in them a revaluation of seventeenth-century poetry, a principled indictment of the poetry and criticism of the nineteenth century, and the outline of a genealogy justifying modernism. The most influential of the essays was the one on "The Metaphysical Poets," and its argument has been made familiar by many retellings: the dramatists of the sixteenth and the poets of the seventeenth centuries "possessed a mechanism of sensibility which could devour any kind of experience"; but at some point in the seventeenth century, "a dissociation of sensibility set in, from which we have never recovered." When, in the eighteenth century, poets "revolted against the ratiocinative," "they thought and felt by fits, unbalanced; they reflected"; and the degeneration culminated in the work of Tennyson and Robert Browning, who "ruminated." But the type of mind for which "a thought . . . was an experience" reemerged in the nineteenth century in the poetry of Baudelaire, Corbière, Laforgue — poets who had "the same essential quality of transmuting ideas into sensations" that Donne had—with the implication that this line is continued in the Anglo-American modernist mode.[38]

We know now, thanks to J. E. Duncan's *The Revival of Metaphysical Poetry* (1959) and Frank Kermode's *Romantic Image* (1957), that Eliot managed, by the remarkable influence of the essays in *Homage to John Dryden*, to receive credit for formulations and critical judgments that were common enough in his own time and that had their roots in the literary values of the century his arguments seemed directed against.[39] And it is not difficult to find further evidence for the thesis that the version of literary history those essays propose would not have struck most of Eliot's contemporaries as particularly iconoclastic. The notion, for instance, hinted at in "The Metaphysical Poets" and elaborated upon elsewhere in Eliot's criticism, that Milton was somehow either the cause or the emblem of a deterioration in the ability of English verse to render complex feeling can be found in an essay by Middleton Murry:

> English blank verse has never recovered from Milton's drastic surgery; he abruptly snapped the true tradition, so that no one, not even Keats, much less Shelley or Swinburne or Browning, has ever been able to pick up the threads again. . . . Read any part of "Paradise Lost" [after reading Shakespeare] . . . and you will discover how much subtlety in the instrument has been lost; in other words, how much capacity to express the finer shades of emotion has been sacrificed.[40]

And the extent to which not only the interest in seventeenth-century poetry, and not only the terms Eliot used to praise that poetry, but even the particular literary genealogy Eliot proposed were things circulating in the contemporary air, is suggested by this passage from a 1919 review by the young Aldous Huxley:

> An author must be *passionné* by his subject, must feel, if he is writing of science or philosophy, that the truths with which he is dealing are in intimate relation with himself. On the rare occasions when this happens, the versified exposition of science or philosophy becomes poetry. It seems to have happened with that strange and almost great poet, Fulke Greville. To him, one feels, the problems of philosophy and statecraft, which occupied his mind, were of vital interest; these abstract intellectual ideas touched him as nearly as love or hatred. . . . Donne, in the same way, felt passionately about abstract ideas; in Blake, too, thought has the quality of emotion. Oddly enough, when we come to the nineteenth century, a period which was conscious and very proud of its scientific achievements, we find no poets who took a sufficiently passionate interest in the new scientific truths to get them into poetry. Tennyson wrote a good deal about science; but his tone is frigid, he was never worked up by it to lyrical fervour. . . .
>
> Perhaps the only poet of the nineteenth century who thoroughly assimilated the science and philosophy of his time, so that it became a part of himself, a condition of all his emotions, an accompaniment in every thought and passion, was Laforgue. Plenty of young men of the generation that was coming to maturity in the early eighties must have read Hartmann's philosophy of the Unconscious. But there can have been few to whom the ideas of Hartmann were such a reality that they were troubled, even in the midst of an embrace, by thoughts of the Unconscious; and there was but one, so far as we know, who gave adequate lyrical utterance to his philosophy-ridden emotions.[41]

The overt argument of Eliot's essay on "The Metaphysical Poets" is an argument about technique; the seventeenth-century conceit is revealed to be the cousin of the nineteenth-century symbol. But the concerns that led Eliot to write the essay were almost certainly not technical. Eliot himself, on the occasion of its republication in 1924, suggested dissatisfaction with his own indirectness. His argument, he explained, properly involved "considerations of politics, education, and theology," matters "which I no longer care to approach in this way."[42] But any other way, by requiring him to enter specific judgments on the issues at hand, would have been less effective. Eliot's theory of the dissociation of sensibility had an extraordinary run precisely because its implications were largely uncontrolled. Eliot himself might use it later to support an argument about religious history involving the English Civil War; but the theory takes on very different permutations when the blame for the dissociation is pinned—as later critics did pin it—on Bacon, on Descartes, or on the rise of capitalism.[43]

The ideological burden is carried in the original essay not by Eliot's own commentary but by the quotations—which is to say, under cover of darkness, since most readers, presented with a passage said to hold some technical interest, will, if the claim strikes them as plausible, skip over the passage. But when we string together three of the strategically crucial quotations, we find a principle of selection in operation that is not merely technical. Eliot cites a passage from Chapman's *The Revenge of Bussy d'Ambois* (1610):

> in this one thing, all the discipline
> Of manners and of manhood is contained;
> A man to join himself with th'Universe
> In his main sway, and make in all things fit
> One with that All, and go on, round as it;
> Not plucking from the whole his wretched part,
> And into straits, or into nought revert,
> Wishing the complete Universe might be
> Subject to such a rag of it as he;
> But to consider great Necessity.

This is contrasted with "some modern passage"[44]—from Browning's "Bishop Blougram's Apology" (1855):

> No, when the fight begins within himself,
> A man's worth is something. God stoops o'er his head,
> Satan looks up between his feet—both tug—
> He's left, himself, i' the middle; the soul wakes
> And grows. Prolong that battle through his life!

And the last quotation in the essay is given to show the persistence of the metaphysical sensibility in the French tradition (it is from Baudelaire's "Le Voyage" [1861]):

> Pour l'enfant, amoureux de cartes et d'estampes,
> L'univers est égal à son vaste appétit.
> Ah, que le monde est grand à la clarté des lampes!
> Aux yeux du souvenir que le monde est petit!

The significance of the comparisons is clearly more than stylistic. In fact, the stylistic analysis—the analysis of the poetry "as poetry"—that would show how the operation of Chapman's brain is unlike the operation of Browning's but like the operation of Baudelaire's, is entirely missing. But if the passages are read for what they say, rather than how they say it, the point is clear enough. The first passage expresses an anti-individualistic ideal that might fairly be called (though in the language of a secular philosophy) Dantesque—"In His Will is our peace"; the second, from the speech of Browning's worldly bishop, describes a Manichean struggle in which the universe is not "round," like the universe in Chapman's lines, but polar, the setting for the individual soul's discovery of its own will and a place where peace is not the desired end; and the third passage expresses a nostalgia for the worldview of the first. It is the irony of the essay that to have placed these passages in the foreground of the argument, and to have explicated them instead of gesturing toward them vaguely as symptoms of their authors' neurological fitness, would have signaled the abandonment of the literary ideology on which Eliot's historical theory was predicated. For it would have meant that what was significant about these writers was not how their brains worked, but what they actually and consciously thought.

Many of Eliot's remarks about the nature of poetry and the shape of the literary tradition were treated by his admirers as discoveries; since the passing of the New Criticism and the school of Leavis, it has been common to think of those "discoveries" as having been more in the nature of inventions. But the distinction is in the end not a particularly useful one, for one of the things literary history seems to teach us about Eliot's early criticism is that he invented his arguments out of what he discovered, in the thought of his own time, to be already there. And to discover what literature is to one's contemporaries is to discover, to the extent that the phrase can make any practical sense, what literature is. It is also to discover something about the sources and the scope of critical power.

This begins to answer what is perhaps the really interesting question, which is how so reductive a group of critical formulations—formulations belonging to a line of aesthetic theorizing which seemed already fatally attenuated and whose philosophical foundations Eliot himself had demonstrated to be factitious—came to be so persuasive. We might enhance the hypothesis about the "already there" nature of Eliot's critical terms with the suggestion that their effectiveness was in fact inseparable from their reductiveness. For the higher the degree of particularity a theory of art has, the more it exposes itself to critique—and there is really no arguing, when all is said and done, with the notion of the objective correlative. It is part of the peculiar design of Eliot's early criticism that the received language of aesthetic theory is used to make arguments whose theoretical content is practically zero—as much as to say, I offer these explanations for my aesthetic preferences, but I am not (though others may be) ready to claim anything of greater significance for them.

Eliot's was a prototypically twentieth-century kind of irony, the irony that "sees through everything." "[T]here is no method," as he put it in a famous and disarming phrase, "except to be very intelligent."[45] In his early writings, this is a posture that, whatever interests it was calculated to conceal, gave his criticism a wonderful forcefulness. In the later criticism, especially in the sociological writings, Eliot's irony takes on something of the quality of an external agent: he cannot seem to get out of the way of his own arguments, he is so eager to qualify them. In *Notes Towards the Definition of Culture* (1948), for instance, efforts to make a thesis about culture issue in some prescriptive advice struggle against—and are, arguably, defeated by—frequent reminders that, properly conceived, culture is an entity so holistic that it cannot really be prescribed for, or even coherently thought about, at all. But there is a continuity between the early and later Eliots, a connection that has to do with the power Eliot habitually granted to the received idea, and it is a continuity postmodernists might do well to contemplate. We are often eager these days to acknowledge that culture is something we can never get outside, but we tend to forget that by the same token it is also something we can never get entirely inside. Our understanding always seems to miss the mark, so that we perpetually make a different thing of what is there regardless of our intentions. If we assume that we can only say what the culture permits us to say—the assumption the attitude of "seeing through everything" compels—we avoid the risk of ascribing to our understanding an objective force it cannot have; but if we ignore the fact that something about the nature of understanding always does place us in a new position relative to what was there, we run the greater risk of becoming the willing victims of our own enlightenment.

From *Discovering Modernism: T. S. Eliot and His Context* (New York: Oxford University Press, 1987): 133-151. Copyright © 1987 by Oxford University Press. Reprinted by permission of Oxford University Press, Inc.

Notes

1. See F. N. Lees, "The Dissociation of Sensibility: Arthur Hallam and T. S. Eliot," *Notes and Queries*, n.s. 14 (1967), 308-9; and Carol T. Christ, "T. S. Eliot and the Victorians," *Modern Philology*, 79 (1981), 159-60.

2. "Preface to the 1928 Edition," *The Sacred Wood: Essays on Poetry and Criticism*, 2d ed. (London: Methuen, 1928), p. viii. This is the edition cited below.

3. "The most remarkable property of [Keats's] poetry . . . is the degree in which it combines the sensuous with the ideal. . . . His body seemed to think; and, on the other hand, he sometimes appears hardly to have known whether he possessed aught but body. His whole nature partook of a sensational character in this respect, namely, that every thought and sentiment came upon him with the suddenness, and appealed to him with the reality of a sensation." [Aubrey Thomas de Vere], *Edinburgh Review*, 90 (July-October 1849), 425-26.

4. "[Donne] belonged to an age when men were not afraid to mate their intellects with their emotions." Rupert Brooke, "John Donne, the Elizabethan," *The Nation*, 12 (15 February 1913), 825. See also Brooke's "John Donne," *Poetry and Drama*, 1 (June 1913), 185-88: "The pageant of the outer world of matter and the mid-region of the passions came to Donne through the brain. The whole composition of the man was made up of brain, soul, and heart in a different proportion from the ordinary prescription. This does not mean that he felt less keenly than others; but when passion shook him, and his being ached for utterance, to relieve the stress, expression came through the intellect" (p. 186).

5. See David J. DeLaura, "Pater and Eliot: The Origin of the Objective Correlative," *Modern Language Quarterly*, 26 (1965), 426-31; R. W. Stallman, ed., *The Critic's Notebook* (Minneapolis: University of Minnesota Press, 1950), p. 116; Pasquale DiPasquale, Jr., "Coleridge's Framework of Objectivity and Eliot's Objective Correlative," *Journal of Aesthetics and Art History*, 26 (1968), 489-500; and René Wellek, *A History of Modern Criticism: 1750-1950*, I (New Haven: Yale University Press, 1955), 253-54.

6. Pound took Eliot in 1916 to see Yeats's *At the Hawk's Well*, the first of the Noh-influenced plays. On the Noh plays and Imagism, see Eliot's "The Noh and the Image," *The Egoist*, 4 (August 1917), 102-3; on the possible influence of the Poundian aesthetic on this aspect of Yeats's work, see Francis J. Thompson, "Ezra in Dublin," *University of Toronto Quarterly*, 21 (1951), 64-77.

7. Ford Madox Hueffer, "From China to Peru," *The Outlook*, 35 (19 June 1915), 800.

8. Richard Aldington, "Modern Poetry and the Imagists," *The Egoist*, I (1 June 1914), 202.

9. John Gould Fletcher, "Three Imagist Poets," *Little Review*, 3 (May 1916), 30.

10. D[ora] M[arsden], "The Work of Miss Rebecca West," *The Egoist*, 5 (October 1918), 115.

11. The immediate problem, as Pound and Hulme seem to have understood it, was that of distinguishing the Image from the late-nineteenth-century Symbol. We can see the kind of explicit transcendentalism the Imagist formula tries to avoid in, for exam-

ple, Yeats's essay on "The Symbolism of Poetry" (1900): "All sounds, all colours, all forms, either because of their preordained energies or because of long association, evoke indefinable and yet precise emotions, or, as I prefer to think, call down among us certain disembodied powers, whose footsteps over our hearts we call emotions" (*Essays and Introductions* [New York: Macmillan, 1961], pp. 156-57). See Ezra Pound, "Status Rerum," *Poetry*, 1 (1913), 123-27, for Pound's effort to dissociate his poetic from Yeats's. Frank Kermode weighs the significance of the distinction between the modernist image and the Romantic symbol, and finds it minimal, in his chapter on Hulme in *Romantic Image* (London: Routledge and Kegan Paul, 1957), pp. 119-37. See also Graham Hough, *Image and Experience: Reflections on a Literary Revolution* (Lincoln: University of Nebraska Press, 1960), where Imagism is defined as "roughly Symbolism without the magic" (p. 9); and Ian Fletcher, "Some Anticipations of Imagism," in *A Catalogue of Imagist Poets* (New York: J. Howard Woolman, 1966), pp. 39-53, which offers a similar definition (Poundian Imagism is "Symbolism with its 'magical' components discounted" [p.43]). This conclusion has been disputed: see Donald Davie, *Ezra Pound: Poet as Sculptor* (New York: Oxford University Press, 1964), pp. 65-67; and Herbert N. Schneidau, *Ezra Pound: The Image and the Real* (Baton Rouge: Louisiana State University Press, 1969). For an account of the metamorphosis of the "soft," "subjective" symbol or impression into the "hard," "objective" Vorticist image, see Michael H. Levenson, *A Genealogy of Modernism: A Study of English Literary Doctrine 1908-1922* (Cambridge: Cambridge University Press, 1984), pp. 103-36.

12. "Hamlet and His Problems," in *The Sacred Wood*, p. 100. The essay appeared originally in *The Athenaeum*, 26 September 1919, pp. 940-41; it is reprinted as "Hamlet" in *Selected Essays*, new ed. (New York: Harcourt, Brace and World, 1950), pp. 121-26. There are slight variations among the three versions.

13. *The Sacred Wood*, p. 101.

14. *The Sacred Wood*, p. 100. *Selected Essays* has "Shakespeare's Hamlet" (p. 124).

15. *Selected Essays*, p. 126. *The Sacred Wood* (p. 102) and the Athenaeum version (p. 941) have "a study to pathologists."

16. *The Sacred Wood*, pp. 101, 102. Eliot's essay on *Hamlet* appeared in September 1919; it is worth noting, in connection with the essay's speculation about the emotional circumstances of Shakespeare's life, that Eliot had already read, in manuscript form, Stephen Dedalus's virtuosic biographical criticism of *Hamlet* in the "Scylla and Charybdis" chapter of *Ulysses*—remarking in a letter to John Quinn, dated 9 July 1919, "I have lived on it ever since I read it." See Robert Adams Day, "Joyce's Waste Land and Eliot's Unknown God," *Wisconsin Literary Monographs*, ed. Eric Rothstein, 4 (Madison, Milwaukee, and London: University of Wisconsin Press, 1971), 180.

17. For instance, in his now well-known remark about *The Waste Land*: "Various critics . . . have considered it, indeed, as an important bit of social criticism. To me it was only the relief of a personal and wholly insignificant grouse against life" (quoted in *The Waste Land: A Facsimile and Transcript of the Original Drafts*, ed. Valerie Eliot [New York: Harcourt Brace Jovanovich, 1971], p. 1); and in his comment, two years before his death, to Herbert Read that his best poetry had cost him dearly in experience (see Peter Ackroyd, *T. S. Eliot: A Life* [New York: Simon and Schuster, 1984], p. 334).

18. "Tradition and the Individual Talent," in *The Sacred Wood*, pp. 55, 56, 57, 58.

19. *The Sacred Wood*, p. 59.

20. The issue of the relation between the poet's experience and the emotional value of the poem was, of course, always a complicated one. The nineteenth-century writer did not consider "sincerity" a purely representational value. When Tennyson insisted that *In Memoriam* was "not an actual biography" (Hallam Tennyson, *Alfred Lord Tennyson: A Memoir* [New York: Macmillan, 1897], 1, 304), he did not mean to say that it was not sincere. Robert Langbaum discusses the problem of the poetic persona and the requirement of sincerity in *The Poetry of Experience: The Dramatic Monologue in Modern Literary Tradition* ([New York: Random House, 1957], esp. pp. 28-35), where he suggests that "*Insincerity* together with its offshoot in Yeats' *mask*, in fact the whole literary attempt since the late nineteenth century to escape from personality, have created a literature in which sincerity and autobiography are encoded, written backwards" (p. 35). What is remarkable about Eliot's critical prescriptions on the matter is that while he continues to tie the aesthetically distinctive character of a given poem to the "real" self of the poet, he has given that self almost nothing to express.

21. "Shorter Notices," *The Egoist*, 5 (June-July 1918), 87. Unsigned.

22. Clive Bell, *Art* (London: Chatto and Windus, 1913), pp. 7-8.

23. Bell, p. 25. Compare Eliot's "The Perfect Critic": "a literary critic should have no emotions except those immediately provoked by a work of art—and these (as I have already hinted) are, when valid, perhaps not to be called emotions at all" (*The Sacred Wood*, pp. 12-13); and "Tradition and the Individual Talent": "The effect of a work of art upon the person who enjoys it is an experience different in kind from any experience not of art" (*The Sacred Wood*, p. 54).

24. Bell, pp. 60-61, 61-62, 59.

25. Marsden, p. 118.

26. *The Sacred Wood*, p. 58.

27. Max Nordau, *Degeneration*, trans. from the 2d German ed. (1895; rpt. New York: Howard Fertig, 1968), p. 324.

28. "When the two gases previously mentioned [oxygen and sulphur dioxide] are mixed in the presence of a filament of platinum, they form sulphurous acid. This combination takes place only if the platinum is present; nevertheless the newly formed acid contains no trace of platinum, and the platinum itself is apparently unaffected; has remained inert, neutral, and unchanged. The mind of the poet is the shred of platinum" (*The Sacred Wood*, p. 54).

29. Ezra Pound, "Affirmations: As for Imagisme," in *Selected Prose 1909-1965*, ed. William Cookson (New York: New Directions, 1973), p. 376. First published in *The New Age*, 16 (January 1915), 349-50.

30. D. H. Lawrence to Edward Garnett, 5 June 1914, in *The Letters of D. H. Lawrence*, eds. George Zytaruk and James T. Boulton, II (Cambridge: Cambridge University Press, 1981), 183.

31. Walter Pater, "Style," in *Appreciations* (London: Macmillan, 1904), pp. 36-37. Compare Matthew Arnold's preface to *Poems* (1853): the poet "needs . . . to be perpetually reminded to prefer his action to everything else; so to treat this, as to permit its inherent excellences to develop themselves, without interruption from the intrusion of his personal peculiarities; most fortunate, when he most entirely succeeds in effacing

himself, and in enabling a noble action to subsist as it did in nature" ("Preface to First Edition of Poems [1853]," in *Irish Essays and Others* [London: Smith, Elder, 1882], pp. 292-93). Eliot's notion of impersonality seems—somewhat surprisingly, given the self-consciously "classical" character of Arnold's preface—closer to Pater's than to Arnold's.

32. "The Perfect Critic," pp. 13, 11.

33. "The Possibility of a Poetic Drama," p. 65.

34. The relations between the author of *The Sacred Wood* and Matthew Arnold on the one hand and Walter Pater on the other are hopelessly tangled. Most discussions of the lines of filiation between Arnold and Eliot as critics concentrate on Eliot's later writings (see, for instance, John Henry Raleigh, *Matthew Arnold and American Culture* [Berkeley and Los Angeles: University of California Press, 1961], pp. 193-219; Ian Gregor, "Eliot and Matthew Arnold," in *Eliot in Perspective: A Symposium*, ed. Graham Martin [New York: Humanities Press, 1970], pp. 267-78; and Roger Kojecy, *T. S. Eliot's Social Criticism* [London: Faber and Faber, 1971], esp. pp. 19-34); I discuss Arnold's presence in *The Sacred Wood* in "The Nineteenth Century in Modernist Criticism," Diss. Columbia University 1980, pp. 73-116.

Echoes of Pater in *The Sacred Wood* are a little more difficult to account for, given that book's general attack on the "impressionistic criticism" of the Paterian school. But they are there; compare, for instance, this statement in Eliot's essay on George Wyndham: "What is permanent and good in Romanticism is curiosity . . . a curiosity which recognizes that any life, if accurately and profoundly penetrated, is interesting and always strange" ("A Romantic Aristocrat," p. 31), with Pater's definition in the postscript to *Appreciations*: "It is the addition of strangeness to beauty, that constitutes the romantic character in art; and the desire of beauty being a fixed element in every artistic organization, it is the addition of curiosity to this desire of beauty, that constitutes the romantic temper" (p. 246). Compare also this passage in the essay on Massinger (only a few sentences after English criticism has been denounced for its unscientific character):

> Reading Shakespeare and several of his contemporaries is pleasure enough, perhaps all the pleasure possible, for most. But if we wish to consummate and refine this pleasure by understanding it, to distil the last drop of it, to press and press the essence of each author, to apply exact measurement to our own sensations, then we must compare; and we cannot compare without parcelling the threads of authorship and influence.

("Philip Massinger," p. 124), with Pater's advice in the preface to *The Renaissance*:

> the function of the aesthetic critic is to distinguish, to analyse, and separate from its adjuncts, the virtue by which a picture, a landscape, a fair personality in life or in a book, produces this special impression of beauty or pleasure, to indicate what the source of that impression is, and under what conditions it is experienced. His end is reached when he has disengaged that virtue, and noted it, as chemist notes some natural element, for himself and others.

(*The Renaissance: Studies in Art and Poetry*, ed. Donald L. Hill [Berkeley and Los Angeles: University of California Press, 1980], pp. xx-xxi). It is hard to see how Eliot's prescription for "The Perfect Critic," with its motto from Gourmont, "Eriger en lois ses impressions personnelles, c'est le grand effort d'un homme s'il est sincère," is in the end different from Pater's—in spite of the effort of that essay to make a meaningful distinction in favor of Arnold's "knowing the object as it really is" against Pater's "knowing one's impression as it really is."

But this sort of inconsistency is only another instance of Eliot's general practice of appropriating whatever is available to suit his own uses, which is why Arnold and Pater often reappear as disguised authorities in his essays a few paragraphs after their influence has been deplored.

35. "A Romantic Aristocrat," p. 30.
36. "A Note on the American Critic," p. 39.
37. "Philip Massinger," p. 129.
38. "The Metaphysical Poets," in *Selected Essays*, pp. 247-49.
39. See Joseph E. Duncan, *The Revival of Metaphysical Poetry: The History of a Style, 1800 to the Present* (Minneapolis: University of Minnesota Press, 1959), pp. 118-29; and Frank Kermode, *Romantic Image* (London: Routledge and Kegan Paul, 1957), esp. pp. 138-61. On the Romantic antecedents of Eliot's nominally anti-Romantic critical formulations, see Edward Lobb, *T. S. Eliot and the Romantic Critical Tradition* (London, Boston, and Henley: Routledge and Kegan Paul, 1981), esp. pp. 60-92.

Parts of Eliot's discussion of the metaphysical poets are in fact rather sharply reminiscent of the preface to *Lyrical Ballads*: "A good deal resides in the richness of association," he remarks of some lines by Lord Herbert of Cherbury, ". . . but the meaning is clear, and the language simple and elegant. It is to be observed that the language of these poets is as a rule simple and pure. . . . The *structure* of the sentences, on the other hand, is sometimes far from simple, but this is not a vice; it is a fidelity to thought and feeling. The effect, at its best, is far less artificial than that of an ode by Gray" ("The Metaphysical Poets," in *Selected Essays*, pp. 244-45). Eliot must have had Arnold's essay on Gray (1880), with its attack on the prosaic quality of the poetry of Pope and Dryden, on his mind here, and not Wordsworth's strictures. It might also be remembered that Eliot's definition of Marvellian wit is made to depend on Coleridge's description of the imagination in chapter fourteen of the *Biographia Literaria* (see "Andrew Marvell," in *Selected Essays*, pp. 256-57). But the relation between "The Metaphysical Poets" and English Romanticism, as Kermode has demonstrated, is much more than a matter of common critical phrases.

40. J. Middleton Murry, "Milton or Shakespeare?" *The Nation and the Athenaeum*, 28 (26 March 1921), 916-17. "The Metaphysical Poets" appeared in October 1921. Eliot's comprehensive attack on Milton came in the 1936 essay ("A Note on the Verse of John Milton," in *Essays and Studies by Members of the English Association*, 21 [Oxford: Clarendon Press, 1936], pp. 32-40), which repeats Murry's argument (though it does not mention Murry) about the deleterious effects of Miltonic blank verse. It is typical of Eliot's relations with Murry that when he performed his famous recantation in the *second* Milton essay (1947; first published in *On Poetry and Poets* [1957]), the

critic he attacked for having too severe a view of Milton's influence was Middleton Murry.

41. A. L. Huxley, "Poetry and Science," *The Athenaeum*, 22 August 1919, p. 783. Standing behind Huxley's view of Laforgue (as it certainly stands behind Eliot's) is Rémy de Gourmont's essay of 1904: "His [Laforgue's] intelligence was very lively, but closely linked to his sensibility. All original intelligences are so composed—they are the expansion, the flowering, of a physiology. But in the process of living, one acquires the faculty of dissociating intelligence from sensibility" ("The Sensibility of Jules Laforgue," in *Selected Writings*, trans. and ed. Glenn S. Burne [Ann Arbor: University of Michigan Press, 1966], p. 199). The connection between literary style and physiological condition was a preoccupation of Gourmont's ("Style is a physiological product, and one of the most constant," he asserts in *Le Problème du style* [1902] [*Selected Writings*, p. 112]). On what Eliot's terminology owed to Gourmont, and how Eliot put that terminology to uses of his own, see F. W. Bateson, "Dissociation of Sensibility," *Essays in Criticism*, 1 (1951), 302-12.

42. Preface to *Homage to John Dryden* (London: Hogarth Press, 1924), p. 9.

43. See Eliot's "Milton II," in *On Poetry and Poets* (New York: Farrar, Straus and Cudahy, 1957), p. 173; L. C. Knights, "Bacon and the Seventeenth-Century Dissociation of Sensibility," *Scrutiny*, 11 (Summer 1943), 268-85; Basil Willey, *The Seventeenth Century Background* (New York: Columbia University Press, 1958), pp. 86-92; and Jürgen Kramer, "T. S. Eliot's Concept of Tradition: A Revaluation," *New German Critique*, 6 (1975), 20-30.

44. *Selected Essays*, p. 246.

45. "The Perfect Critic," in *The Sacred Wood*, p. 11.

Playing at Relationship

John T. Mayer

John T. Mayer attempts to capture the texture of emotional exchanges (actual and potential) or lack of exchange evoked by Eliot's early published and unpublished poems. He interprets "Portrait of a Lady" and "Prufrock" as psychic dramas involving role-playing by reading them against two backgrounds: briefly against several of Eliot's unpublished poems and at greater length in relation to Henry James's short story, "Crapy Cornelia," the rhetoric of late Elizabethan drama (specifically *Othello*), and Henri Bergson's writings about the divided self. For Mayer, Eliot's early poems present a drama of the self that is tempted to engage with others but resists doing so by using roles in defensive ways. He identifies speakers in Eliot's early poems with Narcissus, the mythological figure who became fascinated with himself to the point of self-destruction. Mayer's reading attempts to coordinate the writing with the poet's life by suggesting that particular moments in the poetry represent stages in the writer's personal experience, rather than presenting the kind of poetic mask that Robert Browning used in his dramatic monologues to distinguish his speakers from himself. This kind of turn to the life of the writer in the interpreting of poetry is something that Eliot himself objected to. In order to support his speculative interpretation of the life and of the published works, Mayer expands the interpretive frame to include unpublished poems that Eliot chose not to print. Among the unpublished works, Mayer stresses the importance of Ariadne in "Bacchus and Ariadne" because she presents a self who, having engaged with others (as in her involvement with Theseus, who abandons her in the Greek myth), seems open to transformation. "Portrait of a Lady" is, by contrast, a more realistic presentation of the possibility or impossibility of engagement, with the male figure playing the role of silent sophisticate, a role that Mayer aligns with Eliot. Mayer finds a source and parallel for the poem's self-observation in the rhetoric of *Othello* and other Elizabethan plays, which enables Eliot to produce poems that are not strictly observations, as some of his early poems are, because the language carries a psychological charge. In "Portrait," the form suggests dialogue but presents instead the impossibility of it because of the male speaker's self-defensive attitudes. In Mayer's view, "Prufrock" is a kind of sequel because it reveals role-playing's limits when these attitudes result in a missed life. The Bergsonian conflict of ordinary and deeper self in the poem yields an impasse for the deeper self, which is silenced when Prufrock emerges as Eliot's first hollow man. Not only will the mermaids not sing to him, he cannot sing to them. Mayer identifies Prufrock's dilemma as Eliot's own, but there is a major difference. Eliot did sing, to us, by writing the poems that, rather than refusing expression, actually do dare to speak.   — J.P.R.

"Suite Clownesque" (probably 1910)
"Entretien dans un parc" (February 1911)
"Bacchus and Ariadne: The Second Debate between
the Body and Soul" (February 1911)
"Portrait of a Lady" (1910-1911)
"The Love Song of J. Alfred Prufrock" (1910-1911)

Eliot's finest poems of the early period, "Portrait of a Lady" and "The Love Song of J. Alfred Prufrock," are usually read as social satires, but they gather new force when read as psychic dramas about relationship, self-definition, and role-playing. Although parts of both were written before Eliot sailed for Paris in October 1910, they remained unfinished until the fall of 1911, perhaps because of the experience detailed in the City poems. Once again, the unpublished poems provide an invaluable context against which to set the psychic dramas portrayed in "Portrait" and "Prufrock." The issue they address is that defined in "Bacchus and Ariadne: Second Debate between the Body and Soul," the possibility of breaking out of the chrysalis of self-enclosure into a new life. In "Portrait," game-playing keeps the buried life of both players buried; in "Prufrock," the deep self tries to break through the mask and into life through vocation and relationship. Both poems end in psychic death: in "Portrait," the death of the other ("and besides, the wench is dead") is on behalf of the self; in "Prufrock," the deep self is buried on behalf of the mask.

This quest for life through relationship is shadowed by Narcissus, for Eliot conceives of the self as so fundamental a reality that maintaining its integrity is the law of its being. The Narcissus self finds within consciousness its own sufficiency; otherness threatens this sufficiency, so that relationship is fraught with psychic perils, and even its possibility is problematic. The poems that develop the quest toward otherness implicitly focus on psychic loss, and its possibilities arrange themselves in increasing intensities from superficial concerns about the loss of self-composure (social poise projects inward control) or of privacy (revelation to others risks possession by others), to a fear of the loss of self-possession (the mask protects the core of selfhood or perhaps a hidden self), to outright terror of emasculation or of psychic annihilation.

The need to guard the self against such perils explains why role-playing is so important to Eliot. Role-playing guards the inner life by deflecting relationships from the self to one or several masks. Such psychic play, by multiplying roles, raises a subtler threat of self-annihilation through the dissipation of the self among its roles. This possibility seems to have intensified after Eliot's marriage; he made the condition the basis of "Mélange Adultère de Tout" (1916), and it may have contributed to the breakdown that released *The Waste Land*. In 1910, however, as the unpublished monologue "Suite Clownesque" shows, Eliot thought role-playing a promising strategy of anti-self-consciousness on behalf of limited social contact. The suite format, its ideal of charming, aloof sophistication, its Laforguian comedian with the prominent nose (who recalls the mandarin functionary in "Mandarins 3"), and its master-of-ceremonies tone (as in "Goldfish 2"), connect it with Eliot's other suites from the summer of 1910. In the "Notebook,"

"Suite Clownesque" appears between the first part of "Portrait of a Lady" (which follows "Goldfish") and the complete version of "Prufrock," confirming its connections to them as well: the poem shows how "mandarin" attitudes can be usefully internalized to control one's transactions with others. The mode of internalization is role-playing, the psychic attitude that links "Suite Clownesque," "Portrait," and "Prufrock."

The suite proposes a pose of self-assurance as a way of meeting the world, all that is not-self. This exposition of psychic theatercraft is arranged as a series of turns on stage, perhaps at the vaudeville, perhaps wholly in the mind; its opening "set" of painted colonnades, terra-cotta fawns, and potted palms emphasizes the presence of artifice in life. The first turn introduces the comedian, a *master* of *ceremonies* (we recall Eliot's high regard for mastery and for ceremonial in "Mandarins"), who dominates his audience simply through attitude. Like the hero-mandarin whose physical address gestures psychic power, the comedian (who, we are told, may really be a jellyfish) appears completely in control simply through voice and a set of gestures. The potential of such image-manipulation is clarified by contrasting him with the skill-less group of underage schoolgirls out for a day on the town in the next turn. They arrange themselves carefully in order to support one another; no one is an individual strong enough to stand alone. The comedian is their foil: he gains identity and inner strength from his specific role, whereas they form an impersonal clique without direction, and can only wonder what to do next. By sheer performing skills, he turns a costume and an impertinent stance into power.

In a final turn, the observer imagines himself a blasé sophisticate who appropriates the comedian's self-assurance and parades up Broadway trailed by the girls. Brandishing a cocktail shaker in a hearse, he sings a song of male swagger in syncopated patter.[1] Here is Eliot's dream-self among the women, stylishly in control and quite self-possessed; in the end, he turns into a dapper stroller at the beach, where he looks the girls over, an anticipation of Prufrock. In this ultimate fantasy of success through role-playing, Eliot is in command of himself and the others, at one with the world and the Absolute. He cuts a graceful figure with all eyes on him; for once, the eyes of the others admire rather than torture. This fantasy is too extravagant, and the illusion quickly dies, as the presence of the hearse intimates, in a final call to be serious. Still, Eliot had enough of the performer in him to fancy success in more congenial roles, and in "Portrait" and "Prufrock" he continued to explore the potential of role-playing to manage image and to control others. The poem reminds us how keenly Eliot enjoyed role-playing and how urgently he yearned for the success it promised.

His need for success can be appreciated if we recognize both the intense embarrassment and sense of failure that extreme self-consciousness such as Eliot's causes, and the enormity of the challenge that a relationship poses to the self-enclosed individual. In the unpublished "Entretien dans un parc," written in Paris in 1911, the very thought of beginning one precipitates a psychic crisis. Composed after the earliest fragments of "Portrait" and "Prufrock," but before their completion, it sheds significant light on their psychic plots. Against the romantic backdrop of a spring walk with a companion in the park, a young man struggles to make some kind of decisive move to resolve things between them. His agitated state suggests that a marriage proposal or a break-up is being considered, but this relationship has not even begun. The poem's subtitle, "Situation," carries the sense of "predicament," just as "entretien" suggests not so much a "conversation" (the companion never speaks) as the idea of maintenance and upkeep, but here it is a case of self-maintenance, of keeping the self "maintained." The subtext of the poem is the agony of the Narcissus psyche, for whom the slightest move toward the other constitutes a form of self-betrayal.[2]

Although the "situation" is now a memory, it quickly comes back to life in being recalled, suggesting that some memories are not so much pasts as presences, a precedent for *The Waste Land*. As the couple strolls under the April trees, psyche and landscape interpenetrate: he sees his own uncertainty in the trees. These uncertain April trees are a "psychic image" that interprets consciousness by projecting the interior landscape; they point directly to the insidious streets, ambiguous fog, and etherized patient in "Prufrock." He projects his struggle onto his companion as well, but it is wholly his own, for she is a model of placidity amid his distress. He considers making a romantic gesture, and suddenly seizes her hand. He can act only impulsively, for any gesture toward the other is a break from the self that acknowledges need for the other, and undermines the sufficiency of the self as world. What seems to be at stake is not simply the self's independence, but its fullness of reality. Such an act, for him "the awful daring of a moment's surrender," illuminates the psychic dramas Eliot will play out in "Portrait" and "Prufrock"; it also helps make clear why Eliot's sudden decision several years later to marry a woman he barely knew had to be impulsive: it held the same psychic import.

His gesture releases in him not passion but embarrassment; he senses that he is incompetent in some fundamental way. Having reached out to another, he expects the world to change, and when it does not (recalling the Harvard lyric "When we came home across the hill") and his companion merely smiles at his act of daring, he is disturbed that she is not disturbed. What really distresses him is the possibility of making their two separate selves into a *we*: for when he thinks of this we, he thinks not of a she and an I but of she and myself, language that underscores his obsession with "self." For him, the relationship involves not two persons, but an other and his self, a psychic construct so significant to him that it prevents his "I," the person, from meeting the other as person. He is now consumed by a fear of ridicule, which is really a fear of being literally belittled, diminished. To the Narcissus consciousness, any diminution is a loss of self, the primal reality. For him, the "situation" is psychically threatening, an entrapment: he sees himself in a dead-end street filled with childish graffiti, an epiphany gained through the cityscape. In the city facts before it, consciousness sees itself as it really is, childishly immature and at a psychic impasse.

The poem's final section assumes a pattern that Eliot will repeat in later poems, a speculative "what might have been" segment cut short by the recognition of its pointlessness. The protagonist wonders what would happen if they could escape themselves—that is, escape from their selves. To escape self-awareness is the one thing he cannot do. His situation is that pointedly defined by D. H. Lawrence in *Women in Love*, wherein self-consciousness, the inability to act spontaneously, is the enemy of self-realization: it makes people "grow up crippled, crippled in their souls, crippled in their feelings—so thrown back, so turned back on themselves—incapable . . . of any spontaneous action, always deliberate, always burdened with choice, never carried away."[3] The Narcissus self cannot be "carried away."

"Entretien" marks Eliot's first recognition of the agonies of this self, not the least of which is the need to explain itself. It must explain because it cannot be spontaneous; its explanations are not to the other but to the self, the real object of attention. They often end, as with Prufrock and Gerontion, in resignation and a desire to escape the burden of awareness. This protagonist sets the mode, longing to escape self-consciousness by regressing to the preconscious level of the instinctive burrower, the ant or mole, or by leaping up to God. Since such a leap would reveal his soul, this option is quickly dismissed: for the Narcissus psyche, all self-revelation is immobilizing. Although Eliot considered three formulations of the final line expressing the revelation of aridity, they all emphasize a movement out of closure, an unendurable gesture.

"Entretien" may or may not report a personal experience of Eliot's, but it seems to convey the truth of his psychic life. Better than any of the published poems, it clarifies the meaning of "self-possession" to him: more than self-confidence, it is a sense of command over one's world. Since the Narcissus psyche identifies the self as world, to be self-possessed is to keep the psyche, the soul-world, in possession. The need to do so obsesses the young man in "Portrait of a Lady" and provides that poem's psychic subtext, thus balancing the satiric portrait of the Beacon Hill "*precieuse ridicule*," which in the received version is the poem's point, with a psychic portrait of Eliot himself. If we accept that relationship meant anguish to him, we may read "Prufrock" more sympathetically than as Pound's "study in futility," and we may see young Eliot's own great dare of marriage in a new light, as necessarily impulsive, heroic, and doomed.

The challenge that relationship posed in "Entretien" elicited an immediate response in one of Eliot's most important unpublished monologues, "Bacchus and Ariadne." Indeed, in view of the magnitude of the challenge posed in the former, it is surprising that Eliot, in the very same month, should posit the optimistic reading of the body-soul dualism which he develops in this "Second Debate between the Body and Soul." The poem marks Eliot's first use of myth since "Circe's Palace"; the myth not only sets the debate in the framework of relationship and marriage, but also articulates its mode of reconciliation. The ground for hope eventually proved illusory in Eliot's poetry and during most of his life. Ariadne exerted a special force on Eliot in later poems as a symbol of the deserted woman; here she figures as an emblem of spiritualization for which the desertion is the catalyst. Having given Theseus her love, the thread to escape the labyrinth, and, thus, the means of defining his identity (and eventually, through his mistaken sails, of making him king), Ariadne is rewarded with abandonment on Naxos. In her grief, she attracts the attention of the god Bacchus, who weds her; when she dies, he places her jeweled crown in the heavens to shine forever as a star. Desertion by the ungrateful earthly lover brings Ariadne, through suffering, a godly love. She transcends the physical world by entering fully into it first through love, and then through suffering, and gains an immortal lover who gives her, through metamorphosis, the gift of immortality. As a mythic figure who is first betrayed by love and then saved through suffering, Ariadne is a precedent for the woman in the third Prelude (composed five months later, in July 1911), whose suffering establishes her distinction from the streetwalker in "Rhapsody" (March 1911), who symbolizes the dominance of instinctive passion unless suffering transforms the world of matter.[4]

The relationship of body and soul, of matter and spirit, and the potential for transcendence are shadowed in the poem under the figures of Bacchus and Ariadne, whose lives are said to build up like a wave, unifying them in the tension of their differences, mortal and immortal.[5] But the wave breaks, and they are separated (by Ariadne's death), so that they have not finally broken through the differences between their natures. To the thinker, their marriage suggests the possibility—something that might have happened—of overcoming the unknown tendencies that their differences imply by yielding to something more fundamental than difference, to the flow of life itself that sways within them. The implications of the wave image, with its complex suggestions of an underlying sustaining continuum, a fluctuating surface movement, a building tensional unification, and a breaking that leads to re-formation, are not fully worked out in this unfinished draft, but Eliot seems to have in mind something like Bergson's élan vital as the underlying life force that reveals itself in momentary cresting waves of aspiration and then disappears beneath the surface to build again.

A ring of silence now inhibits these hints of a unity of opposites that the wave image flashes to the thinker almost like signals across a desert, glimpses of a spiritualized force that fuses matter and spirit. In its place comes a different message, the awareness of a world of contact, which focuses those elements of the myth that build relationship not on subtle communication but on the marriage of bodies. Since bodies are physically circumscribed, contact on this level brings a limited kind of communication (such as Ariadne first knew with Theseus) and subjection to time's inevitable erosion of bodies and of whatever the merely physical communicates. The wave and contact images point to losses that time and experience exert on the world of consciousness (anticipating Eliot's later and more concrete formulation of this interaction in "A Cooking Egg").

Still, such considerations produce a flash of hope when the thinker sees that in a world composed of matter and energy, with bodies infused with immaterial force and entelechy, the movement is inevitably outward and upward, symbolized by the butterfly, Psyche, the Soul, breaking out of its chrysalis into freedom and flight. This conceit of biological metamorphosis, of evolution from lower to higher through a physical change of forms, is the poem's final image through which to reconcile the differences of matter and spirit, body and soul, physicality and transcendence. The act of the butterfly bursting from its cell into flight is a compelling expression of the marriage of body and soul; it shows the thinker what the earlier wave image only intimates, and it shows this forthrightly: in its cell, the butterfly passes a necessary stage of development, secure in the confinement that protects the growth of its purest possibility nourished by earth and manure until it bursts forth in full realization. The metamorphosis conceit, rooted in myth, science, and life itself, makes time a source of growth rather than of destruction, and produces in the butterfly a compelling image of the free spirit developed out of matter.

The poem ends with the thinker affirming, triply affirming, that this is the way things are. Repeated assertions of certainty, even when phrased, as these are, as expressions of increasing universality—it is not only like this, it *is* this—inevitably undercut the very certainty that is affirmed, leaving us uncertain whether the thrice-repeated formulas reflect increasing certitude, mere assertiveness, or outright skepticism. Still, what begins in hope may create the very belief that is asserted: the poem's closing ritualistic affirmations may metamorphose hope into acceptance, and acceptance into benediction. One hope that this poem may have represented to Eliot, that of resolving the main issue of the philosophical quest—the relation of body and soul, matter and spirit—through literary means, that is, through myth and image rather than through abstract arguments, may have encouraged him at this halfway point in his Paris year to consider the role of poet as a more effective means of serving the quest for meaning than the role of philosopher. The other hope it embodies, that through relationship and marriage he might solve his overwhelming questions, proved as momentary as the poise of a wave about to break.

"Portrait of a Lady" is Eliot's first major effort to measure realistically the possibilities of relationship for the Narcissus psyche. For one whose self-consciousness strictly restrained the floods of life within him, role-playing offered the hope of limited contact with the other without endangering the security of the self. In 1915, five years after Eliot had ended the relationship on which the poem is based, he admitted to Ezra Pound that while the poem seemed "cruder and awkwarder and more juvenile" every time he copied it, the only "enhancement which time has brought" is that by 1915 "there are two or three other ladies" who could "vie for the honour of having sat for it" (*Letters* 86). Eliot played the silent sophisticate repeatedly in relationships, and "Portrait" forecasts that opposite women he played the role at greater psychic cost to them than to himself. That such results should be seen as an "enhancement" may be sexist rhetoric for Pound's benefit, but at the same time it suggests the self's satisfaction in maintaining itself, in escaping the clutches of the other. Playing the sophisticate is central to "Portrait of a Lady" and "Prufrock," but its importance in these poems has attracted little comment. Yet it is role-playing that accounts for the remarkable combination of influences behind these works—Laforgue, the late Elizabethan drama, and Henry James, which came together in Eliot's mind because of their shared exhibition of the role-playing mentality. The mentality is central to the Jamesian world in which highly self-conscious and refined individuals subtly shift postures in an ever-changing dance of Awareness. In Eliot's poems, the "action" consists almost wholly of Jamesian movements of consciousness; Eliot's lady and man are less polished versions of Osmond and Madame Merle:

> In the manner and tone of these two persons . . . was something indirect and circumspect, as if they had approached each other obliquely and addressed each other by implication. The effect of each appeared to be to intensify to

an appreciable degree the self-consciousness of the other. Madame Merle of course carried off any embarrassment better than her friend; but even Madame Merle had not on this occasion the form she would have liked to have—the perfect self-possession she would have wished to wear for her host. . . . They stood there knowing each other well and each on the whole willing to accept the satisfaction of knowing as a compensation for the inconvenience—whatever it might be—of being known.[6]

Eliot's characters attempt to fashion Jamesian encounters, to approach obliquely, and address by implication. If Eliot's lady fails more often than Madame Merle to wear the mask of perfect self-possession, his young man is never farther from being a young Osmond than when he brashly assumes that he can maintain his composure. Masking and role-playing inform their encounters, although they never come to "know each other well."

The Jamesian ambiance reflects Eliot's temperament, and particular personal and literary experiences. Aiken tells us that the lady's model, Madeleine Moffat, is nothing less than a Jamesian variant of Circe, Eliot's recurrent figure for the destructive woman: "the oh so precious, the oh so exquisite, Madeleine, the Jamesian lady of ladies, the enchantress of the Beacon Hill drawing room . . . like another Circe, had made strange shapes of wild Michael and the Tsetse," shapes reflected in the poem's parrot, dancing bear, and chattering ape—embarrassing, even humiliating transformations.[7] But the poem owes as much to Eliot's reading as it does to Miss Moffat's drawing room; for Eliot, after all, found literature at least as intense as life. James's short story "Crapy Cornelia," which appeared in *Harper's* in October 1909, extensively influenced both poems;[8] it is worth reviewing. Although its plot points to "Prufrock" (a middle-aged bachelor fails to "put the question" to a young widow because she lacks "understanding"), Eliot's debt is mainly to the tale's psychic subtext, a portrayal of inhibiting self-consciousness and self-watching.

The protagonist White-Mason, first seen trying to decide whether to visit the ironically named Mrs. Worthington, embodies Prufrock's fastidiousness (he is repulsed by her parvenu dazzle and by the "riot of the raw" in her surroundings) and painful inhibition (on past visits, he has failed to put the question because of the presence of "others"). Intensely self-conscious, he scrutinizes every act as an advance or a defeat and, like the young man in "Portrait," calculates effects to prove himself in control. Eliot, who explored stage-managing in "Nocturne," "Goldfish," and "Suite Clownesque," would have responded to White-Mason's sense of Mrs. Worthington, "shining" beside a small dark stranger, as a stage-manager: "By a refinement of her perhaps always too visible study of effect" the "dingy little presence" had been provided as a "positive contrast or foil. . . . She might just have planted her mangy lion—not to say her muzzled housedog." White-Mason's theatrical sense turns the room into a set, people and furnishings into props, the whole encounter into a game—a transformation worthy of Laforgue that Eliot exploits in "Suite Clownesque" and in "Portrait." It is significant that the first poems to show Eliot's own sense of such "social" theater, "Conversation Galante," "Humouresque," and "Nocturne," date from November 1909, the month after "Crapy Cornelia" appeared in *Harper's*. Of course, the actors in Eliot's "Portrait" are themselves inveterate stage-managers.

The James story offers a paradigm of the psychic plot of Eliot's poem, encounter as game. It is Mrs. Worthington's social gamesmanship that first attracts White-Mason: "She was 'up' to everything, aware of everything . . . surprised at nothing." Eliot's characters have the same appeal for each other, the self-assurance and snobbery of the "aware" orchestrating exchanges between themselves. As in James, whether their encounters shall remain game or yield relationship is the source of conflict. When White-Mason discovers that the small dark prop beside Mrs. Worthington is his old friend Cornelia, his sole link to the cultivated past, he reconsiders his projected proposal to the brassy Mrs. Worthington. He hesitates, Prufrock-like, with indecision that expresses itself as a self-regarding from outside itself: "It was as if he had sat and watched himself.... Shall I now or shan't I? Will I now or won't I?" Instead of asking his question, he withdraws, rationalizing that the younger woman could not or would not understand his treasured past.

Unlike Prufrock, however, White-Mason is not left alone. In another visit—to Cornelia, who does understand—he proposes an entente cordiale of the spirit:

> By the end of half an hour she had lent herself, all gallantry, to their game.... It was to this tune they proceeded, the least little bit as if they knowingly pretended—he giving her the example and setting the pace of it, and she, poor dear, after a first inevitable shyness . . . falling into step and going whatever length he would.

White-Mason and Cornelia agree to a life of artful conversation: "I can live with you . . . just this way. . . . I'm old. . . . she doesn't know . . . know anything . . . know anything we know."[9] Life that was game becomes dance, a dance of awareness. It is shared and, for them, satisfying. None of Eliot's sensitives gains so much. The story made its way into Eliot's sensibility. White-Mason's theatricality calls up Laforgue's, but it is James who deepens the casual theatricality Eliot practices in his earliest poems into Prufrock's fateful self-contemplation: "It was as if he had sat and watched himself." And it is this self-watching that links Laforgue through James to the most neglected source of Eliot's early form, the late Elizabethan drama.

What interests Eliot in this drama is what he calls "rhetoric," and what is remarkable here is Eliot's unconventional understanding of the term. Rhetoric is not simply a matter of charged language but of a certain type of it, where the "charge" displays a cast of mind. In "'Rhetoric' and Poetic Drama," Eliot singled out only the "rhetoric" of certain speeches, the kind, incidentally, that he found useful for his own verse. In all the passages that he cites, the self watches itself:

The really fine rhetoric of Shakespeare occurs in situations where a character in the play *sees himself* in a dramatic light:

Othello: And say, besides,—that in Aleppo once . . .
Coriolanus: If you have writ your annals true, 'tis there,
              That like an eagle in a dovecote, I
              Fluttered your Volscians in Corioli.
                                            (*SE* 27)

In these speeches, heightened language marks a movement away from communication with another character to intense self-contemplation, as does Timon's rhetoric or that of Sylla's ghost in *Catiline* and of Envy in *The Poetaster*, Eliot's other examples. Such "rhetoric" exhibits the mind's self-regarding, and Eliot uses the same kind of rhetoric in "Portrait" and "Prufrock" for the same purpose. Prufrock constantly sees himself in a dramatic light:

> No! I am not Prince Hamlet, nor was meant to be;
> Am an attendant lord, . . .
>
> . . . though I have wept and fasted, wept and prayed,
> Though I have seen my head [grown slightly bald] brought in
>   upon a platter,
> I am no prophet . . .

as does the young man in "Portrait":

> And I must borrow every changing shape
> to find expression . . . dance, dance
> Like a dancing bear . . .

In such passages, the self is an object—watched, commented on, and even subjected to parenthetical Laforguian diminution.

The rhetoric of Othello's last speech is particularly relevant to "Prufrock" for its model of a state of mind. Indeed, for Prufrock "to be or not to be" the person he wants to be, he has to imitate Othello, not Hamlet. In the passage Eliot cites, Othello cannot accommodate his crime against the innocent Desdemona to his own self-image, so he casts aside the self that wronged her ("Where is this rash and most unfortunate man?" "That's he that was Othello. Here I am") to embrace his former heroic self, which he then characterizes in the striking images that are the "rhetoric" of self-watching:

> . . . one that loved not wisely but too well;
> . . .
> one whose subdued eyes
> Albeit unused to the melting mood,
> Drop tears as fast as the Arabian trees
> Their medicinal gum. . . .

Under Iago's sway, Othello has forgotten how to be Othello, and must recall his traits one by one. He caps his catalogue by describing an extravagant gesture psychically necessary to confirm his recovery of his old self.

> . . . in Aleppo once,
> Where a malignant and a turbaned Turk
> Beat a Venetian and traduced the state,
> I took by the throat the circumcised dog,
> And smote him, thus.

He reenacts the deed by killing his malignant self, Iago's creation, by acting "in character."

In Othello, self-dramatization is so extreme that it leads to physical death, on behalf of psychic wholeness. To recover his heroic self (the self before Iago), which Othello treats as a discarded role, and to assure himself and his Venetian audience, the caretakers of his reputation, that he has not forgotten how to play it, Othello describes the defining act of this self—killing the enemy—and enacts the heroic deed. The idea of performing a special act before a special audience in order to define the self is clearly one scheme Eliot applied to Prufrock, and early on, for Eliot identified the Prince Hamlet passage, which recalls the Othello model of role-description, as one of the poem's earliest passages.[10] Prufrock contemplates other roles—John the Baptist, Lazarus—but, unlike Othello, he fails to dare; this confirms him in the Polonius role he resigns himself to play.

Eliot's use of such "rhetoric" alters the shape of language in the psychic monologue. "Portrait" and "Prufrock" mark a change, from the compressed transcripts of Laforguian mind-play, or short city observations (*Prufrock and Other Observations*), with their mix of observation and instantaneous notation in a kind of stream-of-consciousness flow, to longer utterances whose "rhetoric" of self-objectification projects the role-play and self-regarding exhibited in these poems. It is such psychically charged utterance and not the notational style that shapes the monologues that establish Eliot's reputation.

He first developed this style in "Portrait," in which it is a complex and supple instrument for projecting the convoluted self-consciousness of the young man, Eliot's clearest exemplar of the Narcissus psyche. The unusual format, whereby the lady speaks and he comments silently, indicates the one-sidedness of the relationship, with the man in control and the woman his frustrated victim. Eliot repeated this format in the one-sided "conversation" of "A Game of Chess" to carry the same themes. The device of a voice echoing in consciousness was used in "Humouresque"; in "Portrait," the pseudo-dialogue, whereby the young man narrates the stages of the affair as if to another, interiorizes the action from the man's point of view. The situation is complicated, but so too is his game, which is not the usual social one.

Although the lady suggests Laforgue's Eternal Feminine, who knows the art of every school and never acts except through poses, her efforts are frustrated because this youth is modeled not so much on Laforgue's Pierrot as on Eliot himself—self-absorbed, and fearing relationship as self-violation. His game is a kind of discipline, to learn how to conduct himself in social situations yet remain "self-possessed," uncommitted. On the model of "Suite Clownesque," he masks insecurity behind a front of bravado. The epigraph from *The Jew of Malta*, whose significance has not been understood, reveals his game plan. Like Barrabas, he wants to use role-play to control others:

> We Jews can fawn like spaniels when we please
> And when we grin, we bite; yet are our looks
> As innocent and harmless as a lamb's.

The point of the passage Eliot selected for the epigraph is that it shows Barrabas playing a role, and gaining power and survival through it. He answers the friars out for his gold in the rhetoric of the hardened sinner, the role that their accusations invite him to play:

> —Thou hast committed—
> —Fornication; but that was in another country,
> And besides, the wench is dead.

The epigraph is gambit and response; it trades in deception, exploitation, and violation; it sets the pattern for the exchanges between the lady and the youth as, among other things, a play of respective rhetorics and predicts the outcome of such a relationship.

The man's posing complicates the game in ways that hardly have been recognized.[11] These begin at the very outset when, having begun to set the scene himself, he seems to transfer it to an unnamed "you" so that it can "arrange itself":

> Among the smoke and fog of a December afternoon
> You have the scene arrange itself—as it will seem to do—
> With "I have saved this afternoon for you";

Although this "you" is consistent with Eliot's use throughout the early poetry of the second person in the sense of "one" as a device to escape responsibility, here it is also part of the rhetoric of the sophisticate, whereby the young man mentally addresses himself to a kind of knowing auditor who will recognize his cleverness, approve his gambits, and solve his uncertainties (Are his ideas right or wrong? Should he have the right to smile?). When he suggests that the scene *seems* to arrange itself ("as it will *seem* to do"), he does not mean that the arrangement is illusory, but that it is automatic through the lady's too predictable use of romantic clichés. Although the ambiguity works to let him evade responsibility, it is also an appeal to applaud his sophistication in piercing the lady's "arrangement" of the scene (recalling Mrs. Worthington's), with its four wax candles and darkened room that is her opening gambit, which he wittily deflates as "an atmosphere of Juliet's tomb." He uses the same ploy to open Part II when he points to the predictable bowl of lilacs as a prop. We are set for a multileveled complicated game indeed.

One aspect of this complication is the woman's entrapment by the narrow roles assigned to women in a male-dominated world and her dependence on the man for release. Her situation is similar to that of most women of the day and, indeed, to that of Eliot's mother, whose intellectual energies were channeled first into teaching children and then into domestic routines and child-rearing. The lady is the victim of social and cultural arrangements from which she can hope to be released only by the creation of counterarrangements that appeal to the male. Such arrangements here include the creation of an environment inviting romance, which for this male is a cage of entrapment. The poem insistently points up the contrast between the outdoor public world of male domination—with its "events," "monuments" to male heroes and "public" figures, and "public clocks" that call men to their worldly responsibilities and measure their half-hours of relaxation—and the indoor domestic world of the woman—a single room that is identified by both parties with the life of feelings and, tellingly, with death. The woman's room represents hope to her, the possibility of resurrecting her buried life of feeling; for the man, it is a tomb that threatens to suffocate his self. Indeed, as Lois Cuddy suggests, the whole arrangement of their world and its carefully delineated roles seems mythically rehearsed in the relation of Odysseus and Penelope, whom Joyce would shortly use as the central myth through which to illuminate the arrangement of the modern world. In Homer's world, as in the modern instance, the male leaves home to pursue his own destiny and enters the world dependent on him by journeying over water, whereas the woman spends herself in empty waiting.[12]

Throughout, "rhetoric" indicates the role-playing of each of the characters. At the onset of each encounter, the man plays the sophisticate: "We have been, let us say, to hear the latest Pole / Transmit the Preludes through his hair and fingertips." The role-play shows in the knowing "let us say" and, more obviously, in the pun on "Pole" to "Transmit" the electrical metaphor; assured sophisticates need not demonstrate wit so strenuously. The same is true of the density of musical imagery that follows, more "rhetoric" through which he recognizes the lady as performer, as virtuoso. Although a musical vehicle is a "natural" after a concert, he extends it excessively; these "attenuated tones," "windings," and "ariettes" are the rhetoric of an assumed voice. So too are the repetitious diction and rhythms of her voice, which, although they suggest the snares of a Circe, also have the effect of projecting her real weariness in seeking release from her loneliness, which for her is both pose and actuality.[13]

Against his pose the woman plays a "prelude" to involvement, a genuine relationship of feeling: proposing Chopin as "intimate," she develops her theme through a melodramatic diction (the soul's "bloom" is touched, rubbed, questioned) that is correlative to the intensity of her frustration and of her dependence on him, but this intensity discomforts him through the very forthrightness of its appeal to his feelings. Threatened, he hears a primitive tom-tom warning that wells up from his deepest self and hammers "a prelude of its own" that urges escape.[14] He heeds its call and flees her room-tomb, symbol both of the emotional entrapment she represents and of his burial site should he lose his "self-possession" to a relationship. Outdoors, he regains composure in the "public" city in which he is comfortable in the role of the casual man-about-town ("Let us take the air") who dulls awareness in a "tobacco trance" and escapes female emotional demands through the routines of male camaraderie ("drink our bocks"). The "us" who take the air is the self in its multiple roles, whose contradictions can now be ignored for "half an hour."

Like James's White-Mason, the youth appreciates the lady as a performer, not a person. When she proposes to make the game personal, he reacts instinctively, a cornered male. The primal tom-tom music that she evokes makes it clear that personal involvement represents an elemental threat, to self-survival. If his primitive "prelude" mocks her mannered contriving of effects, its "capricious" nature points up his lack of control over events. The pattern is set for the rest of the relationship: any suggestion of intimacy shatters his poise; his unvarying response is instinctive—fright and flight. He rationalizes his gaucherie but remains ignorant of his fears and of her feelings. His successive returns let her fall prey to the hope he represents, and repeat the pattern of frustration until he tires of it all, when it is too late to end things with grace and without hurt. The form of the monologue, by suggesting dialogue but portraying self-enclosure, effectively dramatizes the young man's self-absorption and the impossibility of dialogue to the Narcissus psyche.

The series of encounters are, in effect, a debate between vulnerability and self-sufficiency, as Eliot explores the potential of rhetoric and manners to bring people together, only to confirm their isolation. With encounters in December, April, and October, the dead seasons dominate and frame the affair. Its wintry beginning forebodes its outcome and mirrors his frozen emotions. April renews nature but not people in Eliot's world; although her buried life cannot be resurrected, it is this spring meeting that brings her most daring emotional overtures and the revelation of his own emotional arrest. In the fall, a final visit devastates his composure and leaves her a posturing mannikin at the tea table. The relationship describes an arc of frozen emotion because his main interest throughout is to play at relationship and learn how to preserve his "self-possession." He never intends to listen to her appeals, so her real feelings cannot break through her rhetoric to be heard. Throughout, it is the woman who attempts to communicate, but the man who turns aside her effort every time by remaining a silent voice.

In December, she appealed for a kind of spiritual intimacy, but it still threatened him. When he returns in April, he is unprepared for the emotional urgency that spring releases in her. As she slowly twists the phallic "lilac stalks," he is alerted; and when her "buried life" erupts, the scene moves by means of polite accusation into epiphany. She tells him that he is ignorant of the life that he "hold[s]" (willfully possesses) in his hands, and when she intimates greater intimacy, her voice is "a broken violin" out of tune with his intentions. Although her rhetoric of flattery is transparent,

> I am always sure that you understand
> My feelings, always sure that you feel,
> Sure that across the gulf you reach your hand.

these obvious untruths (the repetition of "sure") ironically convey his real "Achilles heel," his inability to "reach" out. He recognizes that she has hit on some profound truth about himself that he cannot face, or he would not panic and flee in order to "remain self-possessed." Like Eliot, who is often painfully honest before feelings that he does not comprehend, the man vaguely recognizes that his own Narcissism puts her in an impossible position: "what *can* you receive from me?" (my emphasis). He knows the answer is "Nothing." The "sympathy" she offers is appropriate, being extended to the unconsciously bereaved social self that survives his dead and buried self of feeling. He is honest enough to admit that he is in some way responsible to her, recognizing that "amends" (reparations for injury) are called for, but that he is helpless to make them, for he would have to amend—that is, alter—or remove the faults of his life, and this would make him "cowardly" to his Narcissus self, the self that he must defend at all cost, including the cost to others.

Outdoors, he again plays the man-about-town, as though nothing has happened. He prefers the comics and the sports pages, in which life is cartoon-simple and scores indicate exactly where players stand. He also "remarks" news items that comment on his "situation"—the countess who goes on stage mocks his inhibition by daring to be different; the dance-hall murder, an antisocial act in a social setting, reflects his own antisocial disposition in the social world; a bank defaulter confesses—but the young man admits only self-satisfaction: "I keep my countenance / I remain self-possessed." Earlier, music expressed his disquiet in the face of emotion. Now the tired street piano (which Eliot in "First Caprice" associates with children's voices and the pain of life in the slums) combines with the powerful odor of hyacinths (in the early Harvard lyrics, flowers are love tokens or emblems of passion) to upset his composure by recalling "things that other people have desired." This lyrical moment is the voice of his own buried life, which now cuts across the assumed voice of the man-about-town to acknowledge his awareness of the life of feeling, which in others may cause daring behavior, murder, and even confessions. To this point in the poem, flowers have been associated with intimacy, emotional involvement, and sexual threat, all of which he resists. However, the combined assault of the hyacinths and the "common song" makes him wonder for the first time whether he too may desire things that he dare not confess to himself.

His perplexity is only momentary, and by October, he is "as before." In the final encounter, the relationship ends in a display of the woman's emotional extremity and his own incompetence and inhumanity. He sees a chance to escape because he is going abroad. He mounts stairs, Eliot's well-known image of internal struggle, expecting a polite farewell, but is abashed by the forthrightness of her last appeals. When she thrusts at his inexperience, and raises the one question to be "left unsaid," why they have not "developed," he feels like a person who smiles, and suddenly sees his "expression in a glass." In this arresting mirror image, we see his Narcissus self unmasked, but he is too self-absorbed to profit from a surprising angle of vision on himself. Startled rather than illuminated, he remains "in the dark" but out of "countenance," without a mask to hide behind and forced to borrow every "changing shape" to "find expression." As he scrambles for new masks, he sees that he is a "dancing bear," and he will even "chatter like an ape" rather than reveal genuine feeling. As in "Entretien," reversion to animal consciousness measures the extent of his psychic extremity (the whole point of his playing the game has been to acquire a fitness to survive). These bestial images show him to be a gauche performer and, worse, a dumb creature beyond the pale of human communication.[15] Animals may dance, cry, and chatter, but they do not talk or love. Resisting the temptation to relate, he remains unspeaking, a self-entranced silent voice.

The relationship has bestowed neither sophistication nor self-knowledge. From the safety of his garret abroad, he still plays the game as he weighs the lady's fantasized death in terms of gambit and "advantage." The epigraph that establishes the ambiance of play in the poem also reminds us that in Marlowe it functions to dupe the corrupt: Barrabas's pose of callousness outwits the covetous friars. By treating the lady solely as game and never in earnest, to the point of death, he shows that the game not only corrupts the players, but also robs them of life. His earlier confusion about "things that other people have desired" suggested his possible openness to feeling, but the humiliation of the final encounter signals his desperate retreat to the game mentality as he puzzles over the "right" response. Against the backdrop of a yellow and rose Aesthete evening, life for him is still, and only, a set of gambits and responses: she dies; he sits, pen in hand. The enormity of the difference between death and sitting escapes his notice, and measures the enormity of his insensitivity to her desolation and of his own blindness to the limits of play.

His immersion in the game forecasts the direction of his life, for to see life as game is eventually to lose life as life: "Doubtful, for a while / Not knowing what to feel. . . ." He hangs "for a while" suspended between life and game, treating feeling as a move rather than as real, something manipulated rather than experienced. She does gain an "advantage," for in playing the game as an earnest of relationship, she seems somehow more vital than he, who plays to insulate himself from any life but the play of his mind. Its play now distracts him into total acquiescence in the game. He finds, "now that we talk of dying," that "this music" is successful with a "dying fall." To this point, music associated with relationship struck him as winding, off key. This new music is "successful" not so much because it removes her from his life, but because it signals his own fall from life and his successful return to the insulating embrace of the self. "We," his various voices and masks, confirm his existence in the game-world that in "Prufrock" is a death-in-life world symbolized by human "voices dying." But only "I," his buried self of feeling, questions whether this outcome gives "the right to smile."

"Portrait" is Eliot's first acknowledgment that to play with life is to destroy life. Unlike Prufrock, who almost risks his self-possession, the young man plays without venture of feeling what is for him a game without pain. He is in the end what he was at the outset—self-enclosed, self-obsessed, and self-possessed. He is a youthful Prufrock fascinated by the game's challenge, but ignorant of its deceit, the part of Eliot for whom social rituals promised social contact without self-loss. "Prufrock" is the sequel to "Portrait," and it reveals that playing the game leads to the missed life. Prufrock seeks what the young man always withholds, communication and relationship. But for Prufrock it is too late, for the man has become the mask.

"Prufrock" reflects concerns about self-identity touched on in "Portrait" and in the unpublished "He said: This universe is very clear," whose observer-figure is a collection of attitudes and roles without a core of identity. The compulsive role-player risks psychic division, splitting the self among its roles or into public mask and private self. A greater risk is that in constantly acting from behind "prepared faces," one fails to live. If life is a masquerade, all encounters are mask-to-mask, never face-to-face. Prufrock sees that a world whose rituals bring people together but prevent their meeting is sick; he yearns for a richer existence than he knows. His situation mirrors the tensions implicit in the metamorphosis conceit that Eliot develops in "Bacchus and Ariadne": the masquerade maintains the players' confinement within their socially conditioned roles; Prufrock's deep self wants to break out to otherness and to life. How to express this conflict between mask and self challenged Eliot for over a year, but when he resolved it, he knew that he had written a poem that satisfied him. It proved to be the classic psychic monologue, in which silent voices become psychic drama that ends in psychic death.

Eliot arrived in Paris in the fall of 1910 with the second section of "Portrait," which develops the theme of self-possession, and the "Prince Hamlet" passage of "Prufrock," with its role-playing. He finished both poems by the fall of 1911. "Entretien" (February 1911), which confirms the anguish of self-absorption, may have been the catalyst for exposing in "Prufrock" the limits of role-playing; "Bacchus and Ariadne" turns on the conceit of breaking from a secure but confining stage of development. We recall that in "Goldfish 3," the observer hesitates to disturb his world, distracted by its charms as portrayed in "Mandarins 4"; in "Prufrock" a more knowing protagonist, now split into accommodating masker and disturbed seeker, debates whether to take the risk and "dare / Disturb the universe."

How to unfold this interior drama preoccupied Eliot for some time. The Prince Hamlet passage embodies Eliot's earliest conception of the poem,[16] which exploits the rhetoric of role-playing, as in "Portrait," and the contemplation of model figures, as in "Mandarins." Hamlet embodies Prufrock's aspiration to live—that is, to be or not be; John the Baptist and Lazarus are prophet figures who define his aspiration to disturb the universe; Polonius is the attendant lord whose rhetoric describes the role Prufrock ends up playing. However, the "Prufrock" we know exhibits a more complex delineation of consciousness than that implied in the Prince Hamlet, that is, the Polonius, passage. A role is not another self, an alter-ego addressed as "you": "Let us go then, you and I." Yet Eliot splits Prufrock into contrasting selves, creating what he later called "a *dedoublement* of personality against which the subject struggles."[17]

Prufrock's "you" and "I" originate in something different from Laforguian play, or the use of voices to project different points of view, the method of the unpublished "He said: This universe is very clear." "Portrait" affords the precedent of a one-sided "dialogue" within consciousness, but the source for Prufrock's double self, the poem's most obvious formal feature, has never been traced. It was not Laforgue but Bergson who gave Eliot the idea, a Bergson who thoroughly absorbed Eliot's interest at this time.

Besides *Matter and Memory*, Eliot studied the *Essai sur les données immédiates de la conscience* (an authorized English translation appeared in 1910 under the title *Time and Free Will*), as the numerous citations from both works in Eliot's holograph paper on Bergson in the Houghton Library confirm. In the *Essai*, Bergson argues that the individual experiences two kinds of psychic life, which are really two selves: a superficial self and a fundamental self. The first "comes in contact with the external world at its surface" and grasps reality as empirical data. This is the quotidian self, its time is clock time, and its experience is a succession of separate moments. Below is a deeper self whose "states and changes permeate one another" in an experiential flow, Bergson's "*durée*." Through the process of socialization, by which individuals learn to conduct themselves according to various external codes of family, school, church, business, and other institutional expectations, they adapt their behavior and suppress their own deeper aspirations. The superficial self takes command of daily living, and they move unthinkingly through their daily routines. "As the self thus refracted and thereby broken to pieces, is much better adapted to the requirements of social life in general and language in particular, consciousness prefers it, and gradually loses sight of the fundamental self."[18]

But at times, this suppressed self may "blaze up" in revolt and assert its prerogatives. Because this self remains attuned to profounder truth, it is the self that "ponders and decides" a person's ultimate commitments. A break from the conventional pattern, the pattern of expected behavior, is the deep-seated self asserting itself:

> It is the outer crust bursting, suddenly giving way to an irresistible thrust. Hence in the depths of the self . . . a gradual heating and a sudden boiling over of feelings and ideas, not unperceived, but rather unnoticed. If we turn back to them and carefully scrutinize our memory, we shall see that we had ourselves shaped these ideas, ourselves lived these feelings, but that, through some strange reluctance to exercise our will, we had thrust them back into the darkest depths of our soul whenever they came up to the surface. . . . [Our act of revolt] does not then express some superficial idea, almost external to ourselves, distinct and easy to account for: it agrees with the whole of our most intimate feelings, thoughts and aspirations.[19]

Just such a personal crisis is, of course, the subject of "Prufrock," and the blazing up of the fundamental self into expression is the poem's point of departure. Eliot was familiar with the Bergsonian concept of the double self, and refers to it in his unpublished paper on Bergson. It is this paradigm of personality, with its continual quotidian compromises set against a potential for revolt, that produces Prufrock's "you" and "I." For Eliot, Bergson's description of the revolt of the deep self gave new meaning and depth to the conflict between social conditioning and the seeker's urge to significance that he portrayed in "Mandarins," "Goldfish," and the City poems. This conflict, which he knew mainly from his own experience, has now been given philosophical justification. Since its implications are more elemental than Laforguian play, Jamesian self-watching, and the rhetoric of assumed roles can imply, Eliot used the Bergsonian double self to organize the poem as a whole. When Prufrock's fundamental self "blazes up" to confront his social mask, a psychodrama begins that ultimately fixes his identity and fate.

The main irony of Eliot's title is familiar enough: here is a love song that is never sung to another, that never leaves the self. What has escaped notice is the elaborate counterpoint of silent voices that this song of the self develops within consciousness. The Guido of the epigraph, who, like Prufrock, is obsessed with his image in the eyes of others, admits in the lines that immediately precede those of the epigraph that he knows "each winding way," as Prufrock does the ways of the masquerade. Guido counsels the pope to use deception, a playing with appearances, as a modus operandi. Translated to Prufrock's world, his counsel is to play along with the masquerade and its winding ways, which Prufrock hears in the other voices that sound around and within him.

In Bergson's terms, he needs to break through the outer crust of restrictive, learned behavior that governs the self's transactions with the familiar world, but that immobilizes its deepest feelings. But the habitual behavior that characterizes Bergson's superficial self, which readily adapts to the expectations of society, or, in this case, to the constricting code of the masquerade, is not easily altered. The pressure that the fundamental self exerts toward change and the superficial self's resistance is felt in the dualistic imagery of the first half of the poem. The etherized patient, usually read as Laforguian irony or metaphysical conceit, reflects the tension between the deep self's thrust toward psychic enlargement (the evening spread out against the sky) and the superficial self's numbing rigidity (the etherized patient), although "etherized" rather than "anesthetized" suggests that the aspiring motion (to the ether) affects even the conventional mask.[20] The image also reflects the role conflict between the romantic lover (the expansive evening) and the prophet ministering to a diseased world. The same tension underlies the cat-like fog; active verbs ("rubs," "licked," "leap") reflect the fundamental self's urgency, passive verbs ("let fall," "fell asleep") reflect the superficial self's reluctance and passivity, whereas verbs that imply activity and passivity ("slipped," "lingered," "curled") reflect the tension between the selves. The distinction is symbolically summed up during the meditation on time in the ironic juxtaposing of "murder" and "create," the creative urge of the fundamental self contrasting with the superficial self's compromises that "murder" life.

This conflict also accounts for the contrasting landscapes of the journey; why should the fastidious Prufrock dwell on the sordid world of the slums through which he passes to the fashionable drawing room, the haunt of the superficial self? In the masquerade world of the privileged elite, polite routines dull the pain of living and obscure, like the yellow fog that will shortly be alluded to, the quiet desperation of the participants' lives. The fundamental self calls on the superficial self to "go *through*" the experience that these "muttering" streets voice and by means of it to burst the "shells" of the maskers by penetrating the outer crust of conventional behavior with recognitions drawn from the depths, which have always been "thrust . . . back . . . whenever they came up to the surface."

But the deeper self is resisted by the self conditioned to retreat to the solace of the familiar; we can read the latter's emergence in its transformation of the "muttering retreats" that reveal truth into an "insidious" and "tedious" argument that builds (the rhythms still assert the deep self's presence) into something too "overwhelming" to engage; the tension collapses in the denial of the question ("Oh, do not ask, 'What is it?'") and a pat acceptance of a return to the level of social observance ("Let us go and make our visit"). The first part of the poem is dominated by this rise and fall tension, for as in the "First Debate between the Body and Soul," the debate is not open but implied, particularly in the "come and go" of the psychic pressure toward encounter, against which the comings and goings of the women provide a repeated ironic refrain. Their "talk," a petty voice in counterpoint to the main interior debate, indicates preferred subjects of discussion by the maskers, "almost external to ourselves, distinct and easy to account for." So Michelangelo is reduced to the proportions of the tea table, although for Prufrock, Michelangelo as the celebrator of heroic masculinity remains a disturbing model who raises questions about his adequacy to play enlarged roles. Since he hears this voice in the women's talk, it also carries the sense of the women as judges who impose heroic, that is, impossible, expectations.

Against such concerns, the ambiguous but obscuring fog promises escape, and the *sliding* yellow smoke suggests Prufrock's unconscious slide from encounter into the dream of endless time. The mock-heroic works and days of hands that "lift and drop" a "question" express both the reluctance to drop the mask and routines of the "plate" in order to lift the burden of the overwhelming question, and the eventual dropping of the question, presaged in the first paragraph's "do not ask." "Revisions" rob "visions" of prophetic power, and easily decline into "indecisions." The fog reflects Prufrock's vacillation between encounter and escape; on a deeper level, it suggests the numbing spiritual torpor that is Baudelaire's *ennui*. The masquerade's routines intensify the boredom they seek to circumvent, and induce Eliot's *aboulie*, the particular psychic state that, ironically, combines consciousness of a condition with pervasive indifference to it. This is a variation of the etherized patient, ether bringing loss of feeling through loss of consciousness. It is the state of *aboulie* that Eliot himself knew often in the years leading up to *The Waste Land*.[21] The state gradually dominates Prufrock. To the self-absorbed consciousness, there will always be time, for the press of time is the press of commitments, particularly to others. Time measures the importunities of the real on the self; Prufrock's dream of endless time expresses his unconscious desire to remain self-possessed.

The loosening rhythms of the voice of endless time reduce the tension toward revolt. Prufrock seems to repeat himself when he recalls his dare, but he really hears two voices raising different questions: "Do *I* dare?" and "Do I *dare?*" With the superficial self and its preoccupation with self-image now ascendant, "Let us go" becomes "let us watch," as Prufrock takes time to "wonder" at the figure he cuts before the others. He descends the stair (mounting stairs projects struggle in Eliot; descent projects collapse) before women whose voices, as he hears them, question his adequacy to play the hero ("They will say: 'But how his arms and legs are thin!'") and his virility ("They will say: 'How his hair is growing thin!'"). They voice Prufrock's own projection of himself, for he also sees his formal attire, a Laforguian defense, as ambivalent: his collar "mount[s] firmly" but his tie, at once "rich" and "modest," recalls the dichotomy within himself. The clothes fail to cover his frailty, the thinness of the arms and legs, the weakness of the strength and will. Prufrock would be a hero, but "they"—so he thinks—see only a thin man growing old.

Having used the women to diminish his "vision" of himself as hero, Prufrock plays a kind of anti-Theseus to the women's Ariadne. He reconsiders the "universe" he would "disturb." It is the same world of the endlessly circling daily round that Eliot explored in "Goldfish" and "Preludes," only its particular "evenings, mornings, afternoons" measure out life in meager coffee-spoon servings. Above all this is a world that Prufrock has *known*: he has *known* the evenings, mornings, afternoons of this world; he has *known* the eyes and the arms of the women. He surfeits on knowledge of the familiar, the totally predictable, the too carefully measured, the too narrowly formulated. This is the "Goldfish" world of learned expectations, mannered individuals, and formulated behavior; like the masses bound by their work routines, the elite are bound by their social routines, the need to prepare a "face" and to "murder" other faces as thoughtlessly as they "create" their own. This world inured to feeling crushes the needs of the deep self.

Prufrock's review works for and against encounter. On the one hand, it reveals the masquerade to be a sick world, an etherized patient; but on the other, it suggests the obstacles to the maskers' recognizing their condition, which Prufrock will later use to rationalize his failure in a world that will not understand. Their voices are known by their "dying fall." At the end of "Portrait," the "dying fall" of the music of death signals the young man's entrapment in the death-in-life game. Prufrock's "voices dying" sing the death-life from which he would escape. He knows the maskers' eyes as Bergsonian instruments of social control that fix individuals in categories, "formulate" them to conventional expectations, and pin nonconformists to the wall as "wriggling" specimens of the cost of social defiance.

This sequence of images through which Prufrock relates himself to the masquerade is worth noting as a revelation of unconscious intentions. He knows the masquerade first as boredom (the daily round of the quotidian), then as threat (the piercing, fixing eyes), and finally as ambiguity and contradiction embodied in the women (whose arms convey romance and love, but also physicality and war). The order of these images—evenings, eyes, arms—is the order of Prufrock's priorities: he is more concerned with the masquerade and its oppressiveness than with the women as either threats or lovers. Unconsciously, Prufrock prefers to enlarge himself by playing the prophet who disturbs the universe, rather than the lover who reaches out to the other. The "eyes" and "arms," body parts, undercut the women's attraction as lovers by their lack of humanity. Their sensuality is enclosed ("braceleted"), and when it breaks through, to Prufrock's astonishment ("downed with light brown hair!"), it is called a digression, which it would hardly be if romance were uppermost in his mind. Indeed, the figure of the prophet, of John the Baptist the victim of Salome, seems just below consciousness here, confirming the ascendancy of the prophet over the lover and of the passive victim over the active hero.

These priorities explain why Prufrock's next concern, how to put the overwhelming question (the point of departure in "Entretien" that leads to a final collapse of will), is resolved in the way it is, as the possible gambit of a prophet rather than a lover. Simply to blurt out one's loneliness is unthinkable; Prufrock considers using a third party, the lonely men of the slums: "Shall I say, I have gone . . . / And watched . . . lonely men . . . ?" In the original version of "Prufrock," recorded in the "March Hare," this leads to the lengthy "Pervigilium" that Eliot suppressed; in it, Prufrock plays the prophet to the masquerade, his etherized patient, by assuming the voice of Lazarus and coming "from the dead" to "tell you all." He does so by describing the world of the City poems, particularly "Preludes" and "Rhapsody," whose working-class squalor reveals what the beautiful surface of the masquerade conceals—the desperation of most lives. The "Pervigilium" turns the poem prophetic at its very center. It goes further; by recapitulating the agony of the City series as Prufrock's own experience, it reveals the upheaval that precedes the opening "Let us go" and shows Eliot "ending" the journey traced in the City series by confronting the prophet's role in the life context of his own social world rather than in the private retreat of a bar, as in "The Little Passion."

Prufrock has suffered the same agony as the woman in the third Prelude that gave her "a vision of the street / As the street hardly understands" and that now gives his deepest self a vision of the masquerade that the masquerade must be made to see. So he thinks to take the maskers through these streets—that is, *through* the experience they contain—with their loitering youths, overweight gossiping women, and whimpering children, whose pain is simply their daily lives. As he walks those streets of pain, he turns paranoid and sees the slum-dwellers and their very houses lean together to jeer him. Back in his room, he lies in bed like the woman in the third Prelude and sees the night take form and dart about the room feverishly, until a nauseous dawn stirs the eyes and feet of the city automatons to resume their mindless routines (as in the second Prelude). Meanwhile, stumbling to the window, Prufrock sees an image of his own madness in the form of a blind old drunk in the street, the figure associated in "First Debate" with prophesy and the world of spirit. Suddenly the world falls apart, and his vision ends. The "Pervigilium" is the culmination of the City poems because it presses their materials and images into a vision, though it verges on madness. Still, this is an advance on "The Little Passion," in which the seeker only thinks he may be called to be the prophet. Prufrock has suffered the agony which "The Little Passion" demands of the prophet.

By deleting the "Pervigilium," Eliot vacillates before the task of witness, perhaps for Prufrock's reason, the fear of embarrassment before others, perhaps because he felt that his own vision was, as the "Pervigilium" suggests, a kind of madness. He shortly took up the study of mystical literature to try to sort out the differences between madness and prophesy, idiosyncrasy and authentic vision. Clearly, however, the effect of the deletion is to emphasize the social element in the poem at the expense of the prophetic, as decades of commentaries confirm.[22] Prufrock senses that his paranoid and increasingly frenzied revelation must appear to the maskers to be the ravings of a lunatic, not the raging of a prophet. Eliot retained only the image that ends the "Pervigilium," of "ragged claws / Scuttling" in silent seas, to signal withdrawal before the prophetic role.[23] This crab image recalls the use of burrowers in "Entretien" as a measure of the extremity of the desire to lose self-consciousness by identifying with primitive creatures; in "Entretien" self-consciousness is buried in the earth through the burrowers' imagery, whereas here it is scuttled, deliberately sunk, in silent seas of noncommunicating awareness.

In his "fantasies" in the "Pervigilium," Prufrock recognizes that truth-to-self, the fundamental self of prophesy, entails the death of the social self, the masker. Playing the prophet is also destructive, for the martyred "head [grown slightly bald]" is delivered on the "platter" of social artifact.[24] The voice of the snickering Footman evokes a brave eternal perspective, but it does not remove the fear of the man. Having prepared himself through the agony of the "Pervigilium"—"I have wept and fasted, wept and prayed"—he knows that his refusal to disturb the universe is decisive for his life: the prophet who sees but is silent destroys himself. By remaining a silent voice, Prufrock sees what he "should have been," a pair of ragged claws in a "silent" world. Refusing to be the prophet, he remains the masker "scuttling" without direction and cursed by what might have been.

Prufrock never doubts his calling, and questions its value only after he withdraws before the call. It is a failed prophet and man who turns to rationalization. His "great refusal" collapses tension but not awareness, as the ensuing play of mockery and lethargy makes clear. The "evening," the earlier etherized patient, is now "stretched" and confirmed in its sickness "here beside you and me," his superficial and deep selves, and, on another level, the women as objects and himself as masker, the conventional selves deadened to feeling. Prufrock, who earlier thought to disturb the universe, denies all roles that would "stretch" him: he is no "prophet"; he will not play Lazarus and "tell all," he will not be the Baptist, the prophet as martyr. To assuage guilt and to confirm his life as masker, Prufrock rationalizes that both the masquerade and he are unworthy: no place is set for a prophet among the porcelain. When he accuses the masquerade of impenetrability, his syntax reveals his "malingering" by evading declarative statements for rhetorical questions that implicate but do not accuse. The careful hedging, the groping toward articulation do not convince, but the terrible image of the nerves does; here is the cause of his withdrawal—the sight of the self naked before the world. The fear to dare is finally the Narcissus fear to be revealed.

So Prufrock diminishes himself. Since awareness of his higher calling to prophesy is stifled, only the role of secular hero remains, yet he is not Prince Hamlet but Polonius, the "attendant lord" (both lackey and noble: the old dichotomy between superficial and deep selves). He watches his new self and details its gestures to learn its ways. This self "will do" (it must suffice; it will also "do" by acting its menial tasks, as the "easy tool" of the masquerade); he will "swell a progress," the rhetoric ironically recalling his failure to enlarge himself or the maskers beyond their show; having refused to "start a scene" to disturb the universe, he is "full of high sentence" to rationalize failure and more than "a bit" obtuse to think that he can blunt his yearning for bigger parts.

When he thinks of his "almost ridiculous" figure as that of "the Fool," he vaguely recognizes that his masker role may appear, ironically, to be that of the Shakespearian Fool, truth-teller to kings: it is the one role that his obsession with self-image prevents his playing—for what would "they" think of his dressing in motley? Having refused to enlarge himself and live, he instantly "grows" old. Pathetically, he resigns himself to cultivating appearances: he will roll his trouser bottoms, instead of the universe into a ball. "Do I dare / Disturb the universe" declines into "Do I dare to eat a peach?" The questions one asks define the person one is and can be.

Contemplating this diminished figure and its little life, Prufrock resigns himself to loss. He hears a new voice, the song of the mermaids, and this voice sings what he has lost. Unlike a Prufrock divided within himself and from his world, the sea-girls, even in their name, are one with their world. They sing their lives, and they sing to each other. As they effortlessly ride the waves, they enact themselves naturally, for riding the waves—their natural act, their raison d'être—gestures their affection for their sea-lord. The vision of the mermaids expresses unity, order, and love, fusing body and spirit, male and female, god and creature, nature and art. They harmonize oppositions in union, communion. Hearing their voices singing, each to each but not to him, Prufrock feels excluded and profoundly alienated from this paradigm of fulfillment through action, communication, and relationship. In the mermaids, Prufrock sees what he has lost, sees that he is lost. He lingers with them until called away by the "human" voices of the masquerade who "wake" "us," the fundamental self of aspiration and the superficial self of the quotidian world, in a burial rite, and "we," the two selves that express the potential within the ego for change, "drown." The poem's last line contrasts ironically with its first, the determination of "let us go" ending in psychic death.

The sea imagery here is twofold: the vision of the mermaids; the ideal, is of the sea's surface; "the chambers of the sea," like the earlier "floors of silent seas," is the haunt of fantasy; death-in-life, and the isolated, self-enclosed, chambered self. The use of "chambers" here is richly suggestive: as a room, chamber recalls the "room" of the masquerade, and as a hall for a legislative or judicial body, it emphasizes the formulated rules that govern the comings and goings of the prepared faces, as well as the women as judges; a "chamberlain" is an attendant on a lord, evoking the role to which Prufrock commits himself; a chamber also is a bedroom, recalling Prufrock's romantic aspirations and the sea-girls' riding of the waves; finally, in the sense of a vault (Greek, *kamara*) or an arched roof (Latin, *camera*), chamber emphasizes the entrapment of the self within its own confines of consciousness, where its many voices legislate and mete judgment upon itself. Eliot associates the sea surface on which as a youth he sailed with such delight, with vibrant life images, and the sea's depths with the sailor's ultimate fear, death. Accepting the role of attendant lord, Prufrock opposes the sea lord of Life and momentarily lulls himself into a fantasy world ("the chambers of the sea") in which "we," both selves, "linger" and change is possible. But the iteration of "I" in this section makes clear that what survives is a monistic psyche, that of the mask. Affixing his "prepared face," Prufrock takes his permanent place in the masquerade as the first of Eliot's hollow men.

"Prufrock" is unique in Eliot's *oeuvre*, for it sets forth the archetypal experience that underlies most of his other works. What happens to Prufrock has happened to Gerontion, Tiresias, the protagonist of "Ash-Wednesday," and the voice of the *Four Quartets*, all of whom carry the Prufrockian refusal to dare as their psychic mark of Cain. What sets Prufrock apart is that he alone *experiences* what the others remember: "Footfalls echo in the memory / Down the passage which we did not take / Towards the door we never opened / Into the rose garden." For Prufrock alone, what might have been is what yet may be. He is Eliot's archetype of the great refusal, the man who fears to dare and so misses life. But in the present of the poem, he can act otherwise. "Prufrock" initiates Eliot's obsession with lost opportunity and the missed life. In the poetry that follows, the present is often mean in relation to the lost world. Whether this is real or illusory, a distortion of memory and desire, is problematic: we think the door we never opened leads to the rose garden, not the garden of olives. Only Prufrock experiences the existential terror of the moment of choice. In the event, what might have been may seem what cannot be, but after the event the mind forgets the terror of that moment, and what cannot be becomes in a world of speculation the lost opportunity of what might have been. "Prufrock" reminds us that the inhibiting fears that crowd consciousness at the moment of choice are no less real than the sterile emptiness of its aftermath.

Since Prufrock's failure is the archetype of failure in Eliot's work, we ought to understand it better. Prufrock is often seen as a victim of idealism, of what Eliot calls "the awful separation between potential passion and any actualization possible in life,"[25] a discrepancy he certainly felt keenly. Sometimes such idealism is specified as an idealization of love and of woman, symbolized by the mermaids. However, if the vision of the mermaids idealizes anything, it idealizes life, with women, not men, as its embodiment. The focus of the vision is not the mermaids but their action: they "selve" themselves in Hopkins's sense of the term by serving the sea, as Prufrock might serve his deeper self by disturbing his world. Prufrock is an idealist in asking that life be more than the physical facts show. He sees that the masquerade is a shadow of life; he sees in the mermaids a brave new world. While maskers contrive and disguise, the mermaids sing; the maskers "come and go" in mannered routines, but the mermaids ritualistically serve their god. The mermaids fulfill themselves by being themselves; the maskers bury their selves in their masks. The vision seems to say that the ideal can be realized, but only through fidelity to the deepest impulses of being.

The vision of the mermaids is one of the most lyrically charged passages in Eliot's work. It is so because it is a norm by which to measure not just Prufrock and the maskers, but all human endeavor; it is a norm that Eliot himself likely felt diminished by. Indeed, it may explain the "upheaval" he suffered after completing "Prufrock"; he knew that he had captured an image of the life he wanted, and a paradigm of his failure to achieve it. The life of the mermaids is the good life: it affirms that we embrace life, not withdraw from it, through acts that are natural rather than contrived, spontaneous rather than inhibited, true to self rather than acceptable to others. To live means to act and to risk—to risk the loss of one's image in the eyes of the others, to risk even the loss of the self. To gain life, one may have to risk losing it; in "Prufrock," without risk there is only loss. Prufrock is inhibited, self-conscious, obsessed with image, self-possessed, and afraid, and, at this stage of his life, so too is Eliot. Fear is in the way—the fear to dare, to live honestly, to tell all, to be the Fool. The mermaids will not sing to Prufrock because he will not sing to anyone. His "love song" to himself is a cry of anguish. His silent voices unconsciously speak Eliot's first prophetic utterance, a warning to all who will not dare. Eliot himself was the first to take it seriously.

From *T. S. Eliot's Silent Voices* (New York: Oxford University Press, 1989): 97-129. Copyright © 1989 by Oxford University Press. Reprinted by permission of Oxford University Press, Inc.

Notes

1. In "Suite Clownesque," Eliot employs colloquial speech, lines from popular song, and witty syncopated rhythms more than a decade earlier than in *The Waste Land* and *Sweeney Agonistes*; the musical-stage directions anticipate Vachel Lindsay's use of this technique in "General William Booth Enters Heaven," published in 1913.

2. The Jamesian ambiance suggests that the poem may be based on an experience with Emily Hale, an attempt to clarify their "situation" before Eliot left for Paris, just as the final part of "Portrait of a Lady" reflects his break with Madeleine Moffat before "going abroad."

3. D. H. Lawrence, *Women in Love* (New York: Viking, 1960), p. 34.

4. Ariadne seems to be a forecast-figure for Emily Hale, whom Eliot as early as 1911 possibly recognized as a source of inspiration for his art, his etheralized love, and a figure who would suffer because of him. Like Ariadne and Vivien, Emily would endure desertions, yet be transformed through suffering and through art.

5. On the personal level, this tension of difference is that between the beloved and the poet, on the one hand, and, within the poet, between the lover and the artist, on the other. Eliot will shortly explore this tension in "La Figlia che Piange."

6. Henry James, *Portrait of a Lady*, edited, with introduction, by Leon Edel (Boston: Houghton Mifflin, 1963), pp. 203-204.

7. Conrad Aiken, *Ushant: An Essay* (Cleveland: World Publishing, 1952; reprint, 1962), Cleveland: World-Meridian, p. 186.

8. Grover Smith identifies this source but confines its significance merely to the "outlines" and some "ornamental details" of "Prufrock." See *T. S. Eliot's Poetry and Plays* (Chicago: University of Chicago Press, 1956), p. 15.

9. Quotations are from "Crapy Cornelia," in *Complete Tales of Henry James*, vol. 12, edited, with introduction, by Leon Edel (Philadelphia and New York: Lippincott, 1964), pp. 336, 340, 341-342, 350, 356, 367, 362.

10. See note 16.

11. Piers Gray's analysis offers a stimulating account of the ambiguities of the poem's diction. See *T. S. Eliot's Intellectual and Poetic Development 1909-1922* (Atlantic Highlands, N.J.: Humanities Press, 1982), pp. 13-18. This does not extend to the poem's several rhetorics, however, for Gray's poem is not informed by role-playing. He conflates the "I's" voice with Eliot's own complex awareness, rather than taking it to be that of a neophyte playing at a sophistication he cannot command, and reads the lady's admissions of "feelings of unrest, *loneliness*, and dissatisfaction" as an expression of the kind of Arnoldian sincerity and politeness that honestly admits these things in "decadent Wordsworthian tones" (p. 31). The lady's language is seen to be self-consciously emotive and "ingratiating" (p. 27) but not because it is a strategy; while it does reveal the lady's distress, it is not as sincere and honest as Gray suggests. Still, Gray illuminates important elements that have been overlooked, as, for example, the self-contradictory quality of the poem's ambiguous opening, which prepares us for the young man's "evasion of responsibility" (p. 16).

12. Lois Cuddy develops this view in "Reconsidering Eliot's Women: Images of 'Carefully Caught Regrets' in the Early Poems" (Paper read at the T. S. Eliot Symposium, University of New Hampshire, Durham, New Hampshire, April 28, 1988). She also suggests that the three parts of the poem parallel the story of Odysseus told in Homer and Dante. Part I emphasizes the entrapment of the figures in the respective male and female roles before Odysseus leaves for Troy; Part II coincides with the return from Troy of the "invulnerable hero"; Part III parallels his final journey, as he deserts the woman for another journey over water, and is last seen far from home recalling her likely death. Like Penelope, the lady knows the isolation of years of serving others, serving tea to friends and suitors; to all her forthright offerings of feeling, the young man, like Odysseus, offers no emotional reaction, a typical male strategy for survival in the Greek world. Her pleas are not malicious but pathetic, the revelations of her wasted emotional life. Cuddy accounts for the difference in the ages of Eliot's figures, the young man and the older woman, in mythic terms; Athena makes the returning Odysseus youthful for the reunion—after all, he still has adventures ahead—whereas Penelope has lost her figure and vitality and can look forward only to death. Tennyson's Ulysses also is relatively youthful compared with his "aged wife." Cuddy's paper is in "T. S. Eliot's Classicism: A Study in Allusional Design and Purpose," in Shyamal Bagchee, ed., *T. S. Eliot Annual*, vol. 1 (Atlantic Highlands, N.J.: Humanities Press International, 1989).

13. A. D. Moody, like Gray, regards the lady's sentiments to be transparently her

own, but observes that "they persist insidiously in his very exposing of them" through the graceful flow of "those exquisitely caught hesitations and modulations." See *Thomas Stearns Eliot: Poet* (Cambridge: Cambridge University Press, 1979), p. 21.

14. Gray, too, recognizes the appearance of a new voice here, different from that of the opening gesture and from the "reporting" voice that records cruelly and with fastidious objectivity the lady's own speech. This new voice is said to be a voice of "twisted" lyricism, whose musical metaphor emphasizes the musicality of language. "It is capricious and hence, like the muse, a gift of forces beyond the *conscious* mind, and yet it is monotonous and unwavering, and most of all, quite hostile to the very creativity, the luxuriant anarchy, of the unconscious mind" (*Eliot's Intellectual and Poetic Development*, p. 17). I would argue that it is not the voice of the creative unconscious, but of the deepest instinct of the Narcissus psyche; it is the voice of self-preservation, which must be monotonous in urging its single theme.

15. Gray finds in this passage a recognition of self-disgust, but this is to give the young man too large a capacity for self-knowledge. Indeed, he barely recognizes his own incompetence. Gray's comment that the poem as a whole "plays with the difference between self-possession and being possessed [by] demons" is telling, but it is the reader and not the *I* who recognizes this difference (*Eliot's Intellectual and Poetic Development*, p. 25).

16. "When I went to Paris in the autumn of [1910] I had already written several fragments which were ultimately embodied in the poem.... I think that the passage beginning 'I am not Prince Hamlet,' a passage showing the influence of Laforgue, was one of these fragments which I took with me, but the poem was not completed until the summer of 1911." Eliot to John C. Pope, March 8, 1946, in *American Literature* 18 (January 1947): 319.

17. T. S. Eliot, "A Commentary," *Criterion*, April 12, 1933, p. 469.

18. Henri Bergson, *Time and Free Will*, trans. F. L. Pogson (New York: Macmillan, 1910; reprint, New York: Harper, 1960), pp. 125, 128.

19. Bergson, *Time and Free Will*, pp. 125, 169-170.

20. Stephen Spender calls the image a "symptomatic" simile "not capable of being visualized," and, thus, illustrates the very tendency he decries in recent Eliot criticism "to drain 'Prufrock' of its considerable realism." See *T. S. Eliot* (New York: Viking, 1976), p. 37. Not only can the image be visualized, but it derives from literal fact, the view of Boston across the Charles from Cambridge seen on Eliot's route from Harvard to Beacon Hill. The view today, if the skyscrapers are subtracted, shows that the city, with the bosomy rise of Beacon Hill and the extended length of the Back Bay, resembles a woman lying on a flat surface, the line of the river bank.

21. After his collapse in the fall of 1921 Eliot wrote to Richard Aldington that his bouts of "nerves" were due to "an aboulie and emotional derangement which has been a lifelong affliction." Eliot to Aldington, November 6, 1921, *The Waste Land Facsimile* edition, p. xxii.

22. Lyndall Gordon is right to align "Prufrock" with the third Prelude and several manuscript poems in a vigil cluster, the product of a "period of acute distress in Eliot's life." As we have seen, in the poetry concerned with "vision," the seeker looks to vision as a possible means of accessing spirit, but when he encounters something like it,

he is plagued by its ambiguous nature and by the responsibilities it brings. Gordon's emphasis on the prophetic element in "Prufrock" is a significant step toward our recovering the real thrust of the poem. However, I would put the central conflict somewhat differently; rather than one between "the obligation to cultivate human attachments" and the "prophet's obligation to articulate what he alone knows," I would see Prufrock's fear of self-loss opposing his desire to assume both of these "obligations" (Gordon, *Eliot's Early Years*, pp. 44, 47). Prufrock is a would-be lover, a would-be prophet. For him, as for Eliot, "shyness" and self-absorption cripple the ability both to communicate (whose august form is prophesy) and to love. For Gordon's full discussion, see *Eliot's Early Years* (Oxford: Oxford University Press, 1977), pp. 44-47.

23. "Scuttling" is richly suggestive: as a noun, it is a shallow basket for carrying things, as consciousness is the carrier of awareness; etymologically, it is the diminutive of the Latin *scutum* ("platter"), pointing to the serving plate bearing the head of Prufrock-the-Baptist that announces the end of the prophet, who dies from "scuttling" his prophet-self, leaking the consciousness of this role into the silent sea, where it can never voice itself. Scuttling, in the sense of a quick scurrying motion, is consistent with the superficial self's escapism, as is the typical sideways movement of the crab, which recalls the indirection of the masquerade and of the advice of Guido to the Pope. "Ragged" claws are claws worn to tatters (unlike the carefully dressed Prufrock), perhaps by the stress and strain of the ordeal that the poem dramatizes, which "claws" the deep self and the potential prophet so that the diminished self that survives cannot be represented by the whole crab, but only by the destructive claws of the masker-self.

24. Gordon suggests that Eliot caricatures his own visionary moments "in Prufrock the prophet's crazy fantasies: his head brought in, like John the Baptist's, upon a platter" (*Eliot's Early Years*, p. 47). Although the Pervigilium may suggest this, the images of the scuttling crab and the severed head may not be so crazy: the Baptist loses his head by refusing to play the lover, remaining faithful to his prophet's vision, which will appear to be madness to the ordinary world and to the prophet in his ordinary self.

25. T. S. Eliot, "Beyle and Balzac," *Athenaeum*, May 30, 1919, p. 393.

"Prufrock," "Gerontion," and Fragmented Monologues_____

John Paul Riquelme

In the longer chapter from which this is an excerpt, I discuss *The Waste Land* in more detail, particularly its relation to the elegy and the centrality of Hieronymo, and go on to discuss *Ash-Wednesday* as a mortality ode, by contrast with William Wordsworth's "Immortality" Ode. In the excerpt, I argue for a distinctive swerve in Eliot's poetry from the tendencies of his Romantic precursors. I interpret the early verses, called "Preludes," and "Sweeney Erect" by contrasting them with various poems by Wordsworth. I discuss "Prufrock," "Gerontion," and *The Waste Land* in a related way, by focusing on the typical use in Romantic poetry of several figures of speech, including prosopopoeia (or personification), synecdoche (the substituting of whole for part or part for whole), and apostrophe (address to nonhuman creatures or objects as if they were human, usually starting with "O"). Eliot's modernist transformation of all these tropes challenges the attempt to project a human presence or to grasp a totality as if part and whole were linked within a single organism. In particular, his language challenges the projecting of voice onto the nonhuman and even questions whether voice is adequate and accurate for understanding the nature of individual humans, including poets and their readers. I also trace swerves from the tradition of the dramatic monologue in "Prufrock" and "Gerontion," especially with regard to the continuity of the speaking voice. Instead of continuity, we have discontinuity; instead of speech, we have textualized language; instead of a scene of literal speaking to a silent listener, we have a situation that is ambiguously external or internal and that may involve address to the reader. I trace the dissolution of the self from the early poems into *The Waste Land* by bringing out the way the written disrupts, disfigures, and undermines voice as self, particularly in Eliot's apostrophes, which are both strange and frequent. I argue that Eliot empties

> out the full-throated "O" of apostrophe and turns it into the empty or decayed mouth, suggesting mortality, but the cavernous mouth is still able to produce sounds that constitute a haunting, revealing kind of poetry in Eliot's modernist displacement of Romantic poetic practices.   — J.P.R.

Eliot begins producing alternatives to the self's discourse in the poems he publishes before *The Waste Land*. He does so by using figurative language, syntax, and allusion in ways that generate a self-transforming, self-correcting, inherently differential discourse of wit, a "harmony of dissonances" in which oppositions are reciprocally defining and mutually framing. The imbricated, sometimes antithetical, implications of his styles are the equivalent of a Chinese box or a maze with no exit. They find their ultimate manifestation in the perpetually cross-referential structure of *Four Quartets*. As he develops alternatives to personal discourse in his poetry, Eliot repeatedly and systematically counters the Romantic, particularly the Wordsworthian, emphasis on personal emotion and feeling. The result is an antielegiac body of writing that refuses the Wordsworthian tranquility and consolation that Eliot objects to in "Tradition and the Individual Talent" and in "Matthew Arnold."

Even at the start of his publishing career, the character of Eliot's poetry suggests that the writing process involves neither the self nor an individual, personal voice and that its results need not conform to nineteenth-century poetic forms, including the dramatic monologue and the elegy. The transforming of the dramatic monologue occurs most obviously in "Prufrock," "Gerontion," and *The Waste Land*. In *The Waste Land*, Romantic images and strategies, including the nightingale, prosopopoeia, and apostrophe, are put to use in ways that deter the reader from taking the poem's language to be the voice of a self. Its echoes of Romantic writing are combined with reverberations that present poetry's origin as different from voice. The Romantic echoes are also transformed by Eliot's turn toward an antithetical tradition, revenge tragedy. In *Ash-Wednesday*, the Romantic echoes are taken up into an incantatory, impersonal group discourse in an arrangement keyed to Wordsworth's "Immortality" Ode, which Eliot's poem in many ways reverses. Eliot's refusal to mourn and to be comforted becomes clear when his poetry is compared to Wordsworth's.

"Rhapsody on a Windy Night" has already provided one example of Eliot's early resistance to Romantic conventions concerning poetry as inspired personal utterance. Many of his other early poems also fragment psychologized language and in related ways subvert conventions of Romantic writing. "Preludes" is probably the most pointedly anti-Romantic and, in particular, antielegiac of the early poems. It initiates Eliot's long series of poetic rejections of the elegiac tradition, which reaches one culmination thirty years later in "Little Gidding" 2 when the compound ghost forbids nostalgia and mourning. Along with its musical and temporal meanings, "Preludes"'s title echoes the title of Wordsworth's *The Prelude*, which Eliot transforms by pluralizing. The title encourages a reading of Eliot's poem against the implied background of Romantic poetry, especially Wordsworth's. Like "Rhapsody," "Preludes" evokes and turns from Romantic precursors. The brief, discrete physical descriptions of urban scenes in "Preludes" differ greatly from the longer presentations of nature in *The Prelude*. And they are antithetical to Wordsworth's portrayal of a majestic cityscape in "Composed upon Westminster Bridge."

Since only the last of Eliot's four "Preludes" is longer than a single stanza, it is possible to read the short second and third verse paragraphs of that final prelude as reflecting on the entire sequence. In some published versions of the poems (including *CPP* but not *CP*), these concluding stanzas are set off from the earlier ones by indentation, and in all versions the shifts to first person and to the imperative mood set the two closing stanzas apart from the earlier ones. In the penultimate stanza the deictic character of the phrase, "these images," which can refer to the poetic images that compose "Preludes," invites a self-reflexive reading:

> I am moved by fancies that are curled
> Around these images, and cling:
> The notion of some infinitely gentle
> infinitely suffering thing.
>
> *(CPP* 13)

In their diction, the lines echo various passages in Wordsworth's poetry, including the statement in the third stanza of "Elegiac Stanzas" that "I could have fancied that the mighty Deep / Was even the gentlest of all gentle Things" (Wordsworth 373, l. 12).

The "Elegiac Stanzas" provide a clear example of the poetic strategies and the attitudes that Eliot wrote against. Central elements of this and other Romantic poems, including ekphrasis, apostrophe, personification, and the optimistic consolations of elegy, are taken up and transformed when Eliot produces texts that emphasize attitudes radically at odds with the "patient cheer" of Wordsworth's final stanza. In Wordsworth's poem, the experience of discontinuity, specifically the death by water of the poet's brother, leads to the expression of a loss that is bound up with consolation. Reflecting on the deluded attitudes he held before the death, Wordsworth's speaker says:

> So once it would have been,—'tis so no more;
> I have submitted to a new control:
> A power is gone, which nothing can restore;
> A deep distress hath humanised my Soul.
>
> (Wordsworth 374, ll. 33-36)

The earlier attitudes, which have been presented in several stanzas, include prominently the belief in various continuities and harmonies. Those continuities are emphatically discarded in, among other details, the rhyme of "no more" with "restore." The apparent acceptance of discontinuity, however, is countered by a recompense, itself a form of restoration. The consolation is reflected in the other rhymes, which report that the speaker has found a "new control" for his "Soul." The seemingly radical discontinuity and disorder are, in fact, balanced and contained by a controlling order and power that the experience of loss makes recognizable.

In the second half of "Elegiac Stanzas," the humanizing of the speaker's soul is extended to the painting, which is the ostensible spark for the poem, and to the scene within the painting: the sky, the sea, and Peele Castle in a storm. That extension occurs through apostrophe and personification, recurring elements in Romantic poetry. When the speaker says "O 'tis a passionate Work," whose spirit is both "wise" and "Well chosen," he is referring to the painting, whose artist, Sir George Beaumont, has exercised intelligent control in making the right aesthetic choices. At this point, the ekphrasis provides a way to understand the poem containing the references to the painting, a poem whose author presumably exercises a similar control and expertise in evoking verbally the same intelligent, creative spirit that rules the painting. But that spirit also informs the scene. As Wordsworth presents it, the spirit is not limited to art since it involves all the scenic elements, the castle, the sky, and the sea, including "That Hulk which labours in the deadly swell." Consequently, the apostrophe restores the power whose irretrievable loss was announced a few stanzas earlier. The life that has been lost in the brother's drowning is transferred figurally to the personified castle, which preserves continuity because of its endurance. The castle has a face, a "look with which it braves, / Cased in the unfeeling armour of old time," the ravages of the storm, which do not affect it. That look and face are visible in the painting but also in the poem, whose "humanised" speaker brings the elegy to a close by affirming hope's continuance: "Not without hope we suffer and we mourn" (Wordsworth 374, l. 60). "No more" has become, mournfully, "yet once more" yet once more in a history of repetition that includes [John] Milton's "Lycidas."

There are large contrasts between the figures, images, and attitudes Wordsworth uses in "Elegiac Stanzas" and in his other poems and the ones that Eliot uses in his poetry through *Ash-Wednesday*. While

Wordsworth sees a man in armor within a well-ordered composition, in "Preludes" Eliot sees old women in vacant lots. While Wordsworth employs a painting to suggest a controlling presence that makes hope and consolation possible, in part 2 of *The Waste Land* and in "Sweeney Erect" Eliot uses paintings quite differently. In the depiction of Philomela, as we have seen, there is no suggestion of hope or consolation. The rude forcings there differ sharply from the words and attitudes of "Lycidas" that Eliot echoes in order to counter. "Sweeney Erect" is in part a parody of "Elegiac Stanzas," beginning as it does with the work of a different Beaumont (Francis, co-author with John Fletcher of *The Maid's Tragedy*) from the painter of Peele Castle, and using a rugged, rocky shore and stormy sea as the context for a debased, modern scene. Instead of "this huge Castle, standing here sublime" like a man in armor, Eliot gives us "Sweeney addressed full length to shave / Broad-bottomed, pink from nape to base / . . . / . . . the silhouette / Of Sweeney straddled in the sun" (*CPP* 25-26). Some details of the ekphrastic scene in "Sweeney Erect" return in aspects of *The Waste Land*'s final section. At the end of *The Waste Land* Eliot evokes rather than a castle with a face a ruined chapel and a ruined mouth. While Wordsworth finds a "spirit" in art and in nature, Eliot sees waste and vacancy. Later, in *Ash-Wednesday*, by contrast with the continuity of hope and of mourning that Wordsworth affirms, Eliot finds no cause to hope and no cause even to mourn; Wordsworth's embers from stanza 9 of the "Immortality" Ode have turned to ash in Eliot's "mortality" ode.

The contrast between Wordsworth's informing "spirit" as a presence and the lack of that presence in Eliot's poems emerges in the two poets' differing uses of the word "thing," which occurs in the penultimate stanza of "Preludes." It occurs as well in "A Slumber Did My Spirit Seal," where it pertains to the relation of inorganic to organic substance and to the relation of something once living but now dead to a presence that is a continuing, living "spirit." When Wordsworth uses the word thing in the plural in the third stanza of "Elegiac Stanzas," the predication of extreme gentleness suggests that the thing in question is something living, in fact, a living spirit. Eliot's brief focus on an "infinitely gentle / Infinitely suffering thing" carries momentarily the same implication, which is typical of Wordsworth's writing.

But Eliot does not rest with that implication, which he calls up in order to deny. What is being denied can be clarified by considering another passage from Wordsworth about "things," the following well-known statement from "Tintern Abbey":

> And I have felt
> A presence that disturbs me with the joy
> Of elevated thoughts; a sense sublime
> Of something far more deeply interfused
> Whose dwelling is the light of setting suns,
> And the round ocean and the living air,
> And the blue sky, and in the mind of man:
> A motion and a spirit, that impels
> All thinking things, all objects of all thought,
> And rolls through all things.
> ("Lines" ll. 93-102)

The depth of Eliot's challenge to Wordsworth emerges in his use of the word "thing" to refer not to what Wordsworth's "spirit . . . impels" but to the spirit itself as something that is not wise, sublime, or well-ordered. This change forms part of Eliot's rejection of Wordsworth's optimism, expressed, for instance, at the end of "Elegiac Stanzas." That rejection is evident in the final stanza of "Preludes":

> Wipe your hand across your mouth, and laugh;
> The worlds revolve like ancient women
> Gathering fuel in vacant lots.

The figures in the closing stanzas reverse Wordsworth's in a way that typifies Eliot's undermining of logocentric attitudes, including the notion that the "presence" of a "spirit" both inhabits and transcends material things.

In the lines from "Tintern Abbey," Wordsworth uses metaphor, the aligning of "presence" with "motion" and "spirit," to suggest a synecdoche, the spirit's presence in "all things." Since the lines attribute a consciousness to the entire universe, they provide an example of prosopopoeia as well as synecdoche. In Eliot's version, the words "notion," rather than "motion," and "fancies" indicate the source of a different movement, one localized in the speaker's mind rather than general in the universe or "in the mind of man." The implications of curling and clinging are also reduced by their echoing the close of the third prelude, in which a woman has "curled," meaning uncurled, papers from her hair and in which she "clasped" the soles of her feet in soiled hands. Like Wordsworth, Eliot humanizes the universe, which he pluralizes as "worlds," but he does so in a way that is limited by the bounds of mortality and mutability. Eliot accomplishes his un-Wordsworthian humanizing by using a simile that compares the universe with the decrepitly human, "ancient women," and with an emptiness, "vacant lots," rather than identifying it with a "presence." It evokes vacancy rather than plenitude. The simile still attributes humanity to the universe, but it reverses prosopopoeia, since the aspect of the human involved is not consciousness as spirit but something mortal and subject to decay.

The longer, better known poems, "The Love Song of J. Alfred Prufrock" and "Gerontion," counter the conventions of Romantic poetry in related ways. The celebrated simile at the start of "Prufrock," for instance, in which the evening is compared to "a patient," is an instance of prosopopoeia. As at the end of "Preludes," the figure's Romantic implications are blunted since the patient's "etherised" condition removes mental awareness from the figuration. More obviously than is the case in "Preludes" and "Rhapsody," in the later poems Eliot transforms the conventions of the dramatic monologue. Even though this transformation has been noted by many critics, it is worth emphasizing briefly, since these poems are sometimes still read as examples of the self's discourse within the tradition of the dramatic monologue. They are, on the contrary, examples of the undermining of both that discourse and that tradition. While it is not entirely accurate to say that the dramatic monologue originates with Victorian poets as a reaction against Romantic poetry's emphasis on lyric utterance, the form does become important in the nineteenth century because it provides an alternative to the Romantic lyric. Finding that alternative insufficient, Eliot modifies the dramatic monologue in ways that undercut the impression of a person speaking in a specific scene. He does that in one way by not providing the kind of determinate details about a situation and a person that would enable the reader to link the language readily to a personality or a voice. As Hugh Kenner says of Prufrock, "we have no information about him whatever" (Kenner 35).[1] Some aspects of style in both "Prufrock" and "Gerontion" do give the impression of a voice, but other aspects vitiate that impression in a fashion that differentiates them from Victorian dramatic monologues. Stylistically the poems counter that impression automatically because of the writing's heterogeneity.

Many lines of "Gerontion," including the opening ones, are conversational in character: "Here I am, an old man in a dry month, / Being read to by a boy, waiting for rain" (*CPP* 21). But the poem provides no continuing determinate scene or narrative within which such lines can confidently be placed, though there are sporadic indications of possible scenes and narratives. The relatively disjointed quality of both "Prufrock" and "Gerontion," especially the lack of good continuity between the verse paragraphs, makes it hard to ascribe the language to a speaker, even one who is in the kind of extreme situation mentally or physically that is sometimes portrayed in dramatic monologues. Instead of being located, grounded in a referential way, the language, which is full of dislocations, tends to float; it refuses to be tied to a limiting scene or to a limited meaning. The conversational language is not sustained, for instance, in the lines that follow the opening ones in "Gerontion":

> I was neither at the hot gates
> Nor fought in the warm rain
> Nor knee deep in the salt marsh, heaving a cutlass,
> Bitten by flies, fought.
>
> (*CPP* 21)

We find out where this "I" was not and what it did not do, not where or what it is in any positive sense. The passage gives rise to questions that it does not answer and that are not answered elsewhere in "Gerontion." Stylistically, both the sequence of negatives and the repetition of "fought" at the end of the sentence indicate the composed, written character of the lines rather than the spontaneous utterance of an "I" with a personal voice.

The difficulty of maintaining the illusion of an "I" who speaks becomes greater as "Gerontion" proceeds, for example, in the fifth stanza with its sequence of sentences beginning with the verb "Think," which continues into the next stanza. The sentences may be in the imperative mood. Or the subject of an indicative verb may have been omitted. The grammatical indeterminacy disturbs the statements' coherence in ways that resist resolution. The language pertains not to a character whose name indicates that he is a person but to one who is named artificially. Like a figure in a medieval allegory whose name points to a concept that is abstract and general rather than personal and individual, Gerontion is not a person but one among many possible incarnations of the meaning of his name in Greek, "little old man."

In "Prufrock" there is not as much grammatical disturbance but more indication through rhyme and through repetition of phrases that the language does not represent a conversation or a meditation that might be understood in realistic terms. As Loy D. Martin has suggested, the poem's language represents Prufrock's "inner non-speech" (Martin 234). The impression of something internal, however, as well as the impression of speech, is strongly countered by the language's artificiality. Prufrock's language is not only not necessarily speech, it is also not necessarily internal, as well as not necessarily external. The Popean rhymes, such as "ices" and "crisis" (*CPP* 6), are especially clear indications of the poem's written, constructed character, as are the disjunctions between some of the verse paragraphs. Repeated end rhymes and internal rhymes also give the language a studied quality that marks it as something fabricated, though its artificiality is not that of the poetic conventions Eliot and Pound sought to overturn. The style's obviously crafted rather than ostensibly spontaneous quality is as evident in "Prufrock" as it is in the poems in quatrains Eliot published later along with "Gerontion." In the sixth verse paragraph, for instance, Eliot repeats the end rhymes so frequently that they call attention to themselves despite the irregularity of the verse, especially when he repeats words. In seven lines, there is no alternation in the two rhymes used: dare, stair, hair, thin, chin, pin, thin. The twelve-line stanza also includes the triple repetition of "Do I dare" and the internal rhyming of "decisions and revisions." The style's artificial quality might not be so noticeable in a poem with more narrative continuity to distract the reader from the language's texture. In the context of the relatively discontinuous sequence of the stanzas and together with the ambiguous calling up of a silent listener in the poem's first line, "Prufrock"'s repetitions and other incongruities sometimes create a humorous effect that distinguishes it from its Victorian precursors.

    The complications of "Prufrock" involve from the poem's beginning epigraphs a more direct transformation of the dramatic monologue than does "Gerontion" when the pronouns that "I" uses suggest the presence of an unspecified listener. In many dramatic monologues the listener is also not specified, and the reader is invited to take over the role of listener in a one-sided conversation. In "Prufrock," however, it is not clear whether a real conversation is being dramatically presented, whether the "I" is having an internal colloquy with himself, or whether the reader is being addressed directly. The "you" that is "I"'s counterpart stands in two places at once, both inside and outside Prufrock's mind and inside and outside scenes that can with difficulty be imagined based on the minimal details provided. The reader's situation resembles the position of the viewer of Velásquez's "Las Meninas," in which a mirror invites an identification with the observers of the scene depicted in the painting while the painting's geometry indicates that the illusion of that identification can be sustained only by ignoring obvious details. Reader and viewer stand both inside and outside the frame of an illusion that cannot be sustained.

Two epigraphs from Dante precede and follow the poem's title, one for the entire volume that takes its name from "Prufrock," the other for the poem itself, which stands first in the volume. Together they suggest the oscillation and indeterminacy of Prufrock's position and the reader's. In the first epigraph, Statius mistakes Virgil's shade for a "solid thing" and forgets momentarily what he himself is and can do. In the second, Guido da Montefeltro predicates his address to Dante on the opposite mistake, that Dante is not human and cannot carry his words further. Like Statius and Guido, the reader who tries to pin down the indeterminate identities and locations of "you and I" in the poem will always be mistaken. What is taken for a shade or a figment may be flesh and blood, and what is taken for living flesh may be only a figment in a perpetual instability that marks "Prufrock," like "Rhapsody," as the transforming end of a sequence of poems to which it can be said to belong but some of whose implications it subverts. The subversion occurs largely through the removal of those referential, seemingly stable elements of scene and character that contribute to making the illusion of hearing a personal voice in poetry possible.

Eliot's particular transformation of the dramatic monologue in "Prufrock" depends on the character of the pronouns "you" and "I," which linguists call "shifters" because they are mutually defining and depend for their meanings on the pragmatic context of the discourses in which they occur.[2] Instead of naming something unchanging, these pronouns indicate positions that can be variously occupied. Eliot makes perplexing use of them in some of his best-known poems. In this regard, "Prufrock" is an early anticipation of the Dantesque dialogue of one between the ghost and the poet in "Little Gidding" 2, in which the relation between speaker and listener is one of doubling, oscillation, and, indeterminacy. Though the poems differ substantially, at times both straddle the boundary between monologue and dialogue. In "Little Gidding" the single and the dual voices are taken up into a polylogue because of polyphonic, intertextual qualities of style. As in *The Waste Land*, multiple allusions combined with indeterminate pronoun references create perplexing effects that resist being taken as voice.

Elegy and Revenge, Voice and Writing, Echo and Echolalia in *The Waste Land*

The dissolution of the self is presented in *The Waste Land*, as it is in "Prufrock," through fragmented language and shifting pronoun references. The resulting undermining of voice in the poem is especially marked. Eliot also goes considerably further in *The Waste Land* in subverting nineteenth-century poetic traditions bound up with the determinate, personal self when he transforms the elegy and the lyric as well as the dramatic monologue. Rather than continuing the elegiac tradition in *The Waste Land*, Eliot subverts it. He calls up the vegetation rites that some scholars feel stand behind the structure and the conventions of elegy, but in so doing he creates a background against which his poem's nonelegiac character can be measured. *The Waste Land* challenges the traditions and attitudes of pastoral elegy in its title and in prominent references to Hieronymo, a character from revenge tragedy.

* * *

In *The Waste Land* Eliot specifically evokes writing's potential for undermining voice and self by using styles of speaking and even apparently lyrical language in ways that involve disfiguration and the loss of speech and that reveal the poem's written, constructed, rather than spoken, spontaneous character. The frequent instances of direct address, especially those including apostrophe, emphasize the act of speaking that is a central element of lyric poetry. But the discontinuities created by rapidly changing contexts and by the shifting pronoun references decompose the impression of voice as soon as it is created. Because of the poem's pervasive fragmentation, that impression can even be said to be decomposed before it is created; voice occurs in *The Waste Land* always in the context of writing. The citations and allusions that permeate the poem make it impossible to maintain the illusion of voices speaking as somehow different from writing. Even though apostrophe as a rhetorical device emphasizes the vocal character of language, Eliot counters the vocal effects by embedding them in allusion, as he does also in later poems, such as "Marina"; for example, in the stanza concluding part 1; in the imitation of ragtime songs in part 2, "O O O O," where the O's are also a version of "nothing," which is mentioned one line earlier; in the lines in part 3 from the ballad about Mrs. Porter and her daughter; and in the line quoted right after them from Verlaine's sonnet "Parsifal": "*Et O ces voix d'enfants, chantant dans la coupole!*" (*CPP* 43). Immediately following that citation a counter to the vocative is provided when Philomela's tongueless utterance is reiterated as "jug" six times.

The single apostrophe in *The Waste Land* that seems to be an uncomplicated representation of voice, the one in part 3 beginning "O City city," is only slightly less thoroughly undercut than the other apostrophes because it is longer than they are and appears to contain no citations. It is, in fact, relatively short, only seven lines, and the figuring of the City as a human presence occurs amidst many countering elements in the poem. The citation about music from *The Tempest* that precedes the apostrophe and the highly allusive singing and speaking of the Thames-daughters that follow it provide a context of writing that modifies the vocal effect. The notes also work to undercut the relief suggested in these positive-sounding lines, since the note for line 264 indicates that the Church of Magnus Martyr was likely to be demolished, fated to be defaced and disfigured like much of the rest of the City. As a space, the cavernous interior of the church, its "Inexplicable splendour of Ionian white and gold" (3.265), is more than matched by the "decayed hole" of part 5; its mouthlike space, filled with "white and gold," is placed within the context of various ruined mouths mentioned before and after it.

Because of its quoted, repeated, and ritualized character, like some of the language of *Ash-Wednesday*, the apostrophe to the "Lord" at the conclusion of part 3 creates the impression of group rather than individual utterance. But even that impression is complicated by a truncation that, like the fragmentation of prayer at the end of "The Hollow Men," disrupts the continuities of self and voice. At the end of part 4, the presenting of Phlebas's fate as an exemplum includes a vocative "O you," but this apostrophe asks the listener, a general one rather than an individual, to recognize the fact that everyone who lives will die, in effect, that the fate of everyone is the loss of life and of voice that Phlebas has suffered. "O swallow swallow" at the poem's end works a similar reversal of apostrophe's calling up something living and capable of speech, since, as the note indicates, it alludes to tongueless Philomela's story. The apostrophe is also linked to the allusion to mute Hieronymo, because his line includes a "you" that completes the pattern of "Oh" followed by "you" begun at the end of part 1 and repeated by "O Lord Thou" and "O you" in the conclusions of parts 3 and 4. By the poem's end, apostrophe functions to call up not voice but other texts, other parts of this text, and the physical, though tongueless, production of sounds. In part 5, by means of rhyme and other repetitions of sound, "O" is taken up into a mad, tongueless artist's name, "Hieronymo," into the reiterated no's of the second, third, and sixth stanzas (six occurrences), into the repeated word "only" (seven occurrences), and into the onomatopoeic rendering of a bird's call, not the Romantic nightingale's or even the thrush's but the homely, nonvocal rooster's: "Co co rico co co rico."

The repetition of the long "o" nineteen times in part 5 before the final stanza in "no," "only," and the rooster's call might not be remarkable if repetitions of the sound were not clustered even more insistently in the poem's last verse paragraph. It occurs there at least nine times within five lines: *ascose, foco, Quando,* O swallow swallow, *abolie,*

Hieronymo's. The densest clustering occurs in the line "*Quando fiam uti chelidon*—O swallow swallow" (l. 430), the second half of which involves a multiple chiasmus. It would be tempting to claim that this half-line is exceptional in *The Waste Land* and that it presents a compact instance of multiple chiasmus that is unusual, perhaps unique, in the history of English poetry. Such a claim would be mistaken. The phrase, "maternal lamentation," from the fifth verse paragraph of part 5 (l. 368), for instance, is equally compact and just as complex phonologically. In *The Waste Land*, the unusual and strange become usual.

* * *

The *O* that might represent a whole and the living mouth as source of voice has become in part 5 a hole that is not only empty but mutilated or decayed, and that hole is the context of the poem's whole, the locating of language in a wasted space that in *Ash-Wednesday* is "the hollow round of my skull" (*CPP* 61). In an earlier poem, "Sweeney Erect," that, like part 2 of *The Waste Land* is ekphrastic, Eliot presents the mouth, "This oval O cropped out with teeth" (*CPP* 25), as implicitly a hole in a skull subject to decay. The stanza in which this line occurs alludes to the encounter with the decayed visage of Rousseau in Shelley's "The Triumph of Life":

> That what I thought was an old root which grew
> To strange distortion out of the hill side
> Was indeed one of those deluded crew,
>
> And that the grass, which methought hung so wide
> And white, was but his thin discolored hair,
> And that the holes he vainly sought to hide,
>
> Were or had been eyes. . . .
> (Shelley 367-68, ll. 182-88)

Eliot's mention of "This withered root of knots of hair / Slitted below and gashed with eyes" before the evocation of the mouth includes the word "withered," which occurs prominently in Romantic poetry, for instance, in the opening lines of Shelley's "Epipsychidion" and in Keats's "La Belle Dame Sans Merci." But the word also connects the passage with the depiction of Philomel as one among many "withered stumps of time" (*CPP* 40; *TWL* 2.104). The epigraph at the beginning of "Sweeney Erect" from Beaumont and Fletcher's *The Maid's Tragedy*, in which a mistreated young woman offers herself as the model for a tapestry, reinforces the connection.

The opening lines of "Sweeney Erect" echo the young woman's instructions about how she wishes to be depicted, but Eliot transforms them into instructions for the painting of a landscape:

> Paint me a cavernous waste shore
>   Cast in the unstilled Cyclades,
> Paint me the bold anfractuous rocks
>   Faced by the snarled and yelping seas.

The "cavernous waste" that is also a shore, the rocks, and the snarling are all elements of part 5 of *The Waste Land*, with the snarling transferred from the scene back to the face, though the "red sullen faces" (5.344) are hardly to be taken literally. The phrasing of the instructions is ambiguous, since a preposition has been elided. They mean both "paint for me" this particular scene and "paint me as" this scene. At the end of *The Waste Land*, Eliot follows the instructions and depicts the landscape as a "cavernous waste" that is also the "oval O" of a decayed mouth. The ruined mouths of Philomel, Hieronymo, and Lil—whose problems include not only disfigured looks because of decayed teeth but the debilitating effects of an aborted pregnancy, the removal of a part—are all merged in the dry hole among the rock, "Dead mountain mouth of carious teeth that cannot spit" (l. 339), that is one ultimate form the wasted landscape takes. This "decayed hole among the mountains," with its "empty chapel, only the wind's home," is the mouth as decrepit orifice, inlet and outlet for air. It is the future condition that every mouth and every church, including "Magnus Martyr," ultimately reaches. It is the incongruous, terrifying decayed opposite of Magnus Martyr's "Inexplicable splendour of Ionian white and gold," understood both as paint with gilding and as tooth enamel surrounded by the metal of a repair that cannot be permanent. No lyric, personal, elegiac utterance is possible from such a mouth or in such an unpastoral landscape filled with faces that "sneer and snarl," but murmurs, echoes, and reverberations, as of hollow vessels, are.

From "Echoes and Reverberations, Preludes and Mortality Odes: Antielegiac Stanzas and Fragmented Monologues," *Harmony of Dissonances: T. S. Eliot, Romanticism, and Imagination* (Baltimore: The Johns Hopkins University Press, 1990): 150-160; 181-182; 188-189. Copyright © 1990, The Johns Hopkins University Press. Reprinted with permission of The Johns Hopkins University Press.

Notes

Editor's note: Several substantial notes have been omitted from this reprinting.

1. C. K. Stead agrees that in "Prufrock" "nothing is certain" (Stead, *Pound* 43). In general, Stead's readings of Eliot's poems before *The Waste Land* in this volume support the positions I take with regard to them. His emphasis on the importance of sound is salutary and convincing.

2. The classic study in this regard is Emile Benveniste's *Problèmes de linguistique générale* (Paris: Gallimard, 1966), especially "Structure des relations de personne dans le verbe" (225-36), "La nature des pronoms" (251-57), and "De la subjectivité dans le langage" (258-66). The volume is available in English as *Problems in General Linguistics*, trans. Mary Elizabeth Meek (Coral Gables: University of Miami Press, 1971).

Works Cited

Kenner, Hugh. *The Invisible Poet: T. S. Eliot*. 1960; rept. London: Methuen, 1966.
Martin, Loy D. *Browning's Dramatic Monologues and the Post-Romantic Subject*. Baltimore: Johns Hopkins University Press, 1985.
Stead, C. K. *Pound, Yeats, Eliot and the Modernist Movement*. New Brunswick, N.J.: Rutgers University Press, 1986.

"Unknown terror and mystery":
The Waste Land

Ronald Bush

Ronald Bush provides a reading of *The Waste Land* stressing emotional turbulence that carefully marshals a great deal of biographical detail as part of its commentary on the poem's language, structure, composition, and implications. He does so in part to bring out an immediacy of emotion that he feels other critics have slighted. The power of his reading is less in the biographically speculative comments on passages, which Eliot would have discouraged, than in his compelling evocation of the poem's nightmarish, gothic qualities. He identifies a nightmare pattern in the poem's heterogeneous materials, involving a starkly ambivalent, vividly evoked situation mixing fear and desire that is blocked and transformed in its attempt to reach a climax. The emphasis on nightmare helps to bring out Eliot's affinities with Poe, with French Symbolist writing of the nineteenth century, and with the avant-garde Dada and surrealist tradition of his own time. Bush suggests from the beginning, with an epigraph from Eliot, that rational analysis is not able to dispel the enigma and fear that are central to the poem and to its coming into being. On one hand, Bush has restored a speaker who provides unity to a highly textualized, fragmented, elliptical poem whose sequence appears to be nonlinear, definitely not the continuous sequence of the speaking voice. On the other, Bush is careful always to qualify the notion of *speaker* by reminding us that the language comes from a deeper source than normal speech. He draws helpfully on the manuscript materials for *The Waste Land* published by Eliot's literary executor, his second wife, Valerie Eliot, after Eliot's death. Bush suggestively explains the poem's allusive procedures as in part an ironic strategy for simultaneously drawing on literature as a resource and projecting a self-conscious awareness of literature's limits for dispelling the nightmare. He organizes his reading around two central moments, the scene in the Hyacinth garden in part one and the water dripping song of the hermit thrush in part five, which he discusses respectively in his essay's first and third sections. In the second section, he turns to the work of a psychiatrist who has written about Eliot to bring out the negative character of creativity, by contrast with conventional (and Romantic) notions of positive inspiration. Introducing Eliot's influential concept of the *mythical method*, Bush suggests that the mythical patterning of the poem's details were not part of its gestation. In his essay's first section, Bush compares the hyacinth girl to other important moments in Eliot's poetry and drama. In his essay's third section, he focuses on the emergence of what Eliot called the *auditory imagination* to assert that the music and incantation of part five of *The Waste Land* point forward to Eliot's later poetry and to an ultimate movement beyond the unforgettable memorable nightmare of his most famous poem. The Eliot who in 1948 is critical of Edgar Allan Poe in a major essay is not the same Eliot who wrote *The Waste Land* more than a quarter of a century earlier.

. . . He kept her, as they circulated, from being waylaid, even remarking to her afresh as he had often done before, on the help rendered in such situations by the intrinsic oddity of the London "squash," a thing of vague, slow, senseless eddies, revolving as in fear of some menace of conversation suspended over it, the drop of which, with some consequent refreshing splash or spatter, yet never took place. (Henry James, *The Golden Bowl*)

The idea is to take something familiar, something to which people have emotional associations, and change it enough to make it alien. The most difficult thing of all is to get the ambiences, the cold crispness of Hoth, the swampiness of Dagobah. For Dagobah, I slowed down and used many gull, tern and shorebird sounds, along with sea lions, dolphins and the pump at a water-treatment plant, sounds that kept things low-pitched, croaking, slithering. (Benn Burtt, sound effects expert for *Star Wars*, *New York Times*, June 9, 1980.)

Because the material [of the psychoanalytic novel] is so clearly defined . . . there is no possibility [in it] of tapping the atmosphere of unknown terror and mystery in which our life is passed and which psychoanalysis has not yet analysed. (T. S. Eliot, "London Letter," *The Dial*, September 1922)

From the summer of 1915, when Eliot married Vivien Haigh-Wood and decided for England and a life of poetry, his "inner world of nightmare" had all too many correspondences with the world of outer events. In a gesture of surrender, hoping to overcome his chronic detachment from life, Eliot had in two months courted and wed the sometime governess, sometime painter, sometime ballerina he first met at an Oxford punting party. Yet there was hardly a time when his high-strung and sickly wife was not a problem. And when his parents, who disapproved of the emotional and financial demands Vivien made upon Eliot, summoned him home and threatened to cut off his support (they later half relented), the problems were compounded. The Eliots lived for a while with Bertrand Russell, without whose financial help they could not have gone on. Eliot taught grammar school, but hated it because preparation for teaching invaded even his sleep. He secured a job with Lloyd's bank, but spent almost as much time preparing extension school lectures and working on occasional essays. And he drove himself unmercifully trying to produce the literature that would justify his rebellious behavior and satisfy all "that I have not made a mess of my life."[1] But the more he drove himself, the less he produced. He wrote nothing good enough to publish between mid-1915 and mid-1917, and then after the period of the quatrain poems and "Gerontion" again nothing between summer 1919 and summer 1921.

Almost as soon as they married, Vivien Eliot, who Bertrand Russell said showed "impulses of . . . a Dostojevsky type of cruelty"—she "lives on a knife-edge, and will end as a criminal or a saint"[2]—exacerbated all the internal dissonance Eliot had addressed in his early poetry. At first charmed by Vivien's combination of acute sensitivity and unashamed brashness, Eliot quickly saw it turned against himself. Vivien held him to standards of emotional forthrightness he wished to but could not sustain. According to Lyndall Gordon, there was a "disastrous 'pseudo-honeymoon' at Eastbourne," with Vivien "not far from suicide." Then came the parties at which Vivien, feeling Eliot's disapproval of her lack of restraint, either exaggerated her behavior or publicly accused him of hypocrisy. Just a month after their marriage, Russell watched their *danse macabre* and wrote,

> She is light, a little vulgar, adventurous, full of life—an artist I think he said, but I should have thought her an actress. He is exquisite and listless; she says she married him to stimulate him, but finds she can't do it. Obviously he married in order to be stimulated. I think she will soon be tired of him. She refuses to go to America to see his people, for fear of submarines. He is ashamed of his marriage, and very grateful if one is kind to her. He is the Miss Sands type of American.[3]

Vivien complicated everything. She forced Eliot to quarrel with his parents just when he was feeling anxious over his foreign escape. And she reinforced many of the intricacies of his troubled identity. Like his mother she seemed to adore him in one moment and question his strongest impulses in the next. But Vivien's sarcasm was directed against Eliot's New England self and not its emotional antagonist. The tangled result was that her disapproval was soon compounded with his mother's, threatening both parts of Eliot's delicate equilibrium. Eventually she must have appeared both his just punishment and the very image of the authority he had transgressed. In one vein of his poetry her eyes are telescoped with his mother's, leading to the transformation of Prufrock's "eyes that fix you in a formulated phrase" into *The Hollow Men's* "eyes I dare not meet in dreams." Little wonder that in *The Waste Land*, "the awful daring of a moment's [sexual] surrender" generates feelings of "a broken Coriolanus."

In January 1919, before Eliot and his father had a chance to reconcile, his father died. According to Vivien's diary his reaction was "most terrible."[4] Soon after, he wrote, "This does not weaken the need for a book at all—it really reinforces it—my mother is still alive. . . . a great deal hangs on it for me."[5] In December Eliot mentioned wanting to get started on "a long poem I have had on my mind," and in February he wrote his brother Henry, "I am thinking all the time of my desire to see [mother]. I cannot get away from it. Unless I can really *see* her again I shall never be happy."[6] Just before his mother came with his sister and brother to visit him Eliot began work on his long poem, but her visit stopped him cold. She did not get along with Vivien, whom Eliot whisked away to the country whenever he could. She also had lost none of the force of her New England ideals (she proved "terrifyingly energetic"), and when she left England Eliot, who had passionately desired not confrontation but reassurance and approval, felt once again a failure. By September he was weak and ill, and wrote that he felt extremely "shaky, and seem to have gone down rapidly since my family left."[7] That was when Lloyd's bank gave him leave. In October, attacked by depression, indecisiveness and fear of psychosis, he went alone to Margate for a rest-cure. There, building on fragments he had been collecting since he came to London, he wrote part of *The Waste Land*. According to Valerie Eliot he returned from Margate on November 12, and set out with Vivien on the eighteenth for Paris, where he left Vivien in Pound's care. He then went to Lausanne, where he would place himself in the hands of a Dr. Vittoz and complete the first draft of his poem.[8]

Many times during this period Eliot sensed he was trapped in a bad dream. In 1916 he distinguished his London from his Harvard life by telling Conrad Aiken the latter now seemed "a *dull* nightmare."[9] London with Vivien was anything but dull, and Eliot's confessions to John Quinn in 1922 make it clear that it was difficult for him to dissociate the nightmare within and the nightmare without: he told Quinn that whenever he got tired or worried, he recognized the old symptoms ready to appear, and that he found himself under the strain of trying to suppress a vague but intensely acute horror and apprehension. Perhaps the greatest curse of his life, he said, was the associations imagination suggested with various noises. He could not abide living in a town flat, therefore, because he could never forget the lives and disagreeable personalities of his neighbors.[10]

Eliot's horror and apprehension, his obsession with neighbors' noises and his inflamed perception of noise in general all manifest themselves in the poem he wrote. *The Waste Land* would rehearse some of Eliot's most painful experiences and finger psychological knots that he could not consciously consider. But anxiety blocked him in the fall of 1921, and Conrad Aiken tells us that "although every evening he went home to his flat hoping that he could start writing again, and with every confidence that the material was *there* and waiting, night after night the hope proved illusory: the sharpened pencil lay unused by the untouched sheet of paper."[11] Eliot, however, had to write. He would later gloss Housman's comment, "I have seldom written poetry unless I was rather out of health" with the statement that it revealed "authentic processes of a real poet. . . . I understand that sentence."[12] Poetry was the way he explored and exorcised his discomfort, and in 1921 the burdens of his demon ("[the lyric poet] is haunted by a demon . . . and the words, the poem he makes, are a kind of form of exorcism of this demon")[13] were the worst he had ever known. A memory of the therapeutic effects of composition sent him to his sharpened pencils night after night, and his preoccupation with emotional sincerity, recently honed on the maxims of Rémy de Gourmont, insisted that he confront his demon honestly. Though the poem he was about to write, like his earlier poems, would distance his suffering by raising a moral framework around the demon (that was part of the therapeutic magic), this time the demon would be stronger than the scaffold. Dante's "ordered scale of human emotions" (SW, 168) was very much on Eliot's mind in 1921, as was the indirect mythic presentation of moral states; but even more pressing was a desire to dredge up what he really was and felt.

On the evidence of the manuscripts collected by Valerie Eliot, "The Fire Sermon" was the first full movement of *The Waste Land* Eliot attempted.[14] Out of the fragments he had been collecting since 1914, at Margate Eliot chose a passage already several years old as a starting point:

> London, the swarming life you kill and breed,
> Huddled between the concrete and the sky,
> Responsive to the momentary need,
> Vibrates unconscious to its formal destiny,
>
> Knowing neither how to think, nor how to feel,
> But lives in the awareness of the observing eye.
> Phantasmal gnomes, burrowing in brick and stone and steel!
> Some minds, aberrant from the normal equipoise
> (London, your people is bound upon the wheel!)
> Record the motions of these pavement toys
> And trace the cryptograms that may be curled
> Within these faint perceptions of the noise
> Of the movement, and the lights![15]

This is a programmatic statement, an announcement that at least "The Fire Sermon" would consist of a hypersensitive record of two things—London's teeming crowds and the "cryptogram" of significance curled around them.[16] Eliot's portraits would be the stuff of journalism, his method spiritual analysis, his manner nightmare-gothic, and his emotional subject the emptiness of lives bound upon the wheel of passion and misdirected by the values of the modern city.

That was the program, but the way Eliot phrased it would not do. (Pound later dismissed it with a slash of red ink and a disgusted "B—S.").[17] To conform to the standards Eliot and Pound had been enunciating for several years, Eliot's theme would have to be embodied in comment-free dramatic vignettes. And when Eliot finally conjured these vignettes out of the air, his program fell away and his writing was in the power of his demon. Heeding advice he had recently given others ("the bad poet is usually unconscious where he ought to be conscious, and conscious where he ought to be unconscious. Both errors tend to make him 'personal' "),[18] Eliot seized on images and impressions that had struck his imagination and did not belabor their moral significance.[19] Beginning with "The Fire Sermon," he drew on memories of London formed during the preceding summer, when his attention was sharpened to visionary intensity by the presence of his mother;[20] on scenes from his own life, particularly from his life with Vivien;[21] and on the horrible noises and the disagreeable neighbors he complained of to John Quinn.[22] Through all of these, like wine through water, ran the nightmarish emotional charge of Eliot's vague but intensely acute horror and apprehension of the "unknown terror and mystery in which our life is passed." As Eliot said about Jonson's plays, that was enough to give the fragments a "dominant tone," a "unity of inspiration that radiates into plot and personages alike."[23] What he had sensed at the very bottom of Jonson's constructions became the primary—almost the only—unity of his own poem. To appropriate Richard Poirier on a famous collection of popular songs, the fragments "emanated from some inwardly felt coherence that awaited a merely explicit design, and they would ask to be heard together even without the design."[24]

Some of Eliot's *images trouvailles* were drawn from actual nightmares. When Bertrand Russell, for example, told him about a hallucination Russell had that London Bridge would collapse and sink and the whole great city would "vanish like a morning mist,"[25] Eliot suffused it with the energy of a nursery rhyme gone mad and made it the keynote of his finale. Other images drew on literary nightmares, or combinations of literature and fact, but were no less imaginatively transformed. Out of his recollections of the murdered young women in Dostoyevsky's *Crime and Punishment* and *The Idiot* (and of an actual incident of a man murdering his mistress),[26] Eliot created yet another poetic sequence about the mangling of "La Figlia Che Piange." Participating in the sense of emotional strangulation that suffuses that early poem, the betrayed women in *The Waste Land* also absorb the complex ambivalence associated in Eliot's mind with Vivien. These women anticipate Harry's murdered wife in *The Family Reunion* and Sweeney's murdered neighbor in *Sweeney Agonistes*. They are also the immediate successors of the girl in Eliot's abandoned long poem of the mid-teens, "The Love Song of St. Sebastian," who was strangled by her neophyte-lover between his bleeding knees.[27] Unlike "St. Sebastian," which was to have one strangling episode as centerpiece, *The Waste Land* has many, all brief (some, like "Philomela," nearly invisible). Together they provide an undercurrent to the poem, dominating it the way a buried incident that is too terrifying to confront dominates a nightmare and occasionally breaks its surface. As Hugh Kenner observed many years ago, this buried sequence ties together a number of guilty protagonists and a long list of potential or real corpses: the hyacinth girl, Ophelia, "that corpse you planted last year in your garden," "bones cast in a little low dry garret," and so on.[28]

The subject of *The Waste Land*'s literary borrowings, now that it has been raised, commands a moment's reflection. It should be clear by now that contrary to the assumptions of generations of readers, for Eliot literary borrowings were more appropriations of other people's feelings than tools for ironic comment. He once put it this way: "Immature poets imitate; mature poets steal; bad poets deface what they take, and good poets make it into something better, or at least something different. The good poet welds his theft into a whole of feeling which is unique, utterly different from that from which it was torn" (SW, 125). In *The Waste Land* as elsewhere in his writings, images borrowed from other writers serve the same purpose as images found in everyday life—they provide nuggets of the objective world charged with feelings and untarnished by the deadening, conventional rhetoric of Eliot's personal will. They are thus uncontaminated by the acquired self, rooted in what lies below it and good fodder for a new "whole of feeling." Hence the presence in *The Waste Land* of Ovid's sweet-singing nightingale or Shakespeare's intensely mourned Ophelia.

But there is another way that the literature of the past makes itself felt in *The Waste Land*, a way that also has nothing to do with allusion as we normally think of it. We have seen that in poems like "Burbank with a Baedeker," the resonant poetry of the past is likely to become simply the rhetoric of the present. In *The Waste Land* Eliot's pervasive speaker—if one may use the word "speaker" to describe a vehicle for the "dominant tone" of subconscious feeling—is intensely aware of the literaryness, the rhetorical quality, of his utterance. Much of the poem's poetic sophistication comes from this self-consciousness, which is the enormously subtle dramatization of Eliot reacting against his own inherited disposition to rhetoric.[29] As in not only Eliot's own experience but the fictional lives of Prufrock and Gerontion, one of the terrors of the speaker of *The Waste Land* is that he has forfeited life to books, and is trapped in ways of thinking and feeling acquired through convention. To use Eliot's bitter phrases, his emotional life is a terminal victim of "the pathology of rhetoric" and the "pastness of the past." And so in a sequence like the opening of "The Fire Sermon"—one of the finest and most terrifying passages of the poem—the other horrors of Eliot's nightmare are compounded by a self-consciousness that shadows every attempted escape from an isolated emptiness into the imaginative richness of poetry. In a passage like the following, every allusion has implied quotation marks around it and so renders a self-consciousness on the part of the speaker as much as it alludes to something outside the poem. (Where else in our poetry can a poem like Verlaine's "Parsifal" be sounded—a wondrously passionate poem considered by itself—and yet be charged with the coldness of irony simply by the context of its new surroundings? In "*Et O ces voix d'enfants*" Verlaine expressed indescribable aspiration; here the short line expresses that and also an ironic awareness that poetry is only literature, and to quote poetry is less to relieve genuine feeling than to succumb to monkish temptation.)

> The river's tent is broken: the last fingers of leaf
> Clutch and sink into the wet bank. The wind

Crosses the brown land, unheard. The nymphs are departed.
Sweet Thames, run softly, till I end my song.
The river bears no empty bottles, sandwich papers,
Silk handkerchiefs, cardboard boxes, cigarette ends
Or other testimony of summer nights. The nymphs are departed.
And their friends, the loitering heirs of city directors;
Departed, have left no addresses.
By the waters of Leman I sat down and wept . . .
Sweet Thames, run softly till I end my song,
Sweet Thames, run softly, for I speak not loud or long.
But at my back in a cold blast I hear
The rattle of the bones, and chuckle spread from ear to ear.
A rat crept softly through the vegetation
Dragging its slimy belly on the bank
While I was fishing in the dull canal
On a winter evening round behind the gashouse
Musing upon the king my brother's wreck
And on the king my father's death before him.
White bodies naked on the low damp ground
And bones cast in a little low dry garret,
Rattled by the rat's foot only, year to year.
But at my back from time to time I hear
The sound of horns and motors, which shall bring
Sweeney to Mrs. Porter in the spring.
O the moon shone bright on Mrs. Porter
And on her daughter
They wash their feet in soda water
Et O ces voix d'enfants, chantant dans la coupole!

Below the level of allusion, the passage presents the characteristic emotions of *The Waste Land*. Melancholy, loss, isolation and fear of a meaningless death adhere to "impersonal" objects in a "world" of awareness. The elements of this world arise from observation and memory (sometimes literary), and they strike us as complex sensations that have not been homogenized into a univalent pattern—a nameable feeling. But behind the pieces we sense an emotional logic that is "constantly amalgamating" (SE, 247) fragments into a single vision, and we are drawn into the poem's "point of view." Once we have given ourselves over to the emotional pressure of the poem we accept its coherence as we would accept the sequence of events in a dream, where objects quite often have an order, an emotional charge and a significance very different from the ones they have in waking consciousness. (Think of how often, for example, familiar people or objects terrify us in a nightmare when the same images in our sight or in our daydreams would not make us think twice.)

The opening movement of "The Fire Sermon" is "Hell" as Edward describes it in *The Cocktail Party*:

> What is hell? Hell is oneself,
> Hell is alone, the other figures in it
> *Merely projections.*[30]

It takes its dominant tone from a series of surrealistic images in which subconscious anxiety, as in a bad dream or a psychotic delusion, is projected onto human and non-human objects. Harry, in *The Family Reunion*, describes it this way:

> I could not fit myself together:
> When I was inside the old dream, I felt all the same emotion
> Or lack of emotion, as before: the same loathing
> Diffused, I not a person, in a world not of persons
> But only of contaminating presences.
>
> (CPP, 272)

But what Harry describes, the opening of "The Fire Sermon" presents. In it, emotional fantasies, sometimes of self-loathing, extend through a series of unconnected images in a medium where ego-integration seems to be non-existent. In synechdochic progression, a river, falling leaves, the brown land, bones, a rat, Ferdinand, his brother and his father, Mrs. Porter and her daughter all become extensions of a whole (but not continuous) state of anxiety. Eliot's speaker (if—again—one can use that noun in a case where utterance seems to come from below the level of ordinary speech), projects his feelings of isolation, vanished protection and loss first onto the river, whose tent of leaves is "broken" (the inappropriately violent adjective emphasizes the feeling of grief behind the loss), and then onto the falling leaves, which animistically have fingers that "clutch" for support as they sink into decomposition and oblivion. Then defenselessness becomes a shrinking from attack as the leaves fade into the brown land, "crossed" by the wind. (Ten lines later the crossing wind will become a "cold blast" rattling sensitive bones and, metamorphosed, the insubstantial malevolence of a "chuckle spread from ear to ear.") Still later, after an interlude of deep-seated loss, isolation turns into self-disgust as the "speaker" projects himself into a rat with a human belly creeping softly and loathsomely through the vegetation. (Both rat and vegetation are extensions of the decomposing leaves.) And as this horrified fascination with the process of decomposition increases, the rat's living body merges with a corpse's and the "speaker" apprehends himself first as rotting and sodden flesh, feeling "naked on the low damp ground," and then as dry bones, rattled by the rat's foot as he was rattled before by the cold wind. (In a nightmare one can be both rat and bones.)

In the conclusion of the passage, the threatening vital force which had been apprehended as the wind's blast reasserts itself as raucous sound and the impinging moon, and the poem reacts once again with revulsion, now animating the behavior of Mrs. Porter and her daughter, who insulate themselves in a vivid but ineffective gesture. (According to the bawdier versions of a popular ballad, their "feet" are a euphemism and the soda water is a prophylactic douche; one does not need to know that to feel the compulsive defensiveness in their unexplained washing.)

There is more. The opening of "The Fire Sermon" is not simply an English version of the kind of French poetry that uses symbols to express the ambivalence of the subconscious mind. Eliot's poetry is self-dramatizing. In the way it echoes literature of the past and in its self-conscious use of elevated or colloquial language, it dramatizes a Prufrockian sensibility with a subtlety unavailable to the Eliot of 1911. In the passage we are considering, this sensibility is caught between two double binds: a yearning for the vitality of common life combined with a revulsion from its vulgarity; and an inclination toward poetry combined with a horror of literature. This vacillation, superimposed over the poetry's *progression d'effets*, brings the world of unconscious impulse into contact with the humanized world of language. In "The Fire Sermon" *this* drama begins as the literary word "nymphs" emerges from a series of more or less pure images. As it unfolds, the phrase "the nymphs are departed" suggests Eliot's desire to recuperate his lost sense of fullness in a world of pastoral poetry, and for a moment Eliot appropriates Spenser's voice. "Sweet Thames, run softly, till I end my song." The immediate result is a disgust with modern life worthy of Burbank. Hence the following three lines, where that disgust can be heard in a series of jolting colloquialisms. But both Eliot's poetic nostalgia and his disgust with the quotidian soften in the ninth line: there is a real sorrow in the speaker's statement that the "nymphs" and their vulgar friends have deserted him, a sorrow sounded in the repetition of "departed" twice in two lines. When the speaker reassumes the linguistic personae of the past in the *glissando* of the next three lines, therefore, it strikes us as a gesture taken *faute de mieux*. That is, we sense by this point that Eliot's speaker already has some awareness that the great phrases of the past are as unreal as they are beautiful. As his reminiscence (shall we call it memory?) of Spenser's "Prothalamion" sounds, we detect a note of self-consciousness in the nostalgia, as if the voice inhabiting the lines were feeling its own inauthenticity. When yet a third quotation is added to the

Psalms and to Spenser, this discomfort, which stems from an awareness of the inadequacy of rhetoric to sustain true feeling or ward off grief, explodes in mid-flight. "But at my back," the speaker begins, and we expect to hear the rest of Marvell's immortal lines: "But at my back I always hear / Time's winged chariot hurrying near." Instead, the feeling of desolation which had called up the line swells out into bitterness: even the cherished texts of the past cannot charm away the bleak realities of life. To pretend that they can is a fraud. In Keats's "Ode to a Nightingale," this chilling realization generates yet two more sublime verses: "Adieu! the fancy cannot cheat so well/As she is famed to do, deceiving elf." In *The Waste Land*, the same realization shatters Eliot's poetic continuity, and causes him to interrupt Marvell's lines with a sardonic assertion of the primacy of the here and now:

> But at my back in a cold blast I hear
> The rattle of the bones, and chuckle spread from ear to ear.

Unlike Burbank then, this speaker is aware of the pathology of his rhetoric; all his literary utterances remind him of it. No sooner does he begin to transfigure the death of his father with it in the language of *The Tempest*, than he rebukes himself with an unidealized image of death. The image is close to pure terror; it is his own death as well as his father's that obsesses him:

> While I was fishing in the dull canal
> On a winter evening round behind the gashouse
> Musing upon the king my brother's wreck
> And on the king my father's death before him.
> White bodies on the low damp ground. . . .

The same pattern repeats itself three lines later, only this time the sequence has become more agitated:

> But at my back from time to time I hear
> The sound of horns and motors, which shall bring
> Sweeney to Mrs. Porter in the spring.

This tune is not Spenserian, and its leering swell mocks the legendary powers of music itself. Finally, the last line combines the highest reaches of expressive eloquence with an icy rejection of eloquence itself: "*Et O ces voix d'enfants, chantant dans la coupole!*" Oh those voices. Oh those children's voices.

In passages like this one, then, the anxiety we feel has two sources: a sequence of anxiety-charged images and the increasingly agitated self-laceration of a speaker conscious of his own rhetorical bent. Fueling both is a terrified awareness of death and a near-desperate sense that there is no escape from it. The pattern, moreover, resembles a certain kind of nightmare: a situation both desired and feared arises. Then, fueled by underlying desire, the situation develops. Meanwhile a dream censor is trying to suppress the clarity of the situation and terminates the sequence before the significance of a briefly glimpsed climax can be elaborated.

This configuration describes a great many of the separate vignettes that make up the first three movements of *The Waste Land*. What connects them is precisely what connects the disparate segments of our most distressing dreams. When we do not wake up after our first approach to a piece of heavily charged psychic material, we quite often play out the same pattern in situations that have different manifest elements but draw on the same body of latent content. That is, when the dream censor is able to agitate and then shatter a fantasy that gets too close to some forbidden truth, the forces that initiated the fantasy start the whole struggle again. In each segment, the same impulses reappear veiled in different objects or personae, unifying them from below. A dramatic situation emerges, intensifies mysteriously, reverberates with frightening tension and then, just before the situation is clarified, disperses; then a new situation arises that seems comfortingly different but is in fact the same anew.[31]

I use the analogy of nightmare here with premeditation, but also with some diffidence. There are, of course, other, more subtle, ways of making sense of the tensions, the dramatic unity and the emotional progression of the first three movements of *The Waste Land*, and the best of them use a vocabulary generated to describe related examples of post-romantic poetry.[32] Yet, dealing with a poem whose emotional immediacy has been slighted for so many years, I think it is of real use to apply an analogy drawn from common experience. And I would point out that the analogy is sanctioned by Eliot's own prose.

"The Burial of the Dead" begins as a voice remarks on the cruelty of "Memory and desire." Then, transformed, these feelings are absorbed in a dramatization. But the woman in the dramatization seems unconscious of the desire that conjured her up. We know of it by inference, from the particulars of her vision. She is oblivious to it, and she is just as oblivious to her own anxieties. We read them from the defensive stance of her protestations: why, we must guess, is she so eager not to be identified as Russian? Her interjection, apparently meaningless, is, in Eliot's words, a "tremendous statement, like statements made in our dreams" (SW, 148).

Her appearance in the dream, however, comes to an abrupt end. There is something, apparently, she is afraid to face: "In the mountains, *there* you feel free." Apparently, *here* you do not. Why? Her non sequitur in the next line does not tell us, although it speaks of her uneasiness. But before her uneasiness is allowed to grow the scene is over. It is Marie's evasion that leads to the next verse paragraph, which vibrates with a terror of what cannot be evaded even as we ask ourselves what it has to do with the story we have just heard. The paragraph ends, moreover, with a line (Eliot stole it from "Meditation IV" in Donne's *Devotions*) that represents a threshold over which the poem's voice cannot step: "I will show you fear in a handful of dust."

The next three scenes repeat a sequence the first verse paragraph began: the desolation latent in *Oed' und leer das Meer* is profound enough to foreclose further examination, and the latent content of the thing "One must be so careful [of] these days" is too threatening to name. Finally, in a conclusion that resembles the end of a nightmare sequence, the narrative becomes so agitated it cannot continue, and is shattered by an unexpected incident and a feverish inquisition. Without warning an unexplained encounter verges on some kind of recognition ("There I saw one I knew, and stopped him, crying, 'Stetson!'"), then explodes. There follow three hysterical questions, two lines of reverberating prophesy and then, from out of nowhere, Baudelaire's "You! hypocrite lecteur!"—a fragment which, in context, confronts us like the menacing ravings of a lunatic. Whatever charges Eliot's memory and desire from below has come so close to the surface that the sequence can no longer contain it, and so disintegrates.

At the center of "The Burial of the Dead," and at the center of the nightmare of *The Waste Land*, lies the episode of the Hyacinth garden. Like Marie's summer memory, the episode begins on the note of romantic desire, this time with full-throated song, slightly melancholy, but rising to an unqualified yearning to have the romance of the past restored. Wagner's lyric acts as an epigraph to the drama that follows. As the German suggests a love lost and remembered, the girl who now appears before the speaker recalls a luminous moment when love *renamed* her, and made her part of the spring: "They called me the hyacinth girl." As in "La Figlia," the girl's condition mirrors the speaker's own emotional life, caught for a second in one of its infrequent blossomings. But his moment of self-transcendence—transcending himself through love and transcending his always hollow-sounding voice through images—fades. His qualification "Yet" suggests he is again conscious of himself, and places us at the center of one of Eliot's recurrent obsessions. If his speaker can sustain his love into eternity, if this moment can be made the foundation of a set of permanent values, then his emotional self will have been validated and the warnings of his acquired self will be proved worthless. If, however, the moment cannot be sustained, if the promise of love turns out to be illusory and "the awful separation between potential passion and any actualization possible in life"[33] is as real as he suspected, then the worst of his fears will have been realized, and he will be trapped forever in an emotional waste land where "eyes fix you in a formulated phrase."

What then transpires can only be suggested by a reading alive to the way Eliot's poetry renders small movements of the heart. Eliot's speaker tries to prolong his memory and the feelings attached to it, and we hear his feeling swell in two pronounced spondees: "Your arms full, and your hair wet." But a second caesura introduces the plaintive words "I could not":

> I could not
> Speak and my eyes failed, I was neither
> Living nor dead, and I knew nothing,
> Looking into the heart of light, the silence.
> *Oed' und leer das Meer.*

Could he not speak because speech had been transcended or because the limitation of speech prevented him from fulfilling the moment? Did his eyes fail because he experienced what was beyond vision or because sight prevented him from the vision that he sought? Did he know nothing because worldly knowledge had fallen away or because he understood the nothing that is the ultimate truth? We would need to answer all of these questions if the speaker's statements were not given in the past tense. Since they are, it is clear that the questions they imply are his as much as ours. Looking back at his moment in the garden, the speaker ponders the issues on which his life turns. He has reached a moment like the one Celia describes in *The Cocktail Party*:

> I have thought at moments that the ecstacy is real
> Although those who experience it may have no reality.
> For what happened is remembered like a dream
> In which one is exalted by intensity of loving
> In the spirit, a vibration of delight
> Without desire, for desire is fulfilled

> In the delight of loving. A state one does not know
> When awake. But what, or whom I loved,
> Or what in me was loving, I do not know.
> And if that is all meaningless, I want to be cured
> Of a craving for something I cannot find
> And of the shame of never finding it.
>
> (CPP, 363)

In the Hyacinth garden episode, Eliot dramatizes both Celia's "dream" and her wondering afterwards "if that is all meaningless." Reliving his failure to speak, to see, to know, the voice of *The Waste Land* gives us the agonized speculation of a man asking ultimate questions and being unable—or afraid—to answer. And since the sequence itself not only contains a dream but enacts one, this speculation swells out into another "tremendous statement," cast in a timeless present participle and balanced between the possibilities of nihilism and a mystic vision. Is he "looking into the heart of light" or the "silence"? As Celia puts it,

> Can we only love
> Something created by our own imagination?
> Are we all in fact unloving and unlovable?
> Then one is alone, and if one is alone
> Then lover and beloved are equally unreal
> And the dreamer is no more real than his dreams.
>
> (CPP, 362)

These questions, wrung out of Eliot by the most rigorous discipline of honesty, hang over the first three sections of *The Waste Land* as the "menace of conversation" hangs over James's party in the epigraph to this chapter. They appear to represent Eliot's deepest fears: that we are alone, that what seems our most authentic emotional life is an illusion, that we are consequently worthless, and that reality itself is meaningless.

The Waste Land itself returns continually to that moment and those questions, as if to some feared truth which its speakers would do anything to avoid and yet are doomed to confront. As with a criminal returning to the scene of his crime (a murdered girl, a buried life), all things lead to that. And along the way of this compulsive, nightmarish vacillation, every instrument of answering the doubts, of testing the truth, is itself questioned. Nothing, not the authority of history or of literature or of language itself is allowed to go unsuspected in this horrified interrogation of the moment in the garden. History may be lies, literature may be rhetoric, memory may be illusion, the rambling self may be but an artificial construct, sensation may be hallucination, even language may be a "natural sin."[34] And—uncannily—at the center of this nightmarish questioning stands the figure of Tiresias. How many of Eliot's readers have noticed that the figure he affixed to his disembodied narrator, the figure who unites all the dream's men and all the dream's women, is also at the center of Freud's archetypal myth of the tormented human psyche turned back against itself—the Oedipus myth?[35]

2

One has only to compare the dramatic concentration of the Hyacinth garden episode with Eliot's exploration of the same anxieties in "La Figlia Che Piange" to realize the power of *The Waste Land*. The psychic material once distanced with the aid of Laforguian irony and later with the comic disproportions of the quatrain poems is now isolated and exposed. What had made the earlier poems compelling was the uneasiness that pervaded their formal polish. Deft as they were, and as much as they claimed to be the accounts of an outsider, a double anxiety persistently filled the distance between observed and observer: a Jamesian anxiety that the very fastidiousness which defends the observer from vulgarity also serves to prevent him from participating in what Shakespeare and then Joyce called "life's feast"; and a deeper anxiety that if the observer ever broke through his fastidiousness he would discover the feast was a sham. In Eliot's poems before "Gerontion" the first anxiety makes the observer's distance intolerable. The second renders the thought of giving it up unthinkable. Together they activate the circle of approach and withdrawal that gives Eliot's early poetry its considerable fascination.

In *The Waste Land*, the deeper of these anxieties is brought closer to consciousness than one would have believed possible. It is just below the surface, and the threat of its rising terrifies not only Eliot's "different voices" but also the narrative voice that stands behind them. Even the most unthinking and resistant of the poem's characters find themselves being pushed toward a moment of discovery that will tell them whether the "silence" at the "heart of life" is meaningless or not. Eliot's drama moves from a revulsion from the mode of cultured life to a revulsion from the mode of common life, facing in endless succession the fear that both are shells around a core of emptiness. Even adolescent yearnings—the moment in the Hyacinth garden—constantly threaten to reveal themselves as the ghoulish manifestation of something other than love. At the heart of the poem is a sense of worthlessness, not only the worthlessness of the present but the probable worthlessness of the past and the future. This sense of pervasive worthlessness, called into resurgence by the biographical events recounted at the beginning of this chapter, was undoubtedly at the root of the vague but intensely acute horror and apprehension Eliot told John Quinn in 1922 he had been straining to suppress.[36]

Given the correspondence, moreover, between the never-to-be-repeated intensity of *The Waste Land* and the psychological conditions, amounting to a full-scale breakdown, under which the poem was written, one is compelled to ask whether one was the result of the other. Was *The Waste Land* made possible by a disruption in Eliot's conscious life and a breakdown of his psychological defenses? That, it seems to me, is one of the most interesting of the many problems that surround the poem.

In his case study of Eliot, the psychiatrist Harry Trosman cites two of Eliot's remarks that relate the composition of *The Waste Land* to his emotional breakdown. (Valerie Eliot, who reproduces the first in the

Waste Land Facsimile volume, reports that Eliot told her specifically that he was here "describing his own experience of writing ["What the Thunder Said"]"):

> . . . It is a commonplace that some forms of illness are extremely favourable, not only to religious illumination, but to artistic and literary composition. A piece of writing meditated, apparently without progress, for months or years, may suddenly take shape and word; and in this state long passages may be produced which require little or no retouch.
>
> I know, for instance, that some form of ill-health, debility or anaemia, may . . . produce an efflux of poetry in a way approaching the condition of automatic writing—though, in contrast to the claims sometimes made for the latter, the material has obviously been incubating within the poet, and cannot be suspected of being a present from a friendly or impertinent demon. What one writes in this way may succeed in standing the examination of a more normal state of mind; it gives me the impression, as I have just said, of having undergone a long incubation, though we do not know until the shell breaks what kind of egg we have been sitting on. To me it seems that at these moments, which are characterised by the sudden lifting of the burden of anxiety and fear which presses upon our daily life so steadily that we are unaware of it, what happens is something *negative*: that is to say, not "inspiration" as we commonly think of it, but the breaking down of strong habitual barriers—which tend to reform very quickly. Some obstruction is momentarily whisked away. The accompanying feeling is less like what we know as positive pleasure, than a sudden relief from an intolerable burden.[37]

Based on these remarks and Eliot's psychiatric history, Trosman links the fragmentation and animistic energy of *The Waste Land* to Eliot's disturbance, breakdown and recovery:

> From a psychological point of view, Eliot's achievement lay in utilizing the content of his narcissistic regression for creative purposes. Having experienced a failure in response from need-satisfying and narcissistically

cathected self-objects, he found himself empty, fragmented, and lacking in a sense of self-cohesion. As he began to reintegrate, he turned his previous adversity to poetic advantage. In a highly original manner, and perhaps for the first time in literature, he made narcissistic fragmentation a basis for poetic form and alienation of self legitimate poetic content. The ideational and effective content of his psychic restitution, the expression of his attempt to reconstitute the fragmented elements of the split in his self became the new voice of *The Waste Land*.

Vittoz [the therapist who treated Eliot in Lausanne] was helpful by providing a framework for reintegration, satisfaction in completing simple tasks, and a religious philosophy reminiscent of Eliot's early youth. Vittoz could not, however, provide Eliot with insight into the basis of his disorder, and it is possible that the working out of the poem with the reactivation of experiences from the past, the mixing of memory and desire, and the unification of isolated and fragmented parts of the self may have been a form of partial self-analytic work. When Eliot wrote toward the end of the poem, "These fragments I have shored against my ruins" (line 430), he described a process of partial integration that brought about a relief from his personal grouse against life.[38]

Beneath the jargon of contemporary psychiatry there is a great deal of sense here. It is certainly likely, for example, that the mythic organization of *The Waste Land*, which Eliot imposed on the poem in the last stages of composition,[39] did represent an attempt to "reconstitute" a personal world—to give it a meaning, a shape and an order which were not in the original fragments. Nevertheless, it seems to me that *The Waste Land* is both more and less than the product of reintegration Trosman suggests. For one thing, the subterranean voice of the poem has as much to do with Eliot's theory of poetry as with his breakdown. For another, the final shape of the poem seems to have had more to do with Eliot's collapse than with his recovery.

The Waste Land, we saw, congealed around the intellectual program announced by "London, the swarming life you kill and breed." When

Eliot started to assemble the first of his complete sections, he intended to hold modern life up to spiritual analysis and he consciously chose to present his material as fragments. In no simple sense, then, can we say that the initial fragmentation of the poem was the expression of a disabling emotional disturbance. Eliot, however, did not simply supply examples to illustrate preconceived types of moral decay. *The Waste Land* would be wooden had he done so. Instead, following the procedures described above, he allowed poetic scenes to arise out of *images trouvailles*: observed situations, disconnected mental pictures, overheard sounds, all of which imposed themselves on his imagination. It was at this point in composition that the lock on his unconscious must have broken. Guided by the principle of rigorous emotional honesty that he had been following since his Harvard days, Eliot's habits of composition led him to open a door he could not close. Later he would describe precisely this kind of unexpected marriage of impulse and technique in remarks occasioned by the publication of Ezra Pound's selected poems:

> Those who expect that any good poet should proceed by turning out a series of masterpieces, each similar to the last, only more developed in *every way*, are simply ignorant of the conditions under which the poet must work, especially in our time. The poet's progress is dual. There is the gradual accumulation of experience, like a tantalus jar: it may be only once in five or ten years that experience accumulates to form a new whole and finds its appropriate expression. But if a poet were content to attempt nothing less than always his best, if he insisted on waiting for these unpredictable crystallizations, he would not be ready for them when they came. The development of experience is largely unconscious, subterranean, so that we cannot gauge its progress except once in every five or ten years; but in the meantime the poet must be working; he must be experimenting and trying his technique so that it will be ready, like a well-oiled fire-engine, when the moment comes to strain it to its utmost.[40]

By 1921, Eliot's cultivation of visionary drama, of a "continuous identification of form and feeling,"[41] of the mysteriously charged details of dreams and nightmares, had together managed to weaken the clamp on the impulses of his inner life. Then, combined with the enormous emotional pressure of his family situation, they managed to break it altogether. Supplying portraits for his nightmare, Eliot charged them with his own inner hell and produced the first three sections of *The Waste Land*. Between the time his "strong habitual barriers" had momentarily broken down and the time they reformed, the technical procedures he had made second nature did their job.

Most of what I have described as the poem's nightmare—"The Burial of the Dead," "A Game of Chess" and "The Fire Sermon"—was written or assembled at Margate and just after, in October and November of 1921. In the last two sections, written in the sanitarium at Lausanne, the poem turned from fire to water. That is, in Eliot's words, turned from "anxiety and fear" to "relief from an intolerable burden." The Thames maidens at the end of "The Fire Sermon" anticipate the drowned sailor in "Death by Water" and the releasing of an old self with its interminable tensions. And the last section of the poem—"What the Thunder Said"—strikes us, to quote D. W. Harding, as "corresponding to the precarious situation of a man who has partially recovered from a psychological collapse but remains aware of the formidable obstacles still ahead of him."[42]

When Eliot recovered, however, and the strong barriers were once again in place, he looked at his poem and shuddered. Remembering his return from Lausanne, Eliot would recall that "it was in 1922 that I placed before [Pound] in Paris the manuscript of a sprawling, chaotic poem,"[43] and his words give us a strong sense of how the emotional honesty of his new mirror struck him. The exaggeration of the remark—the draft Pound saw was certainly sprawling, but most of the "chaos" was in Eliot's mind—says a great deal about why Eliot was so willing to give up his work to Pound for alteration.[44] (As it turned out, Pound altered it relatively little.) Having composed one of the most terrifying poems of a terrifying century, Eliot—in Paris and even before—struggled mightily to civilize a "grouse against life" that now seemed objectionable. In August he would write that "Dostoevsky had the gift, a sign of genius in itself, for utilizing his weaknesses; so that epilepsy and hysteria cease to be the defects of an individual and become—as a fundamental weakness can, given the ability to face and study it—the entrance to a genuine and personal universe."[45] And in the last stages of polishing Eliot tried to "utilize" the record of what must have seemed his own "fundamental weakness" by making it part of a moral structure. According to a decade-old pattern, after venting his emotional life, he felt compelled to gather it up and order it in a way his ancestors would approve of.

The Eliot of 1922 was not only a disciple of Rémy de Gourmont but, by turns, also a proponent of Irving Babbitt, T. E. Hulme, Charles Maurras, Georges Sorel and Julien Benda. Even had he been convinced of his poem's emotional coherence, that is to say, allowing *The Waste Land* to suggest moral chaos would have meant repudiating an important part of his character. As Benda put it in a book Eliot called essential, the ideal writer is one who "allows intelligence and judgment to predominate over sentiment in the composition of his work."[46] The problem was how to contain *The Waste Land* within a frame of judgment without vitiating its emotional authority.

Eliot solved his problem by recourse to a technique he had observed in Joyce. In a 1923 review of *Ulysses* that is now as famous as *The Waste Land*, Eliot spoke of "the mythical method":

> In using the myth, in manipulating a continuous parallel between contemporaneity and antiquity, Mr. Joyce is pursuing a method which others must pursue after him. They will not be imitators, any more than the scientist who uses the discoveries of an Einstein in pursuing his own, independent, further investigations. It is simply a way of *controlling*, of *ordering*, of *giving a shape and a significance* to the immense panorama of futility and anarchy which is contemporary history. It is a method already adum-

brated by Mr. Yeats, and of the need for which I believe Mr. Yeats to have been the first contemporary to be conscious. It is a method for which the horoscope is auspicious. Psychology (such as it is, and whether our reaction to it be comic or serious), ethnology, and *The Golden Bough* have concurred to make possible what was impossible even a few years ago. Instead of narrative method, we may now use the mythical method. It is, I seriously believe, a step toward making the modern world possible for art. . . ."[47]

Often as this passage has been invoked to identify the central concerns of *The Waste Land*, the truth is that it belongs to the period when Eliot was reshaping, not composing, his poem. As the words I have emphasized suggest, it points to the way Eliot "controlled" and "ordered" something that was given to him more than it describes how he proceeded from the beginning. As an account of *The Waste Land* as a whole it is a dismal failure, for, as Hugh Kenner has pointed out, "it is difficult to believe that anyone who saw only the first four parts [of *The Waste Land*] in their original form would believe that 'the plan and a good deal of the incidental symbolism' were suggested by Jessie Weston's book on the Grail Legend, or that *The Golden Bough* . . . had much pertinence."[48] It is difficult, as Kenner explains, because the manuscript clearly shows that most of the Frazer and Weston imagery got into the poem only at the very end and that Eliot superimposed this material piecemeal onto sections that had been written earlier. Furthermore, the "myth" exists more in the suggestions of the belated title and in the notes than in the poem itself.

What is remarkable is that Eliot did not ruin his poem in that last reshaping, something for which we have Ezra Pound to thank. In his revision Pound concentrated on local infelicities more than on the integrity of the whole and kept Eliot from brooding about his lack of outline for several crucial days or weeks. What A. Walton Litz has called the "spurious"[49] grail legend plot in *The Waste Land* belongs more to our misreading than to the poem itself. The poem still vibrates much as it did before Eliot framed it, although its mythical overlay emphasizes certain overtones at the expense of others. The chapel perilous, for example, which cryptically appears at line 388, provides one more site where a fearsome ultimate question must be asked, and thus rhymes with the implied and explicit questioning in "The Burial of the Dead."

The final questions we can never answer. It may be, for example, that Eliot had some kind of short-lived religious illumination during the process of re-envisioning the fragments of his poem, and that his reshaping points to the recognition of a pattern in his life that he had not seen before.[50] Whatever the motivation of these last changes, *The Waste Land* survived them. Like *Crime and Punishment* or *The Brothers Karamazov*, though the poem is stamped with the mind of a middle-aged conservative, it claims its authority from the suffering and doubts of a rebellious youth.

3

It becomes increasingly more difficult, though, to say the same about the poetry that followed *The Waste Land*. Whereas Eliot's poetic and critical allegiances had been consistently divided before 1922 between romantic honesty and classical order, internal monologue and controlling myth, in 1922 that balance began to shift. The causes of the shift were many and had to do with new friendships and with Eliot's changing position in London society. But the most important of them seems to have involved Eliot's reaction to having finally achieved the kind of poetry he had for so long been trying to write. Eliot looked back on *The Waste Land* and the state of mind that produced it and saw himself "naked" as even Blake had not dared to be. And, consciously or unconsciously, he decided that he could not, would not continue to write that kind of poetry. He could not strive to write a poetry that continually sensitized his own internal fragmentation and brought him unbearable anxiety. As the next chapter will show, starting in 1922, and before his conversion, Eliot's poetry and criticism ceased to applaud "the transformation of a personality into a personal work of art" (SW, 139) and began envisioning creation as a process in which the poet, through the rigors of akesis, effaces his sensibility in traditional personae, traditional images and traditional patterns of feeling and thought. A token of this turning appeared when Eliot brought out a preface to the second edition of *The Sacred Wood*. In that preface, written in 1928, Eliot explained that he had "passed on to another problem not touched upon in this book: that of the relation of poetry to the spiritual and social life of its time and of other times" (SW, viii). As we shall see, at least for a while the procedure that Eliot chose as best suited to relating poetry to the "spiritual and social life" of its time was the method of *Sweeney Agonistes*, in which myth and the popular imagination were combined to create figures that were unconnected to personal sensibility.

There were other kinds of writing, however, that appealed to Eliot in these years as alternatives to the intense dramatic representation of inner reality. And one of these begins to appear in the last movement of *The Waste Land*. Its emergence was to have profound effects on the remainder of Eliot's career.

As the *Facsimile* volume notes, Eliot wrote Bertrand Russell in October 1922 that "it gives me very great pleasure to know that you like *The Waste Land*, and especially Part V which in my opinion is not only the best part, but the only part that justifies the whole, at all" (129). There is no question that "What the Thunder Said," much of which was written in a sudden fit of emotional release, is enormously moving. Eliot's speaker is here removed from the "swarming life" of London and among the mountains. And even though "There is not even silence in the mountains," the change suggests a condition of momentary release from his recurring nightmare. Where perfumes once "drowned the sense in odours" and the bones once crawled with slime, now "Sweat is dry" (l. 337) and "Dry bones can harm no one" (l. 391). From the first line we have the sense of someone amid a break in an emotional storm straining his faculties for some sign of what will happen next. He is yearning for "a damp gust / Bringing rain" and yet also intensely aware of the possible return of the terrors he has lived with—

relivings of "the frosty silence" in the Hyacinth garden and reappearances of the woman who draws "her long black hair out tight." Line 389 suggests a moment's peace, when the grail quester has finally been given a moment's respite before he asks the doom-laden question that has grown to haunt him. But lines 344 and 345 ("red sullen faces sneer and snarl / From doors of mudcracked houses") tell us we are as much in the world of Browning's "Childe Roland"—a poem Eliot greatly admired[51]—as in the world of Jessie Weston.

As Eliot wrote John Quinn, the greatest curse of his life came from noises and associations noises called up.[52] It is therefore natural that the aura of anticipation in "What the Thunder Said" should be presented through the sense of hearing, and that the great relief of the section be announced by sounds (the hermit-thrush song of lines 357-58, and the tripartite voice of the thunder in the conclusion). The poetry of "What the Thunder Said," in fact, vacillates between highly charged sensations of sound and sight. Moreover, in the twenty-nine lines of the "water-dripping song" (331-59), which Eliot told Ford Madox Ford were the only "*good* lines in *The Waste Land*,"[53] the poetry also hovers between the precise representation of sound and the stylized rhythms of incantation:

> Here is no water but only rock
> Rock and no water and the sandy road
> The road winding above among the mountains
> Which are mountains of rock without water
> If there were water we should stop and drink
> Amongst the rock one cannot stop or think
> Sweat is dry and feet are in the sand
> If there were only water amongst the rock
> Dead mountain mouth of carious teeth that cannot spit
> Here one can neither stand nor lie nor sit
> There is not even silence in the mountains
> But dry sterile thunder without rain

> There is not even solitude in the mountains
> But red sullen faces sneer and snarl
> From doors of mudcracked houses
>
>   If there were water
>   And no rock
>   If there were rock
>   And also water
>   And water
>   A spring
>   A pool among the rock
>   If there were the sound of water only
>   Not the cicada
>   And dry grass singing
>   But sound of water over a rock
>   Where the hermit-thrush sings in the pine trees
>   Drip drop drip drop drop drop drop
>   But there is no water. . . .

This is a repetitive charm. It bespeaks an enormous amount of psychic energy working to displace images into an aural pattern. Both the speaker's anguish in the awful recognition that there is "no water" (once again, a negative pointing to a strong positive desire) and his pained apprehension of the "rock" around him are distanced by hypnotizing incantation. The rhythmic sequence "water . . . rock . . . Rock . . . water . . . road . . . road" lulls us so that we must force ourselves to notice certain clear but unpleasant images:

> Sweat is dry and feet are in the sand
> . . . .
> Dead mountain mouth of carious teeth that cannot spit . . .
> . . . .
>   red sullen faces sneer and snarl
> From doors of mudcracked houses. . . .

"Unknown terror and mystery"

Eliot's music here is a counterpoint between the themes of "rock" and "water," and it resolves itself into the second theme. By the fifth line the phrase "Here is no water" has been transformed into "If there were water," a conjurer's formula that swells in line 338 to "If there were only water." By line 347 the force of desire in the lines is so strong that the charm acquires the rhythm of a litany, a litany which calls into existence a spring, and a pool, but whose strongest magic lies in what follows. For a second, the poem breaks through to the only area of Eliot's visionary geography whose attraction is strong enough to counter the pressure exerted by his anxiety. The place "Where the hermit-thrush sings in the pine trees / Drip drop drip drop drop drop drop" is the emotional terrain of Eliot's childhood, the place where "the wind blows the water white and black" ("Prufrock"), the place where one can hear "The cry of quail and the whirling plover" (*Ash Wednesday*) and the place where one knows the "scent of pine and the woodthrush singing through the fog" ("Marina"). In no other poem, however, is the force of the vision as great as in these lines from *The Waste Land*, where the thrush's song stands as the culmination of an incantatory pattern twenty-eight lines long. Not even in the Hyacinth garden episode do we find an epiphany like this, where every hint of self-consciousness has been effaced by a complex of chiseled image and precisely heard song. The line "drip drop drip drop drop drop drop" is not only an accurate reproduction of the voice of the *Turdus aonalaschkae pallasii*, which Eliot heard as a boy;[54] it is also a piece of pure music which represents complete gratification. It is the only gift of water in the poem. Little wonder that these lines came to Eliot in a great surge of release, or that Eliot should have subsequently felt closer to them than to anything else in his poem.

The "water-dripping song" is a major poetic success. But the cost of that success turned out to be considerable. By introducing so strong a dose of incantation into his poetry, Eliot unleashed a chemical capable of dissolving the delicate balance between music and psychic drama that characterizes the work of his early maturity, a balance which he maintained for a while in common with his fellow modernists. Like Joyce, Pound, Lawrence, Stevens and Woolf, Eliot emerged from his juvenilia into a period where music and internal monologue were held in a powerful but precarious balance. But starting with the "water-dripping song," music—the tendency in post-symbolist verse toward a "musical pattern of sound and a musical pattern of the secondary meanings of the words which compose it"[55]—began to tip the scale. No better description of this changing equilibrium can be offered than Eliot's own: in his first essay on [John] Milton, oblivious to the application of what he said to his own verse, he berated Joyce and Milton for "an auditory imagination abnormally sharpened at the expense of the visual." Eliot went on to say that, in Joyce after the middle of *Ulysses* and in *Paradise Lost*, "the inner meaning is separated from the surface, and tends to become something occult, or at least without effect upon the reader until fully understood" (OPP, 162). In the same essay, he contrasted Milton's involutions to those of Henry James, and concluded:

> The style of James certainly depends for its effect a good deal on the sound of a voice, James's own, painfully explaining. But the complication, with James, is due to a determination not to simplify, and in that simplification lose any of the real intricacies and by-paths of mental movement; whereas the complication of a Miltonic sentence is an active complication . . . deliberately introduced into what was a previously simplified and abstract thought. The dark angel here is not *thinking* or conversing, but making a speech carefully prepared for him; and the arrangement is for the sake of musical value, not for significance. . . . reality is no part of the intention. . . . syntax is determined by the musical significance, by the auditory imagination, rather than by the attempt to follow actual speech or thought. . . . The result with Milton is, in one sense of the word, *rhetoric* (OPP, 160-61).

In Eliot's case the allure of music was slightly different, but the effect was much the same. Starting with a genius for assonance, internal rhyme, and melodious cadence ("There will be time, there will be time / To prepare a face to meet the faces that you meet"), at the beginning of his career Eliot disciplined his propensities toward incantation. As a result of his association with Pound and Imagism, and his admiration for James, Flaubert and Joyce, his verse explored "intricacies and bypaths of mental movement." *The Waste Land* takes Eliot as far along that path as he was to go. The poem, that is, gives us Eliot's maximum push toward what Pound was to call the prose tradition in verse. As such it resembles a number of other modernist masterpieces, typically written in the middle and not at the end of their authors' careers: *The Tower*, *Women in Love*, the first half of *Ulysses*, "Sunday Morning," *To the Lighthouse*.

After *The Waste Land*, Eliot's writing, though it did not abandon the effort to map small movements of feeling and thought, did lose its keenness to dredge up the mind's subterranean reaches. As in the 1936 essay on Milton, Eliot retained a vestige of a distrust for the rhetorical deceptiveness of the auditory imagination, but at the same time allowed it to alter his creative work. As early as 1933 he would write that Matthew Arnold's account of poetry "does not perhaps go deep enough" because Arnold was not

> highly sensitive to the musical qualities of verse. His own occasional bad lapses arouse the suspicion; and so far as I can recollect he never emphasises this virtue of poetic style, this fundamental, in his criticism. What I call the "auditory imagination " is the feeling for syllable and rhythm, penetrating far below the conscious levels of thought and feeling, invigorating every word . . . (UPUC, 118-10).

By 1942 Eliot had so far acceded to the pull of one pole of his literary heritage that he recorded the lessons he had learned *entre deux guerres* under the title of "The Music of Poetry." And of course the major poem of his later years—the work that competes for our admiration with *The Waste Land* even as it calls attention to *The Waste Land's* rejected virtues—is entitled *Four Quartets*. The path to the *Quartets* was one in which Eliot followed his symbolist inclinations to their conclusion. It is littered, however, with what can only be called embarrassments—what Conrad Aiken called "beautiful gibberish":[56]

> Where shall the word be found, where will the word
> Resound? Not here, there is not enough silence
> Not on the sea or on the islands, not
> On the mainland, in the desert or the rain land. . . .
>
> *(Ash Wednesday)*

In his last major critical essay, "From Poe to Valéry" (1948), Eliot by implication locates himself at the end of the symbolist tradition. And nowhere is that essay clearer about how far he had come from *The Waste Land* than in the way it dismisses Poe and Poe's dreaming:

> What is lacking is not brain power, but that maturity of intellect which comes only with the maturing of the man as whole, the development and coordination of his various emotions. I am not concerned with any possible psychological or pathological explanation: it is enough for my purpose to record that the work of Poe is such as I should expect of a man of very exceptional mind and sensibility, whose emotional development has been in some respect arrested at an early age. *His most vivid imaginative realizations are the realization of a dream*: significantly, the ladies in his poems and tales are always ladies lost, or ladies vanishing before they can be embraced. Even in *The Haunted Palace*, where the subject appears to be his own weakness of alcoholism, the disaster has no moral significance; it is treated impersonally as an isolated phenomenon; it has not behind it the terrific force of such lines as those of François Villon when he speaks of his own fallen state (TCC, 35; emphasis mine).

In this passage Eliot characteristically reflects on himself while he analyzes a literary predecessor. In doing so he gives us an emblem of the metamorphosis that divides the two halves of his literary career. Here, to the best of his capabilities, T. S. Eliot, the literary arbiter of the English-speaking world in the year of his Nobel Prize, has left the nightmare-haunted figure of thirty-three-year-old Tom Eliot behind.

From *T. S. Eliot: A Study in Character and Style* (New York: Oxford University Press, 1984): 53-78. Copyright © 1984 by Oxford University Press. Reprinted by permission of Oxford University Press, Inc.

Notes

1. Eliot to John Quinn, 6 January 1919, quoted in *Facs.*, xvi.
2. *The Autobiography of Bertrand Russell: 1914-1944* (Boston: Little, Brown, 1968), p. 64.
3. Ibid., p. 61. The story of Eliot's "pseudo-honeymoon" is also Russell's, as recalled in Lyndall Gordon, *Eliot's Early Years* (Oxford: Oxford University Press, 1977), p. 76.
4. Cited by Richard Ellmann in "The First *Waste Land*," in A. W. Litz, ed., *Eliot in His Time* (Princeton: Princeton University Press, 1973), p. 61.
5. *Facs.*, xvi.
6. Ibid., xviii.
7. Ibid., xxi.
8. Ibid., xxii. On Vittoz, see Harry Trosman, "T. S. Eliot and *The Waste Land*: Psychopathological Antecedents and Transformations," *Archives of General Psychiatry* 30.5 (May 1974), 709-17.
9. *Facs.*, x (emphasis mine).
10. Letter of 21 September 1922, in the Manuscripts Division of the New York Public Library.
11. See the "Prefatory Note" to the reprinting of Aiken's 1923 "An Anatomy of Melancholy" in Allen Tate, ed., *T. S. Eliot: The Man and His Work* (New York: Delacorte Press, 1966), p. 195.
12. Review of *The Name and Nature of Poetry* by A. E. Housman, *Criterion* XIII.50 (October 1933), 154.
13. OPP, 107. For discussion, see above, chapter one.
14. See Grover Smith, "The Meaning of *The Waste Land*," *Mosaic* 6.1 (1972), 127-41, and Hugh Kenner, "The Urban Apocalypse," in Litz, *Eliot in His Time*, pp. 23-49.
15. I cite from Eliot's typed version of a holograph manuscript. See *Facs.*, pp. 42-43 and 36-37. Lyndall Gordon dates the holograph 1917 or 1918 in *Eliot's Early Years*, p. 95.
16. This corresponds to the way Anthony Cronin remembers Eliot explaining the origins of the poem. As far back as 1918, Eliot told Cronin, he had been meditating "a

certain sort of poem about the contemporary world." See "A Conversation with T. S. Eliot about the Connection Between *Ulysses* and *The Waste Land*," in the *Irish Times* for 16 June 1972, p. 10.

17. See *Facs.*, 31.

18. SW, 58 (emphasis mine). Note that Eliot uses the word "personal" here in the special pejorative sense that Gourmont had dissociated (see above, chapter four).

19. See the discussion of *images trouvailles* in chapter four. Conrad Aiken goes further and suggests that Eliot, though he believed his work was "pure calculation of effect," was actually indulging himself in "self-deception." See Joseph Killorin, ed., *Selected Letters of Conrad Aiken* (New Haven: Yale University Press, 1978), pp. 185-86.

20. Eliot first recorded many of these impressions (including his visit to Magnus Martyr on a dreary lunch hour, his living through a "hot rainless spring" and his witnessing an outbreak of flu that "leaves extreme dryness and a bitter taste in the mouth") in 1921 "London Letters" for the *Dial* and the *Nouvelle Revue Française*. A. Walton Litz discusses these letters and their provenance in *"The Waste Land* Fifty Years After" (see *Eliot in His Time*, pp. 13-17), but concludes that they are finally less important for the poem than the reading which shaped Eliot's imagination: Pound, Bradley, James, Conrad, Frazer and Joyce. I would agree that, in themselves, these impressions are only "raw materials," but hesitate to go further. From his first awareness of them to the time they assumed their place in his completed poem, Eliot's privileged moments were shaped as much by the sea-world of his non-literary sensibility as by any of his literary models.

21. As we know from Valerie Eliot's notes to the *Facsimile*, Eliot sketched "Marie" in "The Burial of the Dead" from a woman he had met and shaped some of "The Game of Chess" from his own conversations with Vivien. See *Facs.*, 126.

22. See above, note 10. Another note in the *Facsimile* explains that the last dialogue of "A Game of Chess" was modeled after the words of Eliot's maid, Ellen Kellond (p. 127).

23. See the epigraphs to this chapter and SW, 115.

24. From "Learning from the Beatles," in *The Performing Self: Compositions and Decompositions in the Language of Contemporary Life* (New York: Oxford University Press, 1971), p. 137.

25. *Autobiography*, p. 7. The full passage is worth quoting: "After seeing troop trains departing from Waterloo, I used to have strange visions of London as a place of unreality. I used in imagination to see the bridges collapse and sink, and the whole great city vanish like a morning mist. Its inhabitants began to seem like hallucinations, and I would wonder whether the world in which I thought I had lived was a mere product of my own febrile nightmares. . . . I spoke of this to T. S. Eliot, who put it into *The Waste Land.*"

26. See "Eeldrop and Appleplex I," originally in the May 1917 *Little Review*, reprinted in Margaret Anderson, ed., *The Little Review Anthology* (New York: Horizon, 1953), p. 104: "In Gopsum Street a man murders his mistress."

27. Manuscript in the Berg Collection of the New York Public Library.

28. See Hugh Kenner, *T. S. Eliot: The Invisible Poet* (New York: Citadel, 1959), pp. 161 ff.

29. See chapter two, note 18.

30. CPP, 342 (emphasis mine). For another discussion of this passage, see Gordon, *Eliot's Early Years*, p. 106.

31. My gesture toward *Finnegans Wake* is deliberate. As Margot Norris has argued, much of the opaqueness of that supremely difficult work has to do with how it mimes the way repressed material is approached in a nightmare. See Margot Norris, *The Decentered Universe of Finnegans Wake* (Baltimore: The Johns Hopkins University Press, 1974).

32. See, for example, Donald Davie, "Mr. Eliot," in *The Poet in the Imaginary Museum* (Manchester: Carcanet, 1977), pp. 117-21; Denis Donoghue, "'The Word within a Word,'" in A. D. Moody, ed., *The Waste Land in Different Voices* (London: Edward Arnold, 1974), pp. 185-202; M. L. Rosenthal, "*The Waste Land* as an Open Structure," in Linda Wagner, ed., *T. S. Eliot: A Collection of Criticism* (New York: McGraw-Hill, 1974), pp. 37-48; C. K. Stead, *The New Poetic: Yeats to Eliot* (New York: Harper and Row, 1966), esp. pp. 148-67; and even, in a quirky way, chapter four ("A Dialectical Reading of *The Waste Land*") of Anne C. Bolgan, *What the Thunder Really Said: A Retrospective Essay on the Making of "The Waste Land"* (Montreal: McGill-Queen's University Press, 1973).

33. "Beyle and Balzac," *Athenaeum* 4648 (30 May 1919), 393.

34. "The Post-Georgians," *Athenaeum* 4641 (19 April 1919), 171.

35. But see Cleanth Brooks, *Modern Poetry and the Tradition* (Chapel Hill: North Carolina University Press, 1939; rpt. New York: Oxford University Press, 1965), p. 154, and A. D. Moody, *Thomas Stearns Eliot: Poet* (Cambridge: Cambridge University Press, 1979), p. 292.

36. See above, note 10.

37. Trosman, "T. S. Eliot and *The Waste Land*," 716. I have corrected the accuracy of Trosman's first and restored the full text of Trosman's abbreviated second citation. The first comes from Eliot's essay on Pascal (see SE, 358) and is reproduced in *Facs.*, p. 129. The second comes from UPUC, 144-45.

38. Trosman, "T. S. Eliot and *The Waste Land*," 717.

39. See the Litz and Kenner essays in Litz, *Eliot in His Time*.

40. "Introduction" to *Ezra Pound: Selected Poems* (London: Faber and Gwyer, 1928; rpt. 1973), pp. 15-16.

41. Ibid., p. 19.

42. From D. W. Harding, "What the Thunder Said," in Moody, *The Waste Land in Different Voices*, p. 27.

43. "Ezra Pound" (1946). I cite from a reprint in Walter Sutton, ed., *Ezra Pound: A Collection of Critical Essays* (Englewood Cliffs: Prentice-Hall, 1963), p. 19. In another place Eliot refers to the unfinished *Waste Land* as a "mess": see "From T. S. Eliot," in *The Cantos of Ezra Pound: Some Testimonies* (New York: Farrar and Rinehart, 1933), pp. 16-17.

44. It may also be true, as Trosman suggests, that Pound served as both father-confessor and "narcissistic extension" for Eliot, continuing the role that Eliot's therapist Vittoz had so recently played in Lausanne. See Trosman, "T. S. Eliot and *The Waste Land*," 715.

45. "London Letter," *Dial* LXXIII.3 (September 1922), 331.

46. From *Belphegor* (1918). I cite from the English translation by J. I. Lawson introduced by Irving Babbitt (New York, 1929), p. 129. For Eliot's praise of the book, see "The Idea of a Literary Review," *New Criterion* IV.1 (January 1926), 5.

47. "*Ulysses*, Order, and Myth," *Dial* LXX.5 (November 1923), 483 (emphasis mine).

48. "The Urban Apocalypse," p. 43.

49. "*The Waste Land*: Fifty Years After," p. 6.

50. See below, chapter six, pp. 94-95.

51. See below, chapter six, note 31.

52. See above, note 10.

53. *Facs.*, 129.

54. Eliot's pedantic note to *The Waste Land* is in part humorous, but it is not fundamentally misleading. As John Soldo has pointed out ("The Tempering of T. S. Eliot: 1888-1915," Ph.D. diss., Harvard, 1972), Eliot used a copy of Chapman's *Handbook of Birds of Eastern North America* he received on his fourteenth birthday to identify the hermit-thrush in the neighborhood of the Eliot family summer home on Cape Ann. See Soldo, pp. 182-84.

55. OPP, 26. From "The Music of Poetry" (1942).

56. *Selected Letters*, p. 185. Aiken wrote: "But the skill in the use of time and sound increasingly impresses me, in the later things—Ash Wednesday, for example—there was never a more beautiful gibberish of language, surely? the whole, or detailed, meaning almost nil, but the *effect* lovely."

'The Word Within the World':
Ash-Wednesday and the 'Ariel Poems'

Nancy K. Gish

Nancy K. Gish argues for the centrality of *Ash-Wednesday* (1930) in Eliot's canon, by presenting it as an important hinge and stage of development between the earlier poetry and *Four Quartets*. She undertakes illuminating close readings of four of Eliot's "Ariel" poems, the ones published between 1927 and 1930, and of the six sections of *Ash-Wednesday*, whose elliptical structure she clarifies without ignoring its enigmatic nonlinear quality. In her close readings, she presents significant background material for the poems that is actually also in the poems' foregrounds because the material is so strongly present. She does so by citing and discussing some of Eliot's sources, always by comparison with the meaningful change in details and effects that Eliot creates in his versions. The sources include the sermons of Bishop Lancelot Andrewes, the New Testament of the King James Bible, Dante, and Saint John of the Cross's mystical writings about the dark night of the soul. All these sources were important for Eliot's thinking and for his writing in the specific poems discussed here. The "Ariel" poems were Christmas poems published in illustrated pamphlets by the publisher Faber, where Eliot was an adviser and a key figure. Gish frames her commentary on the longer poem by discussing first the three "Ariel" poems written before it, and then, in her closing, "Marina," which was written after *Ash-Wednesday*. Gish rightly brings out the doubt and sense of limitation expressed by the magus who speaks in "The Journey of the Magi" and by Simeon in "A Song for Simeon," for whom the Christian dispensation comes too late. By contrast, "Marina " evokes a mystic recognition that is not split from human realities. It points forward toward *Four Quartets*. *Ash-Wednesday* presents a dual vision of human love, including sensuality, and mystical aspiration, but they are not reconciled. The speaker has made a choice for the latter but has not moved beyond regret for the loss of the former. Gish's readings bring out the way the earlier speakers are *between* worlds in a static, frustrating way that prevents them from moving forward, while the speaker of the longer poem has made a choice that involves for the moment being *between* and being still but that does not prevent movement. Being in between has been recognized since the emergence of poststructuralism as a distinctive and significant situation for twentieth century art and culture. Gish's essay makes it clear that Eliot contributed to expressing that distinctive aspect of our modernity. She lucidly presents the structure of *Ash-Wednesday* as a nonlinear oscillation between discursive segments and contrasting visions that moves from meditation to renunciation, a vision of spiritual renewal, and a recommitment to the mystic process. As part of the detailed commentary on this elliptical but unforgettable sequence, she regularly draws comparisons with Eliot's earlier and later poems in order to establish *Ash-Wednesday*'s role as a crucial in-between moment. She also cogently discusses how readers who do not share Eliot's Christianity can understand and appreciate the poem. —J.P.R.

With the 'Ariel Poems' Eliot's work becomes more overtly philosophical, the voices less concerned with describing sordid reality and more prone to seek, through thought and prayer, some understanding of their condition. Increasingly, the poems depict a search for some transcendent and eternal value now believed to exist if not yet attained. But if the concepts are more affirmative, experience is often more anguished. As expressions of Christ's coming, 'Journey of the Magi' and 'A Song for Simeon' are peculiarly joyless. Drawing again on Andrewes' 1622 Nativity sermon for the first poem, Eliot dwells less on their great faith than on their 'cold comming' and uncertain reward. What Simeon does see has less force than his regret for what he cannot experience. In each poem we find a puzzling sense of something missed rather than found. Except for 'Marina', they are oddly neutral in tone despite the fulfillment they assume.

United by their concern with transience between two worlds, 'Journey of the Magi', 'A Song for Simeon' and 'Animula' are united also by what Eliot has called 'the Catholic philosophy of disillusion', a tendency 'to look to *death* for what life cannot give'.[1] Essential to this philosophy is the realisation that birth, even Christ's birth, is not sufficient for salvation, that there must also be death if rebirth is to come. The old dispensation is fully consummated and the new begun only with Christ's death. Underlying the feelings and events of the 'Ariel Poems', this 'philosophy of disillusion' determines mood and tone. More important, perhaps, it is tied to one of Eliot's most difficult themes—the meaning of the Incarnation, the moment when timelessness enters time and so gathers all meaning and value to one point. 'Journey of the Magi' and 'A Song for Simeon' focus specifically on the implications of that event and the quality of emotional response to it.

In his 1622 Nativity sermon Bishop Andrewes emphasises five aspects of the Magi's journey: the 'occasion', the 'comming', asking where Christ might be found, finding Christ, and the 'End' or purpose for which He is found. Three of these, the 'comming', finding and 'End', provide a basis for the three sections of 'Journey of the Magi'. Though Eliot uses these events, even drawing on Andrewes' actual words for the first, the changes he makes in his material create a new mood and a new meaning. The source of the first lines is often quoted, but the context in which they occur is also interesting. Andrewes has emphasised that the way was long, unpleasant, difficult, dangerous and cold:

> It was no *summer Progresse*. A cold comming they had of it, at this time of the yeare; just, the worst time of the yeare, to take a journey, and specially a long journey, in. The waies deep, the weather sharp, the daies short, the sunn farthest off *in solstitio brumali*, the very dead of *Winter*. *Venimus*, we are come, if that be one; *Venimus*, We are (now) come, come at this time, that (sure) is another.[2]

Andrewes then describes their feelings about this 'comming':

> All these difficulties they overcame, of a *wearisome, irksome, troublesome, dangerous, unseasonable* journey: And for all this, they *came*. And, came it cheerfully, and quickly; As appeareth, by the speed they made. It was but *Vidimus, Venimus*, with them; They saw, and they *came*: No sooner *saw*, but they set out presently. So, as upon the first appearing of the *Starre* (as it might be, last night) they knew, it was *Balaam's starre*; it called them away, they made ready streight to begin their journey this morning. A signe, they were highly conceited of His *Birth*, believed some great matter of it, that they tooke all these paines, made all this haste, that they might be there to *worship Him*, with all the possible speede they could. Sorie for nothing so much, as that they could not be there soone enough, with the verie first, to do it even this *day*, the *day* of His *Birth*.[3]

In Eliot's version the vivid, concrete images of the journey remain and are amplified. Not only the weather and terrain are hard, but the party itself is unmanageable. What does not remain is the cheerful confidence, the certainty with which these obstacles are overcome:

> There were times we regretted
> The summer palaces on slopes, the terraces,
> And the silken girls bringing sherbet.
> Then the camel men cursing and grumbling
> And running away, and wanting their liquor and women,
> And the night-fires going out, and the lack of shelters,
> And the cities hostile and the towns unfriendly
> And the villages dirty and charging high prices:
> A hard time we had of it.
> At the end we preferred to travel all night,
> Sleeping in snatches,
> With the voices singing in our ears, saying
> That this was all folly.

Though Eliot's Magi come quickly, past great obstacles, their sorrow is not only for delay. They regret the easy, sensual life they have left and are never to regain, the first thing left behind on their journey to Christ. This regret for sensual loss is to remain in *Ash-Wednesday* as a counterpoint to firmly asserted choice. Like that of the Magi, the spiritual journey of the poems as a group retains uncertainty, sorrow and loss even as it moves toward intellectual assurance. For the Magi this is added to the fear that 'this was all folly', that the long journey may lead to nothing. Though they take great pains, it is not here a clear sign that they 'were highly conceited of His *Birth*, believed some great matter of it', for already they feel uncertain. And this foreshadows the ambiguity of their purpose. The Magi come, according to Andrewes, to worship, and that in itself is sufficient End. But Eliot's Magus questions the reason for their coming.

This shift in meaning and tone occurs again in the second and third sections. The strange uncertainty on finding Christ, '. . . it was (you may say) satisfactory', has a basis in Andrewes, but there it serves to re-emphasise their firm faith:

> Weigh, what she found, and what these heere: As poor and unlikely a *birth*, as could be, ever to prove a *King*, or any great matter. No *sight*, to comfort them; Nor a *word*, for which they any whit the wiser: Nothing, worth their travaile. Weigh these togither, and great odds will be found between her faith, and theirs. Theirs, the greater farr.
>
> Well, they will take Him, as they find Him: And, all this notwithstanding, *worship Him* for all that. The *starr* shall make amends for the *Manger*: And, for *stella Ejus*, they will dispense with *Eum*.[4]

Eliot portrays an arrival characterised by similar obscurity and lack of fulfillment. The birth is not even stressed; in its place is a foreshadowing of Christ's death:

> Then at dawn we came down to a temperate valley,
> Wet, below the snowline, smelling of vegetation;
> With a running stream and a water-mill beating the darkness,
> And three trees on the low sky,
> And an old white horse galloped away in the meadow.
> Then we came to a tavern with vine-leaves over the lintel,
> Six hands at an open door dicing for pieces of silver,
> And feet kicking the empty wine-skins.

The circumstances of Christ's birth, which is only 'satisfactory', are not specifically noted. What the Magus remembers are certain images associated with the morning of their arrival. Their meaning is hidden from him, though for the reader they have distinct associations. In *The Use of Poetry and the Use of Criticism* Eliot spoke of such images:

> Why, for all of us, out of all that we have heard, seen, felt, in a lifetime, do certain images recur, charged with emotion, rather than others? The song of one bird, the leap of one fish, at a particular place and time, the scent of one flower, an old woman on a German mountain path, six ruffians seen through an open window playing cards at night at a small French railway junction where there was a water-mill: such memories may have symbolic value, but of what we cannot tell, for they come to represent the depths of feeling into which we cannot peer.[5]

The water-mill and six ruffians playing cards appear in the Magus' memory as a 'water-mill beating the darkness' and 'Six hands at an open door dicing for pieces of silver'. But here a double significance is created. For the Magus they are the 'depths of feeling into which we cannot peer'. For the reader they have a clear symbolic value which now underlies our perception of the Magi and suggests the nature of their plight. They see what they believe is life; we see death already implicit in that event. The trees, images of Calvary; the horse, suggesting the white horse Christ rides in Revelation but here old and galloping away from the speaker; the vine-leaves over the lintel, recalling sacrifice; the soldiers, suggesting those who diced for Christ's robe; and the silver, recalling Judas' betrayal: all create a sense of the agony to come. Since the Jews and the Magi anticipate Christ the conqueror who has not now come, the white horse is particularly suggestive. They are to find instead a poor child doomed to sacrifice. Juxtaposing the sacrificial lamb of the Old Testament and the allusion to Revelation joins the old dispensation and the second coming with the Incarnation, which connects them. After the Incarnation, all time exists in relation to it, and the poem focuses on that significance.

The meaning of Christ's birth is that He must die, but this meaning comes obscurely and darkly to the Magi. At the time of their arrival, they are aware only of certain intense images and a dubious birth. Like Andrewes' Magi they must take Him as they find Him, but their worship is not mentioned, and the star does not make amends. Through this subtle shifting of emphasis and change in mood Eliot conveys their relation to the Christ they have come so far to see. They see Him only; the meaning of the vision remains for them in the impenetrable depths. But it is too intense for forgetting and prevents any return to a former life. The blindness of 'Gerontion' and *The Waste Land* has given way only to another blindness; now the truth is before them but they 'see' its physical manifestation only. Except in 'Marina' Eliot's dramatic figures never do 'see' what they desire. While they think and speak of eternity, they see the world of time. Even Simeon, with this greater understanding, accepts with a kind of resignation a partial and limited vision. The historical position of Simeon and the Magi, however, makes them representative of those who are between two lives. Unable to return, they do not know how to achieve a new life. They have seen Christ's birth—but not His death, and without understanding why, they long for the death that precedes rebirth. Not, like earlier characters, in the Hell of isolation and self disgust, these characters have hardly attained even a purgatory. It is more a limbo, a place without pain but without ecstasy. But they can at least act and choose in limited ways, though the 'End' of their choice remains distant and dim.

The 'End' for which Andrewes' Magi come is to worship. Using the idea of 'End' or purpose as the center of his final stanza, Eliot again shifts its meaning so that the mood changes:

> All this was a long time ago, I remember,
> And I would do it again, but set down
> This set down
> This: were we led all that way for
> Birth or Death? There was a Birth, certainly,
> We had evidence and no doubt. I had seen birth and death,
> But had thought they were different; this Birth was
> Hard and bitter agony for us, like Death, our death.
> We returned to our places, these Kingdoms,
> But no longer at ease here, in the old dispensation,
> With an alien people clutching their gods.
> I should be glad of another death.

The phrase 'set down / This set down / This . . .' has been attributed to Yeats's 'The Adoration of the Magi',[6] but one need not look so far. The phrase occurs in the same sermon by Andrewes. There the context provides an ironic contrast to Eliot's use of it. 'Secondly, set downe this: That, to finde where He is, we must learne of these to ask *Where* He is: Which we full little set ourselves to do.'[7] For Andrewes the Magi are a model, an example to us of great faith and understanding. Here the 'set down' introduces a positive assertion, that from the Magi we can learn how to find where Christ is. In the poem it introduces, oddly, a question, not asking, even, where Christ is but why they were brought to Him.

Since they have seen only a birth, the form of the question leads back to the preceding stanza. Appearing only in the images which are for them obscure, death is yet present and felt. Bearing within it the implication of death in a way they cannot understand, this birth was, for them, 'Like Death, our death'. If one thinks at this point of their place in history, the strange relation is clear. Those who lived before the Incarnation were under the old dispensation. For Christians after Christ's life, the relation of man to God is achieved through imitation of Christ's life and death to this world. For those who lived between His birth and death neither is wholly valid. The Magi, living in this time, feel cut off from their own past, 'But no longer at ease here, in the old dispensation', yet the total Christian experience is not yet available to them. The final line might be taken in several ways. It might mean Christ's death, which would consummate the old way and begin the new; it might mean his own physical death, which would free him from this 'time of tension'. But since 'birth' and 'death' are capitalised when referring to Christ, this death is not His. Read in the light of Eliot's interest in St John of the Cross and in conjunction with 'A Song for Simeon' which specifically mentions the 'saints' stair', it suggests, instead, the mystic death which imitates the death of Christ and allows for a direct relation with God. The earlier emphasis on their regret for sensual delight and the difficulty of their journey strengthens this view. They were, in fact, led all that way for both birth and death; having seen Christ, they cannot return to their first life. Their old life already dead, they have no way of knowing the nature of the new life or the way to attain it since it is not yet fully manifest. Christ must die but has not yet done so. They too must die but know not how.

Like the Magi, Simeon saw Christ's birth when he was already old. Because Simeon is more aware than the Magi of what the Birth means, the implications of his vision are more clear. He sees beyond that event to the suffering which must come before 'the ultimate vision'. The Bible emphasises Simeon's seeing of Christ, promised because of his devotion:

25   And, behold, there was a man in Jerusalem, whose name *was* Simeon; and the same man *was* just and devout, waiting for the consolation of Israel: and the Holy Ghost was upon him.
26   And it was revealed unto him by the Holy Ghost, that he should not see death, before he had seen the Lord's Christ.
27   And he came by the Spirit into the temple: and when the parents brought in the child Jesus, to do for him after the custom of the law,
28   Then took he him up in his arms, and blessed God, and said,
29   Lord, now lettest thou thy servant depart in peace, according to thy word:
30   For mine eyes have seen thy salvation,
31   Which thou hast prepared before the face of all people;
32   A light to lighten the Gentiles, and the glory of thy people Israel.
33   And Joseph and his mother marvelled at those things which were spoken of him.
34   And Simeon blessed them, and said unto Mary his mother, Behold, this *child* is set for the fall and rising again of many in Israel; and for a sign which shall be spoken against;
35   (Yea, a sword shall pierce through thy own soul also,) that the thoughts of many hearts may be revealed.[8]

'A Song for Simeon' lacks this sense of fulfillment; the anticipation of sorrows becomes primary, and Simeon's own thoughts dwell on what he cannot have:

> They shall praise Thee and suffer in every generation
> With glory and derision,
> Light upon light, mounting the saints' stair.
> Not for me the martyrdom, the ecstasy of thought and prayer,
> Not for me the ultimate vision.

Eliot's fascination with the life of saints is evident in this depiction of their higher experience. According to St John of the Cross, to whom

Eliot frequently alludes, the contemplation which guides the soul to God is secret wisdom and is also a ladder.[9] The secret wisdom is the divine illumination of God which is, paradoxically, darkness to the intellect and senses. The ladder is a series of ten steps representing the stages on the mystic path to God. The soul ascends and descends at the same time, for by humbling and lowering itself it is raised and exalted toward God. Contemplation is, then, both light and stairs:

> . . . the principal property involved in calling contemplation a 'ladder' is its being a science of love, which as we said is an infused loving knowledge, that both illumines and enamors the soul, elevating it step by step unto God, its Creator.[10]

'Light upon light, mounting the saints' stair' unites these two aspects of the ladder image. But Simeon sees this ascent, like martyrdom, thought and prayer, as an event for the future. Central to his apprehension of Christ's birth is a meaning only later to be fulfilled. The imagery with which he describes his own life and impending death all suggest the old dispensation where he, like the Magi, remains.

Like many of Eliot's poems, this one begins by establishing a time. Simeon's own life is nearly over, and the fragility of 'a feather on the back of my hand' contrasts with the 'stubborn season' of winter. The first stanza associates Simeon's own death with the destruction of Israel and the need for a new kind of death. The Old Testament prophets frequently describe God's wrathful destruction of Israel as like a great wind or whirlwind. In one instance it leaves the slain covering the earth: '. . . and a great whirlwind shall be raised up from the coasts of the earth. And the slain of the Lord shall be at that day from *one* end of the earth even unto the *other* end of the earth: . . .' (Jeremiah 25:33-34). 'The wind that chills toward the dead land' and the present winter season are also the time when Simeon waits for the 'death wind'. In this context 'dust in sunlight' provides a significant contrast. Reappearing in the *Four Quartets*, this image resembles one used by St John of the

Cross to explain the pure awareness of God in the soul. Although this light is so pure and simple as to be invisible and dark, it is more visible and bright when it reflects off impurities in the soul, just as a ray of sunlight is only seen when filled with dust:

> In observing a ray of sunlight stream through the window, we notice that the more it is pervaded with particles of dust, the clearer and more palpable and sensible it appears to the senses; yet obviously the sun ray in itself is less pure, clear, simple, and perfect in that it is full of so many specks of dust. We also notice that when it is more purified of these specks of dust it seems more obscure and impalpable to the material eye; and the purer it is, the more obscure and inapprehensible it seems to be.[11]

When perfect, the spiritual light of pure inner knowledge of God seems totally dark to the soul, as would a ray of light if it shone on nothing. Achieving such perfect dark knowledge or pure invisible light requires the destruction of all impurities, a total annihilation of self through sensual and spiritual death. As Simeon waits for the physical death of the Old Testament, there is at the same time a waiting for that death of impurity or dust which is mystic apprehension of God. '. . . memory in corners' seems to recall Gerontion remembering an empty past in 'a sleepy corner'. 'Gerontion's' images of death in physical destruction thus provide a background against which to view these other deaths, Simeon's desired peace and the saint's ecstatic martyrdom.

Simeon hopes only for the peace and consolation of knowing Christ has come, justifying his own life because he has fulfilled the Old Law. '. . . he *is* just, he shall surely live, saith the Lord God' (Ezekiel 18:9) of the man who keeps the laws and provides for the poor. Seeing sorrows to come, Simeon asks that his own life be acceptable and that he may have peace. He foresees the persecution of Christians and the passion of Christ, recognising, as the Magi do not, what they mean. He knows also that this birth is death:

> Now at this birth season of decease,
> Let the Infant, the still unspeaking and unspoken Word,
> Grant Israel's consolation
> To one who has eighty years and no to-morrow.

The image of the unspeaking Word is another reference to the Andrewes' phrase used in 'Gerontion'. It also contrasts the mystic experience with Simeon's own experience. In an explanation of the difference between the Old and New Law, St John of the Cross speaks of the Word. In the Old Law it was licit to desire revelation from God because 'at that time faith was not yet perfectly established, nor was the Gospel law inaugurated'.[12] With the Incarnation it is no longer right to ask special revelations because 'In giving us His Son, His only Word (for He possesses no other), He spoke everything to us at once in this sole Word—. . . .'[13] But this includes all of Christ's life and death. 'When Christ dying on the cross exclaimed: Consummatum est (It is consummated) [Jn 19:30], He consummated not these ways alone, but all the other ceremonies and rites of the Old Law.'[14] When we note also that for St John of the Cross the whole mystic experience consists in imitating the death of Christ,[15] we see Simeon's dilemma. The Word has been given, but is still 'unspeaking and unspoken'. For him the ultimate vision granted those who follow Christ's steps is unavailable; there is but 'Israel's consolation', the knowledge that it will be.

Knowing all this, Simeon sees his own life as one of resignation to a lesser order of vision. Like the Magus, he feels weariness rather than joy:

> I am tired with my own life and the lives of those after me,
> I am dying in my own death and the deaths of those after me.

The effect of this is to make Simeon not simply a figure of a strange historical situation but a representative of all those to come after him who are not capable of sainthood. It is physical life of which he is tired and physical death he dies along with others, for spiritual death and life are not to be his.

'Journey of the Magi' and 'A Song for Simeon' use a specific historical time to symbolise a human dilemma—discovering that one is between birth and death and that rebirth requires death to this life. By juxtaposing present and future, Eliot makes the Incarnation a focal point to which all relate and Christ's birth and death the model for all rebirth. The paschal lamb prefigures Christ's sacrifice, a necessary sacrifice which itself prepares for the second coming. And in Simeon's mind the death wind of the Old Testament and the death to come are united by birth. Thus in both poems the vision of birth produces a sense of death without the release such death could bring. Despite the subject of these poems, then, Eliot achieves his effects from a felt negation. If the Incarnation appears to the reader with all its centuries of acquired meaning, it is only uneasily present to the characters. What they express, if not anguish, is clearly not fulfillment, only a subdued loss, a kind of dull unease. What remains vivid is remembered sensual delight or anticipated martyrdom. Thought and feeling are beginning to diverge in these poems in a way to be carried much further in *Ash-Wednesday*. For in all three a timeless vision is asserted while a temporal sorrow is felt. In *Ash-Wednesday* the theme of time finds one resolution; it presents the mystic way of escaping the bond of time altogether. But in order to do so one must traverse the 'time of tension between dying and birth', which troubles Simeon and the Magi, accepting the death of temporal life in order to apprehend eternity. Though it is not a very good poem, 'Animula' is interesting here because it states in a rather flat way the idea central to the first two 'Ariel Poems' and underlying *Ash-Wednesday*.

'Animula' contrasts the soul as it comes from God and as it comes from time. Born into a 'flat world of changing lights and noise' the simple soul is attracted or repelled by pleasure and pain. Eliot portrays the infant's life as one of simple sensuous delight and fantasy. But this gives way increasingly to the burden of moral choice:

> The heavy burden of the growing soul
> Perplexes and offends more, day by day;
> Week by week, offends and perplexes more
> With the imperatives of 'is and seems'
> And may and may not, desire and control.
> The pain of living and the drug of dreams
> Curl up the small soul in the window seat
> Behind the *Encyclopaedia Britannica*.

The soul, confronted by constant change and choice, becomes increasingly uncertain and confused. Life in time is painful and destructive to the soul, leaving it 'Irresolute and selfish, misshapen, lame'. In contrast, true life comes only after death, for this second life is out of time. The opening lines paraphrase a passage in the *Purgatorio* where Dante shows the need for the restraint of law. The simple soul seeks only small pleasures and clings to them unless curbed. Here again Eliot uses the source in a new way, for the small soul in 'Animula' does seek some source of understanding, though without success. Unable to resolve the questions of appearance and reality, desire and control, and caught between the pain of life and escape in dreams, the soul shrivels. In the modern world the only answers offered are facts in the *Encyclopaedia*. But knowledge of this world will not give value judgements, and, unable to distinguish good and ill, the soul rejects even that 'warm reality' it could attain. The good of this world is left behind with its evils, destroying life. It is this which leads to the paradox of life and death, for only in death, which ends temporal life, can there be a birth into true life.

Once this paradox is asserted, 'Living first in the silence after the viaticum,' the poem shifts abruptly to prayer for those who die. Guiterriez, Boudin, this one and that one are important not in themselves but as representatives of all. Floret, slain between the yew trees, suggests mythical associations which expand the moment of death and birth to that of all men. His death between the yew trees provides a visual image for the time between birth and death, since the yew is traditionally associated with both death and immortality. The final line repeats the paradox of death and birth by changing the last word of the traditional prayer from 'death' to 'birth'.

Like 'Journey of the Magi' and 'A Song for Simeon', 'Animula' closes on the union of death and birth. In this case, however, a reason for the association is simply asserted. Because time destroys, only a second life can satisfy, and that is attained only through death. Though 'Animula' is less subtle and effective than the previous 'Ariel' poems, it clearly illustrates the opposition of time and eternity on which all are based. The moment between the yew trees, like the time between Christ's birth and death, is a middle point which all must pass but which is only passed by most in physical destruction. By dying to sense and spirit in this world, the mystic passes through that point in this life, transcending time within the temporal world. Others achieve this true life in God only through physical death. Time and eternity join in the Incarnation, yet to achieve eternity humanity must escape time by physical death or the mystic death to this world.

Ash-Wednesday portrays the mystic's choice, the denial of time and human desire. Yet it is, paradoxically, one of Eliot's most sensual as well as most mystical poems, creating its intense effect by the conflict of willed choice and emotion. In his essay on Dante, T. S. Eliot distinguishes dream from vision, which he calls 'a more significant, interesting, and disciplined kind of dreaming'. 'We take it for granted,' he says, 'that our dreams spring from below: Possibly the quality of our dreams suffers in consequence.'[16] Speaking of the 'Divine Pageant' in the earthly paradise, he reiterates this distinction:

> To those who dislike—not what are popularly called pageants—but the serious pageants of royalty, of the church, of military funerals—the 'pageantry' which we find here and in the *Paradiso* will be tedious; and still more to those, if there be any, who are unmoved by the splendour of the Revelations of St John. It belongs to the world of what I call the *high dream*, and the modern world seems capable only of the *low dream.*[17]

In *Ash-Wednesday* Eliot uses this contrast of high and low dream to portray the meaning of purgation and renunciation. Although the poem moves toward a choice and justification of the *'high dream'*, it gives not only equal space but perhaps more intensity to the *'low dream'*. The rich feeling and poignance of the poem arise from the narrator's yearning after what is not only lost but now known never to have been, what is known to be illusion but still wanted with that paradoxical anguish arising from the separation of thought and feeling. This contrast of low and high dream is both the primary structural device of the poem and the basis for wide divergence in tone and style between sections, from passages of vivid juxtaposed images without logical connective to more abstract and discursive sections developed in the form of logical argument.

Like *The Waste Land* and *Four Quartets*, *Ash-Wednesday* is made up of poems written separately and later put together in a sequence. In each case Eliot selected and arranged to create a whole. That this was so for *Ash-Wednesday* is attested to in a statement he made to Donald Hall:

> Like *The Hollow Men*, it originated out of separate poems . . . Then gradually I came to see it as a sequence. That's one way in which my mind does seem to have worked throughout the years poetically—doing things separately and then seeing the possibility of fusing them together, altering them, and making a kind of whole of them.[18]

If *The Waste Land* is a mass of very disparate pieces drastically cut and abruptly juxtaposed into a partial 'unity', *Four Quartets* is clearly a deliberate sequence of carefully selected recurrent forms, though the idea of a whole came to Eliot only while writing 'East Coker'. *Ash-Wednesday* is between the two, formally as well as chronologically. Though its juxtaposition may seem as abrupt and its sections as discrete, it is in fact truly unified by a single consciousness and a personal quest in a way that Tiresias and the Grail myth only partially unify the earlier work. Moreover, a set of close relations between all the parts emerges more clearly in *Ash-Wednesday*. And, as in *Four Quartets*, this relationship arises partly from a union of idea and emotion relying not solely on fusing the two in images but on alternating evocative and discursive sections. The underlying ideas are articulated overtly through meditation and even logical argument. The personal experience is evoked through unusually intense symbols. The overall pattern of these distinct sections has not been fully explained; it is not, despite the strong reliance on mystic tradition, a recounting of the mystic experience in its chronological order. Nor is it a Dantean movement of descent and reascent into understanding and ecstasy. It is not, in fact, a linear movement at all. Leonard Unger, for example, rightly claimed that the 'ground' upon which 'all the associations occur . . . is the idea of being purified in the purgatorial dark night',[19] and the influence of St John of the Cross is generally acknowledged. But the poem follows no direct line through the mystic experience. Part III, which shows the soul in the first stages of climbing above sensual desire, follows the experience of the dark night of the soul in II rather than, as in mystic experience, precedes it. But there is a sequence, nonetheless, and a structural unity as well as a unity of consciousness. The overall pattern is a movement from renunciation through resignation to renunciation through knowledge and acceptance. We end where we began but at a new level. As in the *Quartets*, this movement arises through both imagery and almost prose-like explanation, what Graham Hough referred to as 'Vision and Doctrine'.[20] For *Ash-Wednesday* rests on a doctrine, though it does not exist to assert one. The movement from resignation to willed acceptance of God's will is a development both intellectual and emotional. The reasons for making it are set out in the more discursive sections of I, V, and VI and constitute not a chronological sequence but a vision of dryness and purgation which allows for the movement from the low dream of III to the high dream of IV. The overall structure, then, moves from meditation on the act of renunciation, through the experience of renunciation and a vision of spiritual renewal to explanation and recommitment to the choice.

The first poem emphasises the need to renounce intellect, will and memory and to turn from the transient to God; the emphasis is on 'because', 'because' there is no hope of regaining secular power or glory or love or even spiritual renewal within time alone. The second poem presents a visionary landscape portraying the desert of the dark night of the soul and the sense of being devoured and desiccated. The fourth is Eliot's version of the earthly paradise, the 'high dream'. Throughout the poems two main themes recur: that time in itself is meaningless and that only the Word, entering time, can give it meaning. These ideas appear explicitly in I and V in passages of discursive explanation and justification. II and IV are both visionary landscapes whose meaning becomes clear through the 'doctrine' in I and V. Poem III, depicting the climbing of the saint's stair, contains a lovely dream-like landscape of natural, earthly beauty, so that the centre of the sequence, III and IV, juxtaposes the low and high dream, human desire and divine love. Poem VI recalls the false dream and returns to the need for renunciation expressed in I. Thus the contrast of false and true dreams at the centre is preceded and succeeded by a kind of reasoning about their meaning and the basis for choice as well as the means of achieving the higher and transcending the lower.

It is perhaps true, as has been claimed, that a total understanding of such religious poetry depends on knowledge of and belief in the doctrines which it uses and the experience it creates. But I think it is possible for a non-believer to possess a religious sensibility without assenting to doctrine. One can understand what it feels like to be empty and dry, to feel what is called 'sin' and long for renewal without in any way defining these experiences in Christian or even religious terms. Nonetheless, their poetic articulation will evoke powerful response in one who knows such feelings. It is necessary, however, if not to believe, to understand the concepts on which a religious understanding of those feelings rests in order to enter a poem using them. In the case of *Ash-*

Wednesday it is necessary to understand, at least in outline, the nature and meaning of the dark night of the soul. Its place in the poem has been fully discussed before;[21] it is enough to point out here that it requires complete renunciation of the world, not only physical but even mental—a kind of chosen death to this life, and it is often described by mystics as like being eaten by a large animal. The surrealist landscape of II thus evokes what the argument of I requires: the sense of becoming nothing, of accepting nothingness. By becoming nothing, according to St John of the Cross, one is filled with God and so, paradoxically, becomes everything. Thus the serenity of achieving peace in God's will comes from losing all will of one's own. The bones are glad to be scattered, and the soul is glad to be nothing because that cuts away all longing for fulfillment in temporal human life, leaving it free to accept the higher vision of divine love. The essential concept underlying this is that time is meaningless, 'time is always time / And place is always and only place'. Only in timelessness, in the unchanging Word, is there meaning. Eliot's concept of time has been called Neo-Platonic, among other things. 'Neo-Platonic' is applicable here in its emphasis on the separation of time and eternity, the notion of the world whirling about the still Word, and the insistence that one must leave the whirling world in order to apprehend the Word. These ideas are embodied in contrasting images of silence and stillness, sound and motion. The high and low dreams are the dreams of timeless perfection and temporal fulfillment, and the poem turns on the choice of one over the other. Ironically, though *Ash-Wednesday* portrays the choice of eternal life, its most intense passages evoke loss. Its failure to satisfy many readers, especially those who decried Eliot's move to the church, is not only, I think, because it posits a doctrine of renunciation of temporal human life but because what is intensely evoked is the loss. The gain is asserted, argued for, prayed for, and chosen; the loss is more deeply felt. In the two dreams, both the nature of the choice and the contrasting moods are revealed.

Assertion, argument, prayer and choice all precede the two dreams.

Poem I is structured as an argument for submission and acceptance; the style is discursive, the tone resigned. There is little concrete imagery and what there is remains general. Yet the form, which suggests a circling motion, effectively conveys an attitude and prepares for the overall movement of the poem. Central to the argument is the idea that time is only time; that is, it contains only what is impermanent and therefore once lost, forever lost. The certainty that time 'is ever sure to bring about . . . loss' now becomes a reason for denying it altogether and seeking a form of experience where gain is certain. The very different mood of *Ash-Wednesday*, despite a theme shared with early poems, depends on this new commitment along with the old nostalgia and longing for human fulfillment. Loss ceases to be a source of satire and becomes instead a poignant memory of what might have been. The opening lines of I, with their reiteration of 'turning', unite the opposed desires for human and divine love. The first line, a translation from Guido Cavalcanti's ballad of farewell to a lady, evokes lost human love. But turning away from the world and towards God is also central to *Ash-Wednesday*. Lancelot Andrewes, in his Ash Wednesday sermon of 1619, focuses on the word:

> Repentance it selfe is nothing els, but *redire ad principia*, a kind of circling; to *returne* to Him by *repentance*, from *whom*, by sinne, we have turned away. And much after a *circle* is this text: beginns with the word turne, and *returnes* about to the same word againe.[22]

Eliot's lines might be said to embody this text, but they are intensified by the dual suggestion of returning to a lover or to God. This ambiguity remains throughout *Ash-Wednesday*: to turn to God one must turn away from the world, but the 'love of created beings' intensifies as they are lost. Power and material success, suggested in the allusion to Shakespeare's sonnet XXIX and the image of the eagle, are also renounced. The eagle has many symbolic associations in mythology and Christian legend—the empire, the church, an aspect of Christ, the soul's flight to God. But in Eliot's poems it is consistently associated with worldly pomp and glory. The speaker, as an aged eagle, combines the qualities of soul which, according to St John of the Cross, must be stripped so that 'Its youth is renewed like the eagle's (Ps. 102:5), clothed in the new man . . . '[23] with the wearied public man whose apparent success has become empty. No longer hoping to regain either the world or desire for it, he renounces the attempt. The 'usual reign' implies the common kind of success, now past and no longer attainable.

Like the first stanza, the second and third begin with 'because', creating a series of premises leading to a definite conclusion. The first 'cause' is loss of passion and power; the second is loss of God, or at least of the awareness of divine rebirth 'where trees flower and springs flow'. This has not yet been defined, but it takes on associations with divine illumination when seen in relation to the vision of IV where the trees do flower and the springs flow. This experience has clearly occurred before, yet it has been 'transitory' and 'infirm' though 'positive' and 'veritable', the one true and real experience. This fleeting moment of reality is to reappear in the *Quartets* as the hint of Incarnation. There it is evoked, here only referred to. But its chief characteristics of being real and positive already separate it from the seemingly ephemeral nature of worldly success. It too, however, is lost and seemingly no longer attainable. The two 'causes' culminate in a third 'cause' which explains both:

> Because I know that time is always time
> And place is always and only place
> And what is actual is actual only for one time
> And only for one place

The loss of both loves, temporal and eternal, is due to the fact that both are apprehended in time and no moment can be retained. 'And what is actual is actual only for one time. . . .' There is a difference between the two, of course, for the eternal remains when not apprehended. It can be known fully only by transcending time. Throughout *Ash-Wednesday* the opposition remains that has already been seen in 'Gerontion', the satires and the first three 'Ariel Poems': time is divorced from eternity, and permanent value can be found only in eternity. Although they are seen to intersect in the Incarnation, that can be apprehended only by renouncing time. Gerontion had lost contact with the Word; the Magi saw and felt its power but could not understand it; Simeon understood but could not accept its meaning for himself. The speaker in *Ash-Wednesday* is involved in the process of understanding and accepting the consequence of this truth, which is to renounce time altogether and to accept the self-annihilation or mystic death which leads to apprehension of eternity.

This renunciation and apprehension follows almost exactly the beginning of mystic experience described by St John of the Cross. According to 'The Dark Night' the soul about to enter this experience loses pleasure in all things, then turns to God 'solicitously and with painful care', for the soul will be concerned only with God. Such souls should give up ideas and thoughts. Describing the act of God in preparing souls for the dark night, St John of the Cross says that he 'divests the faculties, affections, and senses, both spiritual and sensory, interior and exterior. He leaves the intellect in darkness, the will in aridity, the memory in emptiness. . . .'[24] The argument of poem I is almost a restatement of these beginning stages, moving from rejection of all spiritual and physical desire to the need to forget, to give up thought and will. The concluding prayer ('Pray for us now and at the hour of our death') both fulfills the requirement to persevere in prayer while giving up all else and introduces the second poem which is to be an allegory of death—not physical death but the death of sense and spirit which is the dark night of the soul.

The strange, allegorical landscape of poem II directly evokes the experience of the dark night, an experience often compared to being devoured. Despite the violent and terrible images of death, the tone is oddly serene and joyous. Dry bones that remain sing to a Beatrice-like figure who 'honours the Virgin in meditation', and their song is joyous. In the second stanza they sing her praise, attributing to her the mystery of eternity seen by Dante in Beatrice's eyes: the unification of opposites. As Dante sees the alternate natures of the griffin (human and divine) though the griffin remains immovable[25] they see opposites united as an intimation of eternity. Discussing the relation of medieval symbolism to mysticism, H. Flanders Dunbar commented on this idea:

> The unification of opposites is accomplished only in eternity. Man in this world, though granted glimpses of eternity, must live under conditions of time. . . . Dante in the spheres found matter and spirit everywhere united, . . .[26]

The unitive way, the last step in the mystic journey, consists of 'glimpses of things as a whole, each glimpse a foretaste of the Beatific Vision, . . .'[27] which is the ultimate goal of mystic life and the vision in Beatrice's eyes. Thus the bones, though all that is left of a destroyed body, envision eternity and are glad. The mood is created by images as well—white leopards, the cool of the day, the white gown of the lady. All is pure, peaceful and serene. A developed allusion to God's restoration of dry bones intensifies the feeling of renewal and anticipation. After asking 'Can these bones live' God recovers the bones with flesh and breathes life into them. As in the 'Ariel Poems', Eliot modifies the source, changing 'can' to 'shall' and making the bones themselves respond. The question becomes, not God's willingness to restore a nation, but the individual soul's acceptance of nothingness and submission to God. And the bones attribute their own brightness and renunciation of self to the lady. The vision of her nature is the reward for being dissembled and the source of joy in the desert.

She is the lady of silences, set apart from this world where there is 'not enough silence'. Within her all opposition is contained and reconciled. Most important, perhaps, is the union of the single rose with the garden where all love ends. The rose carries many implications throughout Eliot, among them a moment of human love as well as the higher love of Heaven or Dante's multifoliate rose. Here the former has become the latter, as Beatrice was transformed in Dante's mind from a human to a divine love. In the 'Garden', the garden of Eden or the earthly paradise or the desert redeemed, all love 'ends' or achieves its ultimate purpose.

Prayer to the lady divides acceptance of death and anticipation of rebirth. The third section of poem II contains a brief but vivid image of the bones singing in joy and concludes in quiet peace. Deriving again from Ezekiel, it echoes God's promise to the prophet of a restored Israel: 'This is the land which ye shall divide by lot unto the tribes of Israel for inheritance, and these are their portions, saith the Lord God' (Ezekiel 48:29). As the dry bones in the desert offered a symbol for personal death to the world, so their resurrection and inheritance of the land symbolise the rebirth of the soul and its eternal salvation. If the sections of *Ash-Wednesday* followed a chronological order, one would expect III to portray mystic union. Instead, it depicts the soul back in its first stages, wearily climbing the stairs of ascent above physical desire. Overcoming the senses is the first hard stage of mystic experience, occurring long before the death of intellect, will and memory. After the argument for renunciation and the vision of the dark night, the high and low dreams are juxtaposed. This suggests that the experience of II is not presently occurring but is a vision or a dream by which the speaker understands what he must undergo. In the opposing dreams of III and IV, the choice is made clear.

Poem III, originally published under the title, 'Som de Escalina', contains what Eliot means by the 'low dream'. It is none the less lovely. Lilac and blown hair evoke unbearable desire, and the poem does not deny this beauty in the sensual dream, just as Spenser portrays the Bower of Bliss as truly enchanting. It is because of their beauty that the senses enchain. Appropriately, the title is taken from a speech of Arnaut Daniel, who suffers in Purgatory for the sin of lust. He admonishes Dante to be mindful of his pain when Dante reaches the summit of the stairs of Purgatory. At the summit Dante is to see the earthly paradise, and in that image is the basis for Eliot's own 'high dream' of poem IV. The opposed dreams meet in Arnaut Daniel, who, in purgation for desiring the one, prepares for ascent to the other.

Poem III moves from the struggle of ascent to poignant memory of a lost world and culminates in a prayer for help against temptation. Vividly and concretely, the first two sections portray the soul climbing, looking back at the dark and tortuous steps. At each turning of the stair, the soul looks back on the painful ascent:

> At the first turning of the second stair
> I turned and saw below
> The same shape twisted on the banister
> Under the vapour in the fetid air
> Struggling with the devil of the stairs who wears
> The deceitful face of hope and of despair.

Whether 'the same shape' is his own image, recalled in its former pain, or the soul of another on the same journey, it illustrates the difficult early effort to renounce both hope and despair, to move towards silence and darkness. It may also be his sensual self, still struggling but left behind by the soul's willed choice. The devil of the stairs, which has been associated with the 'demon of doubt' Eliot describes as facing Pascal,[28] may also recall the 'angel of Satan' who, according to St John of the Cross, often comes to those who have experienced the dark night of the senses and now must undergo that final and terrible dark night of the spirit. What matters for the poem's emotional impact is the emphasis on struggle and deceit. Hope and despair for the world are surrounded by images of distortion: the shape is twisted, the air fetid, the devil's face deceitful. Yet it is a terrible struggle to resist that force. At the second turning the struggling shapes are left below, and the stair itself is grotesque and disgusting, dark and associated with senility. One cannot go back, only forward, for the past is moribund, 'beyond repair'.

Yet the memory is strange: it represses the unbearable and clings to the illusion of what one wished the past had been. The sudden shift at this point is simply that, the old trick of recalling 'what might have been', the garden known as richly in imagination as if in literal fact. But this is not 'Burnt Norton': no speculation on the mystery of time hedges this round; it is to be illusion only. After the soul has looked back on the conflict with the world and the devil and seen it as hideous, it seems at first odd that the view from the third stair is of sensuous joy. Yet it is not a scene of lust but the dream of a temporal human love which is joyous and fulfilling. The similarity to Prufrock's dreams can hardly be accidental, for Prufrock's failure was seeking happiness in the impermanent. Yet human love rather than mere copulation is perhaps the most difficult to renounce.

 A striking aspect of this passage is its imagery, which recalls the early poems. Seen in relation to the fourth poem, these images take on even greater significance. Both focus on a garden, specific flowers, trees, colours, and the music of flutes. Yet the quality of these images is sharply differentiated—sensual and desiring in one, formal and serene in the other:

>At the first turning of the third stair
>Was a slotted window bellied like the fig's fruit
>And beyond the hawthorn blossom and a pasture scene
>The broadbacked figure drest in blue and green
>Enchanted the maytime with an antique flute.
>Blown hair is sweet, brown hair over the mouth blown,
>Lilac and brown hair;

This is the springtime 'in time's covenant', time of physical rebirth. Sweet music, scent of lilacs, spring colours, the feeling of hair blown over the mouth. Each image suggests fertility and the natural cycle of generation. '. . . bellied like the fig's fruit', the window itself introduces the theme. Leonard Unger sees in this slotted window a suggestion of the female sex organ, but, whether or not one need carry it so far, the fig has associations with pagan fertility rites. According to Frazer,[29] the fig was supposed by East Africans to fertilise women and this was no doubt assumed also by the Romans. An annual ceremony in Greece and Asia Minor celebrated a sacred marriage between fig trees to make them blossom, and Greeks beat human scapegoats personating male and female fig trees on the genitals with fig branches to stimulate generative powers.[30] The hawthorn appears in English legend associated with May Day[31] and was once used to deck doors and porches on May Day in Cornwall.[32] Flute music was considered exciting by the Greeks,[33] and the Death of Adonis (part of a yearly fertility ritual) was mourned to the wailing of a flute.[34] 'Enchanted' is a fitting verb, for the entire scene has an air of pastoral romance, sensuous but natural and compelling. The vulgar or crude or painful does not appear. What Prufrock desired is here created, the association specific in brown hair.

Though sweet, the images are fleeting. Recalled to a sense of higher goals, the narrator shifts the tone with 'distraction'. Distraction, music of the flute, stops and steps of the mind over the third stair. This dream of fulfillment in sensual, temporal life, in the renewal of physical beauty and natural love, is a false dream or at least what Eliot calls the 'low dream'. To love it is to love illusion; to long for it is to slow one's ascent. But the soul can conquer desire: 'Fading, fading', which begins the next line, is still part of the sentence on distraction. And as distractions fade, strength greater than hope or despair comes through faith. The soul, which cannot save itself, need only have faith and God will grant salvation:

> Lord, I am not worthy
> Lord, I am not worthy
> but speak the word only.

These words are said by the priest in Mass just before he consumes Christ's body and blood. The original source is Matthew 8:8, where

Christ has promised to come and heal a centurion's servant. The centurion replies, 'Lord, I am not worthy that thou shouldest come under my roof; but speak the word only, and my servant shall be healed.' The allusion evokes an attitude combining awareness of weakness and unworthiness with trust in God's promise.

As a whole, the third part of *Ash-Wednesday* depicts alternate memories of sensual life: as hideous sin and as joyous participation in the natural rhythm of seasonal rebirth. The seemingly deliberate choice of images recalling early poems suggests both the nature of this dream as natural and sensual, and the transience of all things subject to time. The poem ends not with a promise but with faith and willingness to continue climbing the stair. It is important to remember that this dream is all in the past, seen in memory only. It is seen through a window from the landing of the third stair. The soul is already beyond it, and conflict is wholly inner—the struggle to forget, as well as renounce, desire.

In the fourth poem we are already at the summit, in a cool and tranquil garden like Dante's earthly paradise. The trees, flowers, colours and music remain but are transformed. Blue and green colours of bright spring dress are formalised as liturgical symbol; the fig tree and the hawthorn of cyclic regeneration are replaced by the yew tree of immortality and larkspur that is 'blue of Mary's colour'; fiddles and flutes are borne away or represented by the silent flute of the garden god; and wind blows, not sensuous brown hair, but 'a thousand whispers from the yew'. All is stylised, tranquil and soundless. We are brought from dream to vision, and as in II the serene figure of a woman is central. She is not Mary but represents her, going 'in Mary's colour'. In the opening passage she appears walking between ranks of colours, no longer flowers but abstract ideals. Wearing the white and blue of Mary, she goes among ranks of green and violet, liturgical colours for hope and penitence. We are not told who she is, nor is identification necessary, for like the colours she is idealised, transformed into symbol. Through her image Eliot conveys a quality which defies analysis, for it is non-physical and non-intellectual. Serene and remote, though not aloof, she moves 'among the others', renewing by her very presence the fountains and springs. Two lines suggest her most important quality: 'Talking of trivial things / In ignorance and in knowledge of eternal dolour.' Her wisdom is higher and greater than knowledge of facts and situations. Because she is calm and at peace, she does not need profound speech; her nature is expressed in her manner. Though her form is not described, the formalised setting creates a sense of tranquil nobility and an aura of wisdom transcending speech. Like the Lady of Silences, she contains opposites, ignorance and knowledge being reconciled in a higher innocence and purity. Though she knows eternal dolour, she also does not 'know' it, for her wisdom is of a different order, surpassing ignorance and knowledge.

With Arnaut Daniel's words, the vision shifts abruptly: 'Sovegna vos', 'be mindful', recalls us from purity and holy love to the earthly love for which Daniel suffers in Purgatory. They are related, for the time of suffering restores first innocence:

> Here are the years that walk between, bearing
> Away the fiddles and the flutes, restoring
> One who moves in the time between sleep and waking, wearing
>
> White light folded, sheathed about her, folded.
> The new years walk, restoring
> Through a bright cloud of tears, the years, restoring
> With a new verse the ancient rhyme. Redeem
> The time. Redeem
> The unread vision in the higher dream
> While jewelled unicorns draw by the gilded hearse.

As Beatrice was restored to Dante in her first purity at the summit of the stairway, so this lady represents the restoration of Eden's innocence. 'The years' are quite specific; they are the time that restores, the time of purgatorial suffering. And this vision is a culmination, an earthly paradise reached by climbing the stairs. The years have value, but only in their expiatory function. Through suffering in time, the soul attains perfection which is timeless.

The metaphor of poetry is interesting, for it is at one level literal. In this poem Eliot is restoring Dante's rhyme in a new verse. The *Purgatorio* is renewed, recreated in the modern world though its essence is the same. In another sense it is the essence which is restored, the capacity for vision which Eliot called 'a more significant, interesting, and disciplined kind of dreaming'. It is this capacity which can redeem the time. After the description of years restoring the vision of innocence and the ancient rhyme, the poem shifts suddenly to exhortation, 'Redeem / The time. Redeem / The unread vision in the higher dream.' The sources for this phrase in St Paul and Eliot's own prose are frequently quoted. Both imply that by retaining faith in vision, while the world succumbs to temporal and secular decay, one can redeem the time '. . . so that the Faith may be preserved alive through the dark ages before us; to renew and rebuild civilisation, and save the world from suicide.'[35] This redemption is, thus, for both the individual soul and the world, for while it raises the soul above the world, it keeps alive a knowledge which can later be shared though the vision is now 'unread'. The meaning of the unicorns is ambiguous. The line has been seen as a reference to temporal pomp cheapening and making gaudy the unicorns of chastity. It is *while* the world misreads the vision that one must retain faith in order to redeem the time. Yet in medieval art the unicorn is often depicted with a jewelled collar, and the meaning of the unicorn is not restricted to chastity. It often, like Dante's griffin, symbolises Christ.[36] Nor does 'gilded' necessarily imply specious brilliance. The *Oxford English Dictionary* lists many uses in which it has good connotations. It is probable that the line should be read as part of the higher vision, representing death transformed into more perfect life through Christ. According to Shepard, the unicorn is also associated with monastic life and solitude. This suggests another reading of the line also making it part of restored vision, since monastic solitude is the death of the self but is a death which leads to life. An ironic line seems out of place here; if the mood were to be so broken, it would be difficult to return abruptly to the 'silent sister veiled in white and blue'. Perhaps in either case the formality and idealisation of the image prevent a clash in tone.

The following passage returns to the lady and presents a distinct contrast with the sensual dream of III. Here, most clearly, the two are seen in opposition as temporal and eternal aspiration:

> The silent sister veiled in white and blue
> Between the yews, behind the garden god,
> Whose flute is breathless, bent her head and signed but spoke
>   no word

Here is the figure among trees, the flute, the garden god, yet all is still, even the flute breathless. As in 'Animula', the yew symbolises everlasting life. In English country funerals, mourners carried yew branches to typify immortality.[37] Yew boughs were also used as decorations on Easter and in the Middle Ages were substituted for palms on Palm Sunday. Thus as the images of III resonate with sensual renewal, those of IV are rich with associations of spiritual rebirth. Standing between yews, the lady symbolises the 'time between sleep and waking', the transition from death to life. Her role as contemplative suggests a way of transition other than the physical death described in 'Animula' and portrayed in Floret's death between yews. The presence of a flute suggests music, yet it is, like the music on Keats's Grecian urn, an 'unheard melody'. Indeed, the comparison can be carried further, for like the scenes on the urn, this is suspended in timeless perfection. In 'Burnt Norton' Eliot writes, 'Words move, music moves / Only in time', and his timeless moments are evoked partially by unheard music. As the images of III recall Prufrock's sensual desire, the images of IV anticipate the aspiration, in 'Burnt Norton', for timeless ecstasy.

The lady speaks 'no word', yet her silent gesture is sufficient to renew life:

> But the fountain sprang up and the bird sang down
> Redeem the time, redeem the dream
> The token of the word unheard, unspoken

This suggests a relation of time with the timeless. Rejuvenation of the desert is the token of the timeless word. By purity and holy innocence attained through suffering, time and the dream are redeemed for man. Purgatorial suffering, depicted in the second poem, leads back to the innocence of Eden, and the soul, by regaining innocence, redeems time. The word remains unheard and unspoken because it is eternal, and the speaker is not yet in Paradise. But the dream is a token symbolising his apprehension of the word, an apprehension not attained in any previous poem. The following line implies an eventual manifestation of the word, for it is unspoken 'Till the wind shake a thousand whispers from the yew', until, in other words, entry into eternal life.

IV concludes with a line from a Roman Catholic prayer to Mary, usually said at the end of Mass: 'Turn then, most gracious advocate, thine eyes of mercy towards us. And after this our exile, show unto us the blessed fruit of thy womb, Jesus.' The line, then, implies hope for ultimate vision after a time of sorrow. It is important to note that Eliot does not, in *Ash-Wednesday*, go beyond Dante's earthly paradise into a vision of heaven or an ultimate knowledge. The poem remains with the purgatorial ascent, and even this vision of the lady remains a promise more than a final resolution. Certainly it does not seem to lead towards higher knowledge but to remain a token. In the last two poems the speaker is not moving higher but remains in the time of transition. Like the Magus in 'Journey of the Magi' and Simeon in 'A Song for Simeon' he is between two lives, though unlike them he seems capable of the ultimate vision, willing to accept the struggle which leads to it. Having seen both the low dream and the high dream, he has made the ultimate choice. Yet the poem ends, oddly, not in triumph or even deep conviction but in a plea for help to sustain the choice. And in poem VI the most moving passage is not that plea but the insistent, overwhelming recollection of what was lost without ever having been; and the word itself, 'lost', provides the sad background for the lyric of remembrance.

Poem V is divided into four sections, punctuated three times by God's cry to Israel in Micah 6:3: 'O my people, what have I done unto thee?' This is called by Micah 'the Lord's controversy', for God has done all for His people, yet they turn away. Poem V develops this 'controversy', affirming the presence of the silent word and questioning humanity's ability to find it. The opening section is vivid and powerful, though abstract, gaining intensity through repetition and rhythm, building to a climax. The first full sentence affirms the Word; the second affirms the world's opposition:

> If the lost word is lost, if the spent word is spent
> If the unheard, unspoken
> Word is unspoken, unheard;
> Still is the unspoken word, the Word unheard,
> The Word without a word, the Word within
> The world and for the world;
> And the light shone in darkness and
> Against the Word the unstilled world still whirled
> About the centre of the silent Word.

The style is again discursive, presenting in a clear assertion the relation of Word and world underlying the opposing dreams. Though the Word is lost or ignored, all the world exists in relation to it and it always is. The passage is based on the Gospel of St John, which begins 'In the beginning was the Word' (John 1:1). John 1:5 reads: 'And the light shineth in darkness; and the darkness comprehended it not.' The power of this passage lies in its simplicity and reliance on sound rather than subtle argument. The relation between Word and world, timeless and temporal, resembles that in 'Gerontion' where both exist but seem divorced from one another. Here, however, there is no question that humanity can find the Word. One must blame not historical deception but one's own failure to renounce the impermanent for the sake of God. The reiteration of God's own plea emphasises this, for God has not deserved rejection. If God is rejected, humanity has failed.

Turning from basic assertions to their implications, the speaker asks how the Word is to be found:

> Where shall the word be found, where will the word
> Resound? Not here, there is not enough silence
> Not on the sea or on the islands, not
> On the mainland, in the desert or the rain land,
> For those who walk in darkness
> Both in the day time and in the night time
> The right time and the right place are not here
> No place of grace for those who avoid the face
> No time to rejoice for those who walk among noise and deny
>   the voice

'Here' is no particular place or time but rather place and time themselves. '... Time is always time / And place is always and only place' becomes concrete in all the times and places which have no grace. 'Here' is the temporal world of noise and motion without silence. The emphasis on times, places, seasons, hours and words recalls the preoccupation with specific times in early poems. Those who are caught in time are seen in contrast to the mystic who transcends it.

Strangely enough, the speaker seems to include himself among those who are caught between. Despite the mystic experience of II and the promise of renewal in IV, both V and VI return to the time of tension and uncertainty. The vision of the veiled sister is a positive assurance that a choice is possible, but between those who are caught in time and those who choose renunciation are those who wish to renounce but cannot. The speaker reiterates their question and desire throughout the last two sections of V. They will not go away but cannot pray; they offend but cannot sustain that affirmation when faced with the desert and rocks, the final desert where they must become nothing in order to gain everything and yet they spit 'from the mouth the withered appleseed'. To reject the appleseed is to reject one's participation in sin and so one's own death. 'O my people' recurs, closing the poem on a note of longing for redemption.

Ash-Wednesday turns around a central contrast and returns to the opening conflict, the speaker looking back rather than forward because the choice has been made if not yet carried through. The point is that this choice is an intellectual decision, not a change of feeling. In a sense, what the speaker in *Ash-Wednesday* does is to will this divorce of immediate sensation from intellectual perception in order to achieve peace. The opening lines of VI echo those of I but with 'Although' in place of 'Because'. Since 'Perchè' can be translated either way, the intrinsic ambiguity for English strengthens the poem's structure. We are back to the first choice but on a new plane, a choice now fully understood. Yet having made the choice, 'Although I do not hope to turn again', the speaker is not freed from desire:

> Wavering between the profit and the loss
> In this brief transit where the dreams cross
> The dreamcrossed twilight between birth and dying
> (Bless me father) though I do not wish to wish these things
> From the wide window towards the granite shore
> The white sails still fly seaward, seaward flying
> Unbroken wings

Still in the time of transition, the speaker calls it 'dreamcrossed'. The dreams on which the poem pivots 'cross' here where one must choose between them. The world is beautiful though it is called an illusion. Adjectives describing the speaker as 'lost', 'weak', 'blind', provide an ironic counterpoint to the intense dream of sensual beauty. It is perhaps significant that 'blind' refers again to a specific kind of loss. In *Ash-Wednesday*, for the first time, Eliot depicts one who truly 'sees', if only momentarily, a higher vision. Blindness is simply looking at anything else, looking at 'empty forms' of sensual delight. Sight, sound and smell all give knowledge of impermanence, yet the bent golden-rod and cry of quail and salt savour of sandy earth draw the soul back, and the passage ends with that savour rather than a reminder of 'empty forms'. But the closing prayer for submission does not cancel the evocation of desire. The poem remains between the two worlds despite the clarity and firmness of the final commitment.

In *Ash-Wednesday* Eliot presents a conscious choice, but it is a choice of the mind still at odds with feeling. The narrator seeks the higher dream out of belief and need for peace but cannot cease wanting the world, not its spurious pomp or glory, not the glory of the hummingbird or the ecstasy of the animals but the lilac and sea voices which it should have been. Not until 'Little Gidding' does Eliot find a reconciliation of time and eternity. Here they are utterly opposed, and the low dream of human joy must be as utterly rejected if the earthly paradise is to be attained. The value of time is only in allowing purgation. Yet the poem's most moving passages are not ranks of varied green and jewelled unicorns but of 'brown hair over the mouth blown, / Lilac and brown hair' and 'the bent golden-rod and the lost sea smell'. The narrator's passion is in the world, his peace in the timeless vision, and passion and peace, both deep needs, are as divorced as time and eternity. *Ash-Wednesday*, despite its conceptual coherence, is in one sense a poem at war with itself. It is, nonetheless, the central poem of Eliot's canon looked on now as a whole. Looking back to both 'Prufrock' and 'Gerontion', it rejects the desire of one, transforming the dream of love from human to divine, and rejects the desiccation of the other, transforming Gerontion's dryness of spiritual emptiness which leads to a sleepy corner to the desert of the dark night which leads to spiritual life. Both Gerontion and the narrator of *Ash-Wednesday* are devoured, but the tiger comes to Gerontion in wrath and vengeance at his negation. The leopards in their white purity are agents of purgation, bringing peace and promise. The transcendent vision glimpsed in *Ash-Wednesday* recurs in *Four Quartets* where, in

'Little Gidding' alone, it is not only understood but united with temporal life and seen as inseparable from it. Eliot has been charged with a vision that is non-human and filled with loathing of life.[38] But while his revulsion at sex in the early poems is undeniable, he was acutely sensitive to natural beauty and had an intense sense of time and place. In the inner conflict of the narrator of *Ash-Wednesday* he evoked the paradoxical need for both temporal, earthly beauty and timeless, still serenity. In doing so he achieved a poem not of spiritualised meditation alone but of the anguish of human loss. The complexity, intensity and power of *Ash-Wednesday* arises from that conflict and from the fact that, like Dante, he chooses Beatrice though even the sight of her eyes cannot stop the tears when he knows that Virgil is gone.

If the first three 'Ariel Poems' present a stage of the soul's struggle which leads up to *Ash-Wednesday*, 'Marina' both logically and chronologically follows it. Though it is grouped with 'Journey of the Magi', 'A Song for Simeon' and 'Animula', it was published in 1930 and written after *Ash-Wednesday*. It may seem strange here, for it presents a joyous apprehension of new life miraculously restored, which bears little resemblance to the garden in the desert of *Ash-Wednesday*. It is not specifically Christian, yet it has been described as 'Eliot's one uncompromisingly direct, happy, and assured statement'.[39] The poem creates a mood of wonder and rediscovery, a kind of serene fulfillment. Curiously this fulfillment is derived not from apprehension of timeless perfection but from a temporal and human experience. It is, however, almost dreamlike and seems to lift the speaker beyond himself into some new and wondrous realm. What we have in this poem is the creation of a moment which is to appear again in *Four Quartets*, a moment of time which seems somehow to contain an apprehension of eternity. In *Ash-Wednesday* it was the 'one veritable transitory power', and without looking forward to *Four Quartets* where images from 'Marina' recur and are more clearly defined, this moment of transcendence emerges both in the poem and in Eliot's sources. The poem's title and central situation are based on the recognition scene of Shakespeare's

Pericles. Eliot looked not only to that but to the specific treatment of the play by G. Wilson Knight. In 1930 Eliot sent a copy of 'Marina' to Knight inscribed to him 'with, I hope, some appropriateness',[40] and Knight himself calls 'Marina' 'a perfect poetical commentary on those Shakespearian meanings which I had unveiled'.[41]

Briefly, Knight's thesis is that the later plays express in dramatic form a mystic apprehension of immortality, immortality conceived not as quantity but as quality:

> . . . these miraculous and joyful conquests of life's tragedy are the expression, through the medium of drama, of a state of mind or soul in the writer directly in knowledge—or supposed knowledge—of a mystic and transcendent fact as to the true nature and purpose of the sufferings of humanity . . .
>
> Today we hear from theologians that immortality is a matter of quality and value rather than something which can be measured by time. Canon Streeter asserts that its truth can only be expressed by myth or metaphor. Now the supreme value to man is always Love. What more perfect form, then, could such a myth take than that of the restoration to Pericles of his Thaisa and Marina, so long and so mistakenly supposed lost? It is, indeed, noticeable that these plays do not aim at revealing a temporal survival of death: rather at the thought that death is a delusion. What was thought dead is in reality alive. In them we watch the fine flowers of a mystic state of soul bodied into the forms of drama.[42]

Eliot's 'Marina' evokes this 'mystic state', an intuitive awareness of immortality. Central to 'Marina' is the 'thought that death is a delusion', that with the rediscovery of life it becomes 'unsubstantial'. The poem opens with a series of sea images associated with the time of Marina's loss and recalled by her presence. Though appealing to the senses, the images seem delicate and pure, linking, by their association with Marina, the physical and spiritual. Wind and pine and woodsong fog possess a radiance against which destruction, false glitter, spiritual sloth and lust seem unreal. The physical world divides here into the merely carnal which means death and a natural beauty transfigured by Marina's presence:

> Those who sharpen the tooth of the dog, meaning
> Death
> Those who glitter with the glory of the humming-bird,
>   meaning
> Death
> Those who sit in the stye of contentment, meaning
> Death
> Those who suffer the ecstasy of the animals, meaning
> Death
>
> Are become unsubstantial, reduced by a wind,

Questions create Pericles' sense of wonder at the living Marina who is both less and more vivid than her remembered image. The images of laughter between leaves and hurrying feet under sleep express an inexplicable sense of reality hidden but intense, a reality beyond the grasp of sense yet known through it as the natural world sometimes seems transfigured and radiant. In his cracked and rotting boat Pericles remembers his own youth and the effort of creating: 'I made this.' Like himself it is decaying with time, but Marina's form implies hope and new ships: because of her new life he can resign his own. If there is immortality, it is certainly in value and not in endless life. The continuing life is Marina who is 'Living to live in a world of time beyond me': this is quite different from the timelessness of God, though it may share the quality of transcending decay and death. And that quality, as it is expressed here, is wholly joyous and perfect.

In light of this perfection, it is difficult to understand Eliot's ironic epigraph taken from *Hercules Furens*. Hercules, having unknowingly killed his children in a fit of madness, returns to sanity and recognises what he has done. As Pericles discovers life where he expected death,

Hercules finds death in place of life. Since it is the vision of Marina that remains with us, undiminished by ironic juxtaposition, one is tempted to see the undercutting as directed against Hercules; that is, the poem might show the epigraph to be a false vision of life and death. But that would be to reverse the usual function of Eliot's epigraphs. More likely, Eliot was unable wholly to affirm a transcendence achieved through human love alone. If so, the epigraph stands again as the mind's rejection of feeling, this time even the one rare feeling of profound human fulfillment. But the experience remains intense and affirmative for the speaker of the poem. This moment, in and out of time, human yet transfigured, is woven into the *Four Quartets* and becomes there part of a larger pattern which, in the end, contains both the negative renunciation of time and the affirmation that within time such moments are humanity's contact with eternity. Time and eternity, opposed in *Ash-Wednesday* and the first three 'Ariel Poems', are reconciled in 'Marina' where eternity is a quality or value experienced within time. But such a reconciliation, even discounting the epigraph, does not resolve the conflicts inherent throughout Eliot's previous work. Giving no meaning to the rest of time when that quality is absent, it remains a moving but partial insight. *Four Quartets* focuses specifically on this conflict, reiterating the concepts of time and eternity found throughout the canon and moving towards a completed pattern.

Time in the Poetry of T. S. Eliot: A Study in Structure and Theme. (London: Macmillan, 1981): 58-90. Copyright © 1981 by Nancy K. Gish. Reproduced with permission of Palgrave Macmillan.

Notes

1. T. S. Eliot, 'Dante', in *Selected Essays*, p. 275.
2. Andrewes, 'Sermon 15 Of the Nativitie', p. 109.
3. Ibid., pp. 109-10.
4. Ibid., pp. 114-15.
5. T. S. Eliot, *The Use of Poetry and the Use of Criticism* (2nd edn. London: Faber and Faber, 1964), p. 148.

6. Southam, *A Guide to the Selected Poems of T. S. Eliot*, p. 120.

7. Andrewes, 'Sermon 15 Of the Nativitie', p. 112.

8. The King James Version is used throughout.

9. St John of the Cross, 'The Dark Night', in *The Collected Works of St John of the Cross*, trans. Kieran Kavanaugh and Otilio Rodriguez (London: Thomas Nelson and Sons, 1966), p. 371.

10. Ibid., p. 371.

11. St John of the Cross, 'The Ascent of Mt Carmel', in *The Collected Works of St John of the Cross*, p. 145.

12. Ibid., p. 179.

13. Ibid., p. 179.

14. Ibid., p. 181.

15. Ibid., p. 124.

16. T. S. Eliot, 'Dante', p. 43.

17. Ibid., p. 262.

18. *The Paris Review*, xxi (Spring-Summer 1959), p. 58. Quoted in Kristian Smidt, *The Importance of Recognition: Six Chapters on T. S. Eliot* (Tromsø, 1973), p. 31.

19. Leonard Unger, *T. S. Eliot: Moments and Patterns* (Minneapolis: University of Minnesota Press, 1966), p. 54.

20. Graham Hough, 'Vision and Doctrine in *Four Quartets*', *Critical Quarterly*, xv, no. 2 (Summer 1973), pp. 108-27.

21. Unger, pp. 41-68.

22. Andrewes, 'Sermon 4 Of Repentance: Ash Wednesday 1619', p. 122.

23. St John of the Cross, 'The Dark Night', p. 361.

24. Ibid., p. 333.

25. Dante, *The Purgatorio*, p. 317n.

26. H. Flanders Dunbar, *Symbolism in Medieval Thought and Its Consummation in the Divine Comedy* (New York: Russell & Russell, 1961), pp. 366-8.

27. Ibid., p. 365.

28. B. C. Southam, *A Guide to the Selected Poems of T. S. Eliot* (New York: Harcourt, Brace & World, 1969), p. 113.

29. Sir James Frazer, *The Scapegoat* (Part VI), *The Golden Bough: A Study in Magic and Religion*, ix (12 vols.; 3rd edn. New York: Macmillan, 1935), p. 257.

30. Ibid., p. 257.

31. Frazer, *The Magic Art and the Evolution of Kings* (Part I, ii), *The Golden Bough*, II, p. 52.

32. Ibid., p. 60.

33. Frazer, *Adonis Attis Osiris* (Part IV, i), *The Golden Bough*, V, p. 54.

34. Ibid., p. 225.

35. T. S. Eliot, 'Thoughts After Lambeth', in *Selected Essays*, p. 387.

36. Odell Shepard, *The Lore of the Unicorn* (New York: Barnes and Noble, 1967), p. 81.

37. E. Radford and M. A. Radford, *Encyclopedia of Superstitions*, edited and revised by Christina Hole (rev. edn.; London: Hutchinson, 1961), p. 369.

38. This has been said primarily of the *Four Quartets*. See F. R. Leavis, *The Living*

Principle: 'English' as a Discipline of Thought (New York: Oxford University Press, 1975).

39. G. Wilson Knight, 'T. S. Eliot: Some Literary Impressions', in *T. S. Eliot: The Man and His Work*, p. 249.

40. Ibid., p. 247.

41. Ibid., p. 247.

42. Knight, *Myth and Miracle: An Essay on the Mystic Symbolism of Shakespeare* (London: J. Burrow & Co., 1929), p. 21.

The Soul's Mysterious Errand
Lee Oser

Lee Oser undertakes a reading of *Four Quartets* that establishes both its Emersonian character in an austere spirituality and the significant way that it moves in a religious direction beyond Emerson. Oser argues not only that Eliot's thinking is compatible with salient aspects of the positions taken by Ralph Waldo Emerson, his great nineteenth-century American precursor, but that the compatibility is part of the deeply American character of Eliot's work. Oser points to numerous moments in which Eliot includes references to the new world in his writing at important junctures. His essay's title refers to the quest, common in both writers, for something that is not fully comprehensible. In Eliot's case, the journey, which is both aesthetic and spiritual, requires constant reinvention stylistically, since the end of the journey can never be captured fully in words. Oser's vision of Eliot's late poetic career includes his return to American traditions starting with the closing section of *Ash-Wednesday* and culminating with *Four Quartets*, which Oser reads as spiritual autobiography. One of the Ariel poems, the haunting and memorable "Marina," marks the moment in which Eliot presents America as spiritual frontier. Oser also suggests cogently that in his poems of the 1930s, including "Burnt Norton," the first of the *Quartets*, Eliot is in dialogue with the American poet Hart Crane, whose work Oser compares briefly to Eliot's, especially their common relation to Edgar Allan Poe. Unlike Crane, however, Eliot evokes his family traditions in projecting an idea of America that is beyond the secular. The three later quartets, "East Coker," "Dry Salvages," and "Little Gidding," all written during World War II, are, for Oser, Eliot's most Emersonian writings. In them he presents traditions not as constraining but as enabling. He even turns back to his own earlier writing by alluding to passages from it in the *Quartets* but in transforming ways. Oser brings out well some of the ways in which the text of the *Quartets* is not limited to the words that we read; through echo and allusion it expands the

> boundaries of the poem by creating a larger network of invoked or affiliated writings. The transformation of earlier moments involves, broadly speaking, a movement from the aesthetic in *The Waste Land* to the spiritual in the *Quartets*. In his continuing critique of his own past work, Eliot presents tradition not as the object of nostalgia, as antagonistic critics have sometimes taken it to be, but as always emergent, always in flux, always coming into being anew. In his reading of the second part of "Little Gidding," Oser argues that the memorable scene of instruction that occurs there is an important contribution to American writing, one that goes beyond Emerson but that does not reject him. The essay establishes that Eliot continued to be distinctively American despite transplanting himself to British and European soil. —J.P.R.

Life only avails, not the having lived. Power ceases in the instant of repose; it resides in the moment of transition from a past to a new state, in the shooting of the gulf, in the darting to an aim. This one fact the world hates, that the soul becomes; for that for ever degrades the past, turns all riches to poverty, all reputation to a shame, confounds the saint with the rogue, shoves Jesus and Judas equally aside. Why, then, do we prate of self-reliance? Inasmuch as the soul is present, there will be power not confident but agent. To talk of reliance is a poor external way of speaking. Speak rather of that which relies, because it works and is. (Works, 2:69-70)

Eliot would probably have responded to this celebrated passage from "Self-Reliance" by contending that if you "shove Jesus and Judas equally aside," you will have small matter left for moral argument and the feelings that morality inspires. Such a response would not be unusual: Emerson's inconsistencies in the field of ethics are widely noted. As Stephen Whicher observed, Emerson's "faith in the Soul" could not resolve the conflict between his ideals of power and law, of "life and moral perfection."[1]

Yet even in 1919, a week after telling the readers of the *Athenaeum*, "the essays of Emerson are already an encumbrance," Eliot could write in the same pages: "The Arts insist that a man shall dispose of all that he has, even of his family tree, and follow art alone. For they require that a man be not a member of a family or of a caste or of a party or of a coterie, but simply and solely himself." This is very close to Emerson, and the general sentiment informs not only the Divinity School Address,[2] but the Emersonian culture of New England, including the writings of Charlotte Eliot. In her *Savonarola*, Charlotte dramatizes the moment when the hero finds his calling and his mother realizes that she must lose him:

> *Savonarola:*
>> Go mother, go. I hear the sweet bells chime.
>> And now my father calls thee, It is time
>> That thou depart. So, let me kiss thy hands.
>> Through many years fulfilling love's commands,
>> How beautiful they are! Lay them on me
>> And consecrate my destiny.
>
> *Elena* (anxiously):
>> Thy destiny? My son, with heavy heart
>> I leave thee if I must. I know we part
>> But for a little while, yet fears oppress
>> Vague, undefined. Give me a last caress
>> And then, farewell.[3]

Eliot's high regard for Machiavelli marks yet another point of controversy between him and his mother, whose heritage had made Savonarola—one-time head of the Florentine Republic, victim of Pope Alexander VI, and idealist foil to Machiavelli's political realism—a kind of Puritan saint. But the continuities between mother and son are ultimately more important than their differences. In keeping with his Unitarian and Emersonian parentage, T. S. Eliot in 1919 recasts Christ's injunctions concerning the costs of discipleship (Luke 14:25-35); upholding a family tradition of personal calling, he transfers his activities to the sphere of art.

By 1935, the year of "Burnt Norton," Eliot had fully reclaimed his broader social and religious interests: "To be free we must be stripped, like the sea-god Glaucus, of any number of incrustations of education and frequentation; we must divest ourselves even of our ancestors. But to undertake this stripping of acquired ideas, we must make one assumption: that of the individuality of each human being; we must, in fact, believe in the soul." One should approach these remarks through the context of Eliot's Christian response to the political turmoil of the 1930s.[4] It was in "the needs of the individual soul" that he found a defense against the "regimentation and conformity" that threatened all Western culture (*ICS*, 18). Whereas "a society with a religious basis" would foster individuality, the modern secular nation, whether democratic or fascist or communist ("If you will not have God . . . you should pay your respects to Hitler or Stalin" [*ICS*, 50]), inclined toward "the subduing of free intellectual speculation, and the debauching of the arts by political criteria" (*ICS*, 34); the real issue was not, as was commonly assumed, democracy versus totalitarianism, but paganism versus Christianity. As if to underscore his contention that only a religious culture can tolerate a gadfly, Eliot writes as a Christian apologist in 1935, but he challenges the more traditional Christian public: instead of hymning High-Church conservatism, he alludes ambiguously to a sea god—to a world that is too much with us—and thus conveys the impression that his view of the soul is not predictably orthodox.

But can his view be called Emersonian? The meaning of the word "soul" in "Self-Reliance" poses a crucial problem for students of American literary and intellectual history. Critic Richard Poirier discusses Emerson from a standpoint that is at once pragmatist, mediated by a rather despiritualized version of William James, and theoretical, by way of poststructuralism and Jacques Derrida.[5] For Poirier's Emerson, the soul

> is not to be imagined as an entity; it is more nearly a function, and yet no determination is made as to when the function occurs or from where it ema-

nates. The soul has no determinable there or then, no here or now; rather, as [Emerson's] italics insist, it only *"becomes,"* only promises to make its presence known. That is, the soul appears or occurs only as something we feel compelled to live into or to move toward *as if* it were there. . . .

The creative impulse which is the soul discovers in the very first stages of composition that it wants to reach out beyond any legible form, that it wants to seek the margins, to move beyond limits or fate.[6]

As a reading of Emerson, the passage reflects indirectly on many American writers, not least the Eliot of *Four Quartets*. In his poem's succession of houses—the estate at Burnt Norton, the ephemeral houses of East Coker, the St. Louis home of "The Dry Salvages," and the Anglican church at Little Gidding—Eliot constructs dwellings for what he calls the "soul" and "spirit," then time and again abandons these stopping places in favor of "a moving toward" more adequate moments of insight. But if Poirier is very good at observing the improvisatory brilliance of Emerson's writing, he is willfully blind to the Transcendental and religious dimension of the historical Emerson—I take issue with that "*as if.*" While following Poirier's insights into the soul's "becoming" as in some respect a compositional process, I want to keep hold of the austere spirituality that connects Emerson to Eliot.[7]

In this chapter, I approach Eliot's Emersonianism through what may seem an eccentric hypothesis: that beginning with the final section of *Ash-Wednesday* (discussed in Chapter 5), the expatriate poet and High-Churchman returned to his native traditions in order to set down the spiritual experience that culminated in *Four Quartets*. I explore this ambivalent and difficult return through Eliot's relation to several authors, but chiefly through his likeness to Emerson in their respective discourses on the soul. Matthiessen's much repeated statement, "[Eliot] once remarked to me . . . of his sustained distaste for Emerson," seems to have cut off investigation into the Emersonian aspects of *Four Quartets*. Indeed, one measure of Eliot's success in legislating his academic reception is the absence of Emerson's name from the subject index of Mildred Martin's weighty *A Half-Century of Eliot Criticism*.[8] Here I want to build on my argument of previous chapters, that Emerson was a vital part of Eliot's cultural inheritance. I will develop two focal points: one, where Eliot adapts Emersonianism to his own purposes, and two, where he successfully departs from it, thus challenging American readers, past and present, about what constitutes American poetry.

In "the still point of the turning world" (line 62), the poet of "Burnt Norton" resurrected a concept that had seen earlier use in *Coriolan* 1, "Triumphal March" (1931). Eliot never finished the *Coriolan* sequence, and one may wonder if the plan of that sequence, to describe a spiritual progress in the modern world, failed because his symbolism was inadequate to the task. The still point of *Coriolan* inheres in a supreme and abstract reality, which resembles the Hindus' *Nirguna Brahman*:

> O hidden under the dove's wing, hidden in the turtle's breast,
> Under the palmtree at noon, under the running water
> At the still point of the turning world. O hidden.
> ("Triumphal March" 32-34)[9]

When Emerson wrote his famous poem "Brahma," he imagined a similarly impersonal version of the divine: it was perhaps the utter remove of such high-order abstractions that drove Eliot to change his poetic tack. In *Four Quartets*, the still point continues to be the "hidden" core of reality, knowable only through grace and spiritual discipline; however, as the theme is echoed and elaborated, stillness itself takes on new significance in the poem as the goal of an emergent quest—a quest with visible and personal contours. As a goal, the still point develops affinities with Eliot's symbolism of the New World, a class of symbolism that he was also extending during the 1930s.

In lines 70-78 of the first *Quartet* ("The inner freedom from the practical desire . . ."), the still point retains much of its abstractness.

Eliot carves out a mode of contemplation, which he approaches first in contrast to the "practical," then through a hint of feeling, a "grace of sense / a white light still and moving," then through an abstract series of near paradoxes. Like the "still point" that it explicitly resembles, the "new world" is at this juncture largely conceptual. Only at the end of "Burnt Norton" does it begin to take shape in three dimensions:

> Sudden in a shaft of sunlight
> Even while the dust moves
> There rises the hidden laughter
> Of children in the foliage
> Quick now, here, now, always—
> (*BN* 169-73)

In his short lyric "New Hampshire" (1934), Eliot had described "Children's voices in the orchard / Between the blossom- and the fruit-time" (*CP*, 138). In "Burnt Norton" 1, he deliberately resumes this line of imagery: a 1941 letter to John Hayward refers to "the children in the appletree meaning to tie up New Hampshire and Burnt Norton."[10] At the poem's conclusion, he builds on the images of "New Hampshire" and "Burnt Norton" 1 until they begin to form a theme or pattern, a recurring symbolism of a longed-for paradise that is always "a new world."

I will cast one more backward glance in observing Eliot's symbolism of the New World, as that symbolism developed in the years leading up to *Four Quartets*. Written in 1930, "Marina" dramatizes an anagnorisis that occurs on the New England coast.[11] As in *Four Quartets*, the beauty of a landscape conduces to a moment of spiritual reflection, though here Eliot uses the high romantic trope of the divine wind or afflatus to express a visionary state. The poet leaves behind a world of "Death," identified by preparations for war, by vanity, stasis, and animal pleasure, which

> Are become unsubstantial, reduced by a wind,
> A breath of pine, and the woodsong fog
> By this grace dissolved in place
>
> ("Marina" 14-16)

It would be facile to say that the poet has abandoned Europe for America; rather, he has assimilated America and its redemptive mythology to his own journey. Thus, in writing "Marina," Eliot discovered a more adequate symbol for the movement toward spiritual fulfillment than the still point of *Coriolan*. As *Four Quartets* unfolded, he drew on "Marina" to bring a concrete and affecting reality to the intangible paradox of stillness (the "still and moving"), which consequently became associated with "the frontiers of the spirit."[12] "Marina" was a breakthrough because it portrayed America, the New World, as a spiritual frontier.

One way, rarely if ever explored, of interpreting the *Quartets* is through their relation to Hart Crane's *The Bridge* (1930), where the crossing from an old to a new world is a central theme. Much of Crane's work enters into dialogue with Eliot, and it is virtually certain that Eliot noticed his influence on a younger contemporary whose work he admired. Having published "The Tunnel," the penultimate section of *The Bridge*, in a 1927 issue of the *Criterion*,[13] Eliot may have had his eye on it while composing the tube scene in "Burnt Norton" 3; I will quote Crane, and then Eliot:

> In the car
> the overtone of motion
> underground, the monotone
> of motion is the sound
> of other faces, also underground—
> . . . .
> Toward corners of the floor
> Newspapers wing, revolve and wing.
> Blank windows gargle signals through the roar.[14]

>   Only a flicker
>   Over the strained time-ridden faces
>   Distracted from distraction by distraction
>   Filled with fancies and empty of meaning
>   Tumid apathy with no concentration
>   Men and bits of paper, whirled by the cold wind
>   (*BN* 99-104)

Like Dante before the city of Hell (possibly evoked by the iteration, "Dis . . . dis . . . dis"), Eliot remains spiritually aloof. The train is his symbol of how "the world moves / In appetency, on its metalled ways" (*BN* 124-25), but his is not among the faces beleaguered and run over by time. By comparison, Crane achieves the eerie effect of mechanizing language and his own voice through the repetition of "motion," "tone," and "ground," by personifying (or demonizing) the "blank windows" that "gargle" (the word derives from the Old French *gargouille*, "throat," and is cognate to "gargoyle"), and through the synaesthetic convergence of the "sound" of these words with the entire field of figuration and imagery. Though Crane as narrator merges with his environment and Eliot does not, each writer faces an existential blankness, and each depicts a journey through a dark night of the soul. Through parallels of setting, mood, and theme, Eliot and Crane pursue a conversation about ends that are desired but in doubt, about their respective quests as poets, and about the destination or telos towards which their societies should be directed.

In "The Tunnel" Crane asks: "did you deny the ticket, Poe?";[15] that is, did you, Poe, disavow the physical and spiritual transit, the millennial promise of self and nation? The question is not merely rhetorical and awaits an answer for the reason that "Poe" comprises many figures. He is the historical Edgar Poe, author of "To Helen," "The Raven," and "The City in the Sea," poems that Crane weaves into his own writing. He is also Crane's antiself, a doubter and an agent of irony, "The Tunnel" being the womblike/tomblike space of struggle between the two poets. But Crane has more in mind than competition—he wants to transform his adversary. Rewriting Poe's "Nevermore" as "O evermore," he seeks to change the meaning of Poe's work, to absorb him within the utopian trajectory of *The Bridge*. Granted christological qualities, Poe becomes a kind of martyr who hovers on the brink of resurrection. And it is likely that this new status for Poe takes its epistemological sanction from Eliot's perspective toward literary tradition: "the past should be altered by the present as much as the present is directed by the past."

I want to suggest that Eliot detected a challenge in Crane's question to Poe. During his career Eliot had often championed Poe, and he sympathized with Poe's aversion to the myth of America, the very inspiration of *The Bridge*. On his part, Crane, to judge both from his letters and from his use of *Waste Land* imagery, had grouped Eliot with Poe among the dystopians.[16] Now what was Eliot's answer to Crane? Although the poet of *Four Quartets* refuses to vouchsafe the kind of vision that concludes *The Bridge*, that is, a dream of self, nation, and history redeemed through the mystical power of language, he does not entirely "deny the ticket"—indeed, Eliot shared with both Crane and Poe a belief in that mystical power. Eliot's response to Crane, or to the dialogue that Crane enacts in *The Bridge*, is to correlate the fate of the self neither to America nor to England exclusively, but to a community of the living and the dead in which conventional ideas of nationhood are modified and personalized. Crane, I would argue, had fired Eliot's imagination by replacing the stale rhetoric of nationalism with an America of the spirit. But where Crane had used mythopoesis to connect the past to the present, Eliot turned to his own ancestors: the key to Eliot's community of the living and the dead, and to its central role in the later *Quartets*, is the history of the Eliot family.[17] Implicit in this Eliotic response, finally, is a criticism of Crane's position, insofar as Crane upholds a secular myth of America, while Eliot, in keeping with his cultural writings and theocratic ancestry, rejects a secular basis for even the idea of America, let alone its national reality.

In "East Coker" 1, the poet commences with a theme of houses and beginnings. East Coker is the village in Somerset, England, from which Eliot's forefather, Andrew Eliot, set out for Massachusetts in the years following the Restoration. When he published "East Coker" in the *New English Weekly* in 1940, Eliot wrote *aresse* for *arras* (*EC* 13) in order to follow Sir Thomas Elyot's *The Boke of the Governour* (1531). The poet's namesake and distant ancestor, Sir Thomas was both an East Coker native and a vanguard figure in the English Renaissance. His presence in "East Coker" suggests that the poet is fusing self-inscription with historiography; by alluding to Sir Thomas Elyot, Thomas Stearns Eliot asserts a personal tie to English history and the history of the English language, which developed a perhaps unparalleled range and subtlety in the sixteenth century.

This personalizing of the past differs in spirit from the lesson of Emerson's "History": "The student is to read history actively and not passively" (*Works*, 2:8)—Eliot is devoutly literal in his reading, Emerson more figurative. But the wartime *Quartets* are Eliot's most Emersonian work, for in them he reads public events through the prism of personal experience, without recourse to a poetic mask or persona. "In my beginning is my end" (*EC* 1)—not "In the beginning God created the heaven and the earth," but the cosmological transformed into autobiography. Avoiding self-reliant egotism, the speaker achieves what is more truly Emersonian: a prophetic self-consciousness, extending from the profound to the seemingly trivial. Behind the high and biblical style of "East Coker"'s opening, a private world revolves, replete with personal and familial associations, some of which are quite ordinary. The description of the "rise and fall" of houses evokes a memory of the old Eliot home at 2635 Locust Street, St. Louis, which the family surrendered to a burgeoning warehouse district during T. S. Eliot's Harvard days.[18] The humble "field-mouse" apparently comes from the Eliots' "country house" on Cape Ann.[19]

For the poet of "East Coker," the relation of beginnings to ends inspires a meditation on the act of writing, on literary tradition, and on public and private history. The arras, shaking in the wind like the "bits of paper" in "Burnt Norton" 3, a page from an unbound book, furnishes a locus for this meditation. As commentators have noted, the silent motto on the arras is in one respect that of the Eliot family, which is indeed a motto of silence: "*tacuit et fecit*," "he was silent and acted." Yet, by characterizing the motto as "silent," the poet implies that it too is "removed" from the thoughts, words, and deeds of a living generation. Perhaps we should infer that the motto is superannuated or even simply illegible. More in keeping with the poem's trial of knowing and unknowing, however, is for the motto's silence to recall the silence of all texts until the capable eye confers meaning on them. The motto is silent until illuminated by a pattern of readings, corresponding to a pattern of generational risings and fallings, of beginnings and ends, that directs the progress of the poem's ideal reader, who is the poet in the act of writing and meditating on his writing.

Complicating this larger gestalt, a principle of hermeneutic uncertainty operates in the *Quartets*. By virtue of this uncertainty, the future does not merely repeat the past; the poet can both belong to a family or house, and be freed from the identity that is imposed by houses. He is both part of an established pattern, and freed from that pattern because the pattern is, from his point of view, still forming, not yet fully formed. Thus, after his description of the rural dance at East Coker, Eliot concludes the first section of the poem with lines that liberate him from his ancestral community:

> Dawn points, and another day
> Prepares for heat and silence. Out at sea the dawn wind
> Wrinkles and slides. I am here
> Or there, or elsewhere. In my beginning.
>
> (*EC* 47-50)

Though in one sense the village of East Coker marks his beginning, the poet indicates other beginnings in other places. The gate of his choosing, of being "here / Or there, or elsewhere," remains open. One recalls Poirier's observation: "The soul has no determinable there or then, no here or now. . . ." Determination lingers, however, in the dawn's "point[ing]"—a gesture of fate that singles out the poet, that chooses him, limning his identity so that, coincident with the suggestion of a mysterious destiny, a recognition of otherness literally dawns. This otherness is transcendent, withheld in the antelucan hour, but enduring behind and beyond the play of signification that animates a series of near personifications: "dawn," "day," "heat," "silence," and "wind."

The freedom to unhouse the self has rich American precedents, not least famously in Whitman, who exhorted his readers: "Unscrew the locks from the doors! / Unscrew the doors themselves from the jambs!" (*CPCP*, 50). In the essay "Fate," Emerson observed, "Every spirit makes its house; but afterwards the house confines the spirit" (*Works*, 6:9). The "soul" that waits patiently for "the darkness of God" in "East Coker" 3 enters into a visionary mode rather foreign to our own fin de siècle; but Emerson's "way of life" that "is by abandonment" (*Works*, 2:321-22) constitutes an American negative way with strong parallels in Jonathan Edwards's "rhetoric of negation or apophasis." In the manner of Edwards and Emerson, Eliot explores his *via negativa* with a repetitious tenacity that says he is not wholly satisfied with it; it too will be abandoned:[20]

> You say I am repeating
> Something I have said before. I shall say it again.
> Shall I say it again? In order to arrive there,
> To arrive where you are, to get from where you are not,
>   You must go by a way wherein there is no ecstacy.
> In order to arrive at what you do not know
>   You must go by a way which is the way of ignorance.
> In order to possess what you do not possess
>   You must go by the way of dispossession.
> In order to arrive at what you are not

The Soul's Mysterious Errand

>   You must go through the way in which you are not.
>   And what you do not know is the only thing you know
>   And what you own is what you do not own
>   And where you are is where you are not.
>
>   (*EC* 133-46)

Eliot derived this passage from *The Ascent of Mount Carmel* by St. John of the Cross, the sixteenth-century Spanish mystic. The allusive technique recalls *The Waste Land*, but a notable difference emerges. The Old World of Europe tends in *The Waste Land* to be melancholy—beautiful, but moribund; "staring forms" lean out, "hushing" a room that is "enclosed" in sepulchral air (lines 104-5); such forms conjure a world that, like the House of Usher, might be better lost. It is not to detract from Eliot's historical reach to say that in *Four Quartets* the past lends a momentary framework to experience that is present and unfolding: age-old wisdom is rediscovered and renewed. The mystic's paradoxes do not appear as a set piece or brilliantly preserved relic; they constitute a sympathetic effort of articulative skill within a larger meditation.

Like Emerson in his essays and journals, Eliot in the *Quartets* repeats himself, doubles back on his thoughts, appears in two places at once. For both writers, the innermost self, the soul, goes about its mysterious errand. Repetition is not simply repetition, and arrival not exactly arrival, because they are dual aspects of a journey that cannot be fully comprehended. Throughout the *Quartets*, poetic style is possessed and dispossessed by the poet in what he calls "the intolerable wrestle / With words and meanings" (*EC* 70-71).[21] One might interpret the metaphysical stanzas of "East Coker" 4 (or any of the fourth sections) as one stylistic experiment among many and not the dogmatic heart of the poem. As "rooms," the *stanze* provide a habitation for the soul and an experiment in Christian identity. Here I am certainly not questioning Eliot's religious conviction, I am suggesting that his religious sincerity was closely tied to artistic sincerity, and that as an artist Eliot felt impelled to reinvent himself constantly. Eliot's insistence on stylistic innovation bespeaks his spiritual questing. Emerson asked, "Is not prayer also a study of truth—a sally of the soul into the unfound infinite?" (*Works*, 1:74). In their protean and dynamic aspect, Eliot's stanzas represent a relentless sallying forth of the soul; in their repetition and structure, they mark the basic, material conditions of time and mortality to which the soul must return.[22]

"The Dry Salvages" (1941), the third *Quartet*, dramatizes the metaphor of crossing from an old world to a new. In autobiographical terms, the poet retraces the Atlantic voyages of his English ancestors, Andrew Eliot and Isaac Stearns, who sailed to America in the seventeenth century. Their crossings, and their shared Puritan mission to build a New Israel, acquire fresh significance in light of the poet's journey.

"The Dry Salvages" begins, as do the previous *Quartets*, at the scene of a house, here the Eliot home in St. Louis, near the Mississippi River. In Whitmanian tones of almost painful simplicity, Eliot characterizes the Mississippi as "a strong brown god," a pagan conception that is soon amplified in a description that echoes Tennyson's "Ulysses": "The sea has many voices, / Many gods and many voices" (*DS* 24-25). Paganism is important in this poem; the first hint of pagan themes occurs almost immediately, in the note subjoined to the title: "The Dry Salvages—presumably *les trois sauvages*—is a small group of rocks, with a beacon, off the N.E. coast of Cape Ann, Massachusetts." In lines 26-48 ("The sea howl . . ."), Eliot explores the savage world of river and sea through a synthesis of romantic sublimity and imagist particularity, Pound having applied the latter to the pagan seas of the early *Cantos*. Eliot thus creates his own version of the Homeric voyager sailing by *periploi*, rounding the coast "homewards." Recording the questions—of cosmology, beginnings, ends, and the riddle of time—that the natural world compels the conscious mind to frame, Eliot, following Dante, conceives nature in itself as removed from grace; the "granite teeth" are teeth of primary rock—no subtle change has acted on them. Terror and beauty, the "menace and caress of wave that breaks on water," captivate the imagination, but convey a "distant" cosmos, a "time not our time," while the powers that "howl" and "yelp" are alien to human ears.

Emerson had considered a similar kind of beauty:

> In history, the great moment is, when the savage is just ceasing to be a savage, with all his hairy Pelasgic strength directed on his opening sense of beauty:—and you have Pericles and Phidias,—not yet passed over into Corinthian civility. Everything good in nature and the world is in that moment of transition, when the swarthy juices still flow plentifully from nature, but the astringency or acridity is got out by ethics and humanity. (*Works*, 6:70-71)[23]

At the end of "The Dry Salvages" 1, Eliot approaches what Emerson calls "the great moment," a sublime interlude that challenges Eliot's own religious and social convictions. Emerson selects as his example the golden age of Athens, in the fifth century B.C. Eliot's Ulyssean sailor inhabits a roughly analogous setting, where Pelasgic strength is also directed on an opening sense of beauty—though beauty of a less anthropocentric kind. Unlike Emerson, Eliot does not attach "ethics and humanity" to the moment and place of crossing. To speak of America in its spiritual sense, Emerson's America is the very nexus of transition—one may compare "the imagined land" of Wallace Stevens's "Mrs. Alfred Uruguay." For Emerson's self-reliant individual, America as nature is a source of strength, a birthright. For Eliot, America as nature is a place not fully humanized, where the sunlight of Ithaka yields to a Cimmerian dark, where past and present do not meet, and where ends are very much in doubt. America stands outside the Christian dispensation at this stage in the *Quartets*, Eliot's perspective thus coinciding with that of his seventeenth-century ancestors, who came to build Christ's kingdom among the so-called savages.

In the sestina that begins the next section, the poet owns a profound doubt. His question is age-old: for what purpose do generation after generation undergo the trials of beauty, terror, and death? He loads the question with harrowing and relentless force. As he does so, an intricate pattern of feminine (or double) and triple rhymes establishes itself and unfolds, like a numerical series, with the effect that the lyric's surface makes great demands on the eye, which finds "no end" or resting place, only "addition." Eliot exploits this effect to describe "a future that is . . . liable / Like the past, to have no destination" (*DS* 71-72). The "autumn flowers," the "drifting boat with a slow leakage," the fishermen "forever bailing / Setting and hauling," signify cosmic and personal exhaustion. By juxtaposing his sublime sea lyric with the sestina, the poet suggests that the Emersonian "moment" cannot be sustained as a way of life, that eventually nature and time will crush a man. The sestina's catalog of objects and images fails to cohere spiritually, fails to grant the promise that Whitman, in his poetic catalogs, could triumphantly locate. On the abyss's edge, Eliot can only imagine an "end" to history in "the hardly, barely prayable / Prayer of the one Annunciation" (*DS* 83-84). Thus, in *Four Quartets*, the saving move by consciousness is faith: William James would call this expression of belief a "live hypothesis." From a Christian standpoint, Eliot's challenge was to make the ancient message of the Incarnation new, to dramatize the vitality of a dogmatic truth. The doctrinal theme of course distances him from Emerson. But the severity of his spiritual quest connects Eliot to Emerson's poetic heirs, such as Frost, for whom "the height of poetic thinking" was the "attempt to say matter in terms of spirit and spirit in terms of matter."[24] Eliot takes this attempt to an extreme, before turning to Christian prayer.

"Little Gidding," the final *Quartet*, integrates the many crossings of the larger poem with the theme of Christian pilgrimage. Approaching the church at Little Gidding on a "rough road" in the Huntingdonshire countryside, the poet orders the scene with details conjoining the pedestrian and the numinous:

> When the short day is brightest, with frost and fire,
> The brief sun flames the ice, on pond and ditches,

> In windless cold that is the heart's heat,
> Reflecting in a watery mirror
> A glare that is blindness in the early afternoon.
> And glow more intense than blaze of branch, or brazier,
> Stirs the dumb spirit: no wind, but pentecostal fire
> In the dark time of the year. Between melting and freezing
> The soul's sap quivers. There is no earth smell
> Or smell of living thing. This is the spring time
> But not in time's covenant. Now the hedgerow
> Is blanched for an hour with transitory blossom
> Of snow. . . .
>
> (*LG* 4-16)

It appears that Eliot is echoing his own echo-laden writing, the Belladonna scene from *The Waste Land* (lines 77-89, "The Chair she sat in . . ."). For it is not likely that "branch," "flames," "reflecting," "stirs," and "glow" would have recurred in "Little Gidding," in a passage of nearly identical length to the *Waste Land* passage, purely by chance. Looking at the manuscript record in Helen Gardner's *The Composition of Four Quartets*, one finds that "is blanched" had earlier been "glitters," so that the drafts yield yet another echo of *The Waste Land*.

In his 1941 essay "Rudyard Kipling," Eliot referred to Enobarbus's speech (the point of departure for the Belladonna passage) as "highly decorated," but noted that "the decoration has a purpose beyond its own beauty." This usage of "beyond" is clarified in the essay by Eliot's adoption of Henry James's phrase "the figure in the carpet" to describe the master form suffusing all details, the latent unity emerging out of the variety of a great poet's work, that he saw in Shakespeare (*OPP*, 235-36).[25] Eliot himself pursued such a "figure," and in *Four Quartets* undertook a creative reevaluation of his earlier writing, with the intended result that, in our example, the passages from "Little Gidding" and "A Game of Chess" should modify each other. In a sense, we are met again with Eliot's maxim: "the past should be altered by the present as much as the present is directed by the past."

To what end, precisely, are "Little Gidding" and "A Game of Chess" brought into conjunction? What is the figure in Eliot's carpet? For an answer, I turn once more to Poe, for as Grover Smith has convincingly shown, the language and imagery of the Belladonna scene have a major source in two of Poe's tales, "The Assignation" and "Shadow—a Parable," mentioned by Eliot in a 1921 *Chapbook* article.[26] "Little Gidding" doesn't repeat the same extensive borrowing from Poe that Smith uncovers in *The Waste Land* (though the later Eliot does in fact reecho the "flames," "mirror," "I glare" sequence that Smith observes in a short passage from "Shadow—a Parable"), but verbatim repetition isn't central to my point. I am suggesting that if the Belladonna scene displays Poe's specular opulence, the scene from "Little Gidding" directs Eliot's earlier, Poe-like writing to a more spiritual desideratum. This would accord with the mystical reading of Poe's poetry that Eliot developed in the later 1920s.

Looting Poe's tales for "A Game of Chess," the younger Eliot created a brilliant pastiche, a baroque pleasure-dome for the literary connoisseur. Two decades later, Eliot stresses that such aesthetic experience is not an end in itself, but a means to an end that, however elusive and problematic, remains desirable and mysteriously intact. His impulse is therefore to regard *The Waste Land*'s aestheticism as a prelude to, and hence a part of, the *Quartets*' spiritual autobiography. This autobiography is the true pattern underfoot, the basis for a self-criticism centered upon questions of personal, artistic, and spiritual authority.

Eliot would write soon after the war: "Esthetic sensibility must be extended into spiritual perception, and spiritual perception must be extended into esthetic sensibility and disciplined taste before we are qualified to pass judgment upon decadence or diabolism or nihilism in art" (*NDC* 103). One might say that the two elements of Eliot's chiasmus, "esthetic sensibility" and "spiritual perception," amount roughly to the two halves of Eliot's career, pre- and postconversion. But that is not quite right, because Eliot's aesthetic sensibility was always haunted by his spiritual restlessness. It would therefore be more accurate to say that the two halves of Eliot's career are, to use terms he applied to other poets, immaturity and maturity, for only the mature poet is in a position to judge the relative merits of the different types of art, including types that he had formerly practiced. As his most mature work, *Four Quartets* would express Eliot's aspirations to realize an integrated sensibility, to instantiate the highest principles of taste and judgment through a continuing critique of his past and present writing. An Olympian gambit of this kind must rely upon a comprehensive and highly confident knowledge of one's culture, a knowledge that Eliot cultivated through his views on religion.

In "Little Gidding" 1, thoughts of a "broken king" again recall *The Waste Land* (especially its more Shakespearian moments), as Eliot makes his pilgrimage to the stone church with its memorable history:

> If you came at night like a broken king,
> If you came by day not knowing what you came for,
> It would be the same, when you leave the rough road
> And turn behind the pig-sty to the dull façade
> And the tombstone. And what you thought you came for
> Is only a shell, a husk of meaning
> From which the purpose breaks only when it is fulfilled
> If at all.
>
> (*LG* 26-33)

In a stripped-down, Puritan plain style that is logical and sequential, yet shades toward the use of typology, the poet reflects on the life of Nicholas Ferrar and on Charles I's flight from the Roundheads. As a last bastion of Anglican community before the regicide, Little Gidding embodied English tradition for Eliot.[27] And yet, with that severity of thought that characterizes him, he discovers: "what you thought you came for / Is only a shell, a husk of meaning." Tradition thus has an

Emersonian edge. Shunning mere nostalgia, the poet must build his house anew, must construe identity, knowledge, and consciousness as unfolding rather than fixed. It is not that human history, in its institutions and channels of authority, is corrupting and should be discarded. Rather, it is that what one may choose to keep—a place of prayer, a memorial—reminds one of failure more than triumph. Having failed in the past to live up to our ideals, we must try again; we must purify our motives, and continue the soul's errand in order to fulfill our purposes and recover meaning. Emerson, though a man of many moods, says this over and over again, from "Experience" to "Days."

For the Eliot of *Four Quartets*, poetic language must burn with a purgatorial (and at times pentecostal) "fire" that unites aesthetic sensibility with spiritual perception. In the Dantean passage from "Little Gidding" 2, the place "between three districts where the smoke arose" is a version of purgatory, though the ghost's "brown baked features" add an infernal touch. Evidently, Eliot wanted a purgatorial meeting, but couldn't wholly escape the demonic.[28] With World War II in the very near background, he observes himself in the act of composition; I am reminded of the encounter with Stetson in *The Waste Land*:

> So I assumed a double part, and cried
> And heard another's voice cry: "What! are *you* here?"
> Although we were not. I was still the same,
>   Knowing myself yet being someone other
>   And he a face still forming; yet the words sufficed
> To compel the recognition they preceded.
>   (*LG* 97-102)

Though the words only "suffice," they reveal a prophetic power in "preced[ing]" the thoughts of the poet who writes them, in making him their conduit. The scene is, on the one hand, improvisatory, its pragmatic authority based on "a sense of power and accomplishment in language";[29] on the other hand, it is sustained by a numinous language that embraces the living and the dead. Whether or not we want to ascribe, as Eliot did in some phases, a metaphysical force of fate or destiny to such writing, the use of a scene of instruction, with cultural roots in Dantean and ultimately Virgilian allusiveness, marks one of Eliot's great contributions to American literature. The Emersonian legacy does not entail meetings of this kind.

The ghost's speech is a rather bitter if stately comment on the life of poets, characterized as a hellish purgatory for speech-driven prophets, a slow and painful crossing towards an unseen paradise. The line adapted from Mallarmé, "To purify the dialect of the tribe" (*LG* 127), which Eliot connected in 1928 to "the primitive power of the Word," bespeaks the poet's capacity as a vehicle of fate, while it conveys an ideal of social responsibility that is foreign to Mallarmé's *art poétique*. On a related plane, the ghost's revisiting London streets parallels Eliot's own revisiting England and New England in *Four Quartets*, and points (along with the general delineation of the poet's life, i.e., the life of all poets) to an underlying design of repetition and analogy in Eliot's cosmos. Yet the purport or end of this design, like the truth in poetry itself, cannot be firmly grasped; for this reason the poet's spirit, like the ghost, is "unappeased and peregrine" in a ceaseless pilgrimage.

Despite the "partial horror" of slow decrepitude, the loss of "promise" and the "bitter tastelessness of shadow fruit," the paradise that Eliot seeks throughout the poem, through the purgatory of words and history, is earthly. The union of "the fire and the rose" that ends the *Quartets* suggests a union of spirit and matter, not a reign of paradisal spirit. The Incarnation is the governing idea behind this and similar passages in the poem where the timeless intersects with time, whereas in Emerson, Whitman, and Crane, the Incarnation is assimilated, alongside other biblical and sacramental themes, into syncretic modes of thought. By restoring a formal religiosity that rejects emotional nostalgia, that insists on intellectual substance, Eliot presents a worthy alternative to Emersonian canons. Yet in his concern with the old Puritan ideal of a common errand, Eliot does not follow Dante in imagining heaven, but, like Emerson at the conclusion of *Nature*, devotes himself to a vision of the redeemed earth.

In the final lines of "Little Gidding" ("We shall not cease from exploration . . ."), an American sense of vastness, expressed by imagery of the New World, the longest river and the apple tree, animates a call for exploration that is private and public, voiced in the third-person plural. This new world is no particular place, but an idealized frontier: it is "here, now, always," a perpetual spur to thought, labor, and poetry. Eliot had a similar notion in mind when he wrote in 1939, "we have to remember that the Kingdom of Christ on earth will never be realised, and also that it is always being realised. . . ." (*ICS*, 47). The "children in the apple-tree" (*LG* 248) are the children of Adam, renewed to the innocence that was lost through original sin (Eliot strengthens this suggestion by placing "-fall" at the end of line 247). Poetically, their import has changed, grown more polysemous, since "New Hampshire" and "Burnt Norton," for they hint at the fulfillment of the Eliot family's quest in America, and evoke Christ's equation of "little children" with the kingdom of God (Matt. 19:14). In the final union of "the fire and the rose," the poet enacts a communal prayer for a closure that he cannot achieve by himself: "the fire and the rose are one"—they must be "won" by the collective "we," as well as given from above. As I have suggested, Eliot advances his Christian belief polemically, through dialogue with, among others, Emerson, the non-Christian inheritor of American Puritan culture. Finally, Eliot's vast and vastly refined sensibility is itself the means by which he would persuade us that Christianity is necessity and truth, that history, the history of America, of any and all new worlds, of individuals and their societies, can only cohere, from origin to end, through a Christian grace that leads to a meaning beyond the reach of words. *Four Quartets* is its own best argument for the culture of Western Christendom that it represents.

The "condition of complete simplicity / (Costing not less than everything)" (*LG* 253-54) recalls the imperative of self-surrender that Eliot had put forward in "Tradition and the Individual Talent." But in his refinement of the will to a purgatorial intensity, the poet relies not on tradition so much as on the mysterious destiny of the soul. *Four Quartets* is a record of the soul, and the world of the poem is, in large measure, an image of the soul's becoming. The end of this becoming, the bourne of the soul's transitions, is glimpsed in a vision of an earthly paradise attained through purgatorial fire. The site of this paradise is not determined, but Eliot's final rose harks back with poignancy to the landscape of "The Dry Salvages":

> The salt is on the briar rose,
> The fog is in the fir trees.
>
> (*DS* 25-26)

Here the setting is undoubtedly, as in "Marina," New England. Briar roses are humble flowers, and the salt from the sea air adds to the feeling of commonness. But there is also a touch of surprise in the image, an unexpected combination of textures, while the fog in the fir trees blurs the distant outlines and wakes us to the unfolding possibilities of the concrete and immediate present. In this discovery of the uncommon promise of common things, the poet, like Emerson's blind man "gradually restored to perfect sight," enters the New England of his literal and spiritual ancestors.

From *T. S. Eliot and American Poetry* (Columbia, MO: University of Missouri Press, 1998): 104-125. Copyright © 1998 by the curators of the University of Missouri. Reprinted by permission of the University of Missouri Press.

Notes

1. Stephen Whicher, *Freedom and Fate*, 49. Committed to the social foundation of morals, Eliot arrived at a diametrical remove from what Whicher called Emerson's "radical egoistic anarchism."

2. T. S. Eliot, "A Romantic Patrician," *Athenaeum* 4644 (May 2, 1919), 266-67. In the Divinity School Address, Emerson asks: "Where now sounds the persuasion, that

by its very melody imparadises the heart, and so affirms its own origin in heaven? Where shall I hear words such as in elder ages drew men to leave all and follow—father and mother, house and land, wife and child?" (*Works*, 1:136).

3. Charlotte Eliot, *Savonarola*, 5-6.

4. T. S. Eliot, "Notes on the Way," 89. On the subject of Eliot's cultural politics in the 1930s, see Jeffrey Perl's *Skepticism and Modern Enmity: Before and After Eliot*, 86-112. From an adversarial position, the best analysis of Eliot's cultural writings is Raymond Williams's *Culture and Society, 1780-1950*, 227-43.

5. Poirier's definition of the soul as function echoes a well-known passage from Derrida: "It was necessary to begin thinking that there was no center, that the center could not be thought in the form of present-being, that the center had no natural site, that it was not a fixed locus but a function . . . in which an infinite number of sign-substitutions came into play" (Jacques Derrida, *Writing and Difference*, 280).

6. Richard Poirier, *Poetry and Pragmatism*, 23-25.

7. I am seeking some middle ground in the debate over the poststructuralist Emerson. Michael Lopez advances the cause of poststructuralism during a helpful discussion of Emerson's ties to nineteenth-century romantic thought more generally; see Michael Lopez, "De-transcendentalizing Emerson." Offering a more traditional perspective, Alan Hodder surveys the contentious field of Emerson studies in his fine historicist essay, "'After a High Negative Way': Emerson's 'Self-Reliance' and the Rhetoric of Conversion."

8. Ronald Bush anticipates my line of thought: "No matter how hard the later Eliot tried to accept received dogma and received ritual, his striving betrayed an Emersonian quest to renew and purify the spirit" (Ronald Bush, "'Turned toward Creation': T. S. Eliot, 1988," 1:42). The references are to Matthiessen, *Achievement*, 8, and Mildred Martin, *A Half-Century of Eliot Criticism: An Annotated Bibliography of Books and Articles in English, 1916-1965*. John Clendenning's lonely article of 1967, "Time, Doubt and Vision," is brief but insightful in comparing Eliot and Emerson, with emphasis on "the Boston doubt."

9. Eliot was recalling a poem from his pre-*Waste Land* days, "Hidden under the heron's wing" (*IMH*, 82), which, with its singing "lotos-birds," suggests the influence of Indic religion.

10. Quoted in Helen Gardner, *The Composition of "Four Quartets,"* 29.

11. In 1930, Eliot told a friend that his New England was more closely tied in memory to Maine than to Massachusetts (letter to William Force Stead, June 20, 1930). In another letter of 1930, he said that England couldn't inspire his natural imagery, and that, to write about nature, he had to imagine Missouri and New England (letter to William Force Stead, August 9, 1930).

12. T. S. Eliot, "A Commentary: That Poetry Is Made with Words," *New English Weekly* 15 (April 27, 1939) 27. One may compare Eliot's remark of 1942: "If, as we are aware, only a part of the meaning can be conveyed by paraphrase, that is because the poet is occupied with frontiers of consciousness beyond which words fail, though meanings still exist" (*OPP*, 30).

13. In the *Monthly Criterion* 6 (November 1927), 398-402.

14. Crane, "The Tunnel," 98, 100, in *Poems*.

15. Ibid., 99.

16. For Crane's uses of *Waste Land* imagery in *The Bridge*, see Harvey Gross, *Sound and Form in Modern Poetry*, 217-21.

17. Eliot was intensely conscious of family ancestry. At his Crawford Street flat in the late 1910s he kept a kind of shrine in a corner adorned with family photographs and silhouettes. His letters to his mother give further evidence of his deep concern with ancestry. He wore the family ring, and his nickname, "the elephant," derives in part from an elephant on the family crest. See Ackroyd, *T. S. Eliot*, 91; *LTSE*, 268, 274; and Lyndall Gordon, *Eliot's New Life*, 253. Eliot wrote Herbert Read in 1928 that as a "small boy" he "felt that the U.S.A. up to a hundred years ago was a family extension" (Sir Herbert Read, "T. S. E.—A Memoir," 15). My concern here is to show that Eliot's strong sense both of family and of the United States—as intimately connected to his family's history and identity—emerged as a major force in the symbolism of *Four Quartets*: "When I speak of the family, I have in mind a bond which embraces a longer period of time than this [i.e., longer than two or three generations]: a piety towards the dead, however obscure, and a solicitude for the unborn, however remote" (*NDC* 116).

18. In a letter reminiscent of Henry James's *The American Scene*, Eliot told Stead that the Missouri of his youth had been swept aside by progress (letter to William Force Stead, June 20, 1930). When this author visited the site of the old Eliot home in 1992, he encountered a parking lot—very nearly vacant.

19. Responding to John Hayward's inquiry about the "field-mouse," Eliot wrote: "*Field-mice*. They *did* get into our country house in New England, and very pretty little creatures too: we always restored them to the Land, and only slew the housemice. But the particular point here is that the house is supposed to have been deserted or empty" (his emphasis; quoted in Gardner, *Composition*, 97).

20. Hodder, "'After a High Negative Way,'" 438; Hodder compares Edwards's apophasis to "the *via negativa* of the medieval mystics." I have found Paul Fry's odic genealogy for *Four Quartets* to be very instructive. One of Fry's more general reflections on the nature of odes throws considerable light on the passage at hand: "The quest for voice is by no means confined to the ode; it is possibly the theme of all writing, and it is certainly the theme of the quieter lyrics to which the ode is related in its sphere of concern, the Meditative Lyric and the Conversation Poem. But whereas the lyric that is not an ode seeks voice without fanfare, as if by a spontaneous course of thought, the ode denies itself the illusionism of full-throated ease and writes itself hoarse" (Paul H. Fry, *The Poet's Calling in the English Ode*, 9).

21. Finding that the Eliot of *Four Quartets* accepted "a set poetic structure of the kind he had always struggled to avoid," Ronald Bush avers: "The formal lyrics of . . . 'East Coker' and 'The Dry Salvages' were written to 'fit.' Exchanging the authority of his own voice for the impersonality of an orchestra, Eliot frequently lost his touch. Sometimes, his simulated voices fail to convince" (Ronald Bush, *T. S. Eliot: A Study in Character and Style*, 222). By contrast, I would say that the formal lyrics of "East Coker" and "The Dry Salvages" are spiritual exercises for the personal voice, not impersonal structures.

22. Cf. Elisa New: "The Emersonian afflatus gives the American poet reach. . . .

And yet the poet stretched beyond his limits or past her reach must, in the end, come back to his powerlessness, back to her purblindness" (Elisa New, *The Regenerate Lyric: Theology and Innovation in American Poetry*, 25).

23. Quoted in Bloom, *Poetics*, 312. I am indebted to Bloom's pithy essay "Emerson: Power at the Crossing" to the extent that this chapter originated as a response to it.

24. Robert Frost, *Selected Prose of Robert Frost*, 41.

25. Eliot also used James's phrase with reference to Shakespeare in his introduction to *The Wheel of Fire*. It has a close analogue in Eliot's perspective on rhythm: "Rhythm, of course, is a highly personal matter; it is not a verse form. It is always the real pattern in the carpet, the scheme of organization of thought, feeling, and vocabulary, the way in which everything comes together" (T. S. Eliot, "Marianne Moore," 595).

26. Grover Smith, *"The Waste Land,"* 123-25.

27. See Ronald Schuchard, "'If I think, again, of this place': Eliot, Herbert, and the Way to 'Little Gidding.'" *Words in Time: New Essays on Eliot's Four Quartets*, ed. Edward Lobb (London: Athlone Press, 1993), 52-83.

28. Eliot wrote Hayward: ". . . I wished the effect of the whole [encounter with the ghost] to be Purgatorial which is much more appropriate" (quoted in Gardner, *Composition*, 64-65).

29. Eliot, introduction to *The Wheel of Fire*, xvi.

Fear in the Way:
The Design of Eliot's Drama
Michael Goldman

Michael Goldman presents a structural and thematic overview of all five of Eliot's verse plays, from *Murder in the Cathedral* through *The Elder Statesman*, that emphasizes the place of ghosts and haunting in the plays' action and in our experience of them. Although Goldman focuses primarily on *Murder* and *The Cocktail Party*, widely regarded as Eliot's most successful dramatic works, he links them persuasively to the others through the shift in each from a ghost that can be exorcised to a haunting of a different kind that reaches beyond the central character to other characters and to us. His view provides an alternative to the topics frequently discussed by critics: Eliot's achievement in creating language in verse that audiences can understand without undue effort and the Christian aspects. The ghost is an important figure in Eliot's writing, including in the memorable second part of "Little Gidding," the last of *Four Quartets*, in which the speaker encounters a "familiar compound ghost" in a scene that involves a descent into an underworld. By bringing out the double aspect of the ghosts, which in Eliot are both archaic and familiar, Goldman identifies, without using the term, their *uncanny* aspect, as Sigmund Freud defined the uncanny as both familiar and strange. And he lays the basis, again without using the term, for understanding the plays' *gothic* element, which involves the fear that the characters experience and the dramatic tradition of having ghosts cry out for revenge. Eliot knew the revenge tradition in Elizabethan drama well, wrote about it in his essays, and alludes to it in his poetry. The fear, isolation, and madness evoked by Eliot's plays are all related to a sense of dread that has become pervasive in the modern world as a social and psychological effect of the technology of warfare. As a consequence, the central character's difficulties are all too recognizable to other characters and to the audience. As Goldman suggests,

> Eliot attempted to create plays that subvert the conventions of traditional dramatic plots involving mystery, romance, farce, and melodrama. The attempt is parallel to his subversion of nineteenth-century poetic forms, such as the dramatic monologue, in his non-dramatic poetry. By describing the watching and waiting that typically occurs in Eliot's plays, Goldman helps us to recognize their unusual presentation of action and human agency. Although the waiting cannot be simply identified with the waiting that Samuel Beckett made famous, it is related, and it is equally challenging for the playwright and the audience. In emphasizing the double antithetical character of Eliot's effects, Goldman makes possible a connection to the contradictory implications and effects of Eliot's poems. Eliot merges the experience of knowing with its opposite, not knowing, and with fear in a modern version of Aeschylus' insistence that knowledge comes through suffering. The experience of not knowing is not simple uncertainty but an active experience of ignorance; it involves recognizing that knowledge can be more than grasping determinate, stable facts, concepts, and values. Like Beckett, Eliot mixes the known and the unknown, the threatening and the comic into a haunting tragicomic blend. —J.P.R.

"Nothing is more dramatic than a ghost," says Eliot,[1] and his remark offers an illuminating technical insight into every play he wrote. It also has the virtue of forcing us to think specifically about drama, rather than, say, prosody or moral philosophy. Eliot's own practice as a critic and reputation as a poet have tended to concentrate discussion on either the versification and language of his plays or their Christian implications, and this, while leading to much excellent and valuable criticism, has helped promote a serious misunderstanding of his achievement as a dramatist—as a writer, that is, whose texts are designed to allow a group of actors to shape an audience's experience in a theater over a finite interval of time. The possum-like tone Eliot reverts to in discussing most aspects of his dramaturgy other than verse and idiom has encouraged the notion that in matters of dramatic design, particularly the shaping of the action and the use of dramatic convention, Eliot was content to follow the techniques of the commercial theater, and not always the most up-to-date techniques at that. The picture that emerges seems to be of an Eliot laboring to do indifferently what Noel Coward did well, in the hope that verse meditations on the Christian life might somehow be smuggled to an audience while it was being diverted by boulevard entertainment. But if we allow Eliot the benefit of the doubt and approach his plays as the work of a serious dramatist, we can form quite a different impression of their design and of the originality and value of their achievement.

So I turn to the matter of ghosts in order to stress Eliot's art as a dramatist. Attention to the dramatic value of ghosts in his plays will help us see how they are constructed, what precise use they make of the conventions of drawing-room comedy, and why Eliot's achievement in the theater runs considerably deeper than the creation of a mode of dramatic verse.

Drama probably began with ghosts, with prehistoric impersonations intended to transfigure the malice of spirits—to indulge, placate, or wrestle with the dead, to turn Furies into Eumenides. Ghosts are dramatic because they make for action. By their very nature they stimulate that flow of aggression on which all drama depends. Ghosts haunt us—that is, they bring aggression to bear on us in an especially volatile way, a way that penetrates with particular intensity to our psyche and encourages imitation, encourages us to haunt as we are haunted. They are hard to defend against; they cannot easily be subdued or ignored. They create an unstable situation in the external world because their victims must transfer their aggression to new objects. When a real person hits us we can either hit him back or refuse to. Either reaction may make for drama, but the exchange can easily be enclosed, a balance quickly restored. We cannot hit back at a ghost, however, any more than we can ignore him. The haunting transmits itself through us to a wider world. Thus the classical device of a ghost crying for revenge precipitates the great Elizabethan discoveries as to plot and action—perhaps the greatest discovery being that the ghost could be internalized in the figure of the revenger, who could then be a fully human character—and starring part—while retaining a ghost's peculiar interest and privileges. The ghost makes easy and intense a kind of psychic thrust and counterthrust that connects inner states of feeling—desire, fear, hatred—with movement and change in the external world, the transformation, essential to drama, of activity into action.

A theory of ghosts might make a good theory of drama, and the historical version of this theory might note that at about the point in time when audiences cease to believe in ghosts they begin to be haunted by memories. People have always had memories, of course, but I would suggest that they are not *haunted* by memories much before Rousseau. In any historical period drama must find its proper ghosts, sources for haunting that an audience can accept as both meaningful and mysterious. Today, for example, we are haunted by unconscious memories as well as conscious ones, and by the past in the form of our parents, our bodies, our economic and social milieu. These are the ghosts that walk the modern stage, many of them, perhaps all, first set walking there by Ibsen.

I sketch this theory of the ghost both to suggest how richly sensitive to the art of the drama Eliot's remark is, and also by way of providing a background for his own ghosts and what he does with them. The structure of each of Eliot's plays is built on a double manifestation of ghosts. At first, the play appears to be haunted by spirits that, though in some respects disconcertingly archaic, still bear a clear relation to our own familiar ghosts—the ghosts we have been accustomed since Ibsen to recognize both in drama and in our lives. Gradually—and this is the fundamental process of Eliot's drama—the ghosts are revealed to be very different from what we took them to be. The original ghosts seem to vanish with an ease that is again disconcerting, but their vanishing proves to be a deeper haunting, more personally directed at the audience. They have turned into other, more persistent, ghosts. The most intense and usually the most effective part of Eliot's drama is not the demonstration that the new ghosts are different, but the manifestation of their true power to haunt—their power to haunt in their true capacity.

Eliot gives his spirits many names. But whether he simply calls them ghosts, as in *The Elder Statesman*, or shadows, furies, spectres, phantoms, spooks, guardians, or even saints and martyrs, it is as ghosts that they perform dramatically. They haunt the characters and inspire the action. Like the Furies in *The Family Reunion* they are often quite explicitly associated with myth or legend, but they also conform to ideas a modern audience can accept. They are ghosts of past associations and deeds, of heredity and environment. The guardians in *The Cocktail Party* may seem enigmatic when considered as guardians of souls, but Reilly is quite familiar to us in his professional role as a guardian of psyches. The ghosts are all versions of the "fear in the way"—the phrase from Ecclesiastes that Eliot used as a working title for *Murder in the Cathedral*[2]—a fear that turns out to be both relevant and irrelevant to the concerns of the characters, and that must be met in the course of the action and either accepted or put aside. In fact, the fear in the way of each play is first to be put aside and then accepted. At the end of each play the false ghosts have disappeared and the true ghosts hover with their horror, boredom, and glory over the characters.

Let me very briefly illustrate this by tracing the pattern for each of the plays in turn, from *Murder in the Cathedral* to *The Elder Statesman*. In *Murder in the Cathedral*, the shadows with which Thomas must struggle appear at first to be the Tempters, ghosts of former desires whose enticements to do the wrong thing are quickly dismissed, leaving Thomas to face his real struggle with the temptation to do the right thing for the wrong reason. At the same time there is another spirit in the play haunting the women of Canterbury. It is a fear of Thomas in his capacity as saint and martyr, fear of his coming to Canterbury and of the act of martyrdom to which they are compelled to bear witness. The action of the play demonstrates that this fear is illusory. In one sense the play shows the women are wrong to feel haunted, but in another sense—to which the Knights and the final chorus direct us—the burden of fear and anguish attaching to the figure of St. Thomas remains with them and with us at the end of the play and is indeed revealed only by the play's complete action.

In *The Family Reunion* the pattern is less effectively worked out, but it is simple and clear. The Furies of course begin as Harry's apparent guilt in the death of his wife, the source of his self-loathing and loathing for the human condition. In facing up to them under this aspect, he learns that while their meaning is illusory, they are nevertheless real. They are in fact "bright angels," his Eumenides, whom he must follow. We are left, as in *Murder in the Cathedral*, with a distinctly earthbound chorus burdened by fear and a sense of isolation.

The guardians of *The Cocktail Party* are menacing in a manner that conforms to the prevailing tone of high comedy—they harass Edward with embarrassing questions and surprise visits, they press loathsome concoctions and cryptic advice upon him. It is enough, by Edward's own admission—and this is a point that must be seized in playing—to humiliate him. Their power to humiliate depends of course on the memories and miseries of his relation to Lavinia. Lavinia is described at one point as a phantom; she, brought back from the dead, also haunts Edward as he haunts her. The guardians turn out not to be pests, but, once more, bright angels, yet their power to haunt persists. Most of the complaints Edward and Lavinia bring against each other are disposed of, but their central misery is not. It is Celia who escapes the emptiness and isolation of the ordinary lot, and Edward and Lavinia are left facing both her terrifying example and the absence of transcendent love in their own lives. The mood is hopeful, for their acceptance is a genuine spiritual accomplishment, but a variety of ghosts, of whom Celia must be counted one, haunt the ordinary people who are left behind.

The characters in *The Confidential Clerk* are haunted by disappointments, ghosts of absence—missing children and parents, lost sources of vocation and relatedness. There are also guardian-like figures, Mrs.

Guzzard and Eggerson (though lost children haunt them too), whose riddling style imparts a kind of harassment to the persistent memory of these absent spirits, a method similar to that of the guardians in *The Cocktail Party*, who play teasingly upon what is haunting in Edward's and Lavinia's lives. The missing children and parents function as negative bright angels. Their absence seems to leave Sir Claude and Lady Mulhammer, Lucasta Angel, B. Kaghan, and even Colby lacking a meaningful connection with reality. All the missing links are restored in the last act, where Mrs. Guzzard dominates, but the restored relations are in the end far from Eumenidean, except in the case of Colby. The play's focus narrows to Sir Claude, as Colby slips out with Mrs. Guzzard. Mulhammer, shaken and bewildered, is left with Lucasta, whom he has in effect ignored for most of the play. This is his real daughter and he must accept her, as well as accepting all that he does not have. Again we are left with off-stage transcendence and an ordinary figure on-stage facing the loss and insufficiency of ordinary life.

In *The Elder Statesman*, Lord Claverton tells us that Gomez and Mrs. Carghill are ghosts—ghosts of his past, of past crimes. In all the senses announced at the beginning of the play, their power to haunt Claverton turns out to be illusory; the crimes are not real crimes; their threats are insubstantial. But in another sense the ghosts and what they represent are inexpungeable; to face them they must be accepted, for their power to haunt lies in their reflection of the facts of Claverton's own character, which he must accept if he is to cease to be "hollow." For once, the burden is eased for those left on stage. Monica and Charles are brought closer to each other and to Claverton because his confrontation and acceptance of the ghosts has issued in a transforming love. But the discovery, a version of which has been hinted at in the final tableau of *The Confidential Clerk*, depends on clear-eyed acceptance of a haunting loss and limitation.

The great point about the encounter at the end of *The Elder Statesman*, and the great dramatic surprise, is that Claverton does not make his ghosts disappear or render them innocuous by facing them. They continue to be what they always were, and their power for evil is all the more felt for being more fully faced. The price Claverton pays is his son, Michael, but the meaning of the price, as he tells us, is love. If *The Elder Statesman* goes beyond *The Confidential Clerk* by presenting human love as a path to Divine Love, it is significant that the parent-child relation it requires as a dramatic pivot is much grimmer than that between Sir Claude and his daughter. Lucasta is quite clearly a bright angel, as her name suggests. Michael Claverton is not, and he follows Gomez and Carghill.

The pattern I have been describing is suggestive in a number of ways as to the meaning and method of Eliot's drama. What I wish to stress now is its relation to the convention he finally chose to work in—the convention of boulevard entertainment whose fourth-wall realism and bourgeois milieu sustain the workings of a well-made plot. The exact genre may vary with the mood required, but it is always well-made, whether it be the plot of detection, love-intrigue, farce, or melodrama—always the mechanism of secrets to be discovered, obstacles to be overcome, communications to be rechanneled and restored. It will already be clear that the transition from false ghost to true ghost corresponds to the development in every one of Eliot's plays by which the expectations of the convention are subverted. *The Family Reunion* is not an Agatha Christie-like story of crime and punishment but of sin and expiation. The love-tangles of Edward and Celia, Lavinia and Peter, do not lead to complications in the second and third act. Mrs. Guzzard's revelations do not solve the problems carefully established in the first two acts of *The Confidential Clerk*, but show that the problem as it has been stated is irrelevant, and so on. More important, the change in our understanding of the ghosts develops its special meaning and intensity only by virtue of taking place in this type of setting and growing out of this type of dramatic convention.

The well-made play, particularly the drawing-room comedy or mystery, is characterized by an emphasis on mechanical connectedness. The introduction of any significant element implies that this element will be seen to mesh like a gear with all the other elements of the play, and the action of the play will be the operation of all these gears like a single machine. If the key to a letterbox is called attention to in the first act, a significant letter must be unlocked in the last. This sense of mechanical connectedness extends to the society of the play. The characters' lives, pasts, and appetites act upon each other to a degree of intimacy and efficiency that may fairly be taken, in this genre, as an index of the play's success. The result is not always mechanical drama in any pejorative sense, and the connections I am talking about are not always mechanical in the sense that they are superficial or merely physical. But the impression of efficient and causal interconnection prevails, just as it prevails in the various notions of significant action, of cause and effect—of psychological, biological, social, and economic determinism—that drama of this type reflects.

The haunted characters in Eliot's drawing-room plays are pursued by phantoms of connectedness—actions committed in the past, family secrets, old associations, lovers—the social, sexual, and psychological determinants that are the ghosts of modern drama. But in the end these baleful connections are revealed to be illusory, and the characters are seen to be truly haunted by an inability to connect. The crowded drawing room, the carefully prepared meeting of principals, the statesman's diary are all empty—a cheat and a disappointment. The exact quality of this emptiness is frequently and carefully described—the sudden solitude in a crowded desert, the exacerbated isolation in the midst of an apparent connectedness. It is an isolation that appears inevitable and also miserably unreal because connectedness is felt as the only reality. And here we find the significance of Eliot's convention. This type of isolation cannot be conveyed, for example, on the unlocalized platform of the existential stage, the stage of *Waiting for Godot*. There, isolation represents reality; one is trapped and isolated *in* the real world, the world of one's aloneness, a setting in which the individual, terrified and despairing as he may be, can yet be seen to possess his being. But the sense of isolation from which Eliot's characters suffer—it strikingly resembles that of schizophrenics[3]—is an isolation in unreality. They are trapped in a world of make-believe. In this condition the familiar social world itself is haunting because the very appearance of connectedness only heightens the conviction that one is incapable of connection; one is oneself not real, an empty, worthless, hollow man. The unreal city is oneself and the key confirms the prison.

The dramaturgical point, then, is this. Like the rooms that figure so prominently in *The Waste Land* and the early poems, the drawing room and the dramatic conventions associated with it have a twofold function—they stand for a real world with which the hero is powerless to make contact, and they also stand for the "finite center"[4] of the self in whose unreality the hero is trapped and isolated. In *The Cocktail Party* the isolated cell of the poems has become a modern flat where a man cannot get a moment's privacy, but it confirms a prison still. One achievement of *The Cocktail Party* is its transposition of so much that is haunting in modern life—the horror and boredom and glory that attack and pursue the central sensibility of *The Waste Land*—into the modes of light comedy, but though any production of the play must maintain a proper lightness, it must also be careful not to slight the real pressures that even the most farcical turns of the action apply to the major characters, especially Edward. The first act is a series of humiliations for him, all the more humiliating because they are initiated by the typical raillery and contretemps of drawing-room comedy. And it is exactly this contrast between the convention and his response that allows the play to reveal with lucidity and precision the real sources of humiliation in his life.

Though the later plays are in some respects more profoundly conceived and contain concluding passages of a theatrical beauty quite unique to them, *The Cocktail Party* is still Eliot's most successful play, because in it the vivacity of the author's line-by-line response to his theatrical opportunities is at its height. We feel this most strongly in two ways—first in the interaction of the characters, and second in the use of all the elements in the mise en scène to advance the action and to intensify and render more subtle our experience of it, in particular to heighten our sense that the characters are haunted. In *Poetry and Drama* Eliot complains that too many of *The Cocktail Party*'s characters stand outside the action, but of all his plays it is *The Cocktail Party* whose characters most thoroughly act upon each other in their dialogue.[5] Not surprisingly, *The Cocktail Party* has of all the drawing-room plays the most definite spine, which can be expressed in the phrase *to begin*. From the beginning of the play, when Alex is called upon to begin his story again (the story being drowned, as Julia's soon will be, in the very effort to begin it), until the end, when the bell rings and Lavinia says, "Oh I'm glad. It's begun," the characters are constantly trying to begin and to begin again. And their efforts to begin—if only to leave the room or start a conversation—elaborate the process of haunting and heighten our sense of the fragmentation and isolation of the self that Edward, Lavinia, and Celia experience.

The mise en scène contributes throughout to the sense of an illusory connectedness badgering and isolating the central characters. Take, for example, the strange variety of food that is prepared, consumed, or recommended in the opening scenes. The inadequate tidbits, Alex's culinary fantasies and inedible offerings, the remedies of Norwegian cheese, curry powder, prunes, and alcohol, even the unwanted champagne, all forced upon Edward as he suffers in his constantly interrupted yet unbreakable solitude—these like the genteel disarray of the set, the post-cocktail-party depression (and it has been a badly managed, underfed and underpopulated cocktail party)—like the set, and with a wit and variety that makes the audience alert and sympathetic to nuance, the food plays upon the isolation and debility of the untransfigured individual in the ordinary world. It is a horror and boredom expressed no less exactly than that of the poor women of Canterbury.

All this reinforces the attack Edward undergoes in the course of the first act, the series of humiliations whose insubstantial and amusing surface constantly reminds us how illusory is the ostensibly dense social continuum in which Edward has his being. He cannot be alone for a minute; everyone wants to feed him. He has no privacy; in the nicest way he is interrogated and exposed—but in truth he has nothing but his privacy, and it is a privacy that leaves him with nothing. Left to himself he "moves about restlessly," while the doorbell and the phone keep ringing. Throughout the act, Eliot emphasizes a nagging connection with the outside world by a series of exits and entrances that require Edward to half-leave the stage—to be invisible for an instant, open the door and return with his caller. Edward's world, like drawing-room comedy itself, is a network of insistent social connections which, like his marriage, fail to free him from aloneness and emptiness. In the first scene, he waits his guests and interrupters out, then phones Celia only to receive no answer. The lights go down and come up again. We are immediately aware that no considerable interval has passed; the time elapsed has been pointedly insignificant. Edward sits among the debris as before—potato crisps, glasses, bottles, a forgotten umbrella—playing solitaire.[6]

These examples have all been taken from the first act. Each of the devices referred to—the emphasis on communications, the treatment of food and drink, the behavior of characters when alone—is used in later acts to underline that awareness of transformation which I have argued is essential to Eliot's dramatic technique—awareness that the true nature of the haunting in the play is being revealed. This dramatic imagery is employed with a distinctive wit, a kind of half-explicit mocking of its own recurrence and tendentiousness that sustains the play's tone. Sir Henry's office with its plot-expediting intercom and its carefully scheduled arrangement of exits and entrances contrasts nicely with the nagging persistence of bells and callers in Act One. Similarly, the toasts that are drunk in the course of the play form a sequence that guides our attention from the ordinary to the transcendent. And in the last act we have a cocktail party to contrast with that of the first. The work of the caterers and the new reputation of the Chamberlaynes' parties for good food and drink makes itself felt as a welcome improvement in this ordinary drawing-room world. Even the exits and entrances have been improved—by the presence of a caterer's man who announces the guests. In this world, decent social arrangements still mean much, for they are still the means by which the guardians make their presence known.

As for the behavior of the characters in private, let me take just one example—the moment when Reilly lies down on his couch. In part, this is a joke—a piece of raillery typical of the play but aimed directly at the audience. The couch is one of the indicators by which we have recognized the psychiatrist's office. It has remained empty throughout Reilly's interviews with Edward and Lavinia. Both conventional psychiatry and our conventional dramatic expectations are being mocked. This orchestrates the real shift in expectation, both for us and the characters. The problems of this marriage are not to be located in the usual psychological sources, but in an abiding spiritual deficiency. At the same time the scene marks another transition in the action and in our understanding of the characters. Reilly's moment of exhaustion precedes the entrance of Julia ("Henry, get up") and the interview with Celia; it prepares for our discovery that Reilly does not occupy the highest place in the play's spiritual hierarchy and our dawning sense of what that hierarchy may mean. Again let me stress that the spiritual world is felt as haunting, that it exerts an unsettling and mysterious psychic pressure on the characters. If Reilly's questions and Julia's snooping haunt Edward in the first act, Celia's martyrdom haunts the marital contentment of the last.

The apprehension of a source of haunting and the gradual discovery that the source is very different from what it has been apprehended to be—this pattern of action and feeling is central to Eliot's dramaturgy, and it accounts for an important feature of his dramatic style, or rather for a number of features that together enforce a single theme—that of knowing and not knowing. Take, for example, the motif of the visitor who is both expected and unexpected. The Third and Fourth Tempters both play upon this idea, but it is felt more dramatically in the later plays. Harry is known to be on his way home as *The Family Reunion* opens, but at the point of his first entrance everyone is actively expecting either Arthur or John. Harcourt-Reilly is an unexpected visitor no one is very surprised to see in either the last scene of Act One or in Act Three of *The Cocktail Party*. The arrivals of Lady Elizabeth in the first act and Mrs. Guzzard in the last act of *The Confidential Clerk*, though carefully prepared and discussed extensively in advance, are disconcerting and unexpected when they happen (and both arrivals are heralded by a series of disconcerting messengers).

Also related to the theme of knowing and not knowing is the motif of the crime that is not a crime. The old man Claverton runs over turns out in the third act to have been dead before the accident. Harry Monchonsey did not murder his wife; Lucasta Angel is not Sir Claude Mulhammer's mistress; Edward has not betrayed Celia. In all cases, the revelation is casual, a throwaway defeat of our expectations; it is part of our becoming aware that certain actions and memories do not matter or do not matter for the reasons we thought they did.

Knowing-and-not-knowing is also felt in a recurrent verbal device, prominent as early as *Sweeney Agonistes*—the use of echoing dialogue. This example is from *The Cocktail Party*:

Julia:	Who is he?
Edward:	*I* don't know.
Julia:	*You* don't know?
Edward:	I never saw him before in my life.
Julia:	But how did he come here?
Edward:	*I* don't know.
Julia:	*You* don't know!

As here, the cadence is usually a mocking or riddling one; we may be tempted to put it down to the Possum-mode of mystification. But the device turns a character's words back on himself, suggesting, as the Fourth Tempter suggests to Thomas, that a man may not know what he thinks he knows, and that we in the audience must expect some change in what we think we know. Our words may be riddles even to ourselves. In the drawing-room plays the echoing dialogue is typically both uncomprehending and disconcerting; it confirms a prison but alerts us to a key.

We know and do not know what it is to act and suffer. How do we come to know more? The answer, given in every play, is: *watch and wait*. But watching and waiting imply a crucial dramatic problem, and the success or failure of each of Eliot's plays may be said to hinge on its solution. At some point in the drawing-room plays, the dramatic convention becomes a fragmented background against which certain characters are seen in a new light, isolated in a freshly haunted world. But this means that there is a risk that the continuity of the action may evaporate, sustained as it has been by the apparent connectedness of the play's world and the now-discredited significance of the ghosts haunting it. At the same time there is the danger that the dramatic interest of the central character may evaporate too. The watching and waiting theme requires that at some moment the hero surrender his role as an agent; he must consent to be passive. He is displaced from a central initiating role to become part of the pattern. The moment of surrender may itself make for a good scene; as when Edward accepts his becoming a thing, an object in the hands of masked actors, or Mulhammer gives up control to Eggerson and Guzzard and absorbs the bewildering results. Claverton struggles with a version of this necessity in his first long speech and again accepts it in the strong scene at the end of his play, and Thomas' surrender is perhaps most powerfully felt in his long cry at the moment of death, which Eliot has considerably expanded from the historical records. But essentially what a character accepts at a moment like this is that he must no longer be a *performer*—and this has awkward implications, both for actor and playwright.

Watching and waiting over any period of time is not very dramatic; it is always a problem for an actor, and Eliot cannot be said always to have solved it. At the very end of *The Elder Statesman*, Claverton says, "In becoming no one, I begin to live," but the actor of this often ungrateful role might fairly complain that, instead of becoming no one, the play limits him to *being* no one for most of its length, that he must watch and wait from the beginning. And in *The Family Reunion*, once the interest of the false ghosts peters out and there is no crime to be uncovered, Eliot can devise no action that engages any of the characters; we are treated to a series of explanations that never become encounters. From *The Cocktail Party* on, Eliot is always able to maintain action and encounter, because the haunting function, both false and true, is taken over by real characters who can make their presence felt in a lively way whenever they appear. Reilly, Julia, Guzzard, Carghill, Gomez—these are good parts, not hard to act. But for the last two plays there remains a difficulty in casting the leading roles which makes it problematical whether *The Confidential Clerk* and *The Elder Statesman* will ever receive performances that can test their best values. In many ways they ask more of their actors than they offer in return. Claverton must be played by an actor not only strong but abnormally unselfish, ready to pass honestly through the long passivity of the early acts in order to contribute to the lovely finale. In *The Confidential Clerk* the problem is even more serious. The characterization of Sir Claude as a financier is extremely flimsy, and his lack of definition as a public figure makes the first act dangerously slack. The deep problem, however, is Colby, whose interest lies far too much in the eyes of his beholders. He must be cast against his part; the role must be filled by an immensely engaging, physically robust actor with no suggestion of priggishness or passivity about him. Here, clearly, the production must make up for weaknesses in the text. Whether we shall ever get such a production, however, remains to be seen.

    So far I have been talking mostly about the plays written after *Murder in the Cathedral*, since the subject of ghosts has a special bearing on Eliot's treatment of the drawing-room convention. But my remarks apply to the earlier play as well, for the pattern I have described helps to account for *Murder in the Cathedral*'s dramatic effectiveness and points to meanings that have been overlooked in criticism and production. Let me begin with an objection that is frequently raised against the play: "The determining flaw in *Murder in the Cathedral* is that the imitation of its action is complete at the end of Part One."[7] I do not think this is true to our felt experience of the play, even in a good amateur production, nor to the dramatic intentions clearly indicated in the text.

It is true that by the end of Part One we have seen Thomas accept his martyrdom as part of a pattern to which he must consent for the right reasons, and that we see this acceptance re-enacted both in the sermon and in Part Two, with no modification of theme or deepening of Thomas' response. But the point of the play lies in the re-enactment, since everything is changed *for us* by each re-seeing. The aim of *Murder in the Cathedral* is to make its audience "watch and wait," to "bear witness"—to see the event in several perspectives, each enriching the other, so the pattern may subsist, so the action may be seen as pattern, and so that our own relation to the action, our part of the pattern, may be fully and intensely experienced—and this is not finally accomplished until the very end of the play.

Once more it is a question of knowing and not knowing. Even as the play begins, we know what its climax will be. But by the time we actually see Thomas murdered, after witnessing Part One and the sermon, we see that we knew and did not know. In the same way, the Knights and the Chorus, lacking the knowledge we have, both know and do not know what they are doing and suffering. And of course after the murder, the Knights' speeches show us yet one more aspect of the event that we knew and did not know.

It should be noted at this point that bearing witness, watching the events of the play, is from the first associated both with knowing and not knowing and with fear. In performance we are apt to be unaware of the powerful theatricality of the opening chorus. The theatrical problems of the Women of Canterbury are generally approached by way of voice production and enunciation, and we are grateful—and lucky—if the actresses recruited for the occasion manage to speak clearly and on the beat. Choral acting, as opposed to choral reciting, is usually beyond them. But Eliot understands, as no one except Lorca since the Greeks has understood, that choral writing is writing for the body, and the bodily excitement of the first Chorus derives from the way it joins the feeling of knowing and not knowing to the emotion of fear. The Chorus prefigures the action to come and combines it with a bewildered self-consciousness. We move, they say. We wait. Why do we move and wait as we do? Is it fear, is it the allure of safety, is it even the allure of fear? What kind of fear, what kind of safety? This is exactly the question the play will put about martyrdom, put to Thomas and to us:

> Here let us stand, close by the cathedral. Here let us wait.
> Are we drawn by danger? Is it the knowledge of safety,
>   that draws our feet
> Towards the cathedral? What danger can be
> For us, the poor, the poor women of Canterbury? what
>   tribulation
> With which we are not already familiar? There is no
>   danger
> For us, and there is no safety in the cathedral. Some
>   presage of an act
> Which our eyes are compelled to witness, has forced
>   our feet
> Towards the cathedral. We are forced to bear witness.

The opportunity for the actors is remarkable. The tension between fear and freedom on which the chorus is grounded might fairly be called the root emotion of the theater; it is the same emotion, for instance, that a shaman and his audience share when he begins to impersonate the spirits that are haunting him.[8] The emotion here is intensified through group response, beautifully registered in the language, and profoundly integrated with the action of the play. A crowd of women huddles toward the protection of what it half senses to be a fearful place. The chorus rouses the audience toward the awareness to come, of the church and martyrdom as a painful and difficult shelter.

Thomas is an easier dramatic subject for Eliot than his later heroes, because he remains active all the time he is on stage, aggressive even while he waits and watches. He is supremely connected to this world and the next, secure in his being except for the crisis at the climax of Part One. As far as it bears on Thomas, the pattern of haunting is complete when he says, "Now is my way clear." The true nature of the shadows he must strive with has been revealed to him and he is no longer isolated. We have seen, however, that in the later dramas the pattern of haunting continues to the end of the play and works itself out in the lives of characters for whom such transcendence is not possible. I would like to urge that this pattern is also present in *Murder in the Cathedral*. The sustained pattern of haunting completes the play's design after Thomas' death, and by means of a carefully prepared shift of focus imparts to the whole drama a final richness of impression too easily neglected both in the study and on the stage. As the play finds its structure in our bearing witness to Thomas' martyrdom and, through the Chorus, associates our watching and waiting with a fear that is at times close to panic, so the haunting in the play, the fear in the way of the original title, is finally brought to bear not on Thomas but on the Chorus and on us.

The sequence of events that concludes the play, beginning with the moment the Knights attack Thomas in the cathedral, testifies to Eliot's remarkable control over the resources of his stage. Thomas cries out at length, and the murder continues throughout the entire chorus which begins, "Clear the air! clean the sky!" The stage directions make quite certain of this. The drunken Knights, then, take upwards of three minutes—a very long time on the stage—to hack Thomas to death, while the Chorus chants in terror. Beyond the insistent horror of the act itself there is a further effect of juxtaposition achieved between the murder and the action of the Chorus. Properly acted, the choral text unavoidably suggests that in its terror the Chorus is somehow egging the murderers on, that the continuing blows of the Knights are accomplishing what the violent, physical, heavily accented cries for purgation call for: "Clear the air!

clean the sky! wash the wind! take the stone from the stone, take the skin from the arm, take the muscle from the bone, and wash them. Wash the stone, wash the bone, wash the brain, wash the soul, wash them wash them!" The Chorus brings to a flooding climax the ambivalent current of fear that has haunted the Women of Canterbury from the opening scene—attraction toward Thomas and a powerful aversion from him, fear for and of the martyr. The murder is felt not only as a protracted physical horror but as an action in which the Chorus has participated.

The speeches of the Knights that follow are of course sinister as well as comic.[9] The two effects are connected, as Eliot seems well aware, for our laughter involves us, as their fear has involved the Chorus, in aggression toward Thomas. We laugh with release from the constraints of fancy-dress. In the style they adopt, the Knights voice our own impulse to deflate the bubble of archaism, poetry, and saintliness. We share their animus, and their arguments turn the point against us. They have acted in our interests, as de Morville reminds us. "If there is any guilt whatever in the matter you must share it with us."

It is not the confident Third Priest with his dismissal of the Knights as weak, sad men, who has the last word, but the Women of Canterbury, who acknowledge themselves as types of the common man, weak and sad indeed. At the end they dwell upon their fear, which is no less strong for the transcendence they have witnessed. As in all Eliot's plays, the glimpse of transcendence is in itself a source of fear for those who have been left behind. They make the point the Knights have made in argument and that the choral accompaniment of the murder has powerfully enforced:

> That the sin of the world is upon our heads; that the
>   blood of the martyrs and the agony of the saints
>   Is upon our heads.

I would suggest that everything that happens in the play from the moment the Knights raise their swords has been designed to give these

Fear in the Way

lines a weight of conviction and a dramatic force that I hope I may by now characterize with some precision—as haunting.

The treatment of the Chorus, then, establishes the pattern Eliot was to maintain in his later drama. And the pattern in turn reflects the originality and strength of his writing for the theater. What Eliot discovered was a way to make drama out of the central subject of his poetry and criticism—the calamitous loss of self and imprisonment in self that haunts our era, a disease that may drive the fortunate man to glimpse transcendence, but which even those glimpses cannot cure:

> The enduring is not a substitute for the transient,
> Neither one for the other.
> ("A Note on War Poetry")

The theme pursues Eliot in all his work. In drama, his success was to make the sense of pursuit a ground for action and the theme a source of design, to transmit to his audiences the haunting pressure of "the enduring" on those who, like us, are condemned to roles as actors in a transient world.

From *Eliot in His Time: Essays on the Occasion of the Fiftieth Anniversary of "The Waste Land,"* ed. A. Walton Litz (Princeton, NJ: Princeton University Press, 1973): 155-180. Copyright © 1973 by Princeton University Press, 2001 renewed Princeton University Press. Reprinted by Permission of Princeton University Press.

Notes

1. *Selected Essays*, 3rd ed. (London, 1951), p. 52.
2. See E. Martin Browne, *The Making of T. S. Eliot's Plays* (Cambridge, 1969), pp. 54-55.
3. Laing's account of schizophrenia in *The Divided Self* (London, 1960) makes very interesting reading for the student of Eliot's work. The schizophrenic, we learn, is convinced he has no identity, that he is "hollow" and "unreal." The real world terrifies him, afflicts him with fears of drowning and petrifaction, because it threatens to swamp his identity, to fill up the vacuum of the self. At the same time, because he is unreal, he can

take no real pleasure in the world; it seems to him ghostly or barren. Laing reports the following typical dreams of a schizophrenic patient:

"I found myself in a village. I realize it has been deserted: it is in ruins; there is no life in it. . . ."

". . . I was standing in the middle of a barren landscape. It was absolutely flat. There was no life in sight. The grass was hardly growing. My feet were stuck in mud. . . ."

". . . I was in a lonely place of rocks and sand. I had fled there from something; now I was trying to get back to somewhere but didn't know which way to go . . ."

To deal with this at once unreal and terrifying wasteland, to protect his own vulnerable hollowness, the schizoid personality constructs "false self systems," plausible, usually docile personae that keep the world at a distance, prevent it from encountering the "real" self. He lives forever in a world of make-believe, which only serves to plunge him into a deeper sense of isolation, fragmentation, and worthlessness. Frequently, the schizophrenic believes himself to be invisible.

The clinical point is valuable, not for any suggestions of pathology, but because it points to a source of connection between certain groups of observations and images that are frequently juxtaposed in Eliot's poetry, most notably in *The Waste Land* and the plays. Particularly, there is the connection between, on the one hand, a sense of the world as both unreal and loathsome and, on the other, a deep doubt as to one's identity and capacity to escape from the prison of the self, a petrifying terror of contact with the outside world accompanied by a depressed conviction that such contact is impossible.

Eliot's great and continuing influence on the thought of our age stems in large measure from his portrayal of a crisis in the self, reflected in every phase of modern life, which bears an obvious resemblance to the pathological state Laing has termed "ontological insecurity." Given our inadequate understanding of schizophrenia, the mysteriousness of its etiology and its distressingly high incidence, we might do well to consider whether Eliot's vision does not suggest—as, in their own way, Laing and others in the field are beginning to suggest—that schizophrenia is a spiritual as well as a mental disorder, an affliction of our culture. When Eliot observes that "something happened to the mind of England" between Donne and Tennyson, and that what happened was a divorce between thought and feeling, it is not to be assumed that this is a "projection" of some personal experience of a familiar mental disturbance, a brush of the wing of schizophrenia. But it may be an insight into its causes.

4. See "Leibniz' Monads and Bradley's Finite Centres," in Eliot's *Knowledge and Experience in the Philosophy of F. H. Bradley* (New York, 1964), pp. 198-207. Cf. *The Waste Land*, ll. 411 ff. and Eliot's note on l. 411.

5. Eliot's characters seem at times to have no immediate motivation beyond making themselves clear. The notion of action in drama is notoriously difficult to define, but we may agree that action is locally felt in the line-to-line presence of a psychic thrust, an impulse within the actor pushing out against the other actors and circumstances on stage, and that the interplay of thrusts, the push and pull between actors, is what makes dialogue playable. The thrust to clarity alone is insufficient, and there are too many telltale lines of the what-do-you-mean, explain-yourself variety in the pages of Eliot's drama. Still, in all the plays except *The Family Reunion*, and particularly in *Murder in the Cathedral* and *The Cocktail Party*, the playable thrust is very much in evidence,

and it regularly reveals the presence of what I call ghosts, the haunting forces and persons who humiliate and harry the major characters.

Eliot's characters do achieve a unique clarity of expression, however, and this is an important source of power and originality in the plays. See Professor Kenner's remarkably illuminating discussion of Eliot's drama in *The Invisible Poet* (New York, 1959), pp. 334-36.

6. Later, in the midst of their painful interview, when Celia leaves the room for a moment, "EDWARD goes over to the table and inspects his game of Patience. He moves a card."

7. Denis Donoghue, *The Third Voice* (Princeton, 1959), p. 81.

8. See, for example, Andreas Lommel, *The World of the Early Hunters* (London, 1967), pp. 80-81.

9. Cf. Browne on Henri Fluchère's French production, p. 60.

RESOURCES

Chronology of T. S. Eliot's Life

1888	Born Thomas Stearns Eliot on September 26 to Henry and Charlotte Eliot in St. Louis, Missouri.
1906	Begins undergraduate studies at Harvard University.
1908	Discovers *The Symbolist Movement in Literature* by Arthur Symons.
1911	Completes "The Love Song of J. Alfred Prufrock." Enters graduate program in philosophy at Harvard.
1915	Outbreak of World War I. Publishes "Prufrock" in *Poetry* magazine. Marries Vivien Haigh-Wood.
1916	Completes dissertation on Francis Herbert Bradley but never returns to Harvard for his doctoral degree.
1917	Works at Lloyd's Bank in London. *Prufrock and Other Observations* published by the Egoist Press.
1920	Publishes *Poems* and *The Sacred Wood*, a collection of essays.
1922	Wins the prestigious *Dial* Award for *The Waste Land*. Begins editorship of *The Criterion*.
1925	Publishes "The Hollow Men" in the *Dial*. Leaves Lloyd's Bank and becomes editor at the publishing house of Faber and Gwyer (later Faber and Faber).
1927	Joins the Church of England. Assumes British citizenship.
1930	Publishes *Ash-Wednesday*.
1932	Gives the Charles Eliot Norton Lectures at Harvard. Publishes *Selected Essays: 1917-1932*.
1933	Publishes *The Use of Poetry and the Use of Criticism*.
1934	Publishes *After the Strange Gods* and *The Rock*.

1935	Publishes *Murder in the Cathedral* and *Poems: 1909-1935*. Introduces Marianne Moore's *Selected Poems*.
1939	Publishes *The Family Reunion*. Last issue of *The Criterion* appears.
1943	Publishes *Four Quartets*.
1945	Calls for poets to support Ezra Pound, who had been arrested for pro-fascist radio broadcasts in Rome.
1947	Vivienne Eliot dies in a nursing home after a long illness.
1948	Awarded the Nobel Prize for Literature.
1952	Publishes *The Complete Poems and Plays, 1909-1950*.
1957	Marries Valerie Fletcher, his secretary. Publishes *On Poetry and Poets*.
1959	Publishes *The Elder Statesman*.
1965	Dies on January 4 at his home in London.

Works by T. S. Eliot

Poetry
"The Love Song of J. Alfred Prufrock," 1915
Prufrock and Other Observations, 1917
Poems, 1919
Ara Vos Prec, 1920
The Waste Land, 1922
Poems, 1909-1925, 1925
Ash-Wednesday, 1930
Triumphal March, 1931
Sweeney Agonistes, 1932
Words for Music, 1934
Collected Poems, 1909-1935, 1936
Old Possum's Book of Practical Cats, 1939
Four Quartets, 1943
The Cultivation of Christmas Trees, 1954
Collected Poems, 1909-1962, 1963
Poems Written in Early Youth, 1967
The Complete Poems and Plays, 1969

Nonfiction
Ezra Pound: His Metric and Poetry, 1917
The Sacred Wood, 1920
Homage to John Dryden, 1924
Shakespeare and the Stoicism of Seneca, 1927
For Lancelot Andrewes, 1928
Dante, 1929
Charles Whibley: A Memoir, 1931
Thoughts After Lambeth, 1931
John Dryden: The Poet, the Dramatist, the Critic, 1932
Selected Essays, 1932, 1950
The Use of Poetry and the Use of Criticism, 1933
After Strange Gods, 1934
Elizabethan Essays, 1934
Essays Ancient and Modern, 1936
The Idea of a Christian Society, 1939
The Classics and the Man of Letters, 1942
The Music of Poetry, 1942

Notes Toward the Definition of Culture, 1948
Poetry and Drama, 1951
The Three Voices of Poetry, 1953
Religious Drama: Medieval and Modern, 1954
The Literature of Politics, 1955
The Frontiers of Criticism, 1956
On Poetry and Poets, 1957
Knowledge and Experience in the Philosophy of F. H. Bradley, 1964
To Criticize the Critic, 1965
The Letters of T. S. Eliot: Volume I, 1898-1922, 1988

Drama

Sweeney Agonistes, pb. 1932, pr. 1933
The Rock: A Pageant Play, pr., pb. 1934
Murder in the Cathedral, pr., pb. 1935
The Family Reunion, pr., pb. 1939
The Cocktail Party, pr. 1949, pb. 1950
The Confidential Clerk, pr. 1953, pb. 1954
The Elder Statesman, pr. 1958, pb. 1959
Collected Plays, pb. 1962

Bibliography

Ackroyd, Peter. *T. S. Eliot: A Life*. New York: Simon & Schuster, 1984.

Alderman, Nigel. "'Where Are the Eagles and the Trumpets?' The Strange Case of Eliot's Missing Quatrains." *Twentieth Century Literature* 39 (1993): 129-51.

Alldritt, Keith. *Eliot's Four Quartets: Poetry as Chamber Music*. London and Totowa, NJ: Woburn Press, 1978.

Arrowsmith, William. "Daedal Harmonies: A Dialogue on Eliot and the Classics." *Southern Review* 13, no. 1 (Winter 1977): 1-47.

Bagchee, Shyamal, ed. *T. S. Eliot: A Voice Dissenting: Centenary Essays*. New York: St. Martin's Press, 1990.

Bedient, Calvin. *He Do the Police in Different Voices: "The Waste Land" and Its Protagonists*. Chicago: University of Chicago Press, 1987.

Behr, Caroline. *T. S. Eliot: A Chronology of His Life and Works*. London: Macmillan, 1983.

Blasing, Mutlu Konuk. "*The Waste Land*: Gloss and Glossary." *Essays in Literature* 9 (1982): 97-105.

Bloom, Harold, ed. *T. S. Eliot's "The Waste Land": Bloom's Modern Critical Interpretations*. New York: Chelsea House, 2007.

Brooker, Jewel Spears. *Master and Escape: T. S. Eliot and the Dialectic of Modernism*. Amherst: University of Massachusetts Press, 1994.

Brooker, Jewel Spears, ed. *Approaches to Teaching Eliot's Poetry and Plays*. New York: Modern Language Association, 1988.

Brooker, Jewel Spears, ed. *The Placing of T. S. Eliot*. Columbia, MO: University of Missouri Press, 1991.

Brooker, Jewel Spears, ed. *T. S. Eliot: The Contemporary Reviews*. Cambridge: Cambridge University Press, 2004.

Bush, Ronald. *T. S. Eliot: A Study of Character and Style*. New York: Oxford University Press, 1983.

Bush, Ronald, ed. *T. S. Eliot: The Modernist in History*. Cambridge: Cambridge University Press, 1991.

Cameron, Sharon. *Impersonality: Seven Essays*. Chicago: University of Chicago Press, 2007.

Chinitz, David E. *T. S. Eliot and the Cultural Divide*. Chicago: University of Chicago Press, 2003.

Chinitz, David E. "T. S. Eliot: *The Waste Land*." In *A Companion to Modernist Literature and Culture*, eds. David Bradshaw and Kevin J. H. Dettmar. Oxford: Blackwell, 2006.

Cook, Eleanor. "T. S. Eliot and the Carthaginian Peace." *English Literary History* 46 (1979): 341-55.

Cooper, John Xiros. *The Cambridge Introduction to T. S. Eliot*. Cambridge: Cambridge University Press, 2006.

Cooper, John Xiros. *T. S. Eliot and the Politics of Voice: The Argument of "The Waste Land."* Ann Arbor, MI: UMI Research Press, 1987.

Cowan, Laura. *T. S. Eliot: Man and Poet, Volume I*. Orono, ME: National Poetry Foundation, 1990.

Cuddy, Lois, and David H. Hirsch, eds. *Critical Essays on T. S. Eliot's "The Waste Land."* Boston: G. K. Hall, 1991.

Davidson, Harriet. *T. S. Eliot and Hermeneutics: Absence and Presence in "The Waste Land."* Baton Rouge, LA: Louisiana State University Press, 1985.

Davidson, Harriet, ed. *T. S. Eliot*. London and New York: Longman, 1999.

Dawson, J. L., P. D. Holland, and D. J. McKitterick, eds. *A Concordance to the Complete Poems and Plays of T. S. Eliot*. Ithaca: Cornell University Press, 1995.

Donoghue, Denis. *The Third Voice: Modern British and American Verse Drama*. Princeton, NJ: Princeton University Press, 1959.

Donoghue, Denis. *Words Alone: The Poet T. S. Eliot*. New Haven, CT: Yale University Press, 2000.

Douglas, Paul. "Reading the Wreckage: De-encrypting Eliot's Aesthetics of Empire." *Twentieth Century Literature* 43 (1997): 1-26.

Eliot, Valerie, ed. *The Letters of T. S. Eliot*. New York: Harcourt, Brace, Jovanovich, 1988.

Eliot, Valerie, ed. *The Waste Land: A Facsimile and Transcript of the Original Drafts, Including the Annotations of Ezra Pound*. New York: Harcourt, Brace, Jovanovich, 1971.

Ellman, Richard. *Eminent Domain: Yeats Among Wilde, Joyce, Pound, Eliot and Auden*. New York: Oxford University Press, 1967.

Erwin, Mark. "Wittgenstein and *The Waste Land*." *Philosophy and Literature* 21 (1997): 279-91.

Freed, Lewis. *T. S. Eliot: The Critic as Philosopher*. West Lafayette, IN: Purdue University Press, 1979.

Frye, Northrop. *T. S. Eliot: An Introduction*. Chicago: University of Chicago Press, 1963.

Gallup, David. *T. S. Eliot: A Bibliography*. London: Faber and Faber, 1969.

Gardner, Helen. *The Art of T. S. Eliot*. New York: Dutton, 1950.

Gardner, Helen. *The Composition of "Four Quartets."* London: Faber and Faber, 1978.

Gilbert, Sandra. "'Rats' Alley': The Great War, Modernism, and the (Anti)Pastoral Elegy." *New Literary History* 30 (1999): 179-201.

Gish, Nancy K. *Time in the Poetry of T. S. Eliot: A Study in Structure and Theme*. London: Macmillan, 1981.

Gordon, Lyndall. *Eliot's Early Years*. New York: Oxford University Press, 1977.

Gordon, Lyndall. *T. S. Eliot: An Imperfect Life*. New York: W. W. Norton, 1999.

Grant, Michael. *T. S. Eliot: The Critical Heritage*. Vols. 1-2. London and Boston: Routledge & Kegan Paul, 1982.

Gray, Piers. *T. S. Eliot's Intellectual and Poetic Development, 1909-1922*. Sussex: Harvester Press, 1982.

Habib, M. A. R. *The Early T. S. Eliot and Western Philosophy*. Cambridge: Cambridge University Press, 1999.

Hammer, Langdon. *Hart Crane and Allen Tate: Janus-Faced Modernism*. Princeton, NJ: Princeton University Press, 1993.

Harris, Daniel A. "Language, History, and Text in Eliot's 'Journey of the Magi.'" *PMLA* 95 (1980): 838-56.

Hay, Eloise Knapp. *T. S. Eliot's Negative Way*. Cambridge, MA: Harvard University Press, 1982.

Heaney, Seamus. *The Government of the Tongue: The 1986 T. S. Eliot Memorial Lectures and Other Critical Writings*. London: Faber and Faber, 1989.

Heaney, Seamus. "Learning from Eliot." T. S. Eliot Centenary Lecture, Harvard University, 1988. Pp. 28-41 in *Finders Keepers, Selected Prose 1971-2001*. New York: Farrar, Straus, Giroux, 2002.

Howarth, Herbert. *Notes on Some Figures Behind T. S. Eliot*. Boston: Houghton Mifflin, 1964.

Hughes, Ted. *A Dancer to God: Tributes to T. S. Eliot*. New York: Farrar, Straus, Giroux, 1993.

Jain, Manju. *T. S. Eliot and American Philosophy: The Harvard Years*. Cambridge: Cambridge University Press, 1992.

Jay, Gregory S. *T. S. Eliot and the Poetics of Literary History*. Baton Rouge, LA: Louisiana State University Press, 1983.

Jones, D. E. *The Plays of T. S. Eliot*. Toronto: University of Toronto Press, 1960.

Julius, Anthony. *T. S. Eliot, Anti-Semitism and Literary Form*. Cambridge: Cambridge University Press, 1995.

Kearns, Cleo McNelly. *T. S. Eliot and Indic Traditions: A Study in Poetry and Belief*. New York: Cambridge University Press, 1987.

Kenner, Hugh. *The Invisible Poet: T. S. Eliot*. New York: Harcourt, Brace, 1959.

Kenner, Hugh, ed. *T. S. Eliot: A Collection of Critical Essays*. Englewood Cliffs, NJ: Prentice-Hall, 1962.

Kermode, Frank. *T. S. Eliot: An Appetite for Poetry*. Ann Arbor: University of Michigan Press, 1989.

Koestenbaum, Wayne. "*The Waste Land*: T. S. Eliot's and Ezra Pound's Collaboration on Hysteria." *Twentieth Century Literature* 34 (1988): 113-39.

Laity, Cassandra, and Nancy K. Gish, eds. *Gender, Desire, and Sexuality in T. S. Eliot*. New York: Cambridge University Press, 2004.

Lamos, Colleen. *Deviant Modernism: Sexual and Textual Errancy in T. S. Eliot, James Joyce, and Marcel Proust.* New York: Cambridge University Press, 1999.

Litz, A. Walton, ed. *Eliot in His Time: Essays on the Occasion of the Fiftieth Anniversary of "The Waste Land."* Princeton, NJ: Princeton University Press, 1973.

Lobb, Edward, ed. *Words in Time: New Essays on Eliot's* Four Quartets. London: Athlone Press, 1993.

Longenbach, James. *Modernist Poetics of History.* Princeton, NJ: Princeton University Press, 1987.

Manganiello, Dominic. *T. S. Eliot and Dante.* New York: St. Martin's Press, 1989.

Margolis, John D. *T. S. Eliot's Intellectual Development, 1922-1939.* Chicago: University of Chicago Press, 1972.

Martin, Loy D. *Browning's Dramatic Monologues and the Post-Romantic Subject.* Baltimore: Johns Hopkins University Press, 1985.

Matthiessen, F. O. *The Achievement of T. S. Eliot.* New York: Oxford University Press, 1958.

Mayer, John T. *T. S. Eliot's Silent Voices.* New York: Oxford University Press, 1989.

Menand, Louis. *Discovering Modernism: T. S. Eliot and His Context.* New York: Oxford University Press, 1987.

Michaels, Walter Benn. "Writers Reading: James and Eliot." *Modern Language Notes* 91 (1976): 827-49.

Middleton, Peter. "The Academic Development of *The Waste Land.*" In *Demarcating the Disciplines: Philosophy, Literature, Art*, ed. Samuel Weber. Minneapolis: University of Minnesota Press, 1986.

Miller, James E., Jr. *T. S. Eliot's Personal Waste Land.* Philadelphia: Pennsylvania State University Press, 1977.

Miller, James E., Jr. *T. S. Eliot: The Making of an American Poet, 1888-1922.* Philadelphia: Pennsylvania State University Press, 2005.

Moody, A. D. *The Cambridge Companion to T. S. Eliot.* Cambridge: Cambridge University Press, 1994.

Moody, A. D. *Thomas Stearns Eliot, Poet.* Cambridge: Cambridge University Press, 1979.

Moody, A. D. *Tracing T. S. Eliot's Spirit.* Cambridge: Cambridge University Press, 1996.

Musgrove, Sydney T. *T. S. Eliot and Walt Whitman.* Auckland, New Zealand: Auckland University Press, 1963.

North, Michael. *The Dialect of Modernism: Race, Language, and Twentieth-Century Literature.* Oxford: Oxford University Press, 1994.

North, Michael. *Reading 1922: A Return to the Scene of the Modern.* New York: Oxford University Press, 1999.

North, Michael, ed. *"The Waste Land": Authoritative Text, Contexts, Criticism.* New York: W. W. Norton, 2001.

Oser, Lee. *T. S. Eliot and American Poetry*. Columbia: University of Missouri Press, 1998.

Patterson, Anita. *Race, American Literature and Transnational Modernism*. Cambridge: Cambridge University Press, 2008.

Pearce, Roy Harvey. *The Continuity of American Poetry*. Princeton, NJ: Princeton University Press, 1961.

Perl, Jeffrey M. *Skepticism and Modern Enmity: Before and After Eliot*. Baltimore: Johns Hopkins University Press, 1989.

Pinkney, Tony. *Women in the Poetry of T. S. Eliot: A Psychoanalytic Approach*. London: Macmillan, 1984.

Pollard, Charles W. *New World Modernisms: T. S. Eliot, Derek Walcott, and Kamau Brathwaite*. Charlottesville: University of Virginia Press, 2004.

Raine, Craig. *T. S. Eliot*. New York: Oxford University Press, 2006.

Rainey, Lawrence, ed. *The Annotated Waste Land with Eliot's Contemporary Prose, Second Edition*. New Haven, CT: Yale University Press, 2006.

Rainey, Lawrence, ed. *Modernism: An Anthology*. Oxford: Blackwell, 2005.

Rainey, Lawrence. *Revisiting "The Waste Land."* New Haven, CT: Yale University Press, 2005.

Rajan, Balachandra. *The Overwhelming Question*. Toronto: Toronto University Press, 1976.

Ricks, Christopher. *Decisions and Revisions in T. S. Eliot*. Panizzi Lectures. London: British Library, 2004.

Ricks, Christopher. *T. S. Eliot and Prejudice*. Berkeley and Los Angeles: University of California Press, 1988.

Riquelme, John Paul. *Harmony of Dissonances: T. S. Eliot, Romanticism, and Imagination*. Baltimore: Johns Hopkins University Press, 1991.

Ross, Andrew. "*The Waste Land* and the Fantasy of Interpretation." *Representations* 8 (1984): 134-58.

Rowson, Martin. *The Waste Land*. New York: Harper and Row, 1990.

Schuchard, Ronald. *Eliot's Dark Angel: Intersections of Life and Art*. New York: Oxford University Press, 1999.

Schwartz, Sanford. *The Matrix of Modernism: Pound, Eliot, and Early Twentieth-Century Thought*. Princeton, NJ: Princeton University Press, 1985.

Sigg, Eric. *The American T. S. Eliot: A Study of the Early Writings*. New York: Cambridge University Press, 1989.

Smith, Carol H. *T. S. Eliot's Dramatic Theory and Practice*. Princeton, NJ: Princeton University Press, 1963.

Smith, Grover. *T. S. Eliot's Poetry and Plays: A Study in Sources and Meaning*. 2d ed. Chicago: University of Chicago Press, 1974.

Southam, B. C. *A Student's Guide to the Selected Poems of T. S. Eliot*. 6th ed. London and Boston: Faber and Faber, 1994.

Spender, Stephen. *T. S. Eliot*. Ed. Frank Kermode. New York: Viking, 1976.

Sultan, Stanley. "Eliot and the Concept of Literary Influence." *Southern Review* 21 (1985): 1071-93.

Tate, Allen, ed. *T. S. Eliot: The Man and His Work, a Critical Evaluation by Twenty-Six Distinguished Writers*. New York: Delacorte Press, 1966.

Traversi, Derek. *T. S. Eliot: The Longer Poems*. London: Bodley Head, 1976.

Vendler, Helen. *Coming of Age as a Poet*. Cambridge, MA: Harvard University Press, 2003.

CRITICAL INSIGHTS

About the Editor

John Paul Riquelme is Professor of English at Boston University and Co-director of the Modernism Seminar at the Harvard Humanities Center. His essays on the literature of the long twentieth century, film, humanistic theory, and the gothic tradition, including science fiction, have appeared in *Modernism/Modernity, The James Joyce Quarterly, New Literary History*, and *Modern Fiction Studies*, among other journals. His writings about T. S. Eliot include a full-length study of Eliot's non-dramatic poetry and his prose, *Harmony of Dissonances: T. S. Eliot, Romanticism, and Imagination* (Johns Hopkins University Press, 1991). He has published extensively on James Joyce, Thomas Hardy, and Bram Stoker, including several books: *Teller and Tale in Joyce's Fiction: Oscillating Perspectives* (Johns Hopkins, 1983), the Norton Critical Edition of Joyce's *A Portrait of the Artist as A Young Man* (2007), *Joyce's Dislocutions: Essays on Reading as Translation* (Johns Hopkins, 1984), and editions of *Tess of the d'Urbervilles* (Bedford, 1998) and *Dracula* (Bedford, 2002). His most recent book is *Gothic and Modernism: Essaying Dark Literary Modernity* (Johns Hopkins, 2008), an edited collection that deals with the modern Gothic from Mary Shelley and Bram Stoker through Samuel Beckett, Bret Easton Ellis, and Octavia Butler. He is at work on a book about Oscar Wilde's aesthetic politics and the origins of modernism in 1890s Britain.

About *The Paris Review*

The Paris Review is America's preeminent literary quarterly, dedicated to discovering and publishing the best new voices in fiction, nonfiction, and poetry. The magazine was founded in Paris in 1953 by the young American writers Peter Matthiessen and Doc Humes, and edited there and in New York for its first fifty years by George Plimpton. Over the decades, the *Review* has introduced readers to the earliest writings of Jack Kerouac, Philip Roth, T. C. Boyle, V. S. Naipaul, Ha Jin, Jay McInerney, and Mona Simpson, and published numerous now classic works, including Roth's *Goodbye, Columbus*, Donald Barthelme's *Alice*, Jim Carroll's *Basketball Diaries*, and selections from Samuel Beckett's *Molloy* (his first publication in English). The first chapter of Jeffrey Eugenides's *The Virgin Suicides* appeared in the *Review*'s pages, as well as stories by Edward P. Jones, Rick Moody, David Foster Wallace, Denis Johnson, Jim Shepard, Jim Crace, Lorrie Moore, Jeanette Winterson, and Ann Patchett.

The Paris Review's renowned Writers at Work series of interviews, whose early installments include legendary conversations with E. M. Forster, William Faulkner, and Ernest Hemingway, is one of the landmarks of world literature. The interviews received a George Polk award and were nominated for a Pulitzer Prize. Among the more than three hundred interviewees are Robert Frost, Marianne Moore, W. H. Auden, Elizabeth Bishop, Susan Sontag, and Toni Morrison. Recent issues feature conversations with Salman Rushdie, Joan Didion, Stephen King, Norman Mailer, Kazuo Ishiguro and Umberto Eco. (A complete list of the interviews is available at www.theparisreview.org) In November 2008, Picador will publish the third of a four-volume series of anthologies of *Paris Review* interviews. The first two volumes have received acclaim. *The New York Times* called the Writers at Work series "the most remarkable and extensive interviewing project we possess."

The Paris Review is edited by Philip Gourevitch, who was named to the post in 2005, following the death of George Plimpton two years earlier. Under Gourevitch's leadership, the magazine's international distribution has expanded, paid subscriptions have risen 150 percent, and newsstand distribution has doubled. A new editorial team has published fiction by Andre Aciman, Damon Galgut, Mohsin Hamid, Gish Jen, Richard Price, Said Sayrafiezadeh and Alistair Morgan. Poetry editors Charles Simic, Meghan O'Rourke and Dan Chiasson have selected works by Billy Collins, Jesse Ball, Mary Jo Bang, Sharon Olds, and Mary Karr. Writing published in the magazine has been anthologized in *Best American Short Stories* 2006, 2007 and 2008, *Best American Poetry*, *Best Creative Non-Fiction*, the Pushcart Prize anthology, and *O. Henry Prize Stories*.

The magazine presents two annual awards. The Hadada Award for lifelong contribution to literature has recently been given to William Styron, Joan Didion, Norman Mailer and Peter Matthiessen in 2008. The Plimpton Prize for Fiction given to a new voice in fiction brought to national attention in the pages of *The Paris Review* was presented in 2007 to Benjamin Percy and to Jesse Ball in 2008.

The Paris Review won the 2007 National Magazine Award in photojournalism and the *Los Angeles Times* recently called *The Paris Review* "an American treasure with true international reach."

Since 1999 *The Paris Review* has been published by The Paris Review Foundation, Inc., a not-for-profit 501(c)(3) organization.

The Paris Review is available in digital form to libraries worldwide in selected academic databases exclusively from EBSCO Publishing. Libraries can contact EBSCO at 1-800-653-2726 for details.

For more information on *The Paris Review* or to subscribe, please visit: www.theparisreview.org.

Contributors

John Paul Riquelme is Professor of English at Boston University and Co-director of the Modernism Seminar at Harvard University. He is the author and editor of several critical works including *Harmony of Dissonances: T. S. Eliot, Romanticism, and Imagination*, a study of Eliot's non-dramatic poetry and prose.

R. Baird Shuman, Professor Emeritus of English at the University of Illinois at Urbana-Champaign, has taught at the University of Pennsylvania, Drexel University, San Jose State University, and Duke University. He has published critical studies of Clifford Odets, William Inge, and Robert E. Sherwood. The editor of the thirteen-volume encyclopedia *Great American Writers, 20th Century* (Marshall Cavendish, 2002), he lives in Las Vegas, Nevada.

Gemma Sieff is an editor at *Harper's Magazine*. She lives in New York City.

Neil Heims is a freelance writer and a teacher living in Paris. He received a doctorate from the City University of New York in 1978. He has published over two dozen books and numerous anthology entries on literature. Among the authors about whose work he has written are Milton, Wordsworth, Hawthorne, Charlotte Brontë, Rimbaud, Rilke, Virginia Woolf, Arthur Miller, and Alan Paton. He has written extensively on Shakespeare and edited a number of volumes in a series devoted to Shakespeare criticism through the ages. He has also written biographies of Cervantes, William Blake, Tolstoy, Dostoevsky, Melville, Kafka, Camus, Tolkien, and Allen Ginsberg.

Matthew J. Bolton is a professor of English at Loyola School in New York City, where he also serves as the Dean of Students. Bolton received his Doctor of Philosophy in English from The Graduate Center of the City University of New York (CUNY) in 2005. His dissertation at the university was entitled: "Transcending the Self in Robert Browning and T. S. Eliot." Prior to attaining his Ph.D. at CUNY, Bolton also earned a Master of Philosophy in English (2004) and a Master of Science in English Education (2001). His undergraduate work was done at the State University of New York at Binghamton where he studied English Literature.

Allan Johnson is a Ph.D. student at the University of Leeds, UK, where his current research focuses on theories of literary influence in twentieth-century fiction, with special reference made to the works of Alan Hollinghurst. Originally from the United States, Johnson has served as Theatre Correspondent for *The Record-Courier* in Akron, Ohio. Recent publications include a consideration of architectural space in E. M. Forster's early novels and entries for a dictionary of literary characters.

Louis Menand is a professor of English at Harvard University and a regular contributor to *The New Yorker* and *The New York Review of Books* where he has written on topics ranging from voter behavior to higher education to Bob Dylan. He began his career as an Eliot scholar, publishing his first work, *Discovering Modernism: T. S. Eliot and His Context*, in 1987. His most popular work is *The Metaphysical Club* (2001), which won the Pulitzer Prize for history in 2002. An intellectual portrait of pragmatism's founders, it traces the advent of the uniquely American philosophy and its influence on American society, politics, law, science, education. He is recognized as a leading scholar of American studies, and in 2002 published a collection of essays titled *American Studies*. His other works include *The Cambridge History of Literary Criticism, Volume 7: Modernism and the New Criticism*, co-ed. (2000); *The Future of Academic Freedom*, ed. (1997); and *Pragmatism: A Reader*, ed. (1996).

John T. Mayer is Professor Emeritus at the College of the Holy Cross and has written extensively on T. S. Eliot. His books include *T. S. Eliot's Silent Voices*, a critical study of Eliot's early and unpublished poems (1989).

Ronald Bush has taught at Harvard, Cal Tech, and Oxford, where he is currently the Drue Heinz Professor of American Literature. His scholarly work has encompassed American and Anglo-American literature, modernist primitivism, Jewish-American literature, culture, and identity. His essays have appeared in *ANQ*, *Textual Practice*, *English Language Notes*, and the *Wallace Stevens Journal*. His books include *T. S. Eliot: The Modernist in History*, ed. (1991); *T. S. Eliot: A Study in Character and Style* (1983); and *The Genesis of Ezra Pound's Cantos* (1976). He is presently at work on a biography of James Joyce.

Nancy K. Gish is a Professor of English and women's studies at the University of Southern Maine. She has received a fellowship from the National Endowment for the Humanities, and seen her work published in *Contemporary Literature* and *English Studies*. Her works include *Gender, Desire, and Sexuality in T. S. Eliot* (2004), ed.; *Hugh MacDiarmid, Man and Poet* (1992), ed.; and *Time in the Poetry of T. S. Eliot* (1981).

Lee Oser is an Associate Professor at College of the Holy Cross and author of several books on modernist literature. His essays have appeared in *World Literature Today*, *Southwest Review*, *Southern Review*, and *Modern Philology*. His most recent work, *The Return of Christian Humanism: Chesterton, Eliot, Tolkien, and the Romance of History* (2007), is a study of Christian humanism's influence on twentieth-century writers. He is also the author of *The Ethics of Modernism* (2007), a study of the ethics and aesthetics that informed modernist literature; *T. S. Eliot and American Poetry* (1998), an analysis of American poetry's impact on Eliot, as well as how his work shaped later generations of American poets; and *Out of What Chaos* (2007), a novel about the religious conversion of a Portland, Oregon, musician.

Michael Goldman is Emeritus Professor at Princeton University. He is recognized as one of one of the most respected American drama critics, and has twice won the George Jean Nathan Award for Dramatic Criticism. He has received fellowships from the National Endowment for the Humanities, the Guggenheim Foundation, and the American Council for Learned Societies. He has published widely on Shakespeare, Ibsen, Eliot, and dramatic criticism in journals like *Modern Philology* and *Modern Drama*, and his poetry has appeared in *The New Yorker, Atlantic Monthly*, and *Kenyon*

Review. He has written a number of critical books including *On Drama: Boundaries of Genre, Borders of Self* (2000) and *Ibsen: The Dramaturgy of Fear* (1998). He has also published two books of poetry, *First Poems* (1965) and *At the Edge* (1969), and written two plays, "Walking Toward the River in the Sun" and "Elegaterooneyrismusissimus."

Acknowledgments

"T. S. Eliot" by R. Baird Shuman. From *Dictionary of World Biography: The 20th Century* (Pasadena, CA: Salem Press, 1999): 1058-1061. Copyright © 1999 by Salem Press, Inc.

"The *Paris Review* Perspective" by Gemma Sieff. Copyright © 2008 by Gemma Sieff. Special appreciation goes to Christopher Cox and Nathaniel Rich, editors for *The Paris Review*.

"'Poetry as Poetry,'" by Louis Menand. From *Discovering Modernism: T. S. Eliot and His Context* (1987) by Louis Menand. Copyright © 1987 by Oxford University Press. Reprinted by permission of Oxford University Press, Inc.

"Playing at Relationship" by John T. Mayer. From *T. S. Eliot's Silent Voices* (1989) by John T. Mayer. Copyright © 1989 by Oxford University Press. Reprinted by permission of Oxford University Press, Inc.

"'Prufrock,' 'Gerontion,' and Fragmented Monologues" by John Paul Riquelme. From *Harmony of Dissonances: T. S. Eliot, Romanticism, and Imagination* by John Paul Riquelme. Copyright © 1990, The Johns Hopkins University Press. Reprinted with permission of The Johns Hopkins University Press.

"'Unknown terror and mystery': *The Waste Land*," by Ronald Bush. From *T. S. Eliot, A Study in Character and Style* (1984) by Ronald Bush. Copyright © 1984 by Oxford University Press. Reprinted by permission of Oxford University Press, Inc.

"'The World Within the World': *Ash-Wednesday* and the 'Ariel Poems,'" by Nancy K. Gish. From *Time in the Poetry of T. S. Eliot: A Study in Structure and Theme* by Nancy K. Gish. Copyright © 1981 by Nancy K. Gish. Reproduced with permission of Palgrave Macmillan.

"The Soul's Mysterious Errand," by Lee Oser. Reprinted from *T. S. Eliot and American Poetry* by Lee Oser, by permission of the University of Missouri Press. Copyright © 1998 by the Curators of the University of Missouri.

"Fear in the Way: The Design of Eliot's Drama," by Michael Goldman. From *Eliot in His Time: Essays on the Occasion of the Fiftieth Anniversary of "The Waste Land,"* ed. A. Walton Litz. Copyright © 1973 by Princeton University Press, 2001 renewed Princeton University Press. Reprinted by permission of Princeton University Press.

Index

Ackroyd, Peter, 44
Adams, Henry, 33
Adams, John, 24
Adonais (Shelley), 33
"Adoration of the Magi" (Yeats), 231
Aeschylus, 295
Aesthetics, 267, 285-287; aesthetic emotion, 104; ambitions, 23; effects, 98; essays on, 96; standard, 95; theory, 29, 31, 115
African-American writers, 49
After Strange Gods (Eliot), 41
Aiken, Conrad, 34, 36, 188-189, 219
Alain-Fournier, 34
Aldington, Richard, 97
Alldritt, Keith, 47
Allston, Washington, 96
"Andrew Marvell" (Eliot), 58
Andrewes, Lancelot; sermons, 224, 244
"Animula" (Eliot), 237-238, 255, 261; Catholic philosophy of disillusion in, 226; symbolism in, 255; theme of time in, 237, 239; union of death and birth in, 239
Annotated Waste Land with Eliot's Contemporary Prose, The (Rainey), 44
Anti-Romanticism, 95, 168
"Antitradition Futuriste, L'" (Apollinaire), 107
Antony and Cleopatra (Shakespeare), 83
Apollinaire, Guillaume, 107
Approaches to Teaching Eliot's Poetry and Plays (Brooker), 45
"Ariel" poems, 267; Christmas, 224; theme of time in, 239, 246, 264
Aristotle, 109
Armstrong, Isobel, 57
Arnold, Matthew, 57, 66, 69, 119-120, 218
Arrowsmith, William, 48

Art, view of, 100
Art (Bell), 104
Ash-Wednesday (Eliot), 15, 35, 160, 216, 219, 224-225, 228, 237, 239-241, 244, 248, 252, 256, 259-261, 271; American traditions in, 267; blindness in, 259; centrality of, 224; conflict in, 261; conversion in, 39; dark night of the soul in, 243; elliptical structure of, 224; eternal life in, 243; hope and mourning in, 168, 171; images in, 170; language, 180-181; loss in, 244; surrender in, 17; theme of time in, 237, 246, 264; transcendence in, 261; transcendent vision in, 260; writing of, 240
"Assignation, The" (Poe), 285
At the Hawk's Well (Yeats), 117
Athenaeum, The (magazine), 268
Auditory imagination, 185, 217-218
"Aunt Helen" (Eliot), 37

Babbitt, Irving, influence of, 23, 29, 33
Bacon, Francis, 30, 113
Bagehot, Walter, 60
Barthes, Roland, 6
Baudelaire, Charles, 111, 114, 153, 201
Beckett, Samuel, 5, 295
Bedient, Calvin, 46
Behr, Caroline, 44
Bell, Clive, 104-105; metaphysical hypothesis, 104
Benda, Julien, 210
Bentley, Joseph, 79
Bergson, Henri, 34, 131, 149, 155; divided-self writings, 123, 149-151
Berryman, John, 42
Bible, 224, 232; Old Testament, 230, 234-235, 237

"Bishop Blougram's Apology" (Browning), 114
Blake, William, 112, 212
Blast (magazine), 37
Bloom, Harold, 57
Boke of the Governour, The (Elyot), 277
Book of Common Prayer, 77
"Boston Evening Transcript, The" (Eliot), 37
Botticelli, 96
Bradley, F. H., 4
Bridge, The (Crane), 274, 276
Brodsky, Joseph, 50
Brooke, Rupert, 95, 117
Brooker, Jewel Spears, 44-45, 79
Brooks, Van Wyck, 33
Brothers Karamazov, The (Dostoyevsky), 212
Browning, Robert, 33, 55, 57-63, 66-67, 69, 111, 114, 123; dramatic monologue, 55, 62, 64, 66, 69
"Burbank with a Baedeker" (Eliot), 42, 193
"Burial of the Dead, The" (Eliot, *The Waste Land*), 77-78, 81, 86, 88, 209; memory and desire in, 200; narrative voice, 78, 85, 88; nightmare in, 201; questioning in, 212; Stetson in, 82, 85
"Buried Life, The" (Arnold), 69
"Burnt Norton" (Eliot), 250, 255, 267, 270, 272, 274, 289; imagery in, 273, 278
Burtt, Benn, 185
Bush, Ronald, 46

Calvinism, 28
Cambridge Companion to T. S. Eliot, The (Moody), 45
Cambridge Introduction to T. S. Eliot, The (Cooper), 44
Cantos, The (Pound), 109
Capitalism, 113

Carey, John, 81
Caribbean writers, 49
Cathay (Pound), 96
Catholic Anthology (Pound), 37
Cats (musical), 51
Cavalcanti, Guido, 244
Cavalier poets, 58
Chapman, George, 57, 114
"Childe Roland to the Dark Tower Came" (Browning), 64, 214
Chinitz, David, 46-49
Christ, Carol T., 58, 63
Christianity, 232, 235, 242, 244, 261; dispensation, 224; influence on Eliot, 17, 25, 27, 46, 270, 280, 282, 289, 294-295
"Circe's Palace" (Eliot), 130
"City in the Sea, The" (Poe), 275
Cocktail Party, The (Eliot), 195, 202, 294, 315; guardians in, 298-300; isolation in, 303; knowing and not knowing theme, 307; Lavinia in, 304; success of, 303; unexpected visitor in, 307
Coleridge, Samuel Taylor, 96, 109
"Composed upon Westminster Bridge" (Wordsworth), 168
Composition of Four Quartets, The (Gardner), 284
Concordance to the Complete Poems and Plays of T. S. Eliot, A (Dawson), 44
Confidential Clerk, The (Eliot), 301; characters in, 299, 309; Eggerson in, 300, 308; Elizabeth in, 307; ghosts of absence in, 299-300; Mrs. Guzzard in, 301, 307-308
"Conversation Galante" (Eliot), 135
"Cooking Egg, A" (Eliot), 131
Cooper, John Xiros, 44
Corbière, Tristan, 111

Cowan, Laura, 45
Coward, Noel, 296
Crane, Hart, 267, 274-276, 288
"Crapy Cornelia" (Eliot), 123, 134-135
Crime and Punishment (Dostoyevsky), 191, 212
Criterion, The (journal), 4, 24, 29, 38, 40
Culture and Society (Williams), 42

Dada, 5, 46, 184
Dalí, Salvador, 5
Dante, 4, 16, 177, 247-248, 252-254, 256, 275, 281, 287-288; Eliot on, 48, 239; high and low dream in, 248; images in, 254; influence of, 23, 31, 35, 48, 177, 189, 224, 238, 261
Dawson, J. L., 44
"Death by Water" (Eliot, *The Waste Land*), 209; burial at sea, 87; drowned sailor in, 81
Decline of the West, The (Spengler), 40
"Degeneration" (Nordau), 106
Depersonalization, 32, 35
Derrida, Jacques, 270
Descartes, René, 113
Deviant modernism, 42
Dial, The (journal), 3, 38, 40, 48
Dialect of Modernism: Race, Language, and Twentieth-Century Literature, The (North), 49
Dickens, Charles, 74-75
Dissociation of sensibility, 4, 55, 57-58, 93-94, 106, 110, 113
Dobrée, Bonamy, 76
Doctrine of impersonality, 104
Donne, John, 3, 23, 31-32, 94-95, 111-112, 200
Donoghue, Denis, 46-47
Dostoyevsky, Fyodor, 186, 191, 210
Double entendres, 35
Dramatic monologue, vii, 5, 33, 55, 60, 66, 69, 123, 166, 174, 176-177; deconstruction of, 55, 66, 167, 173, 178
"Dry Salvages" (Eliot), 267, 282; crossing from old world to new in, 281; landscape of, 271, 281, 290
Duchamp, Marcel, 5
Dunbar, H. Flanders, 247

"East Coker" (Eliot), 240, 267, 279-280; biblical style, 277; theme of houses and beginnings, 277
Edwards, Jonathan, 279
Egoist, The (magazine), 27, 38, 97, 102
Ehrenpreis, Irvin, 15
Elder Statesman, The (Eliot); ghosts in, 294, 298; Gomez in, 300-301, 309; Lord Claverton in, 300, 308-309; Michael in, 301; Monica in, 300
"Elegiac Stanzas" (Wordsworth), 169-172
Eliot, Abigail Adams Cranch (grandmother), 24
Eliot, Andrew, 24, 277, 281
Eliot, Charles William, 24
Eliot, Charlotte (mother), 25, 27, 269
Eliot, Henry (brother), 188
Eliot, Henry Ware (father), 26
Eliot, T. S.; childhood, 216; collected works, 44; critics, 41, 43-45, 47-48; death, 6-7, 45, 49-50, 184; drama, 47, 294; early critical essays, 57-58, 94, 110, 115; epigraphs, 41, 48, 146, 151, 182, 184, 263-264; fame, 4; financial straits, 38; gender studies, 42; influence of, 3-4, 38, 40, 43, 50, 55; influences on, 23, 25, 27, 29, 31, 33, 35-36, 49; jazz, 49; man of letters, 29; marriage, 37, 109, 125, 130, 186-187; mental illness, 205; poetry, 46-47, 93; popular culture, 49; religious faith,

39, 41, 46; self-discipline, 23; sources, 224, 261
Eliot, Thomas Ware (uncle), 27
Eliot, Valerie (second wife), 44, 50, 184, 188-189, 205
Eliot, Vivien Haigh-Wood (first wife), 37, 186-188, 191-192; diary, 187; marriage, 186-187
Eliot, William Greenleaf (grandfather), 23-24; sermons and lectures, 26
Ellmann, Richard, 45
Elyot, Thomas, 277
Emerson, Ralph Waldo, 271-272, 279, 281-282, 287-288; influence of, 267-271, 277, 283, 289
England, Eliot in, 36
English Civil War, 113
"Entretien" (Eliot), 129-130, 146, 148, 155, 157
"Epipsychidion" (Shelley), 182
Essai sur les données immédiates de la conscience. See *Time and Free Will*
Europe, Eliot in, 34
"Experience and the Objects of Knowledge in the Philosophy of F.H. Bradley" (Eliot), 97
Ezra Pound: His Metric and Poetry (Eliot), 96

Faber and Faber (publisher), 4, 24, 38, 40, 50, 224
Family Reunion, The (Eliot), 192, 195, 301, 309; Furies in, 298-299; Harry in, 299, 307; isolation in, 299; unexpected visitor in, 307
"Fate" (Emerson), 279
"Figlia Che Piange, La" (Eliot), 191, 204
"Fire Sermon, The" (Eliot, *The Waste Land*), 74, 81, 84, 86-88, 189, 195, 197, 209; homosexual burlesque in, 80; London's crowds in, 190-191;

loss and isolation in, 197; nightmare in, 193, 209; water, 85
"First Debate between the Body and Soul" (Eliot), 156; rise and fall tension in, 152
Flaubert, Gustav, 109, 218
Fletcher, John Gould, 97, 171, 182
Ford, Ford Madox, 96, 214
Four Quartets (Eliot), 15, 41, 46, 51, 75, 219, 224, 240-241, 261, 271, 278, 280; ghosts in, 294; Greek epigraphs in, 41, 48; imagery in, 234; Incarnation in, 245; landscape, 273; spirituality of, 267-268, 271-272; structure of, 167, 280; symbolism in, 272-273; symmetrical utterances in, 16; time in, 261, 264; transcendent vision in, 260; voice of, 41, 160, 277; writing of, 240
Frazer, James, 23, 35
Freud, Sigmund, 3, 204, 294
"From Poe to Valéry" (Eliot), 219
Frye, Northrop, 44
Futurism, 107-108

"Game of Chess, A" (Eliot, *The Waste Land), 284-285*; faceless woman in, 84; Lil in, 84; narrative voice in, 82-83; nightmare in, 209; one-sided conversation in, 139; orderly and disorderly in, 82; rats' alley in, 85; repeated images and phrases in, 82, 86
Gardner, Helen, 284
Garnett, Edward, 107
"Gerontion" (Eliot), 15, 129, 160, 167, 173, 176, 186, 193, 204, 236, 260; allegory, 175; anti-Semitic references in, 42; blindness in, 230; dramatic monologue in, 166; images of death in, 235; language in, 166, 174, 175; theme of time in, 246, 257

Gide, André, 34
Gish, Nancy K., 46, 49
Goethe, Johann Wolfgang von, 96
Golden Bough, The (Frazer), 23, 35
Golden Bowl, The (James), 185
"Goldfish 2" (Eliot), 125, 135, 150, 154
"Goldfish 3" (Eliot), 148
Goldman, Michael, 47
Gordon, Lyndall, 44, 187
Gourmont, Rémy de, 121-122, 189, 210
Government of the Tongue, The (Heaney), 50
Grant, Michael, 44
Greville, Fulke, 112

Habib, M. A. R., 47
Half-Century of Eliot Criticism, A (Martin), 272
Hall, Donald, 240
Hallam, Arthur, 94, 98
Hamlet (Shakespeare), 99, 105
"Hamlet and His Problems" (Eliot), 93, 96, 99-101
Harding, D. W., 209
Hartmann, Edward von, 112
Harvard University, 4, 23-24, 28-31, 33-36, 277
Haughton, Hugh, 50
Hayward, John, 273
Heaney, Seamus, 50
Hellström, Gustaf, 3
Heraclitus, 47-48
Hogarth Press, 110
"Hollow Men, The" (Eliot), 17; brutalized consciousness, 15; prayer in, 180
Hollow Men, The (Eliot), 187, 240
Homage to John Dryden (Eliot), 110-111
Homosexuality, 35
Hough, Graham, 241
Hughes, Ted, 50
Hulme, T. E., 210

Humanists, 23, 30
"Humouresque" (Eliot), 135; voice echoing in, 139
Huxley, Aldous, 112
"Hysteria" (Eliot), 37

Idea of a Christian Society, The (Eliot), 46
Idiot, The (Dostoyevsky), 191
Imagination; auditory, 185, 217-218; minimalist theory of, 98
Imagism, 36, 97-98, 218
Imagist, 93, 96-99, 101
Impersonality, 94, 101, 106, 120
"In a Station of the Metro" (Pound), 97
In Memoriam (Tennyson), 33
Intellectuals and the Masses, The (Carey), 81
Interior monologue, 56, 67
Invisible Poet: T. S. Eliot, The (Kenner), 46
Ironists, 23, 33

Jacobean dramatists, 110
Jain, Manju, 47
James, Henry, 33, 109, 123, 133-136, 143, 151; style of, 217
James, William, 270, 283-284
John of the Cross, Saint, 232-233, 235-236, 241, 243, 245-246, 249; mystical writings, 224, 280
Jones, D. E., 47
Jonson, Ben, 191
"Journey of the Magi, The" (Eliot), 224-226, 256, 261; Catholic philosophy of disillusion in, 226; union of death and birth in, 237, 239
Joyce, James, 6, 48, 56, 142, 204, 210, 217-218
Julius, Anthony, 48

Index

Kearns, Cleo, 48
Keats, John, 58, 95, 111, 117, 182, 255
Kenner, Hugh, 45-46, 174, 192, 211
Kermode, Frank, 47, 118
Knight, G. Wilson, 262

"La Belle Dame Sans Merci" (Keats), 182
Laforgue, Jules, 33, 35, 111-112, 122, 125, 133, 135-137, 139, 149, 151, 154; irony, 23, 31
Laity, Cassandra, 49
Lamos, Colleen, 49
Langbaum, Robert, 47
Lawrence, D. H., 107-108, 217; sexual relations, 109
Lectures on Art (Ruskin), 96
Lectures to Young Women (Eliot, W. G.), 26
"Leisure Time" (Eliot, W. G.), 26
Levenson, Michael, 47
Levy, William Turner, 27
Lewis, Windham, 37
Life of Archer Alexander: From Slavery to Freedom (Eliot, W. G.), 26
Literary History of America, A (Wendell), 30
"Little Gidding" (Eliot), 178, 267, 284-285; Christian pilgrimage in, 283, 286; ghosts in, 294; imagery of, 284, 287, 289; voices in, 168, 178
Little Review, The (magazine), 97
Litz, A. Walton, 45, 47, 211, 221
Lloyd Webber, Andrew, 50
London, Eliot in, 36
"London Letter" (Eliot), 186, 221
Love, 35
"Love Song of J. Alfred Prufrock, The" (Eliot), 15, 55, 61-62, 66-67, 70-71, 100, 129, 133-134, 147, 150, 153, 155-159, 161, 216, 260; dramatic monologue in, 166, 177; irony in, 151; language, 166-167, 173-175, 178; mermaids in, 159-160, 162; Narcissus psyche in, 123, 125, 127-129, 133, 139, 143, 145-146, 158; opening of, 5; psychic drama, 123-124, 126-128, 151, 160; quest for life through relationship in, 125; related to other works, 126, 130, 138-139; role-playing's limits in, 124, 126-127, 147-149; sea imagery in, 159-160; self-possession in, 135-137, 147, 151, 153-155, 162; voice, 176; writing of, 35, 139, 161
"Love Song of St. Sebastian, the" (Eliot), 192
Lowell, Amy, 97
Lowell, Robert, 42
"Lycidas" (Milton), 170-171

Machiavelli, Niccolò, 269
Magritte, René, 5
Mallarmé, Stéphane, 288
"Mandarins 3" (Eliot), 125
"Mandarins 4" (Eliot), 126, 148, 150
Manganiello, Dominic, 48
Margolis, John D., 48
"Marina" (Eliot), 216, 224-225, 230, 261-262, 267; landscape of, 273, 290; mystic recognition in, 224, 262, 274; theme of time in, 264
Marsden, Dora, 97, 105
Martin, Loy, 47
Martin, Mildred, 272
Marvell, Andrew, 85
Massinger, Philip, 109-110
Matter and Memory (Bergson), 149
"Matthew Arnold" (Eliot), 167
Maurras, Charles, 34-35, 42, 210
Mayer, John T., 46
"Mélange Adultère de Tout" (Eliot), 125

Menand, Louis, 16, 47, 63
Metaphysical poets, 3-4, 23, 31-32, 50, 57, 95, 121
"Metaphysical Poets, The" (Eliot), 32, 57-58, 75, 110-112
Middleton, Peter, 46
Miller, James, 49
Milton, John, 4, 55, 111, 170-171, 217; essay on, 217-218; influence of, 94
Modernism, 5, 7, 17, 45, 47, 49-50, 55, 59, 75-77, 93-94, 101, 110; "deviant," 42; early, 56, 95; forerunners of, 106; writers, 6
Moffatt, Adelaine, 68
Monroe, Harriet, 36-37
Moody, A. D., 45-46
"Mr. Apollinax" (Eliot), 37
Murder in the Cathedral (Eliot), 310; fear and freedom in, 298-299, 311; ghosts in, 294, 309, 315; shadows in, 298, 312; success of, 294; Thomas in, 298, 307-308, 310-313
Murry, John Middleton, 111
"Music of Poetry, The" (Eliot), 218
Myth, 35
Mythical method, 48, 185, 210-211

Neilson, William Allan, 32
"New Hampshire" (Eliot), 289; images of, 273
Nineteenth century; critical essays, 6, 57-58; poetic forms, 167, 174, 178; poetry, 41, 47, 55, 58; texts, 3
Nobel Prize for Literature, 3, 18, 23, 39, 41, 50, 220
"Nocturne" (Eliot), 135; stage-managing in, 135
Nordau, Max, 106
North, Michael, 46-47, 49
Notes Towards the Definition of Culture (Eliot), 116

Objective correlative, 23, 32, 93, 96, 98-101, 103-104, 115
"Ode to a Nightingale" (Keats), 198
Old Possum's Book of Practical Cats (Eliot), 16, 51
Oser, Lee, 46-47
Othello (Shakespeare), 123, 138
Our Mutual Friend (Dickens), 74-75
Outlook, The (newspaper), 96

Paradise Lost (Milton), 111, 217
Paris, Eliot in, 34
"Parsifal" (Verlaine), 179, 193
Pater, Walter, 96, 103, 107-109, 120-121; essay on "Style", 106
Patterson, Anita, 47, 49
Pearce, Roy Harvey, 47
"Perfect Critic, The" (Eliot), 109, 119, 121
Pericles (Shakespeare), 262
Perl, Jeffrey, 47
Perse, Saint-John, 49
Peter, John, 42, 49
Philosophy, 35
Plath, Sylvia, 42
Poe, Edgar Allan, 5, 185, 219, 267, 275-276, 285
Poetic procedure, 96; depersonalization, 32, 35; experience, 32-33; language, 5-6, 55; masks, 55, 61
Poirier, Richard, 191, 270-271, 279
Pollard, Charles, 49
"Portrait of a Lady" (Eliot), 35, 37, 56, 67, 69-71, 147; engagement in, 123; game-playing, 125, 135; language of, 137, 139, 148; music of death in, 125, 155; Narcissus psyche in, 139; obsession in, 129; psychic drama, 123-124, 127-128, 133; quest for life through relationship in, 133; related to other works, 126-127, 133, 135,

147; self-observation, 147; social satire, 124; writing of, 35, 139, 148
Postmodernism, 45, 47, 116
Poststructural readings, viii, 45-46, 270, 291
Poststructuralism, 225
Pound, Ezra, 16, 36, 56, 68, 96-97, 107, 133, 188, 190, 208-209, 211, 217-218, 221; aesthetic and political enthusiasms, 109; influence of, 38; study in futility, 130; theory of poetry, 108; "vortex," 36
"Preludes (I–IV)" (Eliot), 37, 168, 171-172; anti-Romanticism, 168, 173; images, 168, 171
Pre-Raphaelites, 29, 31
"Prothalamion" (Spenser), 197
Prufrock and Other Observations (Eliot), 139
Purgatorio (Dante), 35, 238, 254
Puritanism, 27

Quinn, John, 118, 188, 191, 205, 214

Rahv, Philip, 16
Rainbow, The (Lawrence), 107
Raine, Craig, 48
Rainey, Lawrence, 44, 46
"Raven, The" (Poe), 275
Realism, 55, 64
Renaissance, The (Pater), 96, 108, 120
Revenge of Bussy d'Ambois, The (Chapman), 113
Revenge tradition, 294, 296
Revisionism, 95, 109
Revisiting "The Waste Land" (Rainey), 46
Revival of Metaphysical Poetry, The (Duncan), 111
"Rhapsody on a Windy Night" (Eliot), 37, 51, 168, 173, 177

"Rhetoric and Poetic Drama" (Eliot), 136
Ricks, Christopher, 48, 50
Rivière, Jacques, 34
Romantic Image (Kermode), 47, 111
Romanticism, 4, 55, 61, 93-94, 120; British, 4, 94, 121; imagination, 55; optimism, 30; poets, 23, 31-32, 58, 168-170, 173-174, 182
Rousseau, Jean Jacques, 29, 181, 297
"Rudyard Kipling" (Eliot), 284
Russell, Bertrand, 37-38, 186-187, 191, 213; financial help, 186

Sacred Wood, The (Eliot), 95, 109-110, 120; preface to, 213; vocabulary in, 109
Salem witch trials, 24
Santayana, George, 33
Sassoon, Siegfried, 16
Satyricon (Petronius), 76
Savonarola (Eliot, C.), 27, 269
Schiller, Friedrich, 96
Schuchard, Ronald, 38, 50
Schwartz, Sanford, 47
"Second Debate between the Body and Soul" (Eliot), 130
"Self-Reliance" (Emerson), 268
Seventeeth century, 58; poets, 3, 57-58, 110-111
"Shadow—a Parable" (Eliot), 285
Shakespeare, William, 35, 99-102, 105, 111, 118, 120, 123, 137-138, 159, 179, 192, 204, 244, 284, 286
Shame of the Cities, The (Steffens), 28
Shaw, Fiona, 51
Shelley, Percy Bysshe, 58, 111, 181-182
Sigg, Eric, 47
"Slumber Did My Spirit Seal, A" (Wordsworth), 171
Smith, Carol, 47
Smith, Grover, 48

"Song for Simeon, A" (Eliot), 225-226, 232-233, 256, 261; Catholic philosophy of disillusion in, 226; Christian dispensation in, 224; union of death and birth in, 237, 239
Sorel, Georges, 210
Southam, B. C., 44
Spender, Stephen, 46, 50
Spengler, Oswald, 40
Spenser, Edmund, 85, 197, 248
Stearns, Isaac, 281
Stevens, Wallace, 217, 282
Student's Guide to the Selected Poems of T. S. Eliot, A (Southam), 44
"Suite Clownesque" shows, 125-126, 135, 140; stage-managing in, 135
"Sunday Morning" (Stevens), 218
Sweeney Agonistes (Eliot), 47, 192, 213; knowing and not knowing theme, 307
"Sweeney among the Nightingales" (Eliot), 48
"Sweeney Erect" (Eliot), 181-182; paintings in, 171
Swinburne, Algernon Charles, 109, 111
"Symbolism of Poetry, The" (Yeats), 118
Symbolist Movement in Literature, The (Symons), 33
Symbolist poets, 23, 31, 33-34, 57
Symons, Arthur, 33

T. S. Eliot (Frye), 44
T. S. Eliot: Man and Poet (Cowan), 45
T. S. Eliot: The Critical Heritage (Grant), 44
T. S. Eliot Prize, 50
Tate, Allen, 45
Tempest, The (Shakespeare), 179, 198
Tennyson, Alfred, 33, 57-58, 63, 94, 111-112, 119, 281
Thackeray, William Makepeaace, 109
"The Triumph of Life" (Shelley), 181

Time and Free Will (Bergson), 149
Times Literary Supplement (magazine), 110
"Tintern Abbey" (Wordsworth), 172-173
"To Helen" (Poe), 275
To the Lighthouse (Woolf), 218
Towson, Martin, 50
"Tradition and the Individual Talent" (Eliot), 3, 93, 102-103, 105-107, 119, 167; meditation on creativity in, 5; writing, 28, 32
Tristan und Isolde (Wagner), 79
Trosman, Harry, 205-207, 222
Turgenev, Ivan, 27
Twentieth-century writing, 3-4, 55-56, 70; irony, 115; principles of, 95; theorists, 98
Tzara, Tristan, 46

Ulysses (Joyce), 56, 118, 217-218, 221; Eliot on, 48, 56, 70, 210
Unitarianism, 17, 25, 27, 31
Untergrand des Abendlandes. See *Decline of the West, The*
Use of Poetry and the Use of Criticism, The (Eliot), 229

Verdenal, Jean, 35, 71
Verlaine, Paul, 179, 193
Verse drama, viii, 4, 47-48, 294
Victorian poetry, 55-60, 62, 64, 69, 174
"Vortex" (Pound), 107
Vorticism, 36-37, 103
"Voyage, Le" (Baudelaire), 114

Wagner, Richard, 79
Waiting for Godot (Beckett), 302
Warner, Deborah, 51
Waste Land, The (Eliot), 15, 30, 35, 63, 67, 70-71, 93, 125, 127, 153, 185, 189, 192-194, 198, 203-206, 210-

213, 218-219, 240, 280, 284, 303, 315; aestheticism, 268, 285; allusions in, 74, 76, 81, 85, 178-180; Belladonna scene from, 284; betrayed women in, 192; biographical details in, 184; blindness in, 230; Buddha in, 74, 84, 87; Cumean Sibyl in, 74, 76, 80, 85; death and destruction in, 74, 77, 85-86; emotional turbulence in, 184; Fire Sermon in, 189; graphic novel version, 50; Hyacinth garden in, 185, 201, 203-205, 214, 216; hyacinth girl in, 79, 81, 83; images in, 77-78, 80, 82, 85-86, 88, 167, 171, 192, 208, 216, 276, 285; influences on, 24; language in, 74, 77, 166-167, 178, 184; literary borrowings, 192; Madame Sosostris in, 80, 82, 85-87; Marie in, 74, 78, 80, 83, 88; nightmare in, 184-185, 201, 209, 221; pessimistic character of, 40, 46; publication, 38, 41, 56; sexual surrender in, 187; speaker in, 193, 203, 205, 207; spiritual condition in, 109; structure of, 184, 207, 211-212; stylized rhythms of, 214; success of, 3, 40; symbolism, 211; three movements of, 199-200; Tiresias in, 74, 76, 78, 81, 85-87; voice in, 74-79, 82, 85, 88; water dripping song in, 185, 214, 216-217; writing of, 74, 188, 207, 240

Wendell, Barrett, 30-31

West, Rebecca, 97, 105

Weston, Jessie, 211, 214

"What the Thunder Said" (Eliot, *The Waste Land*), 88, 209, 214; emotion in, 213; images in, 86; rhythms in, 86; writing in, 206

Whicher, Stephen, 268

Whitman, Walt, 279, 281, 283, 288

Wilde, Oscar, 29

William Greenleaf Eliot: Minister, Educator, Philanthropist (Eliot, C.), 25

Williams, Raymond, 42

Wit in nineteenth-century poetry, 55

Women in Love (Lawrence), 218

Wood, Michael, 16-17

Woolf, Leonard, 24

Woolf, Virginia, 6, 24, 38, 56, 70, 217

Wordsworth, William, 23, 31, 58, 61, 166-173; definition of poetry, 32; "Immortality" Ode, 168, 171

World War I, 4, 17, 36, 56, 71, 75, 77-79, 81-83, 85

World War II, 4, 24, 42, 71, 267, 287

Yeats, William Butler, 36, 48, 118-119, 211

S Eliot